Fodor's
PUERTO RICO

Welcome to Puerto Rico

It's easy to have a Caribbean vacation on Puerto Rico, but this tropical island offers much more than sun and sand. In the exciting city of San Juan, you're sure to find your scene whether it's art museums, posh boutiques, or trendy bars. Nearby, the lush El Yunque rain forest provides a peaceful retreat from urban diversions. Colonial towns such as Ponce and San Germán bring history to life in centuries-old churches and plazas. Nighttime is always right for salsa dancing and piña coladas, and no matter where you stay, you're never far from the beach of your dreams.

TOP REASONS TO GO

★ **Dining:** From Nuevo Latino restaurants to simple spots serving comida criolla.

★ **Old San Juan:** Cobblestone streets, cafés, and boutique hotels in a charming neighborhood.

★ **Beaches:** From lively resort-fronted strands to remote coves with calm waters.

★ **El Yunque:** The only tropical rain forest managed by the U.S. Forest Service.

★ **History:** Sixteenth century fortifications such as El Morro and La Muralla still stand.

★ **Vieques and Culebra:** Laid-back islands with unspoiled beauty and quiet towns.

Contents

MAPS

Fodor's Features

Chapter 1

EXPERIENCE PUERTO RICO

1 A Day Trip to Culebra and Playa Flamenco

Culebra is a relatively short, 45-minute ferry ride from Ceiba and is home to Playa Flamenco, a beach known for its white sand and stunningly turquoise water. The beach itself doesn't offer many services outside of the overpriced drinks, so bring snacks for the day. The UV Rays are extra strong, so bring sunscreen. *(Ch. 5)*

2 Surfing in Rincón

Rincón is the place to surf on the west coast. Domes Beach is popular beach for morning surf sessions; Tres Palmas consistently serves up big waves. For beginners, Maria's is great when waves are smaller. *(Ch. 7)*

3 Taking in the Views from El Morro

El Castillo de San Felipe del Morro, more commonly known as simply El Morro, was constructed in the late 1400s to protect San Juan from pirates. Walk around to see the towering walls and the waves crashing at its base. *(Ch. 3)*

4 Parque de las Cavernas del Río Camuy

This hidden gem is the third-largest underground cave system in the world, filled with waterfalls and rushing water (though the caverns were heavily damaged by Hurricane Maria in 2017). *(Ch. 6)*

5 Desecheo Island

Desecheo Island is an uninhabited island off the west coast of Puerto Rico, a former bombing range that offers beautiful dive sites teeming with marine life. *(Ch. 7)*

6 Relaxing on Seven Seas Beach

Seven Seas Beach in Fajardo is ideal for mellow beach days thanks to its calm, reef-protected waters and mangrove-shaded, semi-private feel. *(Ch. 4)*

7 Eating Fresh Fish in Boquerón

This Cabo Rojo beach town is filled with food stands, bars, and restaurants, making it the perfect place to go out with friends for some beers and fresh seafood. *(Ch. 7)*

8 Spend a night out in La Placita de Santurce

This classic hub of San Juan nightlife has a festive, block-party vibe that encourages bar-hopping while you listen to ever-present music. You can start or end your night here. *(Ch. 3)*

9 Strolling through Old San Juan

The colorful apartments and narrow streets of Old San Juan are iconic. Though swarmed with tourists, it's also popular with locals, who frequent the many bars and restaurants. *(Ch. 3)*

10 Salsa Dancing

Puerto Ricans grow up dancing salsa, so if you want to keep up with the locals, you'll need to pick up a few steps. Take a crash course, or practice your steps at a salsa bar. *(Ch. 3)*

11 Ron del Barrilito Distillery

Not often seen outside the island, Ron del Barrilito has been around since 1880 and is a favorite in Puerto Rico. Call ahead, and you can visit the distillery. *(Ch. 3)*

12 Visiting the Kioskos

Luquillo's *kioskos* (food stalls) are lined up in a row, making them the perfect place to sample all of Puerto Rico's favorite *frituras* (fried foods) and grab a cold drink. *(Ch. 4)*

13 Luquillo's Beaches

While surfers flock to Playa la Pared, families often prefer the more full-service Balneario La Monserrate, and swimmers are drawn to the swaying palm trees and calm waters of Playa Costa Azul. *(Ch. 4)*

14 Hike El Yunque National Forest

The only U.S. tropical rain forest (still being cleaned up post–Hurricane Maria) is packed full of flowing waterfalls, cool rivers, and beautiful mountain views, not to mention a variety of hiking trails. *(Ch. 4)*

15 Bar-Hopping in Esperanza, Vieques

Vieques is a great spot if you like to relax in a simple local bar with a stiff cocktail or cheap beer. Calle Flamboyan in Esperanza has several places to choose from, including the famous Duffy's. *(Ch. 5)*

16 Visiting a Local Coffee Farm

Hacienda Buena Vista, in the southern town of Ponce, has played an important role in Puerto Rico's coffee industry and still plants, harvests, and processes its coffee and cacao crops. *(Ch. 8)*

17 Refugio Nacional de Vida Silvestre de Culebra

The bird-watcher's paradise, managed by the U.S. Fish and Wildlife Service, is home to over 50,000 birds and 13 different species, as well as leatherback sea turtles. *(Ch. 5)*

18 Kayaking in Puerto Mosquito

The blue-glowing waters of Vieques' most notable bioluminescent bay (there are three here) are a truly incredible sight as long as you visit on a dark night, ideally during a new moon phase. *(Ch. 5)*

19 Driving the Island

Do it in a day, or do it slowly over the course of several days, but leave from San Juan and circumnavigate the island to see beautiful beach views, green mountains, expansive valleys, and so much more. *(Ch. 4, 6, 7, 8)*

20 Arecibo Observatory

Built within a gigantic, natural limestone sinkhole (and operated by the U.S. NSF), Arecibo's radio telescope is 1,000 feet in diameter, 167 feet deep, and covers around 20 acres of land. *(Ch. 6)*

WHAT'S WHERE

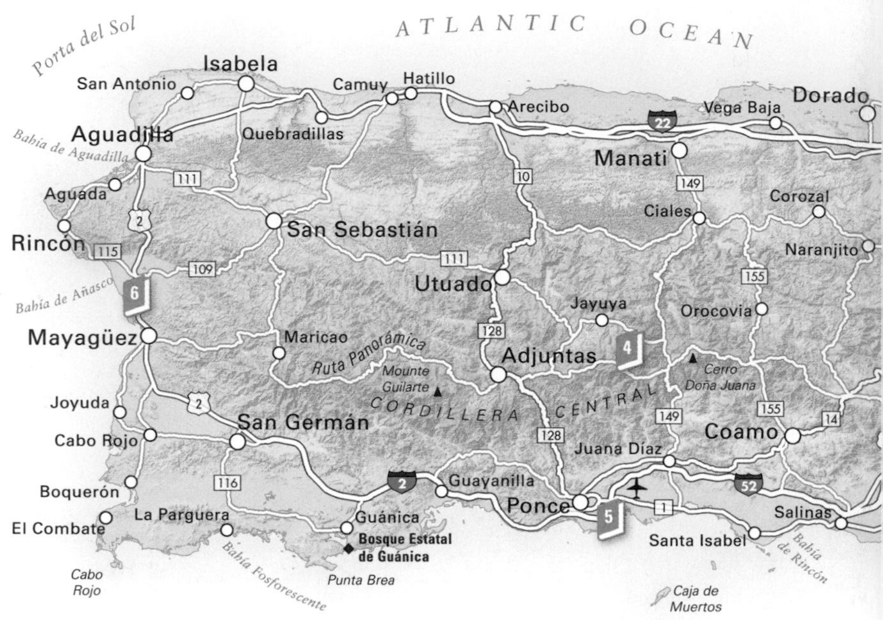

1 San Juan. The capital has tremendous museums, a vivacious bar scene, restaurants from the earthy to the trendy, plus fabulous boutiques and galleries. Old San Juan is a visual delight of forts, churches, convents, and cobbled streets dating back centuries. Hotels concentrate in the beach-lined Condado and Isla Verde districts, where the nightlife sizzles.

2 El Yunque and the Northeast. El Yunque is the most popular day trip from San Juan: hiking trails snake through this tropical rain forest, leading to hidden pools and mountaintop *miradores* (lookouts). Luquillo has one of the island's best-known beaches, the Balneario La Monserrate. Westward, Reserva Natural Las Cabezas de San Juan teems with wildlife in several distinct ecosystems, including mangroves. Fajardo is a base for exploring exquisite offshore cays, including Isla Palominos.

3 Vieques and Culebra. Once used by U.S. armed forces for military exercises, this pair of sand-fringed isles is now famous for their jaw-dropping beaches. Boutique hotels and trendy eateries have popped up alongside beachy bars on Vieques; Culebra remains less developed and sleepier. Ecotourism is big, with popular activities including snorkeling, diving, kayaking, and visits to the stunning bioluminescent bay in Vieques.

4 The North Coast and the Cordillera Central. Puerto Rico's north coast is an easy drive from San Juan, convenient for day trips, while the rugged mountain spine that runs the length of the island is festooned with forest.

5 Rincón and the Porta del Sol. The jagged coastline of the west is renowned for world-class surfing, centered on Rincón, where dozens of beaches beckon those who like to hang 10. Cabo Rojo offers great birding. Architecture buffs appreciate the grandeur of downtown Mayagüez.

6 Ponce and the Porta Caribe. The southern coast is studded with tropical dry forests, such as Bosque Estatal de Guánica, a destination for hikers and birders. The colonial center of Ponce has one of the finest art museums in the Caribbean, and the hilltop town of San Germán charms visitors. Offshore, "The Wall" offers scuba divers the raptures of the deep.

10 Things to Eat and Drink in Puerto Rico

FLAN
While flan is another favorite throughout Latin America, it's the most iconic dessert of Puerto Rico. This creamy custard-based dessert comes in a number of flavors, including caramel, cheese flan made with cream cheese, and coconut flan made with coconut milk.

MOFONGO
While the national dish of Puerto Rico is officially *arroz con gandules* (rice with pigeon peas), most locals will tell you mofongo is the standout dish of the Island of Enchantment. Plantains are fried and then mashed together with garlic, oil, and salt, then stuffed, usually with chicken or shrimp.

MALTA
As its name suggests, Malta is a malt beverage, a lightly carbonated soft drink made from hops, barley, and water. Malta, however, is nonalcoholic. High in vitamin B, malt-based beverages are said to metabolize carbs and fat into energy while helping to regulate appetite. There might still be hope for our fried food–filled bellies!

QUESITO
Quesitos, or "little cheeses," are long sticks of puff pastry filled with sweetened cream cheese and are a breakfast favorite. They are usually topped with a dusting of powdered sugar, or with a thin, sweet glaze. A popular variation of the quesito includes guava along with the cream cheese filling.

EMPANADILLAS
Empanadas, or *empanadillas,* are another go-to snack in Puerto Rico. These halfmoon–shape flaky pastries are stuffed and then fried. The filling is traditionally chicken or ground beef, but it's also possible to find them stuffed with shrimp or crab.

PASTELES
Similar to tamales, *pasteles* are made by enclosing adobo pork in green banana masa, and then wrapping that in banana leaves. While tamales are traditionally steamed, Puerto Rican pasteles are boiled.

AREPAS
Typically, *arepas* are made of corn flour and are toasted or grilled on a stove top. Puerto Rican arepas, however, are made with wheat flour and are then fried. Arepas in Puerto Rico are a specialty of the Fajardo coastal region and are stuffed with seafood like shrimp or octopus.

TRIPLETA
The *tripleta* is sometimes referred to as the Puerto Rican version of a Cubano sandwich. Each tripleta will vary from the next, but they are generally made with a combination of three grilled meats served on a slightly sweet bread and topped with *papitas,* small and thin crispy fries.

COFFEE
The coffee in Puerto Rico is rich, bold, and flavorful. Coffee was Puerto Rico's largest export once upon a time, and while that's no longer the case, the island's coffee retains its top-notch quality. Coffee is typically served in one of three ways: *pocillo,* the local term for an espresso; *cortadito,* an espresso with steamed milk; or *café con leche,* a large cup of coffee and milk similar to a latte.

MAVÍ
Found throughout the Caribbean islands, *maví* is a drink made from the fermented bark of the Mauby tree. The tree bark is boiled together with ginger and cinnamon, mixed with sugar, and then left to ferment for several hours. Maví is often compared to root beer and is a specialty of Puerto Rico's southern region.

10 Things to Buy in Puerto Rico

ARTESANÍA
Artesanía are handmade works, also known as artistas del patio. Examples include art carved out of coconuts, lace dresses, *santos* (the figures of saints used in home altars), or even furniture. Some popular elements often displayed on these crafts are the Puerto Rican flag and the Taíno sun.

HAMMOCK
The Taíno people, the original natives of the island, are rumored to have invented the hammock (*hamaca* in Taíno). Hammocks are incredibly easy to come by in Puerto Rico. You can find canvas or denim hammocks. Alternatively, you can get a handwoven cotton hammock in artisan or craft shops.

PIQUE
Unlike the commonly blended hot sauces we're used to, pique is made by combining chili peppers, herbs, and seasonings and putting them to steep in vinegar. There aren't really a standard set of ingredients; each version is unique, and it can be added to basically any type of food to give it a little zing. Homemade pique is often served in restaurants and food stands, but you can also by it in supermarkets.

PILÓN
This type of wooden mortar and pestle is used to grind together different ingredients. As with many typical "Puerto Rican" things, the pilón was originally used by the Taíno and is a culinary staple on the island. Once the coffee bean was introduced to the island, the pilón was even used to process beans.

PANDERETA

The *pandereta* is a handheld percussion instrument similar to a tambourine, except that it doesn't have cymbals. Panderetas, also known as panderos, are the key instrument in plena, a genre of music created by agricultural workers in Puerto Rico's southernmost region, and they come in three different sizes.

CIGARS

Puerto Rico was once one of the world's top exporters of tobacco, and cigar making remains a tradition despite the industry's decline in the last 60–70 years. There are three types of tobacco native to the island, the most famous of which is Hoja Prieta. Don Collins is the best-known brand.

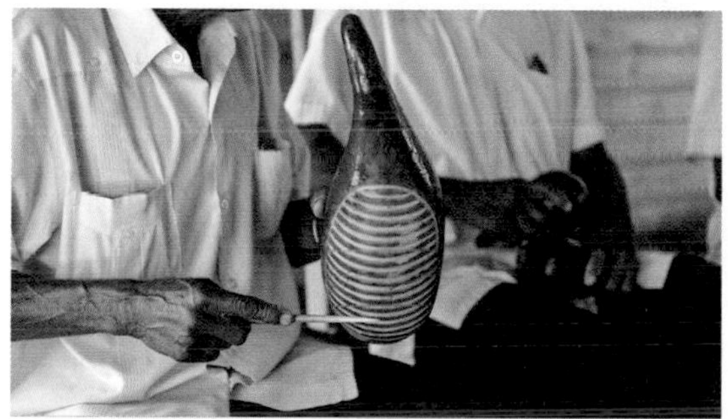

GÜIRO

A popular instrument in Puerto Rico, güiros are made from hollowed-out gourds with parallel ridges carved into one side. The music is made by running a "scraper," a stick or metal tine, up and down the ridges. They are believed to have originated with the Taíno or Arawak people.

COFFEE

More than a century ago, Puerto Rico was actually one the world's largest coffee exporters. Although only 1% of the island's coffee is exported today, Puerto Rico's rich, bold, dark coffee is often rated as some of the best in the world. The mountain city of Yauco is one of the island's more famous coffee producers.

RUM

While many of Puerto Rico's export industries have faded out, one remains steadfast: rum. Rum continues to be Puerto Rico's main export. Don Q is a local favorite, said to be the best rum on the island. Palo Viejo, Caliche, Ron del Barrilito, and Ron Llave are popular brands, as is Bacardí.

ADOBO

In 1966, Goya Foods released a seasoning called adobo, which has now become a household necessity in any Puerto Rican home. There are nearly a dozen varieties of adobo seasoning, each meant to be used with a different type of food such as beef, chicken, fish, etc. If you're looking for a food souvenir, adobo can be found at any grocery store.

Beaches of Puerto Rico

PUNTA TUNA BEACH
Punta Tuna Beach is on Puerto Rico's southeast coast. Strong currents make it unsafe to swim here, but this is a beautiful place to relax with a book or take a long walk on the beach. This is also home to the Punta Tuna Reserve, a nesting site for turtles. Nesting season is from March to July. *(Ch. 8)*

CAYO ICACOS
Cayo Icacos is one of about 10 small islands that make up the Cordillera Nature Reserve just off the coast of Puerto Rico. Icacos can only be reached by boat, and the ride is a short 15–20 minutes, but it has no facilities, so you'll need to bring along whatever you might need for the day. *(Ch. 4)*

DOMES BEACH
Rincón is a tourist hot spot on Puerto Rico's west coast, and Domes beach is one of its most popular. This beach gets its name from the dome-shape building there, which used to be a nuclear plant. Domes beach is also well-known surfing spot. You can see whales here in the winter. *(Ch. 7)*

BORÍNQUEN BEACH
On the west coast, this big, beautiful stretch of white sand leads to large rocks and a cliff that juts into the sea. The water can be too rough and choppy for swimming in the winter, but the summer months are great for swimming and snorkeling but beware of sea urchins along the rocky walls. During low tide, you'll find a small cave at the far end as well as the ruins of a lighthouse. *(Ch. 7)*

FLAMENCO BEACH
Flamenco Beach's claim to fame is a #2 rating on the Discovery Channel's list of best beaches in the world, making it a source of pride for Puerto Ricans. And rightfully so. This crescent-shape whitesand Culebra beach with crystal-clear turquoise waters is a swoon-worthy spot made for social media. It's a popular weekend daytrip for both locals and visitors. *(Ch. 5)*

ISLA VERDE BEACH
San Juan's best beach is technically not in San Juan but rather in Carolina, where the airport is. It's made up of three different beaches, each with its own unique vibe. The first, El Alambique, is the most lively, with hotels, restaurants, and water sports. Pine Grove beach sits between two large hotels and is a popular surf spot. Balneario de Carolina is the third. *(Ch. 3)*

Flamenco Beach

MAR CHIQUITA

The beaches along Puerto Rico's northern coast are unique in that many of them are formed from natural pools surrounded by limestone walls that protect these swimming holes from the rough waters of the Atlantic Ocean. Food trucks selling all of the local fave fried goodies are always set up here, and arts vendors come out on the weekends when the beach is busier. The water gets rough in the winter months, and swimming may not always be a good idea. *(Ch. 6)*

POZO DE LAS MUJERES

Pozo de las Mujeres is another natural swimming hole protected by rock formations, and this beach is almost split in two. On the left-hand side, the water is shallow, calm, and protected from the rougher waters outside the natural barricade. On the right-hand side, however, the rocks do not form a protective barrier and the water is much rougher. *(Ch. 6)*

PLAYA PEÑA BLANCA

Swimming in the crystal clear waters of Peña Blanca is best in the summer months during low tide. In the winter months, the waters reach the rocks around the beach, eliminating the already fairly small shoreline. *(Ch. 7)*

PLAYA SUCIA

Playa Sucia, in the southwest, actually means "dirty beach." While it can be dirty from seaweed on occasion, the water is usually a beautiful turquoise, and this beach is known as one of the most beautiful on the island. Playa Sucia is also home to a lighthouse, Faro de los Morrillos, as well as limestone cliffs and caves. The only downside is the access via a rutted dirt road. *(Ch. 7)*

Puerto Rico Today

If you've heard there's trouble in paradise, it's true: Puerto Rico has been reeling from an economic crisis that's been years in the making. The problems became more acute in 2015, when the island's government began defaulting on debt payments. The impact on citizens has been profound—with cost-of-living increases that aren't matched by increases in salaries, and cuts in many services, especially those provided or subsidized by the government. Hurricane Maria, which battered the island in 2017, deepened the crisis, impacting tourism, the island's most important industry, profoundly. Many hotels and attractions were closed for months, and island infrastructure was severely affected. Visitors to the island may notice some lingering effects, especially beyond San Juan, and should call ahead to confirm that the key points of interest they want to visit are open.

ZIKA VIRUS

Puerto Rico's first confirmed case of Zika virus was reported in 2015, and by 2016, the mosquito-borne illness reached epidemic proportions on the island. The Centers for Disease Control (CDC) estimated that at least one-quarter of the population had been exposed to the virus. As of 2018, however, the number of new cases decreased dramatically, and the island declared that its epidemic was over. Travelers are advised by the CDC to take all the usual precautions against mosquito bites. The organization warns pregnant women against travel to areas where incidents of Zika have been reported. As of this writing, the CDC did not have an active travel alert related to Zika in Puerto Rico.

THE STATUS ISSUE

Puerto Rico is a commonwealth of the United States, a complicated status that extends U.S. citizenship to Puerto Ricans, but without all of its benefits. The island's government holds a "status" referendum periodically to assess Puerto Ricans' current preferences: do they want to remain a commonwealth, pursue independence, or seek statehood? Results are in no way binding, and the U.S. Congress would be required to enact legislation to allow a change in status. The most recent referendum was held in June 2017, and a small portion of the population voted overwhelmingly in favor of statehood.

SOME CARIBBEAN COMPETITION

The "opening" of Cuba to American citizens has long been an issue of concern for the Puerto Rican tourism industry, which feared that its Caribbean neighbor would not only draw travelers away from the island because of its former forbidden status, but also because of its geographical proximity: Cuba is closer to the United States than Puerto Rico is. The fact remains, however, that for travelers who don't want to worry about passports, visas, and currency exchange, Puerto Rico remains the easiest option.

AN ENTREPRENEURIAL, ARTISANAL MOMENT

Despite doom-and-gloom news about the economy, a growing number of younger Puerto Ricans understand that the current crisis brings enormous opportunity. Exciting entrepreneurial ventures touch every sector of the economy, from tech to tourism, and from agricultural to artisan-powered design. For visitors, this means new-to-Puerto-Rico options like treehouse "glamping," pet-friendly accommodations and businesses, and cutting-edge bars and restaurants.

Kids and Family

Puerto Rico is a family-friendly island with no end of fun things for kids to see and do, including cave exploration, snorkeling with marine turtles, and nighttime excursions to bioluminescent lagoons. Many resort hotels arrange children's activities or have kids' clubs, freeing parents for romantic beach strolls and candlelit dinners.

CHOOSING A PLACE TO STAY

Resort hotels make a point of catering to family needs. Most offer free rooms to children under 12 and can provide cribs. Here are a few questions to help you gauge the level of family-friendliness:

Are there discounted meals and activities? Do restaurants have kids' menus? Are there children's programs, and is there an age range? A children's pool?

El Conquistador, a Waldorf Astoria Resort, near Fajardo, has a long list of facilities for children, including the sensational Coquí Water Park. On the south coast, **Copamarina Beach Resort and Spa** has a children's pool and playground, plus kayaks, pedal boats, tennis, and heaps of other activities.

Condos and vacation rentals offer an inexpensive option, especially for larger families. They typically have multiple bedrooms, and you can cook for yourselves. **ESJ Towers,** in Isla Verde, is right on the best beach in San Juan.

THINGS TO DO

Vacationing in the Caribbean is all about the outdoors. Kids may even forget video games when they see the options: snorkeling, whale-watching, body boarding, and cave exploring. And the list of great beaches is nearly endless. The wave action around Rincón can get a little rough for youngsters, but Vieques and Culebra have the most fantastic, reef-protected sands, which are good for snorkeling, and kids can also go kayaking and fishing. Of course, many beaches have riptides, so do play it safe and heed posted warnings, such as red flags.

Parque de las Cavernas de Río Camuy. This huge cavern will leave kids wide-eyed. They'll have fun trying to discern imaginary figures in the surreal dripstone formations. And they'll also enjoy a number of not-so-imaginary figures, like the tiny *coquí* frogs hopping around the cavern entrance, crabs and blind fish in the underground river, and bats flitting about overhead. The tram ride to reach the caverns is icing on the cake.

Arecibo Lighthouse and Historical Park. Local families flock to this small theme park built around Los Morrillos lighthouse. It has a museum on seafaring—and that includes pirates. In winter, kids can look for whales from the lighthouse observation platform. The playground has a pirate cave and replica galleon, as well as a Taíno village.

History You Can See

PRECOLONIAL PUERTO RICO

The Taínos were the indigenous group that populated the island prior to its "discovery" by Christopher Columbus on his second trip to the New World in 1493. The Taínos' name for the island was Borinquen, and even today Puerto Ricans honor their Taíno heritage by referring to themselves as *boricuas*.

What to See: The island's two main ceremonial centers—**Tibes** and **Caguana**—have preserved the limited artifacts of Taíno culture that have been discovered over the years. At Tibes, just north of Ponce, visitors can see reproductions of the *bohíos* in which Taínos lived, as well as fields believed to have served as ritual sites.

Closer to San Juan, those curious to get a window into the Taíno world can visit **La Cueva de María de la Cruz,** a cave in Loíza where archaeologists discovered Taíno artifacts in the mid-20th century. Entry to the cave is free; the site is unstaffed.

COLONIAL PUERTO RICO

Columbus arrived in 1493, and the Spanish crown controlled the island—though with a determinedly laissez-faire approach—until the Spanish-American War of 1898 ended with the concession of Puerto Rico to the United States. The first Spanish governor of the island was Juan Ponce de León, the explorer famous for his legendary pursuit of the elusive fountain of youth. Spain's Queen Isabella charged Ponce de León with the task of "compel[ling] and forc[ing] the Indians to work for the Christian inhabitants." According to the late historian and archaeologist Ricardo Alegría, the Taínos were decimated, refusing to resist the Spanish conquistadores because they believed that Spaniards were immortal; thus, taking up arms against them was futile.

By the 1530s, Africans had been brought to the island for slave labor; they built San Juan's two biggest fortresses, Castillo San Felipe del Morro and Castillo San Cristóbal, massive construction projects that took more than 250 years of intense, arduous labor. Slavery in Puerto Rico was finally abolished in 1873.

What to See: Built in 1521, **Casa Blanca** was the intended home of Juan Ponce de León, who never actually lived here. His descendants, however, called the Old San Juan property home for 250 years.

Castillo San Felipe del Morro and **Castillo San Cristóbal** aren't San Juan's only forts—there's also Fortín San Gerónimo del Boquerón, just behind the Caribe Hilton, and the Fortín El Cañuelo on Goat Island, visible across San Juan Bay—but they're certainly the largest and most impressive. Both offer commanding views of the Atlantic from their upper levels.

Built between 1533 and 1540, **La Fortaleza** was intended to serve as a perch from which the Bay of San Juan could be monitored and protected. Its strategic limitations were soon discovered, though, and the UNESCO-recognized structure is home to Puerto Rico's governor, as it has been since the late 16th century. Guided tours allow the public to glimpse how the governor lives.

A predominantly Afro–Puerto Rican town, **Loíza** was founded in 1719 and was populated by escaped slaves. Separated from the mainland by the Río Grande, the town remained geographically and socially isolated until the mid-1970s, allowing many Afro–Puerto Rican traditions to be preserved. Called the "capital of tradition," Loíza is home to popular *bomba* and *plena* music and dance, and is famous for *vejigantes* (coconut masks), used during annual festivals (⇨ *see also the "Masks of Puerto Rico" feature in Chapter 8*). Although it's most lively in early July, when the Santiago Apóstol festival is under way, a visit at any other time of year should include a stop at **San Patricio,** one of the island's oldest churches and home to what may be the only black St. Patrick statue in the world.

THE TRANSITION TO THE COMMONWEALTH

Puerto Rico became a U.S. territory in 1898. Although few would argue that life was better under the Spanish, many have had misgivings about the transfer. As Puerto Rican historians Kal Wagenheim and Olga Jiménez de Wagenheim remarked, "The invasion of Puerto Rico [by the U.S.] ended four centuries of oppressive Spanish colonial rule, only to replace it with a more subtle brand of colonialism."

Although the island was now part of the United States, Puerto Ricans were without formal citizenship for more than a decade. The educational system underwent frequent upheavals during this time, as did the structure of island government, in accordance with U.S.-imposed policies which reflected evolving defense and economic interests. Even when U.S. citizenship was granted with the Jones–Shafroth Act (1917), this development did little to resolve the ambiguous relationship between Puerto Rico and the United States; citizenship for Puerto Ricans was not, after all, conferred with all the rights and privileges enjoyed by state citizens. Puerto Ricans don't, for example, have a voting representative in Congress, nor can they vote for president. The island became a commonwealth (or a "free associated state") in 1952, but this made little difference in the day-to-day lives of the islanders.

Fierce debates continue among Puerto Ricans about the status of the island. Of the three major political parties, one is in favor of statehood, one prefers being a commonwealth, and the third advocates independence.

What to See: Built between 1919 and 1929, Puerto Rico's Beaux Arts–style **Capitolio** building is an often-overlooked site that shouldn't be missed. Its rotunda is inlaid with colorful mosaic tiles depicting the major periods of Puerto Rican history, and the Puerto Rican Constitution is displayed in glass cases. Busts of important Puerto Rican politicians are also on display. Visitors will often encounter protesters on the Capitolio steps; citizens gather here frequently in peaceful protest against government policies.

Las Mercedes Cemetery, in Ponce, is the final resting place of some of Puerto Rico's most important and celebrated politicians, among them Don Luis A. Ferré, former governor and founder of the Museo de Arte de Ponce. The grand tombstones and mausoleums in this cemetery are photo-worthy, as are the bones resting within your reach in open crypts at the back of the cemetery. **■ TIP→ Every town has its own culture trolley (often free), offering a historic guided tour of the area's highlights. Stops can generally be found in the town's plaza, in front of the city hall.**

What to Read and Watch Before Your Trip

Puerto Rico is often used as a stand-in location to film movies set in different, harder-to-access places, like Vietnam or Cuba—which doesn't do justice to a land so beautiful in its own right. Works that do focus on Puerto Rico show a vibrant, diverse island full of rebellion and resilience.

MOVIE: *AMISTAD*

This Steven Spielberg film is based on the true story of an 1839 slave uprising aboard a ship on its way from Cuba to the United States. Amid some debate of its historical accuracy, the movie frames the legal battle following the uprising as of great importance to United States history and the mounting tensions around slavery. The scenes set in Africa—at a slave fortress and beyond—were all filmed around San Juan.

BOOK/MOVIE: *THE RUM DIARY* BY HUNTER S. THOMPSON

Hunter S. Thompson's lost novel, found after his death by friend Johnny Depp (who went on to produce and star in the movie), is loosely based on the chunk of time Thompson spent living in San Juan, in the late 1950s and '60s, among American expat journalists and businessmen. It's the story of an American who moves to Puerto Rico to write for a sports paper, and is full of typical Thompson-esque hijinks, investigative reporting, party drugs, and drinking binges.

MOVIE: *MALA MALA*

This 2014 documentary is comprised of several stories from within the Puerto Rican LGBTQ+ community, including those of drag queens, transgender individuals, and others across a spectrum of gender identities. Among the film's stars is April Carrion, who later became a contestant in *RuPaul's Drag Race*. It played at several film festivals, receiving with praise for the way it represents the communities at its focus.

MOVIE: *RUNNER RUNNER*

While this feature film's named setting is Costa Rica, all scenes were shot in Puerto Rico. In the plot, Justin Timberlake gets caught up in a high-stakes cheating scheme at an online poker site and travels to Costa Rica to find the owner, Ben Affleck. Instead, Timberlake is drawn further into the scheme until he finds it virtually impossible to get out. It's mostly your run-of-the-mill thriller, with an expensive cast and plenty of plot holes, but the scenes of Puerto Rican coasts and cities are lovely.

BOOK: *MUNDO CRUEL: STORIES* BY LUIS NEGRÓN

Negrón's collection of stories describe growing up homosexual in Puerto Rico, an experience often tangled up in religion, secrecy, and violence. Negrón, born in Guayama, sets his stories in the Santurce district of San Juan. Originally published in Spanish, the 2010 collection won the Lambda Literary Award for Gay Fiction.

BOOK: *WAR AGAINST ALL PUERTO RICANS: REVOLUTION AND TERROR IN AMERICA'S COLONY* BY NELSON A. DENIS

Author and attorney Nelson A. Denis pieces together interviews, testimonies, and personal accounts to explain the unsuccessful 1950 political uprising against the United States—a violent event central to Puerto Rican political history, yet rarely covered in textbooks. The main character is Pedro Albizu Campos, a Harvard Law graduate, agricultural organizer, and head of the Nationalist party responsible for the insurrection. Denis, the child of a Puerto Rican mother and Cuban father, became fascinated by Albizu Campos and the lack of literature about him while studying at Harvard. Through its focus on this event, the book paints a much larger picture of the United

States's complicated, often problematic involvement in Puerto Rico.

BOOK: *WHEN I WAS PUERTO RICAN* BY ESMERALDA SANTIAGO

Santiago's 1993 autobiography about growing up both in San Juan and in rural Macun, is the first book of a series (followed by *Almost a Woman* and *The Turkish Lover*) about her life. There's seldom a story about Puerto Rico that doesn't involve a central character making a move to the mainland, and much of the book deals with her mother's decision (and the subsequent transition) to move the family to New York City.

MOVIE: *THE MAN WITH MY FACE*

In perhaps the only film noir ever set in Puerto Rico, a man returns home from a trip to find that an eerie double of himself has taken his place. It's a fun black-and-white thriller, and the scenes of San Juan are some of the film's best characteristics.

BOOK: *SILENT DANCING* BY JUDITH ORTIZ COFER

Judith Ortiz Cofer's lyrical work explores her life spent back and forth between Puerto Rico and United States, and the mixed cultural identity it has produced for her. Silent Dancing is a mixed-genre ode to Puerto Rico and the author's memories of her childhood spent there. Her other book, *The Latin Deli,* explores the lives of women living among each other in Paterson, New Jersey—but longing for their former island home.

BOOK: *SONG OF THE SIMPLE TRUTH: THE COMPLETE POEMS OF JULIA DE BURGOS* BY JULIA DE BURGOS

Burgos (1914–1953) was born in Carolina, Puerto Rico, attended the University of Puerto Rico, and later lived in Cuba and New York City. Also a key early feminist and political activist, Burgos is widely considered one of Puerto Rico's greatest poets. The book (originally in Spanish and translated into English) includes a biographical introduction and more than 200 of her poems.

MOVIE: *MARUJA*

This 1959 film became a Puerto Rican classic, telling the story of the obsession around a beautiful woman in a small town. It was filmed in the northern valley of Bayamón. While the plot is somewhat corny, it's a beautiful depiction of rural 1950s life in Puerto Rico. It's also the first feature film known to use an all local Puerto Rican cast, and created stars out of many of the actors in it.

Weddings and Honeymoons

Many other Caribbean destinations make a big pitch as wedding destinations, and Puerto Rico often gets overlooked. But it has all the ingredients of a spectacular place to wed and/or honeymoon. Gorgeous beaches dissolving into warm turquoise waters and a sensual tropical climate induce romance, and many an enamored couple has tied the knot here on the spur of the moment.

CHOOSING THE PERFECT PLACE

You can be as stylish or as informal as you wish. Although Puerto Rico has fewer ritzy beach resorts than many other islands, there's no shortage of exquisite boutique hotels with just the right ambience to inspire "I do." In San Juan, Villa Herencia and El Convento have just the right romantic style. In Rincón the Horned Dorset Primavera exudes honeymoon chic, and the Hix Island House on Vieques will suit honeymooners seeking a reclusive escape. Also consider Copamarina Beach Resort, which has spa- and diving-themed packages for honeymooners. Many larger hotels have their own wedding planners to take care of all arrangements—a distinct advantage over smaller hotels if you're seeking to wed on the island.

GETTING YOUR LICENSES

You must get an application from the Demographic Registry Office, which is in the Plaza Las Américas Mall in the Hato Rey neighborhood of San Juan. There are no special residency requirements, but U.S. citizens must produce a birth certificate, as well as a driver's license or other state-issued photo identification. Non-U.S. citizens must produce a valid passport for identification purposes. Medical certificates that conform to the requirements for marriage in your state of residence are required; these can be completed by your own doctor, but must be valid for 10 days beyond their issue date.

Both you and your intended must appear together at the office to purchase a marriage license; the cost is $20. A judge or any member of the clergy may then perform your ceremony. The fee is usually between $150 and $350. Most large hotels on the island have marriage coordinators who can explain the necessary paperwork and help you complete it on time for your marriage ceremony.

Chapter 2

TRAVEL SMART PUERTO RICO

Updated by
Julie Schweitert Collazo

★ **CAPITAL:**
San Juan

POPULATION:
3.68 million

LANGUAGE:
Spanish and English

€ **CURRENCY:**
U.S. Dollar

AREA CODE:
787, 939

⚠ **EMERGENCIES:**
911

DRIVING:
On the right

ELECTRICITY:
120–220 v/60 cycles; plugs have two or three rectangular prongs

TIME:
One hour later than New York (the same during daylight saving time)

WEB RESOURCES:
www.prtourism.com
www.discoverpuertorico.com

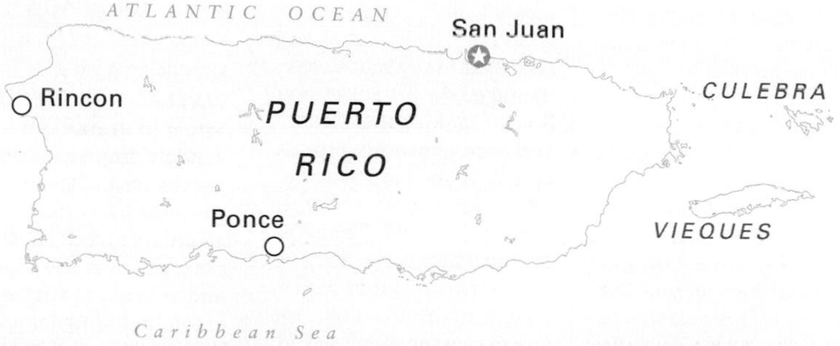

10 Things You Need to Know Before You Go

IT'S HEAVILY INFLUENCED BY THE UNITED STATES

It's surprising that many people still think Puerto Rico is an independent nation, but it's actually a U.S. commonwealth. This also means that it's heavily influenced by all things American, including fast-food chains, department stores, car repair companies, and more. This also means three things that will simplify your trip (and therefore your life, am I right?): One, you don't need a passport, so if your government-issued ID is sufficient to allow you to fly, that's all you need (you do undergo an agricultural inspection on your return trip, but no customs or immigration in either direction). Two, Puerto Rico uses the same electrical outlets as the U.S., so there's no need for convertors or adaptors. Three, Puerto Rico's currency is the U.S. dollar, so there's no need to worry about currency exchange, though you might be charged a foreign-transaction fee by the ATM (though likely not by a credit card).

LEARN A BIT OF SPANISH

Despite Puerto Rico's official relationship with the United States, Spanish remains the most commonly used language on the island. While most people do speak English in the more touristy areas, you can expect to find many areas of the island where this isn't quite the case. Additionally, it's important to be aware that the English language often conjures insecurity and feelings of inferiority for some of the older generations who don't know English as well or at all. Learning some basic Spanish before a trip to Puerto Rico will not only simplify things for you, but it can also serve as a sign of respect for the local people.

RENT A CAR

Public transportation is practically nonexistent in Puerto Rico, and what is offered is confined to a pretty small area within the San Juan metro area. If you want to explore more of the island, renting a car is the best way to do it. As you plan your travel to different parts of the island, be aware that the center of the island is full of mountains (and that many roads were damaged during Hurricane Maria), making it difficult and time-consuming to cut across. If you plan to drive from east to west, you will need to do so via the north or south highways. Also, be sure to carry a bit of cash on you; many areas require you to pay for parking, and often cash is the only way to do so.

SOMETIMES YOU JUST NEED A BOAT

While a car grants you the flexibility and freedom to see much more of the island, many of Puerto Rico's most iconic beach attractions can only be accessed by boat. In some cases you can take a ferry, but in other cases you will need to either rent a boat or book a boat excursion. Either way, some of the best spots simply aren't reachable without a boat. It's disappointing, we feel your pain, and that's why we've made this list of Puerto Rico's beaches that includes many driveable options.

IT'S NOT CHEAP

The slow-paced rest and relaxation of island life doesn't come without a price. Many islands face economic issues due to the need to import most products, and Puerto Rico faces extra challenges set forth by U.S. shipping regulations. This means that prices usually include a markup and quite high taxes. The cost of living in Puerto Rico is actually higher than the average cost of living in the U.S., so budget accordingly.

KIOSKOS ARE A WALLET'S BEST FRIEND

Street food stalls and vendors, known as kioskos, are the best place to get the most local and most affordable food. These are set up all over the island and are easy to spot. Many areas, including Luquillo, Loíza, and Ponce, have their own kiosko area where you can find a whole line of one kiosk after the other, each with its own number, serving either local Puerto Rican food or a mix of more "American" food, like pizza and hamburgers.

DID SOMEONE SAY FRIED EVERYTHING?

The local diet of Puerto Rico doesn't offer many options for healthconscious travelers. Nearly every dish or snack contains some kind of meat, and the majority of food is served fried. This isn't the most food-friendly destination for vegetarians or vegans, either. While you will still be able to find things to eat, you may miss out on most of the local flavors if you're unable to eat meat, or if you have a strong aversion to all things fried.

TEMPERATURES MAY VARY

Although Puerto Rico is located in the Caribbean, it can get quite breezy and chilly, particularly in the mountainous areas where many of the rivers and waterfalls are found. High season, from December to April, brings the coolest temperatures of the year. It doesn't necessarily get cold, especially during the day, but temperatures do drop at night, and the breeze coming in from the ocean can also create a bit of a wind chill. Be sure to pack something a bit warmer that you can easily throw on when needed.

DON'T GET YOUR METRICS TWISTED

One thing that may strike you as confusing once in Puerto Rico is the fact that the island uses a mix of both the metric and U.S. customary measurement systems. For example, distances are marked in kilometers, while speed limits are marked in miles per hour. Additionally, gas is sold in liters rather than gallons. This can be confusing, especially if you only have familiarity with one of these systems. Download a unit converter to your phone if you're concerned this may be an issue for you.

IT RAINS IN THE RAIN FOREST

It kind of seems selfexplanatory that it rains in the rain forest, but a common complaint from people working in tourism is that tourists always complain about the rain in El Yunque, which is Puerto Rico's rain forest. Expect the weather there to be wetter than elsewhere on the island. If you plan to make a trip to El Yunque during your time in Puerto Rico, be sure to pack closed-toe shoes suitable for trekking in muddy conditions, as well as a rain jacket, poncho, or some other form of protective gear.

PUERTO RICO, POSTHURRICANE MARIA

Although it's been almost two years since Hurricane Maria devastated the island, Puerto Rico is still struggling to get back on its feet in many ways, particularly outside of San Juan. Most of El Yunque is still closed, with only one short trail open at this time. Be advised to use caution while driving—many of the stoplights are still broken, some signage has blown away and was never replaced, the roads are marked with massive potholes, there is poor lighting as many streetlights are out, and there are many one-way streets that don't come up as such in your GPS. Business has resumed as usual for most tourist attractions and activities, but some information you find online may be outdated (and a few major attractions and hotels are still closed), so do look for sources that were either written or updated post-Maria.

Getting Here and Around

Air Travel

Nonstop flights to San Juan are approximately 3¾ hours from New York; 2½ hours from Miami; 3½ hours from Atlanta; 3¾ hours from Boston; 4½ hours from Chicago; and 4½ hours from Dallas.

There are dozens of daily flights to Puerto Rico from the United States, and connections are particularly good from the East Coast, although there are a few nonstop flights from the Midwest as well. San Juan's international airport is a major regional hub, so many travelers headed elsewhere in the Caribbean make connections here. Because of the number of flights, fares to San Juan are among the most reasonably priced to the region.

AIRPORTS

The island's main airport is Aeropuerto Internacional Luis Muñoz Marín (SJU), 20 minutes east of Old San Juan in the neighborhood of Isla Verde. San Juan's secondary airport is the small Fernando L. Ribas-Dominicci Airport (SIG), also called Isla Grande, near the city's Miramar section. From either airport you can catch flights to Culebra and Vieques, and from SJU you can also connect to other destinations in Puerto Rico and throughout the Caribbean.

Other Puerto Rican airports include Aeropuerto Internacional Rafael Hernández (BQN) in the northwestern town of Aguadilla; Aeropuerto Eugenio María de Hostos (MAZ) in the west-coast community of Mayagüez; Mercedita (PSE) in the south-coast town of Ponce; José Aponte de la Torre (RVR) in the east-coast town of Ceiba; Antonio Rivera Rodríguez (VQS) on Vieques; and Aeropuerto Benjamin Rivera Noriega (CPX) on Culebra.

GROUND TRANSPORTATION

Before arriving, check with your hotel about transfers: except in San Juan, where it's not allowed, some hotels and resorts offer transport from the airport (fee or no fee) to their guests; some larger resorts run shuttles regularly. Otherwise, your best bets are *taxis turísticos* (tourist taxis). Uniformed officials at the airport can help you make arrangements. They will give you a slip with your exact fare to hand to the driver. Rates are based on your destination: the base rate for a taxi turístico is $10 to Isla Verde, $15 to Condado, and $19 to Old San Juan. There's a $1 charge for each bag handled by the driver, and other fees, too, including a fuel surcharge (currently at $2 per ride), an "airport fee" (currently $1 per ride to or from the airport), and fees for rides with more than five passengers ($2 for each additional passenger up to seven passengers), as well as a nighttime surcharge ($1 per ride, 10 pm–6 am).

FLIGHTS TO PUERTO RICO

San Juan's busy Aeropuerto Internacional Luis Muñoz Marín receives flights from all major American carriers. American Airlines flies nonstop from Charlotte, Chicago, Dallas/Fort Worth, Miami, and Philadelphia. Delta flies nonstop from Atlanta and New York–JFK. JetBlue flies nonstop from Boston, Fort Lauderdale, Hartford, Newark, New York–JFK, Orlando, Tampa, and Washington National. Southwest flies nonstop from Baltimore/Washington, Chicago-Midway, Fort Lauderdale, Houston–Hobby, Newark, Orlando, and Tampa. Spirit Air flies nonstop from Fort Lauderdale and Orlando. United flies nonstop from Chicago, Cleveland, Houston, Newark, and Washington, D.C.–Reagan National.

It used to be that travelers arriving at San Juan's international airport had to transfer to nearby Aeropuerto Fernando

L. Ribas-Dominicci (known as Isla Grande Airport) to take a flight to Vieques or Culebra. These days, all carriers servicing the islands run flights from the international airport as well. (That said, if you don't mind changing airports, flights to Vieques and Culebra are much cheaper from Isla Grande than they are from SJU—and even cheaper, by as much as half, from Ceiba, about a 90-minute drive from San Juan.) Air Flamenco and Vieques Air Link offer daily flights from both airports in San Juan, as well as from Ceiba, to Vieques and Culebra. Cape Air flies between the international airport and Culebra, Mayagüez, and Vieques.

San Juan is not the only gateway into Puerto Rico. If you're headed to the western part of the island, you can fly directly into Aguadilla. United flies here from Newark; JetBlue flies here from Ft. Lauderdale, New York–JFK, and Orlando; and Spirit Air flies nonstop from Fort Lauderdale. If the southern coast is your goal, JetBlue flies to Ponce from New York–JFK and Orlando.

FLIGHTS TO THE CARIBBEAN

Puerto Rico is also a good spot from which to hop to other Caribbean islands. Cape Air connects San Juan to St. Thomas, St. Croix, Tortola, and Virgin Gorda. Seaborne Airlines departs from San Juan International to Anguilla, Antigua, Dominica, La Romana (Dominican Republic), Martinique, Nevis, Pointe a Pitre, Punta Cana (Dominican Republic), Santo Domingo (Dominican Republic), St. Croix, St. Kitts, St. Maarten, St. Thomas, Tortola, and Virgin Gorda. JetBlue offers direct flights from SJU to St. Thomas, St. Croix, Punta Cana, Santo Domingo, and Santiago.

Bus Travel

The Autoridad Metropolitana de Autobuses (AMA) operates buses that thread through San Juan, running in exclusive lanes on major thoroughfares and stopping at signs marked "Parada." Destinations are indicated above the windshield. Bus B-21 will take you from Condado to Old San Juan, and Bus A-5 runs from San Juan through Santurce and the beach area of Isla Verde. Note that bus service has been reduced significantly due to the island's financial crisis. Service starts at around 5 am and generally continues until 9 pm, but buses are not viewed by visitors as an efficient or easy way of getting around San Juan. Fares are 75¢ and are paid in exact change upon entering the bus. Most buses are air-conditioned and have wheelchair lifts and lockdowns.

There's no bus system covering the rest of the island. If you do not have a rental car, your best bet is to travel by *públicos,* which are usually shared 17-passenger vans. They have license plates ending in "P" or "PD," and they scoot around the island, stopping at a terminal in each town's main plaza. They operate primarily during the day; routes and fares are fixed by the Public Service Commission, but schedules aren't set, so you have to call ahead. The público system is centered around San Juan, so if you aren't beginning or ending your trip in San Juan, it may not be much use to you.

Car Travel

Several well-marked multilane highways link the major population centers on Puerto Rico. Route 26 is the main artery through San Juan, connecting Condado and Old San Juan to Isla Verde and the airport. Route 22, which runs east–west between San Juan and Camuy,

Getting Here and Around

and Route 52, which runs north–south between San Juan and Ponce, are toll roads. Route 2, a smaller highway, travels west from San Juan toward Rincón, and Route 3 heads east toward Fajardo. The latter can be mind-numbingly slow, so consider taking Route 66, a toll road that bypasses the worst of the traffic. Note that most toll plazas are cashless, so the EZ-Pass option is usually a worthwhile convenience—some companies, including Payless, even offer unlimited toll use for a flat daily rate.

Five highways are particularly noteworthy for their scenery and vistas. The island's tourism authorities have even given them special names. The Ruta Panorámica (Panoramic Route) runs east–west through the Cordillera Central. The Ruta Cotorra (Puerto Rican Parrot Route) travels along the north coast. The Ruta Paso Fino (Paso Fino Horse Route, after a horse breed) takes you north–south and west along the south coast. The Ruta Coquí, named for the famous Puerto Rican tree frog, runs along the east coast. And the Ruta Flamboyán, named after the island tree, goes from San Juan through the mountains to the east coast. Note, however, that signposting for all of these highways tends to be poor and inconsistent.

GASOLINE

All types of fuel—regular, super premium, and diesel—are available by the liter. Most stations are self-service. Hours vary, but stations generally operate daily from early in the morning until 10 or 11 pm; in metro areas many are open 24 hours. In the Cordillera Central and other rural areas stations are few and far between, so plan accordingly. In cities you can pay with cash and bank or credit cards; in more remote areas, cash is occasionally your only option. Note, too, that you cannot pay at the pump, even with a debit or credit card; you'll need to go inside the station to pay before pumping.

From	To	Rte./Distance
San Juan	Aguadilla	Rte. 22/81 miles (130 km)
San Juan	El Yunque	Rte. 3/35 miles (55 km)
San Juan	Fajardo	Rte. 3/36 miles (59 km)
San Juan	Mayagüez	Rte. 22/98 miles (160 km)
San Juan	Ponce	Rte. 52/73 miles (117 km)

ROAD CONDITIONS

Puerto Rico has some of the Caribbean's best roads, but potholes, sharp turns, speed bumps, sudden gradient changes, and poor lighting can sometimes make driving difficult, especially outside of the metropolitan area. Be particularly cautious when driving after heavy rains or hurricanes; roads and bridges might be washed out or damaged. Many mountain roads are very narrow and steep, with unmarked curves and cliffs. Locals are familiar with such roads and often drive at high speeds, which can give you quite a scare. When traveling on a narrow, curving road, it's best to honk your horn before you take any sharp turn. Roads—even major ones—are often poorly marked, if at all.

Traffic around cities—particularly San Juan, Ponce, and Mayagüez—is heavy during rush hours (weekdays 7–10 am and 3–7 pm).

ROADSIDE EMERGENCIES

In an emergency, dial ☎ *911*. If your car breaks down, call the rental company for a replacement. Before renting, make sure you investigate the company's policy regarding replacement vehicles and repairs out on the island, and ask about surcharges that might be incurred if you break down in a rural area and need a new car.

RULES OF THE ROAD

U.S. driving laws apply in Puerto Rico. Street and highway signs are most often in Spanish. They also use international symbols, but brushing up on a few key Spanish terms before your trip will help. The following words and phrases are especially useful: *calle sin salida* (dead-end street), *carril* (lane), *cruce de peatones* (pedestrian crossing), *cuidado* (caution), *desvío* (detour), *estación de peaje* (tollbooth), *no entre* (do not enter), *no estacione* (no parking), *salida* (exit), *tránsito* (one-way), *zona escolar* (school zone).

Distances are posted in kilometers (1 mile = 1.6 km), but speed limits are posted in miles per hour. Speeding and drunk-driving penalties are much the same as on the U.S. mainland. Police cars often travel with their lights flashing, so it's difficult to know when they're trying to pull you over. If the siren is on, move to the right lane to get out of the way. If the lights are on, it's best to pull over—but make sure that the vehicle is a *marked* police car before doing so.

Ferry Travel

The Autoridad de Transporte Marítimo (Maritime Transportation Authority) runs passenger ferries from Fajardo to Culebra and Vieques. Service is from the ferry terminal in Fajardo, about a 90-minute drive from San Juan. Advance reservations are not accepted. There are a limited number of seats on the ferries, so get to the terminal with plenty of time to spare; this means arriving an hour or two ahead of the departure time in Fajardo, somewhat less in Vieques and Culebra. In Fajardo the ticket counter is in the small building across the street from the actual terminal. In Vieques and Culebra the ticket counters are at the entrance to the terminals. There are food kiosks at Fajardo and Vieques that are open even for the early-morning departures. Culebra has casual eateries within a short walking distance of the ferry.

The Fajardo–Vieques passenger ferry departs from Vieques daily at 9:30, 1, 4:30, and 8, returning at 6:30, 11, 3, and 6; tickets for the 90-minute journey are $2 each way. The Fajardo–Culebra ferry leaves Culebra daily at 9, 3, and 7, returning at 6:30, 1, and 5; the 90-minute trip costs $2.25. Note that schedules and service can change without advance notice due to weather and other circumstances.

Before You Go

 Passport

All visitors to the United States require a passport that is valid for six months beyond your expected period of stay. U.S. citizens do not need a passport to visit Puerto Rico, which is considered part of the United States for immigration purposes.

 Visa

Except for citizens of Canada and Bermuda, most visitors to the United States must have a visa. If you are from one of the 38 designated members of the Visa Waiver Program, then you only require an ESTA (Electronic System for Travel Authorization) as long as you are staying for 90 days or less. However, some changes were made in the Visa Waiver Program in 2015, and nationals of Visa Waiver nations who have traveled to Iran, Iraq, Libya, Somalia, Sudan, Syria, or Yemen no longer qualify for ESTA. Also, if you have been denied a visa to visit the United States, your application for the ESTA program most likely will be denied.

 Immunizations

There are no immunization requirements for visitors traveling to Puerto Rico for tourism.

 U.S. Embassy/Consulate

There are no foreign embassies in Puerto Rico, but several countries have consulates.

 Visitor Information

In addition to the Puerto Rico Tourism Company's *¡Qué Pasa!*, pick up the Puerto Rico Hotel and Tourism Association's *Bienvenidos*—both magazines are published in English and Spanish. In them you can find a wealth of information about the island and its activities. They are free and available at tourism offices and hotel desks; some hotels provide copies in guest rooms. The Puerto Rico Tourism Company has information centers at the airport, and in Old San Juan, Ponce, Aguadilla, and Cabo Rojo. Most island towns also have a small tourism office, usually in the city hall.

 When to Go

Low Season: From August to late October, temperatures can climb to oppressive heights and the weather grows muggy, with a high risk of tropical storms. Many upscale hotels offer deep discounts.

Shoulder Season: From late April to July and November to mid-December, hotel prices drop 20%–50% from high season. There's a chance of scattered showers, but expect sun-kissed days and fewer crowds.

High Season: From mid-December through mid-April, the weather is typically sunny and warm. Good hotels are often booked far in advance, everything is open, and prices are highest.

Essentials

Addresses

Addresses in Puerto Rico (especially in and around San Juan) can be confusing, because Spanish terms like *avenida* and *calle* are used interchangeably with English terms like *avenue* and *street.* This means that the shopping strip in Old San Juan may be called Calle Cristo or Cristo Street. (And it might just be called "Cristo," as it is on many maps.) A highway is often called an *expreso,* and an alley or pedestrian-only street is labeled a *paseo.*

Outside a metropolitan area, addresses are most often given by the kilometer mark along the road. That means that the address for Parque de las Cavernas del Río Camuy, south of Arecibo, is given as Route 129, Kilometer 18.9.

Dining

Throughout the island you can find everything from French haute cuisine to sushi bars, as well as superb local eateries serving *comida criolla,* or traditional Puerto Rican food. Note that the *mesón gastronómico* label is used by the government to recognize restaurants that preserve culinary traditions. By law, every menu has a written warning about the dangers of consuming raw foods; therefore, if you want something medium rare, you need to be specific about how you'd like it cooked. *For information on food-related health issues, see Health/ Safety below.* The restaurants we list are the cream of the crop in each price category.

MEALS AND MEALTIMES

Puerto Ricans' eating habits mirror those of their counterparts on the mainland United States. They eat breakfast, lunch, and dinner, although they don't tend to drink as much coffee throughout the day. Instead, islanders like a steaming, high-test *café con leche* in the morning and another between 2 and 4 pm, perhaps alongside a local pastry or other sweet treat. They may finish a meal with coffee, but they never drink coffee *during* a meal.

People tend to eat dinner late in Puerto Rico. Many restaurants don't open until 6 pm, and you may find yourself alone in the restaurant before 7; from 8 onward, it may be quite busy.

Unless otherwise noted, restaurants listed in this guide are open daily for lunch and dinner.

RESERVATIONS AND DRESS

Regardless of where you are, it's a good idea to make a reservation if you can. In some places, it's expected. We mention reservations specifically only when they're essential (there's no other way you'll get a table) or when they are not accepted. For popular restaurants, book as far ahead as you can (often 30 days), and reconfirm as soon as you arrive. (Large parties should always call ahead to check the reservations policy.) We mention dress only when men are required to wear a jacket or a jacket and tie.

Puerto Ricans generally dress up to go out, particularly in the evening. And always remember: beach attire is only for the beach.

WINES, BEER, AND SPIRITS

Puerto Rico isn't a notable producer of wine, but it does make several well-crafted local beers and, of course, lots of rum. Legends trace the birthplace of the piña colada to several San Juan establishments. Puerto Rican rum is popular mixed with cola (known as a *Cuba libre*), soda, tonic, fruit juice, or water—or served on the rocks or even straight. Look for Bacardi, Don Q, Palo Viejo, Caliche, and Barrilito. The drinking age in Puerto Rico is 18.

Essentials

What It Costs

	$	$$	$$$	$$$$
AT DINNER				
	Under $13	$13–$20	$21–$30	Over $30

Lodging

San Juan's high-rise hotels on the Condado and Isla Verde beach strips cater primarily to the cruise-ship and casino crowd, although some also target business travelers and families. Outside San Juan, particularly on the east coast, you'll find self-contained luxury resorts that cover hundreds of acres. In the west, southwest, and south—as well as on the islands of Vieques and Culebra—smaller inns, villas, condominiums, and government-sponsored *paradores* are the norm.

Most hotels and other lodgings require you to give your credit-card details before they will confirm your reservation. If you don't feel comfortable emailing this information, ask if you can call it in or fax it (some places even prefer faxes). However you book, get confirmation in writing and have a copy of it handy when you check in.

Be sure you understand the hotel's cancellation policy. Some places allow you to cancel without any kind of penalty—even if you prepaid to secure a discounted rate—if you cancel at least 24 hours in advance. Others require you to cancel a week in advance or penalize you the cost of one night. Small inns and B&Bs are most likely to require you to cancel far in advance. Note that hotels in Puerto Rico add a hotel tax to your bill; the tax varies by hotel type, so ask at the time of booking if the amount is not clear. Many hotels, even if they do not market themselves as all-inclusive resorts, also add a resort fee, typically charged as a daily rate. Most hotels allow children under a certain age to stay in their parents' room at no extra charge, but others do charge for them as extra adults; be sure to learn the cutoff age for discounts.

HOTELS

In the most expensive hotels, your room will be large enough for two to move around comfortably, with two double beds or one queen- or king-size bed, air-conditioning, a phone, Wi-Fi or other Internet access, a private bath, an in-room safe, cable TV, a hair dryer, iron and ironing board, room service, shampoo and toiletries, and possibly a view of the water. There will be a concierge and at least one hotel restaurant and lounge, a pool, a shop, and an exercise room or spa. In Puerto Rico's smaller inns, rooms will have private baths, air-conditioning or fans, a double to king-size bed, possibly room service, and breakfast (continental or full) included in the rate. Most also have Wi-Fi or other Internet access in guest rooms, although some have Wi-Fi in public areas only. In some smaller hotels, several rooms share baths—it's a good idea to ask before booking. All hotels listed in this guide have private baths unless otherwise noted.

In Puerto Rico smoking is prohibited in public places, including restaurants, bars, cafés, casinos, and hotel common areas.

PARADORES

Some *paradores* are rural inns offering no-frills apartments, and others are large hotels; all must meet certain standards, such as proximity to an attraction or beach. Most have a small restaurant that serves local cuisine. They're often good bargains (usually $85–$125 per night for a double room). The Puerto Rico Tourism Company's website lists all paradores with their contact information. Small Hotels of Puerto Rico, a branch of the

Puerto Rico Hotel & Tourism Association, is a marketing arm for more than 20 small hotels islandwide. The organization occasionally has package deals including casino coupons and LeLoLai (a cultural show) tickets.

What It Costs

$	$$	$$$	$$$$
FOR TWO PEOPLE			
Under $150	$150–$250	$251–$350	Over $350

Health/Safety

The most common types of illnesses are caused by contaminated food and water. Make sure food has been thoroughly cooked and is served to you fresh and hot; avoid vegetables and fruits that you haven't washed (in bottled or purified water) or peeled yourself. If you have problems, mild cases of traveler's diarrhea may respond to Imodium (known generically as loperamide) or Pepto-Bismol. Be sure to drink plenty of fluids; if you can't keep fluids down, seek medical help immediately.

Infectious diseases can be airborne or passed via mosquitoes and ticks and through direct or indirect physical contact with animals or people. Some, including Norwalk-like viruses that affect your digestive tract, can be passed along through contaminated food. Condoms can help prevent most sexually transmitted diseases, but they aren't absolutely reliable and their quality varies from country to country. Speak with your physician and/or check the Centers for Disease Control and Prevention (CDC) or World Health Organization (WHO) websites for health alerts, particularly if you're pregnant, traveling with children, or have a chronic illness.

SPECIFIC HEALTH ISSUES IN PUERTO RICO

Dengue fever, a mosquito-borne disease, is a reality in the Caribbean. Puerto Rico has experienced several recent epidemics, most recently in 2010 and 2012. Virulent forms of the virus can cause high fever, joint pain, nausea, rashes, and occasionally death, but the most common strain is relatively mild, causing mostly flulike symptoms. Most cases were reported in urban areas far from the usual tourist destinations.

In 2015, the island also reported its first cases of another mosquito-borne virus, **Zika,** which poses serious risks to pregnant women and children in particular. The CDC issued travel warnings for Puerto Rico and other countries where Zika has been reported, but those warnings have since expired (and the number of new cases is down dramatically); check the CDC website for current warnings.

To prevent against mosquito-borne diseases, the U.S. Centers for Disease Control and Prevention (CDC) advises the use of an insect repellent with DEET and clothing that covers the arms and legs. While it's especially important to do this at dusk, when mosquitoes are most active, some mosquitoes are also active durling daytime hours.

Health care in Puerto Rico is among the best in the Caribbean, but expect long waits and often a less-than-pleasant bedside manner. If you require treatment, it is likely you will be charged in cash, even if you have active health insurance. Be sure to obtain a receipt for services that you can submit to your insurer. At all hospitals and medical centers you can find English-speaking medical staff, and

Essentials

many large hotels have an English-speaking doctor on call.

Tap water on the island is generally fine for drinking, but avoid drinking it after storms (when the water supply can become mixed with sewage). Thoroughly wash or peel produce you buy in markets before eating it.

Do not fly within 24 hours of scuba diving.

OVER-THE-COUNTER REMEDIES

All the U.S. brands of sunscreen and over-the-counter medicines (for example, Tylenol, Advil, Robitussin, and Nyquil) are available in pharmacies, supermarkets, and convenience stores.

SAFETY

San Juan, Mayagüez, and Ponce, like most other big cities, have their share of crime, so guard your wallet or purse in markets, on buses, and in other crowded areas. Avoid beaches at night, when muggings have been known to occur even in Condado and Isla Verde. Don't leave anything unattended on the beach. If you must keep valuables in your vehicle, put them in the trunk. Always lock your car. The exception is at the beaches of Vieques, where rental-car agencies advise you to leave the car unlocked so thieves don't break the windows to search for valuables. (This happens extremely rarely, but it does happen.)

We recommend that women carry only a handbag that closes completely and wear it bandolier-style (over one shoulder and across your chest). Open-style bags and those allowed to dangle from one shoulder are prime targets for pickpockets and purse snatchers. Avoid walking anywhere alone at night.

Money

Puerto Rico, which is a commonwealth of the United States, uses the U.S. dollar as its official currency. Prices for most items are comparable to those in the States, and that includes restaurants and hotel rates. As in many places, city prices tend to be higher than those in rural areas, but you're not going to go broke staying in the city: soft drinks or a cup of coffee run about $1–$2; a local beer in a bar, $3–$5; museum admission, $5–$10. Prices listed here are for adults. ATMs are prevalent in San Juan but may be scarce in rural areas. Substantially reduced fees are almost always available for children, students, and senior citizens.

TAXES

You must pay a tax on your hotel room rate: 11% for hotels with casinos, 9% for other hotels, and 7% for government-approved paradores. Ask your hotel before booking. The tax, in addition to each hotel's discretionary service charge (5%–16%), can add a hefty 12%–27% to your bill. The island's sales tax was raised from 7% to 11.5% (the highest in the U.S.) in 2015.

Tipping

Some hotels (usually those classified as resorts) automatically add a 5%–16% service charge to your bill. Check ahead to confirm whether this charge is built into the room rate or will be tacked on at checkout. Tips are expected—and appreciated—by restaurant waitstaff (15%–20%), hotel porters ($1 per bag), maids ($1–$2 per day), and taxi drivers (10%–15%).

On The Calendar

JANUARY

Fiestas de la Calle San Sebastián (*San Sebastián Street Festival*). The January festival features four nights of live music as well as food festivals and *cabezudos* parades, where folk legends are caricatured in oversize masks. 🌐 *www.discoverpuertorico.com/en/experiences/culture.*

FEBRUARY–MARCH

Carnival. In the days preceding Lent, Ponce celebrates Carnival with flamboyant costumes, parades, and music. 🌐 *www.visitponce.com.*

Casals Festival. Every year, San Juan honors world-renowned cellist Pablo Casals, who lived in Puerto Rico for nearly three decades until his death. Classical music performances feature the Puerto Rico Symphony Orchestra, as well as local and international soloists, trios, and quartets. ☎ *787/723–5005.*

Heineken JazzFest. The annual Heineken JazzFest attracts some 15,000 aficionados to San Juan for four days of outdoor concerts by the likes of Michel Camilo and Eddie Palmieri.

Jayuya Fiesta del Café. One of several coffee festivals held annually around the island, Jayuya's Fiesta del Café features all the usual activities at these types of events, but is notable for *la colada del café,* which organizers contend is the largest coffeepot on the island, brewing up to 100 pounds of coffee at once. 🎟 *Free*

Saborea Puerto Rico. Puerto Rico's largest culinary event is a three-day extravaganza held at Escambrón Beach in San Juan. It includes presentations by island and international chefs, as well as food from local restaurants, featuring beer, wine, and rum tastings. 🌐 *saboreapuertorico.com.*

JUNE–JULY

Aibonito Flower Festival. This popular festival displays incredible tropical foliage, including countless varieties of colorful orchids and ginger plants. There's also plenty of food and music.

Puerto Rico Restaurant Week (*PRRW*). This one-week islandwide dining celebration, held every June, is the perfect opportunity to visit top restaurants and enjoy specially priced prix-fixe menus as well as lunch and dinner menus. 🌐 *www.prrestaurantweek.com.*

SEPTEMBER

Puerto Rico Symphony Orchestra. The annual season of the Puerto Rico Symphony Orchestra begins in San Juan with classical and pop performances by the island's finest orchestra. ☎ *787/723–5005.*

NOVEMBER

Festival de Café (*Coffee Harvest Festival*). The mountain towns of Maricao and Yauco host the annual Festival de Café. Performers play music, and artisans and home cooks sell their crafts and regional foods.

Festival del Mundillo (*Bobbin Lace Festival*). Moca's Festival del Mundillo showcases delicate woven lace with demonstrations and exhibits.

DECEMBER

Festival de las Máscaras. The annual Festival de las Máscaras honors the mask-making traditions of Hatillo, where colorful masks used in religious processions have been crafted for centuries.

Helpful Phrases in Spanish (Puerto Rico)

BASICS

Hello	Hola	**oh**-lah
Yes/no	Sí/no	see/no
Please	Por favor	pore fah-**vore**
May I?	¿Me permite?	may pair-**mee**-tay
Thank you	Gracias	**Grah**-see-as
You're welcome	De nada	day **nah**-dah
I'm sorry	Lo siento	lo see-**en**-toh
Good morning!	¡Buenos días!	**bway**-nohs **dee**-ahs
Good evening!	¡Buenas noches!	**bway**-nahs **no**-chess
Good-bye!	¡Adiós!/¡Hasta luego!	ah-dee-**ohss/ah** -stah **lwe**-go
Mr./Mrs.	Señor/Señora	sen-**yor**/ sen-**yohr**-ah
Miss	Señorita	sen-yo-**ree**-tah
Pleased to meet you	Mucho gusto	**moo**-cho **goose**-toh
How are you?	¿Cómo está usted?	**ko**-mo es-**tah** oo-**sted**

NUMBERS

one	un, uno	oon, **oo**-no
two	dos	dos
three	tres	tress
four	cuatro	**kwah**-tro
five	cinco	**sink**-oh
six	seis	saice
seven	siete	see-**et**-eh
eight	ocho	**o**-cho
nine	nueve	new-**eh**-vey
ten	diez	dee-**es**
eleven	once	**ohn**-seh
twelve	doce	**doh**-seh
thirteen	trece	**treh**-seh
fourteen	catorce	ka-**tohr**-seh
fifteen	quince	**keen**-seh
sixteen	dieciséis	dee-**es**-ee-**saice**
seventeen	diecisiete	dee-**es**-ee-see-**et**-eh
eighteen	dieciocho	dee-**es**-ee-**o**-cho
nineteen	diecinueve	dee-**es**-ee-new-**ev**-eh
twenty	veinte	**vain**-teh
twenty-one	veinte y uno/ veintiuno	**vain**-te-**oo**-noh
thirty	treinta	**train**-tah
forty	cuarenta	kwah-**ren**-tah
fifty	cincuenta	seen-**kwen**-tah
sixty	sesenta	sess-**en**-tah
seventy	setenta	set-**en**-tah
eighty	ochenta	oh-**chen**-tah
ninety	noventa	no-**ven**-tah
one hundred	cien	see-**en**
one thousand	mil	meel
one million	un millón	oon meel-**yohn**

COLORS

black	negro	**neh**-groh
blue	azul	ah-**sool**
brown	café	kah-**feh**
green	verde	**ver**-deh
orange	naranja	na-**rahn**-hah
red	rojo	**roh**-hoh
white	blanco	**blahn**-koh
yellow	amarillo	ah-mah-**ree**-yoh

DAYS OF THE WEEK

Sunday	domingo	doe-**meen**-goh
Monday	lunes	**loo**-ness
Tuesday	martes	**mahr**-tess
Wednesday	miércoles	me-**air**-koh-less
Thursday	jueves	hoo-**ev**-ess
Friday	viernes	vee-**air**-ness
Saturday	sábado	**sah**-bah-doh

MONTHS

January	enero	eh-**neh**-roh
February	febrero	feh-**breh**-roh
March	marzo	**mahr**-soh
April	abril	ah-**breel**
May	mayo	**my**-oh
June	junio	**hoo**-nee-oh
July	julio	**hoo**-lee-yoh
August	agosto	ah-**ghost**-toh
September	septiembre	sep-tee-**em**-breh
October	octubre	oak-**too**-breh
November	noviembre	no-vee-**em**-breh
December	diciembre	dee-see-**em**-breh

USEFUL WORDS AND PHRASES

Do you speak English?	¿Habla usted inglés?	**ah**-blah oos-**ted** in-**glehs**
I don't speak Spanish.	No hablo español	no **ah**-bloh es-pahn-**yol**
I don't understand.	No entiendo	no en-tee-**en**-doh
I understand.	Entiendo	en-tee-**en**-doh
I don't know.	No sé	no **seh**
I'm American.	Soy americano (americana)	soy ah-meh-ree-**kah**-no (ah-meh-ree-**kah**-nah)
What's your name?	¿Cómo se llama usted?	koh-mo seh **yah**-mah oos-**ted**
My name is . . .	Me llamo . . .	may **yah**-moh
What time is it?	¿Qué hora es?	keh **o**-rah es
How?	¿Cómo?	**koh**-mo
When?	¿Cuándo?	**kwahn**-doh
Yesterday	Ayer	ah-**yehr**
Today	hoy	oy
Tomorrow	mañana	mahn-**yah**-nah

Tonight	Esta noche	**es**-tah **no**-cheh
What?	¿Qué?	keh
What is it?	¿Qué es esto?	keh es **es**-toh
Why?	¿Por qué?	pore **keh**
Who?	¿Quién?	kee-**yen**
Where is . . .	¿Dónde está . . .	**dohn**-deh es-**tah**
. . . the train station?	la estación del tren?	la es-tah-see-**on** del trehn
. . . the subway station?	la estación del tren subterráneo?	la **es-ta-see-on** del trehn la es-ta-see-**on** soob-teh-**rrahn**-eh-oh
. . . the bus stop?	la parada del autobus?	la pah-**rah**-dah del ow-toh-**boos**
. . . the terminal? (airport)	el aeropuerto	el air-oh-**pwar**-toh
. . . the post office?	la oficina de correos?	la oh-fee-**see**- nah deh koh-**rreh**-os
. . . the bank?	el banco?	el **bahn**-koh
. . . the hotel?	el hotel?	el oh-**tel**
. . . the museum?	el museo?	el moo-**seh**-oh
. . . the hospital?	el hospital?	el ohss-pee-**tal**
. . . the elevator?	el ascensor?	el ah-sen-**sohr**
Where are the restrooms?	el baño?	el **bahn**-yoh
Here/there	Aquí/allá	ah-**key**/ah-**yah**
Open/closed	Abierto/cerrado	ah-bee-**er**-toh/ser-**ah**-doh
Left/right	Izquierda/derecha	iss-key-**eh**-dah/dare-**eh**-chah
Is it near?	¿Está cerca?	es-**tah sehr**-kah
Is it far?	¿Está lejos?	es-**tah leh**-hoss
I'd like . . .	Quisiera . . .	kee-see-**ehr**-ah
. . . a room	un cuarto/una habitación	oon **kwahr** toh/**oo**-nah ah-bee-tah-see-**on**
. . . the key	la llave	lah **yah**-veh
. . . a newspaper	un periódico	oon pehr-ee-**oh**-dee-koh
. . . a stamp	un sello de correo	oon **seh**-yo deh korr-**eh**-oh
I'd like to buy . . .	Quisiera comprar . . .	kee-see-**ehr**-ah kohm-**prahr**
. . . soap	jabón	hah-**bohn**
. . . suntan lotion	Loción bronceadora	loh-see-**ohn** brohn-seh-ah-**do**-rah
. . . envelopes	sobres	**so**-brehs
. . . writing paper	papel	pah-**pel**
. . . a postcard	una tarjeta postal	**oon**-ah tar-**het**-ah post-**ahl**
. . . a ticket		
How much is it?	¿Cuánto cuesta?	**kwahn**-toh **kwes**-tah
It's expensive/cheap	Está caro/barato	es-**tah kah**-roh/bah-**rah**-toh
A little/a lot	Un poquito/mucho	oon poh-**kee**-toh/**moo**-choh
More/less	Más/menos	mahss/**men**-ohss
Enough/too (much)	Suficiente/	soo-fee-see-**en**-teh/
I am ill/sick	Estoy enfermo(a)	es-**toy** en-**fehr**-moh(mah)
Call a doctor	Llame a un medico	**ya**-meh ah oon **med**-ee-koh
Help!	Socorro	soh-**koh**-roh
Stop!	Pare	**pah**-reh

DINING OUT

I'd like to reserve a table . . .	Quisiera reservar una mesa . . .	kee-**syeh**-rah rreh-sehr-**bahr oo** nah **meh**-sah . . .
. . . for two people.	para dos personas.	**pah**-rah dohs pehr-**soh**-nahs
. . . for this evening.	para esta noche.	**pah**-rah **ehs**-tah **noh**-cheh
. . . for 8 PM	para las ocho de la noche.	**pah**-rah lahs **oh**-choh deh lah **noh**-cheh
A bottle of . . .	Una botella de . . .	**oo**-nah bo-**teh**-yah deh
A cup of . . .	Una taza de . . .	**oo**-nah **tah**-sah deh
A glass of . . .	Un vaso de . . .	oon **vah**-so deh
Bill/check	La cuenta	lah **kwen**-tah
Bread	El pan	el pahn
Breakfast	El desayuno	el deh-sah-**yoon**-oh
Butter	La mantequilla	lah man-teh-**kee**-yah
Coffee	Café	kah-**feh**
Dinner	La cena	lah **seh**-nah
Fork	El tenedor	el ten-eh-**dor**
I don't eat meat	No como carne	noh koh-moh **kahr**-neh
I cannot eat . . .	No puedo comer . . .	noh **pweh**-doh koh-**mehr**
I'd like to order . . .	Quiero ordenar . . .	**kee** yehr oh **ohr**-deh-nahr
I'd like . . .	Me gustaría . . .	Meh goo-stah-**ee**-ah
I'm hungry/thirsty	Tengo hambre.	**Tehn**-goh **hahm**-breh
Is service/the tip included?	¿Está incluida la propina?	es-**tah** in-cloo-**ee**-dah lah pro-**pee**-nah
Knife	El cuchillo	el koo-**chee**-yo
Lunch	La comida	lah koh-**mee**-dah
Menu	La carta, el menú	lah **cart**-ah, el meh-**noo**
Napkin	La servilleta	lah sehr-vee-**yet**-ah
Pepper	La pimienta	lah pee-mee-**en**-tah
Plate	plato	
Please give me . . .	Por favor déme . . .	pore fah-**vor** **deh**-meh
Salt	La sal	lah sahl
Spoon	Una cuchara	**oo**-nah koo-**chah**-rah
Sugar	El ázucar	el ah-**su**-kar
Tea	té	teh
Water	agua	**ah**-gwah
Wine	vino	**vee**-noh

Great Itineraries

Colonial Treasures

More than almost any other island in the Caribbean except Cuba, Puerto Rico has a trove of well-preserved colonial cities. Old San Juan is the best known—and it's a must-see for anyone interested in the region's rich history—but the southern coast also has some gems, from the graceful square in Coamo to the churches of San Germán, to the heady mix of Neoclassical and art deco masterpieces in Ponce.

DAY 1: OLD SAN JUAN

If you truly want to experience Old San Juan, make sure you stay within the city walls. El Convento, once a Carmelite convent, is one of Old San Juan's most luxurious lodgings. **The Gallery Inn,** whose mascot is a cockatoo named Campeche, has the most personality, while **Da House** is cheap and funky. After you drop off your suitcases, hit the cobblestone streets. Make sure to stroll along the city walls and visit one of the forts—most people pick **Castillo San Felipe del Morro,** but the nearby **Castillo San Cristóbal** is equally impressive. Old San Juan isn't just for sightseeing: when the sun goes down, the streets light up, turning this historic neighborhood into a nightlife center. For dinner, head to Calle Fortaleza, where you'll find some of the city's best restaurants; then while away the night at one of the happening bars or clubs.

Logistics: Believe us when we tell you that you don't want the headache of parking in Old San Juan. At San Juan's Aeropuerto Internacional Luis Muñoz Marín, take a *taxi turístico* (tourist taxi) to your hotel. The streets here were made for walking, and that's just what you'll do. Wait to pick up your car when you're ready to leave the city for the countryside.

DAY 2: COAMO

Head south from San Juan, and if you get an early enough start, take a short detour to Guayama, where you'll find the gorgeous **Casa Cautiño.** This 19th-century manor house, transformed into a museum, is one of Puerto Rico's most beautifully restored colonial-era structures. Continue west to Coamo, known for its thermal springs. On Coamo's lovely main square is the gleaming white **Iglesia San Blas de Illescas,** one of the island's oldest churches. In terms of distance, Coamo isn't so far from San Juan—only about 60 miles (96 km)—so you don't have to leave at the crack of dawn to have most of a day to explore the town.

Logistics: Head south from San Juan toward Ponce on Route 52 (toll road). For a detour, pick up Route 15 near Cayey and follow it south to Guayama. From there, you can take Route 3 (which runs into Route 1 at Salinas) west to Santa Isabel; then turn north on Route 153 to reach Coamo.

DAY 3: PONCE

Your destination on your third day is Ponce, the "Pearl of the South." You'll know you've arrived when you drive through the massive letters spelling the name of the city. The main square, the Plaza de las Delicias, is a delight: here you'll find the **Catedral de Nuestra Señora de Guadalupe,** a church dating from 1835, and **Parque de Bombas,** a firehouse from 1882, painted in bold red and black stripes. There are several museums around the city, but the most interesting is the **Casa Wiechers-Villaronga,** a small house built in 1911. In a city filled with Neoclassical confections, this is one of the most elaborate. Strolling the downtown streets, you'll also marvel at Neoclassical and art deco architecture. Don't miss the **Museo de Arte de Ponce,** one of the Caribbean's best art museums.

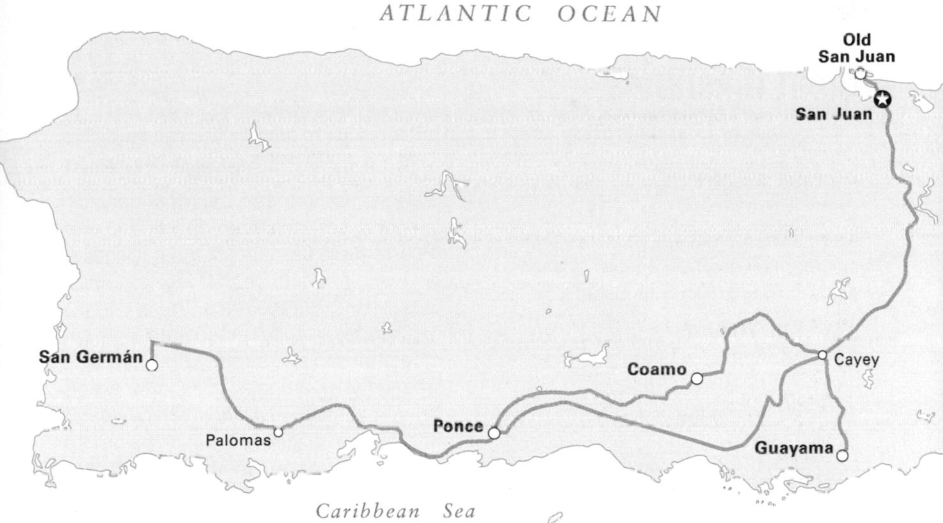

Logistics: From Coamo, follow Route 14 to Ponce; to continue downtown, take Route 12.

DAY 4: SAN GERMÁN

Less than an hour west of Ponce is San Germán, a must-see for anyone interested in the colonial era. The best place to start a tour of San Germán is Plazuela Santo Domingo, the small park in the center of the historic district, which itself is listed on the National Register of Historic Places. At the eastern edge of the park is the **Capilla de Santo Domingo de Porta Coeli.** This chapel, at the top of some steep stone steps, is now a museum of religious art. Stroll west past the delightful assemblage of buildings of every architectural style from mission to Victorian. Make sure to see the other gorgeous church, the **Iglesia San Germán de Auxerre,** a few blocks north.

Logistics: San Germán is easy to reach—simply take Route 2 west from Ponce. When you reach Route 122, head south into town.

DAY 5: SAN JUAN

If you have time on your way back to San Juan, stop for lunch at one of the open-air eateries near Guavate, off Route 52. You can try the famous *lechón,* a whole pig roasted on a spit.

Tips

If you're staying in Old San Juan, pick up your rental car at one of the hotel desks. You'll avoid an expensive taxi ride back to the airport.

Pack comfortable shoes for exploring these colonial-era cities. You'll be glad you brought sneakers after a few hours traipsing around on cobblestone streets.

Old San Juan is hillier than it first appears, and in Ponce avoid walking to Castillo Serrallés—a steep hike through an unsavory area. Take advantage of the free trolleys, which depart from main plazas and will take you to the most popular tourist sites in both cities.

Logistics: From San Germán take Route 2 until you reach Ponce. Exit onto Route 52; a toll road takes you all the way to San Juan.

Great Itineraries

Island Hopping

If you have a week for your trip, this itinerary will give you a taste of each of eastern Puerto Rico's highlights.

DAY 1: EL YUNQUE

East of San Juan is El Yunque, the undulating rain forest that covers much of the eastern edge of the island. It's a highlight of any trip to Puerto Rico, and you can still have a memorable time with only one day to spend there. Several of the trails can be hiked in an hour or less, including one that leads to some spectacular waterfalls, the **Cascada La Mina.** Spend the night in Río Grande; our favorite hotel along this stretch of shoreline is the luxurious **St. Regis Bahia Beach Resort,** known for its Robert Trent Jones golf course, beautiful private beach, and first-rate service.

Logistics: Take Route 3 east from San Juan; then head south on Route 191, which leads through El Yunque.

DAY 2: RESERVA NATURAL LAS CABEZAS DE SAN JUAN

Next stop: Fajardo, on the northeastern tip of the island. Drop your stuff off at your hotel—we prefer smaller accommodations like the **Fajardo Inn**—then head out on a tour (reserve ahead) of the mangrove forests of the **Reserva Natural Las Cabezas de San Juan.** Exploring this area isn't just a daytime experience, however. For a very different view of Las Cabezas, you may want to return at night, when you can paddle through its bioluminescent bay in a kayak. Companies offer trips nightly, although the experience is more dramatic under a moonless sky. In the afternoon, take a boat excursion from Fajardo to **Isla Palomino.**

Logistics: Continue on Route 3 to Fajardo, where Route 987 leads to Las Cabezas de San Juan.

DAYS 3 AND 4: CULEBRA

Culebra has some of the most beautiful, powdery-soft beaches you'll find in all of Puerto Rico. It's a small, quiet island, so you won't find much to do except relax—but then, that's the draw. There are no big hotels or fancy restaurants, only small guesthouses and some villas. If this sounds like getting a little too far away from it all, then skip Culebra and spend more time on Vieques, which has more resorts, better restaurants, and plenty of eco-centric activities. If you want to visit both islands, you can fly between Culebra and Vieques, but note that there's no ferry link.

Logistics: Drop off your rental car in Fajardo (or in Ceiba, if you're flying)—you'll want to rent a sturdier four-wheel-drive vehicle once you get to Culebra, and you can't take a rental car on the ferry anyway. Take the 90-minute ferry trip from Fajardo—or a 10-minute puddle-jumper flight—to the island from Ceiba. (We recommend taking the plane; the views are spectacular.)

DAYS 5 AND 6: VIEQUES

Close to the U.S. Virgin Islands—in terms of both atmosphere and geography—Vieques has an entirely different feel from the rest of Puerto Rico. If you've never been, we strongly recommend you spend at least one night there. The beaches are seemingly endless, the snorkeling is remarkable, and the **Puerto Mosquito Bioluminescent Bay** is one of nature's best shows. One great way to explore the island is on a bicycle tour arranged by a local operator.

Logistics: You'll want to fly between Culebra and Vieques—there are scheduled direct flights between the islands. For ferry service, you'll need to return to Fajardo first; there are no ferries between the islands.

DAY 7: SAN JUAN

From Vieques, take a puddle-jumper flight back to San Juan (or to Ceiba's airport to pick up your rental car). If you want to spend a day in Old San Juan, fly into Aeropuerto Fernando L. Ribas-Dominicci; it's a short taxi ride from the airport's Isla Grande location to Old San Juan's colonial heart.

Logistics: If you are connecting to a flight back home, make sure your flight to San Juan is headed to Aeropuerto Internacional Luis Muñoz Marín. If instead you're flying to San Juan's regional airport, Aeropuerto Fernando L. Ribas-Dominicci, you'll have to take a taxi between the airports.

Tips

Don't plan on taking your rental car to Vieques or Culebra—it's not allowed.

Check to see if you have to reserve in advance for certain tours, such as the daily trip to Fajardo's Reserva Natural Las Cabezas de San Juan.

Vieques and Culebra are both popular weekend destinations for Puerto Ricans, so ferries can get very crowded and sometimes difficult to board. If possible, plan your travel for a weekday.

Contacts

Air Travel

U.S. AIRLINE CONTACTS American Airlines. *800/433–7300* *www.aa.com*. **Delta Airlines.** *800/221–1212 U.S. reservations, 800/241–4141 international reservations* *www.delta.com*. **JetBlue.** *800/538–2583* *www.jetblue.com*. **Southwest Airlines.** *800/435–9792* *www.southwest.com*. **Spirit Airlines.** *801/401–2222* *www.spirit.com*. **United Airlines.** *800/864–8331* *www.united.com*.

REGIONAL AIRLINE CONTACTS Air Flamenco. *787/724–1818* *www.airflamenco.net*. **Cape Air.** *800/227–3247* *www.capeair.com*. **Seaborne Airlines.** *787/946–7800 in San Juan* *www.seaborneairlines.com*. **Vieques Air Link.** *787/741–8331, 888/901–9247* *www.viequesairlink.com*.

AIRPORT CONTACTS Aeropuerto Antonio Rivera Rodríguez. *787/741–0515* . **Aeropuerto Benjamin Rivera Noriega.** *787/742–0022* . **Aeropuerto Eugenio María de Hostos.** *787/833–0148*. **Aeropuerto Fernando L. Ribas-Dominicci.** *Isla Grande* *787/729–8715*. **Aeropuerto Internacional Luis Muñoz Marín.** *787/289–7240* *www.aeropuertosju.com*. **Aeropuerto José Aponte de la Torre.** *787/729–8462*. **Aeropuerto Mercedita.** *787/842–6292*. **Aeropuerto Rafael Hernández.** *787/890–6075*.

Bus Travel

Autoridad Metropolitana de Autobuses. *787/294–0500*.

Ferry Travel

Autoridad de Transporte Marítimo. *787/497–7740* *www.dtop.gov.pr*.

Lodging

RENTAL CONTACTS Island West Properties. *787/823–2323* *www.island-west.com* **Puerto Rico Vacation Apartments.** *787/727–1591, 800/266–3639* *www.sanjuanvacationpr.com* **Rainbow Realty.** *787/741–4312, 787/435–2063* *www.viequesrainbowrealty.com*.

PARADOR CONTACTS Puerto Rico Tourism Company. *787/721–2400, 800/866–7827* *www.discoverpuertorico.com*. **Small Hotels of Puerto Rico.** *www.puertoricosmallhotels.com*.

Visitor Information

Puerto Rico Tourism Company. *787/522–5960* *www.discoverpuertorico.com*.

Chapter 3

SAN JUAN

Updated by
Paulina Salach

Sights	Restaurants	Hotels	Shopping	Nightlife
★★★★☆	★★★★★	★★★★☆	★★☆☆☆	★★★★☆

WELCOME TO SAN JUAN

TOP REASONS TO GO

★ **Take a stroll:** Wander the cobblestone streets of Old San Juan. The fortifications and governor's mansion are UNESCO World Heritage sites.

★ **Climb a battlement:** Explore Castillo San Felipe del Morro, the 16th-century fortress that dominates the waterfront; rangers provide fascinating insight.

★ **Shop:** Head to Condado's Avenida Ashford, where you'll find most of the city's designer boutiques, including that of Nono Maldonado, one of the island's homegrown talents.

★ **Catch some rays:** Take it easy at San Juan's best beach, Balneario de Carolina, at the eastern tip of Isla Verde. Take time to parasail.

★ **Dine on the strip:** Dine at Marmalade, just one of many stellar restaurants along the eastern end of Calle Fortaleza, a trendy strip that locals call "SoFo."

San Juan's metro area stretches 19 km (12 miles) along Puerto Rico's north coast. Mapping the city is rather like working a jigsaw puzzle; neighborhoods are irregular in shape and sometimes overlap. The areas most visited by tourists run along the coast.

1 Old San Juan. Still enclosed by its original fortified city walls, this enclave of blue-cobblestone streets is superbly preserved, with more than 800 structures of historic importance, many dating back to the 16th century. Many of the city's best restaurants and bars are here, as well as boutiques offering everything from cigars to designer clothing. Laid out in an easy-to-navigate grid, Old San Juan has enough sights and shops to enthrall for days.

2 Puerta de Tierra. Just east of the Old City, Puerta de Tierra is home to a few notable hotels, a nice public beach, and several parks.

3 Condado. The most vibrant pedestrian area outside Old San Juan, Condado is home to hotels, restaurants, shops, and residences of the city's moneyed elite. Its main street is Avenida Ashford.

4 Miramar and Isla Grande. Bordering Santurce and across the bay from Condado, is Miramar. Isla Grande has the city's municipal airport and the San Juan Convention Center.

5 Santurce and Hato Rey. South of Condado and Ocean Park, Santurce—home of the city's main art museums and galleries—melds into

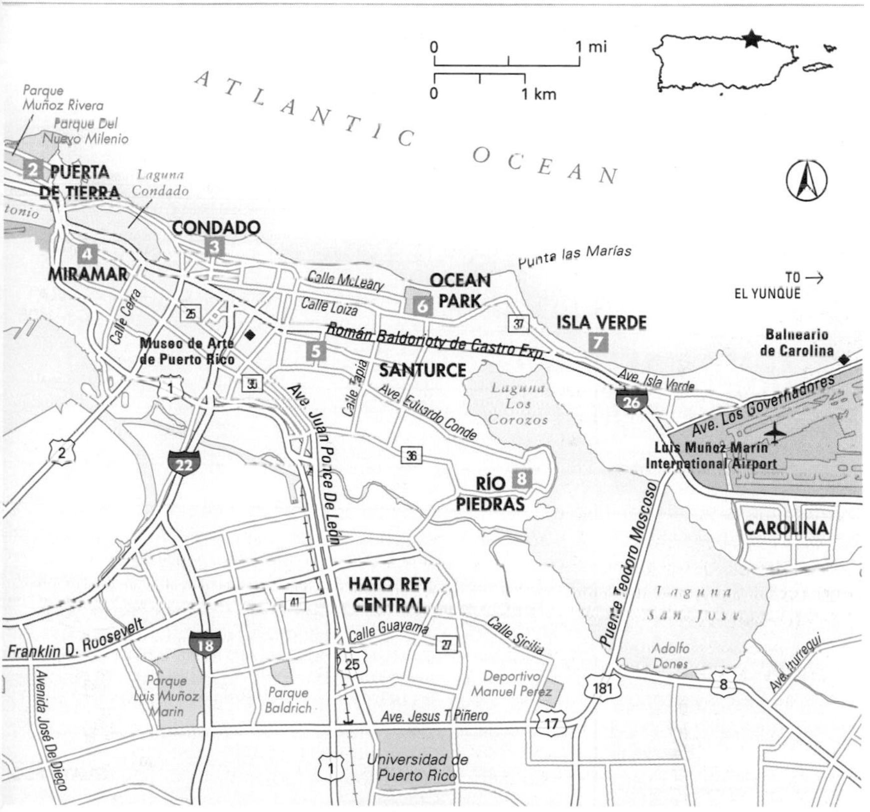

Hato Rey, the city's business and banking district.

6 Ocean Park. Partially gated, this primarily residential area east of Condado nevertheless has a few small hotels and popular restaurants.

7 Isla Verde and Carolina. Home to Puerto Rico's international airport, this area east of Ocean Park is also where you'll find many of the city's large hotels, many of its top nightclubs, and its best beach.

8 Río Piedras. The mostly residential Río Piedras area is home to the Universidad de Puerto Rico.

9 Cataño. Primarily industrial, Cataño is best known as the sight of the Bacardí rum distillery.

10 Guaynabo. A mix of residential and industrial areas, this neighborhood is worth visiting for its historical sights, including the island's first settlement.

11 Bayamón. This suburb has one of San Juan's larger malls.

Puerto Rico's capital is most commonly associated with the colonial streets and forts of Old San Juan, but that's only part of the picture. San Juan is a major metropolis, radiating out from the bay on the Atlantic Ocean discovered by Juan Ponce de León. The city may be rooted in the past, but it has its eye on the future. Locals go about their business surrounded by colonial architecture and towering modern structures.

By 1508 the explorer Juan Ponce de León had established a colony in an area now known as Caparra, southeast of present-day San Juan. He later moved the settlement north to a more hospitable peninsular location. In 1521, after he became the first colonial governor, Ponce de León switched the name of the island—then called San Juan Bautista, in honor of St. John the Baptist—with that of the settlement of Puerto Rico, or "rich port."

Defended by the imposing Castillo San Felipe del Morro (El Morro) and Castillo San Cristóbal, Puerto Rico's administrative and population center remained firmly in Spain's hands until 1898, when it came under U.S. control after the Spanish-American War. Centuries of Spanish rule left an indelible imprint on the city, particularly in the walled area now known as Old San Juan. The area is filled with cobblestone streets and brightly painted colonial-era structures, and its fortifications have been designated a UNESCO World Heritage Site.

Old San Juan is a monument to the past, but most of the rest of the city is planted firmly in the 21st century and draws migrants from all over the island and beyond to jobs in business and industry. The city captivates residents and visitors alike with its vibrant lifestyle as well as its balmy beaches, pulsing nightclubs, creative cocktail bars, globe-spanning restaurants, and world-class museums. Once you set foot in this city, you may never want to leave.

Planning

WHEN TO GO

During high season (mid-December–mid-April) hotels tend to crowd up (but only rarely sell out completely), and rates are a bit higher than in the off-season. Fall and spring are less expensive, plus the weather's still fantastic and the tourist crush less intense. However, a winter visit may allow you to participate in many of San Juan's annual events—in particular,

If You Like

Architecture

San Juan has been under construction for nearly 500 years, as evinced by the city's wide range of architectural styles. The Old City's Spanish colonial row houses—brick construction with plaster facades painted in pastel blues, oranges, and yellows—line narrow streets and alleys paved with *adoquines* (blue-gray stones originally used as ballast in Spanish ships). Several churches, including the Catedral de San Juan Bautista and Iglesia San José, were built in the 16th century, the latter in the ornate Gothic style. The massive, white marble Capitolio, home of Puerto Rico's legislature, was completed in 1929. And firmly rooted in the 21st century are the gleaming high-rise resorts along the beaches in Condado and Isla Verde and the glistening steel-and-glass towers in the business and financial district of Hato Rey.

Music

Music is a source of Puerto Rican pride and an inescapable part of nearly every festival, holiday, party, and even political protest. The brash Latin sound is best characterized in the music and dance of *salsa*, which shares not only its name with the word "sauce" but also its zesty, hot flavor. A fusion of West African percussion, jazz (especially swing and big band), and other Latin beats (mambo, merengue, flamenco, cha-cha, rumba), salsa music is sexy and primal. Dancers are expected to let go of all inhibitions. Most nightspots, including restaurants, offer live music several nights a week, especially Friday and Saturday.

Nightlife

As befits a metropolitan capital city, San Juan has a wide variety of restaurants and bars for people with all sorts of palates and party habits. Old San Juan, Condado, and the up-and-coming arts district of Santurce are big nighttime destinations. Many of the newer establishments have set their tables on terraces, the beach, indoor patios, or streetside to take advantage of the late-night atmosphere. Clubs and bars stay open into the wee hours of morning, closing only when the last patron leaves.

the lively Christmas celebrations, which extend through mid-January. The Fiestas de la Calle San Sebastián, held in Old San Juan every January, consist of several nights of live music, food festivals, and *cabezudos* (giant heads on daily parade). The Heineken JazzFest, each spring, is the Caribbean's showcase for local and international talent.

San Juan's weather is moderate and tropical year-round, with an average temperature of about 82°F (26°C). And although it's true that much of summer and fall is considered hurricane season, San Juan is still an attractive destination during those months: room rates are at their lowest, restaurant reservations are easier to come by, and fewer tourists roam the streets.

GETTING HERE AND AROUND

AIR TRAVEL

American, Delta, Frontier, JetBlue, Southwest, Spirit, Sun Country, and United fly to San Juan from the Unites States.

International carriers include Air Canada from Toronto, Air France from Paris, British Airways from London, Iberia and Air Europa from Madrid, and Condor from Germany. Air Flamenco and Vieques

Air Link offer daily flights from SJU and Isla Grande Airport (SIG) in San Juan to Vieques and Culebra. Cape Air flies between SJU and Vieques.

AIRPORTS Aeropuerto Fernando L. Ribas Dominicci (*SIG*). ✉ *Calle Lindbergh* ☎ *787/729–8715.* **Aeropuerto Internacional Luis Muñoz Marín** (*SJU*). ☎ *787/253–2329* 🌐 *www.aeropuertosju.com.*

AIRPORT TRANSFERS

Before you leave for Puerto Rico, check with your hotel about transfers; many larger hotels offer transport from the airport (sometimes free) to their guests. Otherwise, your best bet is a *taxi turístico* (tourist taxi). Uniformed officials at the airport can help you make arrangements; they will give you a slip with your exact fare written on it to hand to the driver. Rates are based on your destination: a taxi turístico costs $10 to Isla Verde, $15 to Condado, and $19 to Old San Juan and the cruise-ship piers. There's a $1 charge for each bag handled by the driver.

The Baldorioty de Castro Expressway (Route 26) runs from the airport into the city. Exits are clearly marked along the way, although you should check with your hotel to determine which one is best for you to take. Plan on 25–30 minutes for the drive from the airport all the way west to Old San Juan.

BUS AND TROLLEY TRAVEL

The Municipio de San Juan operates free trolleys throughout Old San Juan. Trolleys run along three routes beginning at Pier 4, on Calle Gilberto Concepción de Gracia and running to the two forts plus Plaza de Armas.

The Autoridad Metroplitana de Autobuses (AMA) maintains a network of bus routes throughout San Juan, running in exclusive lanes on major thoroughfares and stopping at signs marked "Parada." Destinations are displayed above their windshields. Bus B-21 runs through Condado all the way to Plaza Las Américas in Hato Rey. Bus A-5 runs from San Juan through Santurce and the beach area of Isla Verde. Fares are 75¢ and must be paid in exact change upon entering the bus. Most buses are air-conditioned and have wheelchair lifts and lock-downs. However, they are slow and inefficient and not suitable for most vacationers.

CONTACTS AMA (*Autoridad Metropolitana de Autobuses*). ☎ *787/294–0500* 🌐 *act.dtop.pr.gov.*

CAR TRAVEL

Although car rentals are inexpensive (as little as $15 per day if booked in advance), we don't recommend that you rent a car if confining your stay to San Juan. (At most, you might want to rent a car for a day trip elsewhere on the island.) Parking is difficult—particularly in Old San Juan—and most hotels charge hefty rates (at least $20 per day); also, traffic can be very heavy. With relatively reasonable taxi and Uber rates, it simply doesn't pay to rent a car unless you are leaving the city.

The main highways into San Juan are Route 26 from the east (it becomes the Baldorioty de Castro Expressway after passing the airport), Route 22 (José de Diego Expressway) from the west, and Route 52 (Luis A. Ferré Expressway) from the south.

MAJOR CAR-RENTAL CONTACTS Avis. ✉ *San Juan International Airport, Terminal Bldg., Carolina* ☎ *787/253–5926* 🌐 *www.avis.com.* **Hertz.** ✉ *Luis Muñoz Marín International Airport, Salvador Caro Ave., Carolina* ☎ *787/791–0840* 🌐 *www.hertz.com.* **National.** ✉ *Luis Muñoz Marín International Airport, Salvador Caro Ave., Carolina* ☎ *787/791–1805* 🌐 *www.nationalcar.com.* **Thrifty.** ✉ *10030 Marginal Los Angeles, Carolina* ☎ *787/253–2525* 🌐 *www.thrifty.com/loc/ll/pr/carolina/carolina/10030-marginal-los-angeles.*

LOCAL AGENCIES Charlie Car Rental. ✉ *6050 Isla Verde Ave., Carolina* ☎ *787/728–2418* 🌐 *www.charliecars.com.* **Vias.** ✉ *Hotel Villa del Sol, 4 Rosa*

St., Isla Verde ☎ 787/791–4120 ⊕ www.viascarrental.com.

TAXI TRAVEL

Taxis turísticos—painted white, with the *garita* (sentry box) logo—run from the airport and cruise-ship piers to Isla Verde, Condado, Ocean Park, and Old San Juan. They charge set rates based on zones (usually $10–$20); make sure to agree on a price before you get inside. City tours start at $36 per hour.

Although you can hail cabs on the street, virtually every San Juan hotel has taxis waiting outside to transport guests; if none are available, have one called. (Once called, taxis may charge an extra $1 for the pickup.)

Uber, the popular ride-sharing company, has entered the Puerto Rico market and operates in the San Juan metro area. Fares are generally lower than those of traditional taxis, and cars are readily available. Uber is not allowed to pick up at the airport, but it can drop you off.

CONTACTS Go Puerto Rico Shuttle. ☎ *787/400–2100* ⊕ *www.puertoricoshuttle.com* **Metro Taxi.** ☎ *787/725–2870.*

TRAIN TRAVEL

The Tren Urbano, an elevated light-rail system, travels throughout the metropolitan area, with stops at the University of Puerto Rico and Bayamón, but does not stop near the main tourist areas or at the airport, so you're unlikely to ride it on a typical visit. The fare is 75¢, which includes transfers to city buses. The system runs 5:30 am–11 pm and is operated by the Alternativa de Transporte Integrado (ATI).

BEACHES

Just because you're staying in the city doesn't mean you'll have to forgo time on the *playa*. Indeed, San Juan's beaches are among the island's best. With 365 different beaches in Puerto Rico, choosing where to spread out your towel might seem like a daunting task, but that decision is easier now that seven have been designated with a Blue Flag. Chosen by the Foundation for Environmental Education, a nonprofit agency, Blue Flag beaches have to meet more than 30 criteria, focusing on water quality, the presence of a trained staff, and the availability of facilities such as water fountains and restrooms.

Two beaches on the east side of the island, Seven Seas in Fajardo and Luquillo Beach, made the cut. More surprisingly, two of the beaches are in San Juan: Balneario El Escambrón in Puerta de Tierra, and Balneario de Carolina in Isla Verde. A fifth is Punta Salinas in nearby Toa Baja. This means that five of Puerto Rico's finest beaches are within an hour's drive of the capital. The other two Blue Flag beaches are in the west and south: Boquerón in Cabo Rojo and Pelicano Beach in Ponce.

HOTELS

San Juan prides itself on its plentiful clean and comfortable accommodations, and hoteliers, by and large, aim to please. Big hotels and resorts, several with casinos, and a few smaller establishments line the sandy strands along Condado and Isla Verde. If you want to do little but relax on the beach, enjoy ample resort amenities, and partake in lively nightlife, either area is a good option. Between them, the Ocean Park neighborhood has homey inns, as do Miramar and Santurce, although the latter two areas aren't directly on the beach. They're likely to be more popular with independent travelers, artistic types, and anyone who wants to stay a little bit off the beaten tourist track. Old San Juan has fewer lodging options, only one of which has a casino, but most of the city's best boutique hotels are here. If you're a history or architecture buff or looking for a unique romantic experience, definitely stay in one of these colonial inns; many of their structures date back several hundred years, and you'll feel as if you've been transported to another era (even though most have flat-screen televisions and Wi-Fi). Keep in mind, though, that these buildings are old and Puerto Rico's climate is tropical, so minor inconveniences like room mustiness or ongoing repairs are possible. Also consider Old San Juan if you're in town for a cruise, since the main cruise piers are within walking distance. Wherever you stay, keep in mind that all guest rooms are now no-smoking.

Staying in a self-catering apartment or condo has advantages over a resort, especially for families, mainly due to the considerable autonomy of more residential lodging. For example, the option to cook for yourself means you can eat when and what you want. Several companies represent such properties in San Juan. When booking, be sure to ask about maid service, swimming pools, and any other amenities that are important to you.

AirBnB rentals are abundant in San Juan (and throughout Puerto Rico) and have become very popular with travelers. You can rent everything from from low-budget apartments to mansions near the beach to colonial homes in Old San Juan—the options are varied. If you decide to rent through AirBnB or any other online service, ensure that you complete your rental through the company; you run greater risks and do not receive any buyer protection by making side deals with home or apartment owners.

PRICES

Room rates generally aren't inexpensive: for a high-end beach-resort room, expect to pay at least $200–$300 for a double in high season (roughly mid-November–mid-April); for smaller inns and hotels, doubles start at $100–$150. As a rule, if your room is less than $50 in high season, then the quality of the hotel might be questionable. Some hotels include breakast in their basic rates, but most hotels offer no other meal plans. There are no all-inclusive resorts in San Juan.

What It Costs In U.S. Dollars

$	$$	$$$	$$$$
FOR TWO PEOPLE			
under $150	$150–$250	$251–$350	over $350

Hotel reviews have been shortened. For full information, visit Fodors.com.

APARTMENT RENTALS

Caleta 64 Apartments
Four nicely furnished boutique apartments are just steps from the cathedral and Calle Cristo. ✉ *64 Caleta de San Juan, Old San Juan* ☎ *787/667–4926* 🌐 *www.caleta64.com.*

RESTAURANTS

In cosmopolitan San Juan, European, Asian, Middle Eastern, and chic fusion eateries vie for your attention, with family-owned restaurants specializing in seafood or *comida criolla* (creole cooking, or local Puerto Rican food). U.S. chains such as McDonald's and Subway compete with chains like Pollo Tropical and El Mesón, which specialize in local cuisine. Many of the most innovative chefs here have restaurants in the city's large hotels, but don't be shy about venturing into stand-alone establishments—many concentrated in Condado and along Calles Fortaleza and San Sebastián in Old San Juan. Old San Juan is also home to a number of notable new restaurants and cafés, offering more artisanal-style cuisine—crop-to-cup coffee, rustic homemade pizzas, and creative vegetarian food—at affordable prices. There's a radiant pride in what the local land can provide, and these enthusiastic young restaurateurs are redefining what Puerto Rican food is, bite by tasty bite.

The dress code varies greatly from place to place, although a restaurant's price category can be taken as a good indication. For less expensive places anything but beachwear is fine; ritzier spots will expect collared shirts and long pants for men ("jacket and tie" requirements are rare) and chic attire for women. When in doubt, do as the Puerto Ricans often do and dress up.

For breakfast outside of your hotel, cafés or *panaderías* (local bakeries) are your best bets. It's rare for such establishments to close between breakfast and lunch; it's slightly more common for restaurants to close between lunch and dinner. Although some places don't accept reservations, it's always a good idea to make them for dinner whenever possible. This is especially true during the busy season from November through April and on weekends at any time of the year.

Restaurant reviews have been shortened. For full information, visit Fodors.com.

What It Costs In U.S. Dollars

	$	$$	$$$	$$$$
AT DINNER	under $12	$12–$20	$21–$30	over $30

NIGHTLIFE

From Thursday through Sunday it's as if there's a celebration going on nearly everywhere in San Juan. Be sure you dress to party, particularly on Friday and Saturday nights; Puerto Ricans have flair, and both men and women love getting dressed up to go out. Bars are usually casual, but if you have on jeans, sneakers, and a T-shirt, you may be refused entry at nightclubs and discos.

Well dressed visitors and locals alike often mingle in the lobby bars of large hotels, many of which feature bands in the evening. Some hotels also have clubs with shows and/or dancing; the cover generally starts at $10. Casino rules have been relaxed, injecting life into what was once a conservative hotel-gaming scene, but you still won't be allowed in wearing a tank top or shorts. There are more games, plus such gambling perks as free drinks and live music.

In Old San Juan, Calle San Sebastián is lined with bars and restaurants. Salsa music blaring from jukeboxes in cut-rate pool halls competes with mellow Latin jazz in top-flight nightspots. The young and the beautiful often socialize in Plaza San José. Mid-January sees the Fiestas de la Calle San Sebastián, one of the Caribbean's best street parties.

Young professionals as well as a slightly older bohemian crowd fill Santurce, San Juan's historical downtown area, until the wee hours. The revitalized Plaza del Mercado (Calle Dos Hermanos at Calle Capital) has structures—many painted in bright colors—dating from the 1930s or earlier. On weekend nights the area's streets are closed to vehicular traffic. You can wander from dive bars to trendy nightspots and sway to music that pours from countless open-air establishments and the marketplace's front plaza.

Several publications will tell you what's happening in San Juan. *¡Qué Pasa!,* the official visitors' guide, has current listings of events in the city and out on the island. *Bienvenidos,* published by the Puerto Rico Hotel & Tourism Association, is also helpful.

There are also publications for Spanish-speaking visitors, including the weekend section of Spanish-language newspaper *El Nuevo Día*; the paper also gives a weekly rundown of events on its website (🌐 *www.elnuevodia.com*). *Sal!* (🌐 *www.sal.pr*) reviews restaurants and includes articles about dining and nightlife; it's also available as a free downloadable app (iOS) and can be used in either English or Spanish.

PERFORMING ARTS

San Juan is arguably one of the most important cultural centers of the Caribbean, known both for its homegrown culture and the healthy influx of visiting artists that the local population supports. The city hosts the Puerto Rico Symphony Orchestra, the world-renowned Pablo Casals classical music festival in winter, and an annual series of opera concerts. Many hit plays in New York and other large markets get produced locally, and there are often three or four other local theatrical productions taking place on any given weekend, many of them downright adventurous.

MAJOR EVENTS

The Casals Festival

FESTIVALS | The Casals Festival has been bringing some of the most important figures in classical music to San Juan ever since Pablo Casals, the famous cellist, conductor, and composer, started the festival in 1957. Casals went on to direct it until his death in 1973, and it has continued to serve as a vibrant stage for top-notch classical performers since then. Most of the shows are held at the Centro de Bellas Artes Luis A. Ferré, but performances are also at the University of Puerto Rico and other venues. The festival takes place from mid-February through mid-March. Tickets are available at the box office of the Centro de Bellas Artes Luis A. Ferré and through 🌐 *ticketpop.com.* ✉ *Luis A. Ferré Performing Arts Center, 22 Av. Ponce de León, Santurce* ☎ *787/918–1106* 🌐 *ticketpop.com.*

Puerto Rico Heineken Jazz Fest

FESTIVALS | San Juan is a great place to hear jazz, particularly Latin jazz, and the annual Puerto Rico Heineken Jazz Fest, which takes place in March at Bahía Urbana, is one of the best opportunities for it. Each year's festival is dedicated to a particular musician; honorees have included Chick Corea, Mongo Santamaria, and Dizzy Gillespie. ✉ *Baha Urbana* ☎ *866/994–0001, 787/294–0001.*

Saborea Puerto Rico

CULTURAL FESTIVALS | If you love all things gastronomy, you'll thoroughly enjoy the Saborea Puerto Rico food festival held every spring. This highly anticipated four-day culinary extravaganza brings together chefs from all over the Island and abroad. Watch chefs prepare dishes at the demo kitchen, sample an array of foods at the tasting pavilion, and listen to live music—all while enjoying the unbeatable beachfront setting. ✉ *Balneario de Carolina, Calle Av. Boca de Cangrejos* 🌐 *www.saboreapuertorico.com.*

TICKETS

Two major outlets sell tickets for events throughout Puerto Rico.

Ticket Center

TICKETS | With ticket counters available in many of the malls on the island, Ticket Center is a convenient way to score seats to most large-scale events. ☎ *787/792–5000* 🌐 *www.tcpr.com.*

Ticketpop

TICKETS | A fast and easy method to purchase tickets online for major concerts, sporting events, and other shows. ☎ *866/994–0001, 787/294–0001* 🌐 *www.ticketpop.com.*

SHOPPING

In Old San Juan, Calle Fortaleza and Calle San Francisco have everything from T-shirt emporiums to jewelry stores to shops that specialize in made-to-order Panama hats. Running perpendicular to those streets is Calle Cristo, lined with factory-outlet stores, including Coach, Dooney & Burke, Guess, and Tommy Hilfiger. On weekends, artisans sell their wares at stalls around Paseo de la Princesa.

With many stores selling luxury items and designer fashions, the shopping spirit in Condado is reminiscent of that in Miami. Avenida Ashford is considered the heart of San Juan's fashion district. High-end chain stores such as Ferragamo and Gucci huddle together in a formerly derelict shopping strip, betting that the newly renovated luxury hotel La Concha will attract people ready to plunk down their platinum cards. A little farther west along Avenida Ashford are the one-of-a-kind clothing retailers that make this neighborhood worth a visit.

Just as in most other American cities, however, the real shopping occurs in the mall, and Plaza Las Américas—the largest in the Caribbean—is not to be missed. Known to locals simply as "Plaza," it's often host to artisan crafts fairs, art exhibitions, antiques shows, live Latin music, and pageants, depending on the time of year. For high-end shopping at stores like Saks and Louis Vuitton, head to the newer Mall of San Juan.

Thanks to Puerto Rico's vibrant arts scene, numerous galleries and studios are opening, and many are doing so in Santurce, Puerta de Tierra, and other neighborhoods outside the walls of Old San Juan.

ACTIVITIES

Many of San Juan's most enjoyable outdoor activities take place in and around the water. With miles of beach stretching across Isla Verde, Ocean Park, and Condado, there's a full range of water sports, including sailing, kayaking, windsurfing, paddleboarding, kiteboarding, Jet Skiing, deep-sea fishing, scuba diving, and snorkeling.

Land-based activities include biking, tennis, and walking or jogging at local parks. With a bit of effort—meaning a short drive out of the city—you'll discover a world of championship golf courses and rain-forest trails perfect for hiking. Baseball is big in Puerto Rico, and the players are world-class; many are recruited from local teams to play in the U.S. major leagues. The season runs October through February, and games are played in venues all over the island.

BIKING

Automobile traffic makes bike travel somewhat risky, mostly because most streets lack dedicated bike lanes—plus, all those fumes can be hard to take. That said, recreational cyclists are increasingly donning their helmets and wheeling through the streets, albeit with great care.

Your best bet for a safe and enjoyable experience is to book a bike tour through an outfitter. One popular 45-minute journey takes riders from the cobblestone streets of Old San Juan to Condado. It passes El Capitolio and runs through either Parque del Tercer Milenio (oceanside) or Parque Luis Muñoz Rivera, by way of the Caribe Hilton Hotel and over Puente Dos Hermanos (Dos Hermanos Bridge) onto Avenida Ashford. The truly ambitious can continue east to Ocean Park, Isla Verde, and right on out of town to the eastern community of Piñones and its beachside bike path.

Rent the Bicycle

BICYCLING | For about $27 per day, this friendly operation offers bicycle rental with free delivery to all major San Juan hotels. They also offer guided tours of Old San Juan and greater San Juan beaches and parks. The bilingual guides are authorized by the National Park Service to give tours of the forts. ✉ *Capitolio Plaza, 100 Calle del Muelle, Suite 205, Old San Juan* ☎ *787/661–2728* 🌐 *www.rentthebicycle.com.*

FISHING

Puerto Rico's waters are home to large game fish such as snook, wahoo, dorado, tuna, and barracuda; as many as 30 world records for catches have been set off the island's shores. Prices for fishing expeditions vary, but they tend to include all your bait and tackle, as well as refreshments, and start at $600 (for a boat with as many as six people) for a half-day trip to around $1,000 for a full day, or around $200 per person for a full day on a split charter.

GOLF

Puerto Rico is the birthplace of golf legend and raconteur Chi Chi Rodriguez, and he had to hone his craft somewhere. The island has more than a dozen courses, including some of championship caliber; several make good day trips from San Juan. Be sure to call ahead for details on reserving a tee time; hours vary, and several hotel courses allow only guests to play or give preference to them. Greens fees start at $25 and go as high as $190.

Three golf clubs are within fairly easy striking distance of San Juan. The four 18-hole golf courses at **TPC Dorado Beach** are just west of San Juan. More options lie farther to the east of the city. The **Wyndham Gardens at Palmas del Mar Country Club** has two good golf courses. And the spectacular **Wyndham Grand Río Mar Beach Resort & Spa** has a clubhouse with a proshop and two restaurants set between two 18-hole courses.

HIKING

El Yunque is the only tropical rain forest within the U.S. National Forest system. The park is officially known as the Bosque Nacional del Caribe (Caribbean National Forest) and is a great day trip from San Juan, about an hour's drive east.

SURFING

Although the west-coast beaches around Isabela and Rincón are considered *the* places to surf in Puerto Rico, San Juan was actually the place where the sport got its start on the island. In 1958 legendary surfers Gary Hoyt and José Rodríguez Reyes began surfing at the beach in front of Bus Stop 2½, facing El Capitolio. This spot is known for big waves, but the conditions must be nearly perfect to surf it. Today many surfers head to Puerta de Tierra and a spot known as La Ocho (in front of Bus Stop 8). Another, called the Pressure Point, is behind the Caribe Hilton Hotel.

In Condado you can surf La Punta, a reef break behind the Presbyterian Hospital, with either surfboards or body boards. In Isla Verde, white water on the horizon means that the waves are good at Pine Grove, the beach break near the Ritz-Carlton. East of the city, in Piñones, the Caballo has deep-to-shallow-water shelf waves that require a big-wave board known as a "gun." Surf culture frowns upon aficionados who divulge the best spots to outsiders; if you're lucky, though, maybe you'll make a few friends who'll let you in on where to find the best waves.

TOURS

Debbie's Journeys in Puerto Rico

GUIDED TOURS | Debbie Molina runs private and public walking tours of Old San Juan specializing in history and architecture and special holiday trips that let you experience a local Thanksgiving or Christmas. ✉ *San Juan* ☎ *787/605–9060* 🌐 *www.hellotourguide.com* 🎟 *From $25.*

Flavors of San Juan

WALKING TOURS | These friendly, well-informed guides can take you on walking tours of Old San Juan, combining visits to restaurants that are off the beaten path with a cultural and historical introduction to the city. ✉ *Calle Recinto Sur, Old San Juan* ☎ *787/964–2447* 🌐 *www.sanjuanfoodtours.com* 🎟 *From $80.*

Sailing Dreams Yacht Charters

BOAT TOURS | Captain Judith will take you on an unforgettable sailing tour in the Bay of San Juan. Choose from day, evening, and private tours. Refreshments and appetizers are provided. ✉ *San Juan Marina, Slip 64, 482 Av. Manuel Fernandez Juncos* ☎ *787/519–5000* 🌐 *www.sailingdreamspr.com* 🎟 *From $99.*

Segway Tours of Puerto Rico

SPECIAL-INTEREST | This company offers group tours of the city's historic district, using Segways for fun and easy transport. ✉ *Pier 2, Old San Juan*

☎ 787/598-9455 🌐 www.segwaytourspr.com 💵 From $60.

★ **Spoon Food Tours**

SPECIAL-INTEREST | FAMILY | Get to know Puerto Rico with Spoon, a local tourism company specializing in authentic culinary and cultural tours. From walking and driving food tours to cocktail tours and mixology and cooking classes, this company offers travelers a unique opportunity to experience the gastronomy, culture, and history of Puerto Rico. You'll eat delicious local food, try fantastic cocktails, and mingle with locals while learning along the way. It's a great way to immerse yourself in the culture, sipping and savoring your way through Puerto Rico with your passionate, epicurean guide. Take a tour at the beginning of your stay so that you can take advantage of all the recommendations provided by your guide. Email in advance of your trip, and the staff will be happy to provide suggestions of other things to do on the island. ✉ *Old San Juan* ☎ *787/598–6008* 🌐 *www.spoonfoodtours.com* 💵 *From $75.*

VISITOR INFORMATION

You'll find Puerto Rico Tourism Company information officers (identified by their caps and shirts with company patch) near the baggage-claim areas at Luis Muñoz Marín International Airport.

In Old San Juan the tourism headquarters is at the old city jail, La Princesa; its main information bureau is opposite Pier 1 on Calle Tanca at Calle Gilberto Concepción de Gracia. Be sure to pick up a free copy of *¡Qué Pasa!,* the official visitor guide. Information officers are posted around Old San Juan (near the cruise-ship piers and at the Catedral de San Juan Bautista) during the day.

La Oficina de Turismo del Municipio de San Juan, run by the city, has information bureaus in Old San Juan and in Condado.

CONTACTS Oficina de Turismo del Municipio de San Juan. ✉ *Alcaldía, Plaza de Armas, 153 Calle San Francisco, Old San Juan* ☎ *787/480–2548.* **Discover Puerto Rico DMO.** ✉ *Ochoa Bldg., Calle Tanca and Calle Comercio, across from Pier 1, Old San Juan* ☎ *787/721–2400* 🌐 *www.puertoricodmo.com/DMOLanding.*

Old San Juan

Old San Juan's 16th-century cobblestone streets, ornate Spanish town houses with wrought-iron balconies, ancient plazas, and eclectic museums together form a repository of the island's colorful history. Founded in 1521 by the Spanish explorer Juan Ponce de León, Old San Juan sits on an islet separated from the "new" parts of the city by a couple of miles and a few centuries. Today, however, it is culturally youthful and vibrant, reflecting the sensibilities of the stylish professionals, bohemian art crowd, and university students who people its streets. You'll find more streetfront cafés and innovative restaurants, more contemporary art galleries, more musicians playing in plazas, than anywhere else in San Juan.

Old San Juan slopes north, uphill, to Calle Norzagaray, which runs along the Atlantic shoreline and connects Castillo San Cristóbal to El Morro, the islet's twin fortifications. On the north side of Calle Norzagaray you'll find a small neighborhood wedged between the city walls and the ocean—this is La Perla, a rough area you'd be wise to avoid. The west end of the Old San Juan overlooks the bay, and it's here that the rugged, towering walls of the original city are most evident. On the south side, along Calle Gilberto Concepción de Gracia, you'll find cruise ships and commercial piers jutting into San Juan Harbor.

GETTING AROUND

If you try to explore Old San Juan by car, you'll likely find yourself sitting in traffic much of the day—especially on weekends, when police change traffic patterns. Old San Juan is a walking city, with narrow one-way streets, narrower alleys, little parking, and sights and shops packed together in an area hardly larger than one square mile. Some of the streets are steep and many are paved with cobblestones, so wear comfortable shoes as well as a hat and sunscreen—and drink plenty of water.

In Old San Juan, free trolleys can take you around, and the tourist board can provide you with a copy of *¡Qué Pasa!* as well as a map, which contains a self-guided walking tour.

Ferry: The ferry between Old San Juan and Cataño is operated by the Autoridad de Transporte Marítimo. It costs a mere 50¢ one-way and runs every 30 minutes daily 6 am–10 pm. The ferry, which departs Pier 2, is the one to take if you wish to visit the Bacardí rum factory.

Parking: If you can't avoid taking a car into Old San Juan, park at La Puntilla, at the head of Paseo de la Princesa. It's an outdoor lot with the cheapest rates, at less than $5 for all-day parking. You could also try the Felisa Rincón de Gautier lot on Calle Gilberto Concepción de Gracia or the Frank Santaella lot between Paseo de Covadonga and Calle Gilberto Concepción de Gracia. Parking starts at around $1 or so for the first hour. Many lots open early and close late; some are even open 24 hours a day, like the Felisa Rincón parking garage (known as "Doña Fela" to locals).

Trolleys: Free trolleys swing through Old San Juan all day, every day; they depart the main bus terminal area across from Pier 4 and take one of three routes. One route heads north to Calle Norzagaray, then west to El Morro, dropping you off at the long footpath leading to the fort. Then it retraces its route past Castillo San Cristóbal, west to Plaza de Armas, east on Fortaleza, west on Recinto Sur, and then back along Calle Gilberto Concepción de Gracia (also called Calle la Marina) to the piers. A second route takes you east to the Puerta de Tierra district, then via Castillo San Cristóbal to El Morro, then via Calle Norzagaray and Plaza Colón and back to the piers. The third route follows a figure 8 from Pier 4 north on Tanca, then west along San Francisco and east on Fortaleza, returning via Plaza Colón. The trolleys make regular stops (at 24 signs marked "Parada") along the way. When you're finished touring, taxis can be found in several spots: in front of Pier 2, near the Catedral de San Juan Bautista, on the Plaza de Armas, or in Plaza Colón. A map of trolley routes is available from the Puerto Rico Tourism Company information offices.

CONTACTS Autoridad de Transporte Marítimo. ☎ *787/497–7740.*

SAFETY

Old San Juan is generally safe, but keep in mind that pickpockets visit the same places as tourists. Keep money and credit cards out of back pockets, and avoid carrying open handbags. Avoid the Perla district and, if walking, stick to well-policed areas and well-lighted streets by night. Women should take licensed taxis at night.

TIMING

Old San Juan is a small neighborhood, approximately seven city blocks north to south and eight east to west. In strictly geographical terms, it's easily traversed in a day. But to truly appreciate the numerous plazas, museums, boutiques, galleries, and cafés requires two or three days. *For a great half-day itinerary, see "Walking Old San Juan."*

Sights

Capilla del Cristo

RELIGIOUS SITE | According to legend, in 1753 a young horseman named Baltazar Montañez got carried away during festivities in honor of San Juan Bautista (St. John the Baptist), raced down Calle

Old San Juan's Cementerio Santa María Magdelena de Pazzis is one of the city's best-kept secrets and offers a peaceful respite from the bustle of the busy streets.

Cristo, and plunged over its steep precipice. Historical records maintain the man died, but legend contends that he lived. (Another version of the story has it that the horse miraculously stopped before plunging over the cliff.) Regardless, this chapel was built partly to prevent further calamities. Inside is a small silver altar dedicated to the Christ of Miracles. Above the altar hang two religious paintings by Puerto Rico's famous painter José Campeche. You can peer in through the wrought-iron gates, which are usually closed. ✉ *Calle Cristo, at the end, Old San Juan* 🎫 *Free.*

Casa Alcaldía de San Juan (*San Juan City Hall*)

GOVERNMENT BUILDING | San Juan's city hall was built between 1602 and 1789. In 1841, extensive alterations made it resemble Madrid's city hall, with arcades, towers, balconies, and an inner courtyard. Renovations have refreshed the facade and some interior rooms, but the architecture remains true to its colonial style. Only the patios are open to public viewings. A municipal tourist information center and an art gallery with rotating exhibits are in the lobby. Call ahead to schedule a tree tour. ✉ *153 Calle San Francisco, Plaza de Armas, Old San Juan* ☎ *787/480–2910* 🌐 *www.sanjuanciudadpatria.com* 🎫 *Free* 🕑 *Closed weekends.*

Casa Blanca

HOUSE | The original structure here was a wooden house built in 1521 as a home for Ponce de León; he died in Cuba without ever living here. His descendants occupied the house's sturdier replacement, a lovely colonial mansion with tile floors and beamed ceilings, for more than 250 years. It was the home of the U.S. Army commander in Puerto Rico from the end of the Spanish-American War in 1898 to 1966. Several rooms decorated with colonial-era furnishings are open to the public. A guide will show you around, and then you can explore on your own. Don't miss the stairway descending from one of the bedrooms. (Despite local lore, this leads to a small room and not to a tunnel to nearby El Morro.) The lush garden, complete with watchtower, is a quiet place to unwind. ✉ *1 Calle San Sebastián, Old San Juan* ☎ *787/725–1454* 🎫 *$3* ⏲ *Closed Mon. and Tues.*

Casa de Ramón Power y Giralt
MUSEUM | FAMILY | The restored home of 18th-century naval hero Don Ramón Power y Giralt is now the headquarters of the Conservation Trust of Puerto Rico. On-site are several displays highlighting the physical, cultural, and historical importance of land and properties on the island under the trust's aegis. The goal of the trust is to increase the amount of protected lands in Puerto Rico from (currently) 8% to 33% by the year 2033. Displays are in Spanish but there are note cards in English to the changing exhibitions. A gift shop sells toys, Puerto Rican candies, and eco-friendly souvenirs. ✉ *155 Calle Tetuán, Old San Juan* ☎ *787/722–5882* 🌐 *paralanaturaleza.org* 🎫 *Free* ⏲ *Closed Sun. and Mon.*

★ **Castillo San Cristóbal**
MILITARY SITE | FAMILY | This huge stone fortress, built between 1634 and 1790, guarded the city from land attacks from the east. The largest Spanish fortification in the New World, San Cristóbal was known in the 17th and 18th centuries as the Gibraltar of the West Indies. Five freestanding structures divided by dry moats are connected by tunnels. You're free to explore the gun turrets (with cannon in situ), officers' quarters, re-created 18th-century barracks, and gloomy passageways. Along with El Morro, San Cristóbal is a National Historic Site administered by the U.S. National Park Service; it's a UNESCO World Heritage Site as well. Rangers conduct tours in Spanish and English. ✉ *Calle Norzagaray at Av. Muñoz Rivera, Old San Juan* ☎ *787/729–6777* 🌐 *www.nps.gov/saju* 🎫 *$7, includes Castillo San Felipe del Morro.*

★ **Castillo San Felipe del Morro** (*El Morro*)
HISTORIC SITE | FAMILY | At the northwestern tip of the Old San Juan, El Morro (the promontory) was built by the Spaniards between 1539 and 1786. Rising 140 feet above the sea, the massive six-level fortress was built to protect the port and has a commanding view of the harbor. It is a labyrinth of cannon batteries, ramps, barracks, turrets, towers, and tunnels, through which you're free to wander. The cannon emplacement walls and the dank secret passageways are a wonder of engineering. A small but enlightening museum displays ancient Spanish guns and other armaments, military uniforms, and blueprints for Spanish forts in the Americas, although Castillo San Cristóbal has more extensive and impressive exhibits. There's also a gift shop. The fort is a National Historic Site administered by the U.S. National Park Service, and a UNESCO World Heritage Site as well. Various tours and a video are available in English. ✉ *Calle del Morro, Old San Juan* ☎ *787/729–6960* 🌐 *www.nps.gov/saju* 🎫 *$7, includes Castillo San Cristóbal.*

Catedral de San Juan Bautista
RELIGIOUS SITE | The Catholic shrine of Puerto Rico had humble beginnings in the early 1520s as a thatch-roofed wooden structure. After a hurricane destroyed the church, it was rebuilt in 1540, when it was given a graceful circular staircase and vaulted Gothic ceilings. Most of the work on the present cathedral, however, was done in the 19th century. The remains of Ponce de León are behind a marble tomb in the wall near the transept, on the north side. The trompe-l'oeil work on the inside of the dome is breathtaking. Unfortunately, many of the other frescoes have suffered water damage. ✉ *151 Calle Cristo, Old San Juan* ☎ *787/722–0861* 🎫 *$1 suggested donation.*

Cementerio Santa María Magdalena de Pazzis
CEMETERY | One of Old San Juan's best-kept secrets, this remarkable cemetery provides a peaceful respite from the bustle of the city. Sandwiched

between El Morro and La Perla, it offers a panoramic view of the Atlantic Ocean and an enviable resting place for the many notable figures fortunate enough to be buried here. Dating back to the early 1800s, the cemetery was originally administered by Carmelite nuns. Today you can stop by the ornate tombs (many of which are topped with graceful marble sculptures) to pay your respects to an illustrious group of Puerto Rican political figures, intellectuals, artists, and revolutionaries, including José Celso Barbosa, José Ferrer, Pedro Albizu Campos, Rafael Hernández, Ricardo Alegría, and others. ⚠ **While a robust police presence has made this area bordering La Perla safer, it's still a good idea to avoid coming after hours or at night.** ✉ *West end of Calle Norzagaray, Old San Juan* 🎫 *Free.*

Fundación Felisa Rincón de Gautier

MUSEUM | This tiny but fascinating museum honors Felisa Rincón de Gautier, who served as San Juan's mayor from 1946 to 1968. Throughout her life, "Doña Felisa" worked tirelessly on various public causes, including women's voting rights and health care for the poor. Her preschools, known as Escuelas Maternas, were used as the model for the United States' Head Start program. Extremely well connected politically, both on the island and abroad, she was an egalitarian figure who rose to power at a time when women and politics were not mentioned in the same breath. Even if you have no interest in her story, you'll get a peek inside one of the historic houses of Old San Juan. Guided tours in English or Spanish are available. ✉ *51 Caleta de San Juan, Old San Juan* ☎ *787/724–7239* 🌐 *www.museofelisarincon.com* 🎫 *Free* 🕓 *Closed Sun. and Mon.*

Fundación Nacional Para la Cultura Popular

MUSEUM | This nonprofit foundation serves many functions: museum, performance space, dance and music school, and archive dedicated to preserving the contributions Puerto Ricans have made to music, dance, television, theater, film, and other culture. In a 300-year-old building once used by the Spanish as a meteorological lookout, you can visit a rotating exhibition, come in the evening to hear live Latin music, or take a *bomba* or *plena* dance class. A small store sells music by Puerto Ricans in every genre, from classical to salsa. Signed posters from El Gran Combo, Tito Puente, and Willie Colón—as well as Ricky Martin's platinum record—line the walls. Check the website or call ahead for the performance schedule. ✉ *56 Calle Fortaleza, Old San Juan* ☎ *787/724–7165* 🌐 *www.prpop.org* 🎫 *Free* 🕓 *Closed Sun. and Mon.*

La Fortaleza

GOVERNMENT BUILDING | Sitting atop the fortified city walls overlooking the harbor, La Fortaleza was built between 1533 and 1540 as a fortress, but it proved insufficient, mainly because it was built inside the bay. It was attacked numerous times and occupied twice, by the British in 1598 and the Dutch in 1625. When the city's other fortifications were finished, this became the governor's palace. Changes made over the past four centuries have resulted in the current eclectic yet eye-pleasing collection of marble and mahogany, medieval towers, and stained-glass galleries. Still the official residence of the island's governor, it is the Western Hemisphere's oldest executive mansion in continual use. Guided tours of the gardens and exterior are conducted several times a day in English and Spanish; call ahead, as the schedule changes daily. Proper attire is required: no sleeveless shirts or very short shorts. Tours begin near the main gate in a yellow building called the Real Audiencia, housing the Oficina Estatal de Preservación Histórica. ✉ *West end of Calle Fortaleza, Old San Juan* ☎ *787/721–7000* 🌐 *www.fortaleza.pr.gov* 🎫 *Free* 🕓 *Closed weekends.*

Hear your footsteps echo throughout Castillo San Felipe's vast network of tunnels, designed to amplify the sounds of approaching enemies.

Museo de las Américas

MUSEUM | On the second floor of the imposing former military barracks, Cuartel de Ballajá, this museum houses four permanent exhibits: Folk Arts, African Heritage, the Indian in America, and Conquest and Colonization. You'll also find a number of temporary exhibitions of works by regional and international artists. A wide range of handicrafts is available in the gift shop. ✉ *Calle Norzagaray and Calle del Morro, Old San Juan* ☎ *787/724–5052* 🌐 *www.museolasamericas.org* 🎫 *$6* 🕓 *Closed Mon.*

Museo de San Juan

MUSEUM | A bustling marketplace in 1857, this handsome building now houses the small San Juan Museum. You'll find rotating exhibits of Puerto Rican art, plus tableaux and audiovisual shows that present the island's history. Concerts and other cultural events take place in the huge interior courtyard. Stop by on Saturday morning to check out the small but lively farmers' market. ✉ *150 Calle Norzagaray, at Calle MacArthur, Old San Juan* ☎ *787/480–3530* 🎫 *Free* 🕓 *Closed Mon.*

Museo La Casa del Libro

MUSEUM | Dedicated to the artistry of the printed word, this museum counts among its holdings approximately 400 books printed before the 15th century—one of the larger such collections in the Western Hemisphere. It also owns two royal decrees from King Ferdinand and Queen Isabella that date back to 1493, the year Columbus first reached Puerto Rico. Because the museum is in a temporary location while long-term restorations to the permanent building are under way, only a small portion of the 6,000-piece collection is on display: you can see a page from the Gutenberg Bible and a 12th-century lunar-cycle calendar, which is impressive and worth a quick look. The gift shop has a terrific collection of posters that draws customers from all over the world. ✉ *255 Calle Cristo, Old San Juan* ☎ *787/723–0354* 🌐 *www.lacasadellibro.org* 🎫 *$4.50* 🕓 *Closed Sun. and Mon.*

Parque de las Palomas

CITY PARK | **FAMILY** | The small, newly renovated park bordering Old San Juan's Capilla del Cristo has a large stone wall with pigeonholes cut into it. Hundreds of *palomas* (pigeons) roost here, and the park is full of cooing local children chasing the well-fed birds. Stop to enjoy the wide views over Paseo de la Princesa and the San Juan bay. ✉ *End of Calle Cristo, Old San Juan.*

Paseo de la Princesa

PROMENADE | Built in the mid-19th century to honor the Spanish princess of Asturias, this street has a broad pedestrian walkway and is spruced up with flowers, trees, benches, and streetlamps. Unfurling westward from Plaza del Inmigrante along the base of the fortified city walls, it leads to the Fuente Raíces, a striking fountain depicting the various ethnic groups of Puerto Rico. Take a seat and watch the boats zip across the water. Beyond the fountain is the beginning of Paseo del Morro, a well-paved shoreline path that hugs Old San Juan's walls and leads past the city gate at Calle San Juan and continues to the tip of the headland, beneath El Morro. ✉ *Paseo de la Princesa, Old San Juan.*

Plaza de Armas

PLAZA | The Old City's original main square was once used as military drilling grounds. Bordered by Calles San Francisco, Rafael Cordero, San José, and Cruz, it has a fountain with 19th-century statues representing the four seasons as well as a bandstand, a small café, and a kiosk selling snacks and fruit frappés. The Alcaldía commands the north side. This is a popular, bustling meeting place, often filled with artists sketching caricatures, pedestrians in line at the food stands, and hundreds of pigeons waiting for handouts. ✉ *Calle San José, Old San Juan.*

Plaza Colón

PLAZA | A statue of Christopher Columbus stands atop a soaring column and fountain in this bustling Old San Juan square, kitty-corner to Castillo San Cristóbal. Once called St. James Square, it was renamed in 1893 to honor the 400th anniversary of Columbus's arrival in Puerto Rico; bronze plaques on the statue's base relate episodes in his life. Local artisans often line the plaza, so it's a good place for souvenirs. Cool off with a fresh fruit frappé or smoothie at the kiosk. ✉ *Old San Juan.*

Plazuela La Rogativa

PLAZA | According to legend, the British, while laying siege to the city in 1797, mistook the flaming torches of a *rogativa* (religious procession) for Spanish reinforcements and beat a hasty retreat. In this little plaza, a monument of a bishop and three women commemorates the legend. The striking contemporary statue was created in 1971 by the artist Lindsay Daen to mark the Old City's 450th anniversary. The fine view of La Fortaleza and the harbor is a bonus. ✉ *Caleta de las Monjas, Old San Juan.*

Puerta de San Juan

ARCHAEOLOGICAL SITE | Dating back to 1520, this was one of the five original entrances to the city and is the only one still in its original state. The massive gate, painted a brilliant shade of red, gave access from the port and welcomed diplomats into the city. It resembles a tunnel because it passes through La Muralla, the 20-foot-thick city walls. ✉ *Paseo de la Princesa, Old San Juan.*

Restaurants

Café Berlin

$$ | **INTERNATIONAL** | **FAMILY** | A handful of tables spill onto a sidewalk deck lighted with tiny lights at this bohemian and romantic restaurant overlooking Plaza Colón. There's something on the international menu for everyone, including a good selection of vegan and vegetarian dishes. **Known for:** breakfast; variety of vegan and vegetarian choices; street-side

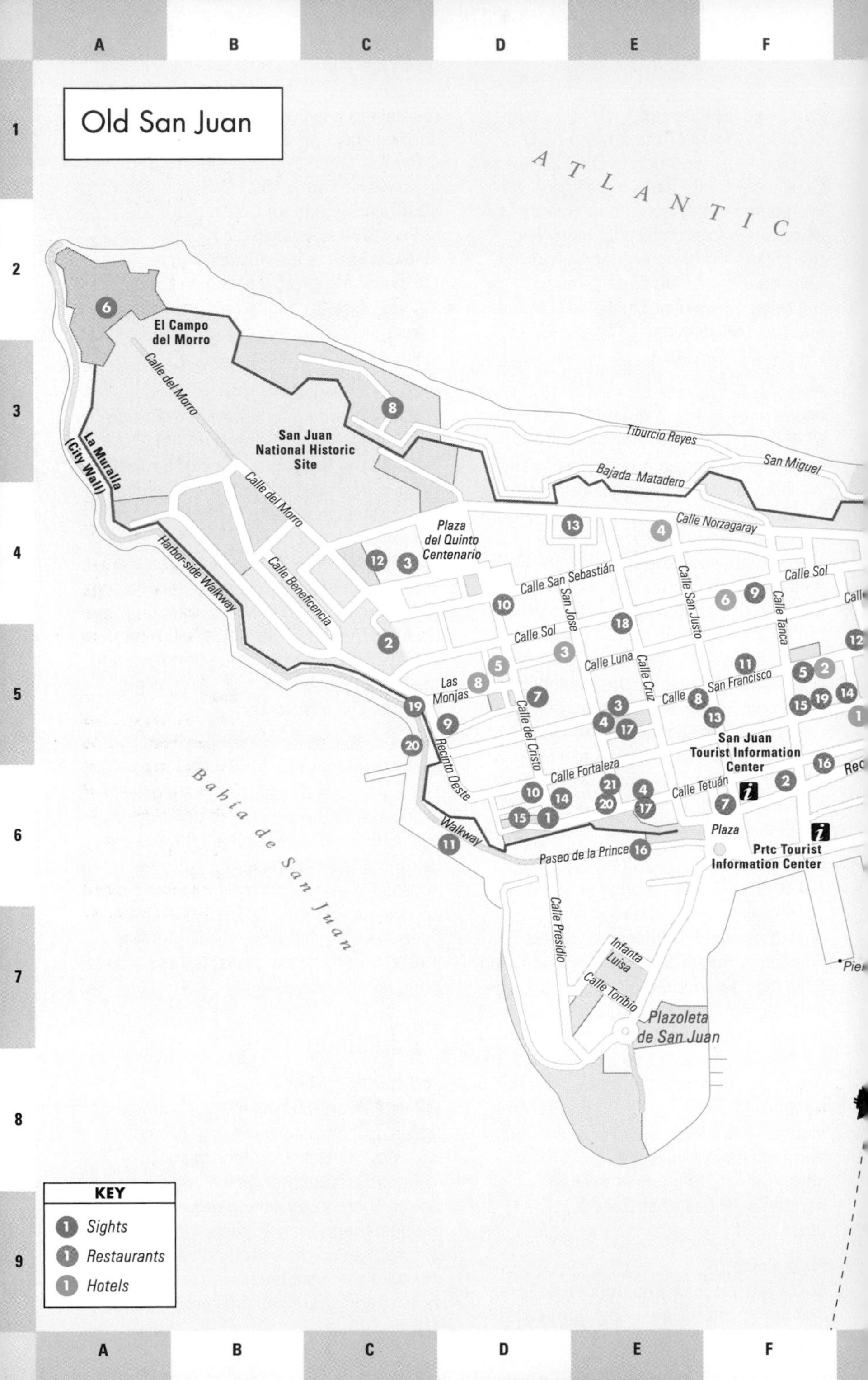
Old San Juan
A B C D E F
1 2 3 4 5 6 7 8 9
ATLANTIC
El Campo del Morro
Calle del Morro
San Juan National Historic Site
La Muralla (City Wall)
Harbor-side Walkway
Calle Beneficencia
Plaza del Quinto Centenario
Tiburcio Reyes
San Miguel
Bajada Matadero
Calle Norzagaray
Calle San Sebastián
San Jose
Calle San Justo
Calle Sol
Calle Tanca
Calle Luna
Calle Cruz
Calle San Francisco
Las Monjas
Calle del Cristo
Recinto Oeste
Calle Fortaleza
Calle Tetuán
San Juan Tourist Information Center
Plaza
Prtc Tourist Information Center
Bahía de San Juan
Walkway
Paseo de la Prince
Calle Presidio
Infanta Luisa
Calle Toribio
Plazoleta de San Juan
KEY
Sights
Restaurants
Hotels

OCEAN
La Muralla (City Wall)
Calle Luna
Calle O'Donnell
Visitors Center
Muñoz Rivera
Plaza de Colón
Calle Fortaleza
Ponce de Léon
Paseo Covadonga
Frank Santaella Parking Garage
Erumbaugh St.
Recinto Sur
Comercio
Pershing
Gen. Harcing
Terminal de Guaguas (Bus Terminal)
Free Trolley
Calle del Muelle
Paseo Gilberto Concepcion de Graci
San Juan Cruise Ship Ports
Pier 2
Pier 3
Pier 4
Pier 1
Bahía de San Juan
FERRY TO CATAÑO
0 1/4 mi
0 250 m

Sights

1 Capilla del Cristo........ D6
2 Casa Alcadía de San Juan.................C5
3 Casa Blanca.............. E5
4 Casa de Ramón Power y Giralt............ E6
5 Castillo San Cristóbal.....I4
6 Castillo San Felipe del Morro A2
7 Catedral de San Juan Bautista...... D5
8 Cementerio Santa María Magdalena de Pazzi.....C3
9 Fundación Felisa Rincón de Gautier D5
10 Fundación Nacional Parala Cultura Popular. D6
11 La Fortaleza D6
12 Museo de las Américas C4
13 Museo de San Juan..... E4
14 Museo la Casa del Libro.................. D6
15 Parque de las Palomas D6
16 Paseo de la Princesa.... E6
17 Plaza de Armas E5
18 Plaza Colón.............. G5
19 Plazuela La Rogativa.... C5
20 Puerta de San Juan C5

Restaurants

1 Café Berlin............... G4
2 Café Cuatro Sombras.......... F6
3 Café Don Ruiz C4
4 Café 4 Estaciones........ E5
5 Cafeteria Mallorca F5
6 Caficultura.............. G4
7 Carli's Fine Bistro & Piano............ F6
8 Casa Cortés Chocobar................. E5
9 El Jibarito................. F4
10 El Patio de Sam D4
11 La Bombonera F5
12 La Madre G5
13 La Mallorquina........... F5
14 Marmalade.............. G5
15 Pirilo Pizza Rustica F5
16 Raíces...................... F5
17 Señor Paleta E6
18 St. Germain Bistro & Café............. E5
19 Trois Cent Onze F5
20 Verde Mesa E6
21 Waffle-era Tea Room E6

Hotels

1 CasaBlanca Hotel G5
2 Da House Hotel F5
3 Decanter Hotel.......... D5
4 The Gallery Inn........... E4
5 Hotel El Convento....... D5
6 La Terraza de San Juan.............. F4
7 Sheraton Old San Juan Hotel.......... G6
8 Villa Herencia Hotel D5

dining. *Average main: $19 ✉ 407 Calle San Francisco, Old San Juan ☎ 787/722–5205 🌐 www.cafeberlinpr.com.*

★ Café Cuatro Sombras

$ | CAFÉ | If you want to try local, single-origin, shade-grown coffee, this micro-roastery and café is the place to do it. Owners Pablo Muñoz and Mariana Suárez grow their beans in the mountains of Yauco on a hacienda that has been in the Muñoz family since 1846. **Known for:** locally grown coffee; pastries and sandwiches; coffee tastings. *Average main: $7 ✉ 259 Calle Recinto Sur, Old San Juan ☎ 787/724–9955 🌐 www.cuatrosombras.com ⏲ No dinner.*

Café Don Ruiz

$ | CAFÉ |FAMILY | Tucked away in the corner of the old Spanish military barracks, Café Don Ruiz serves some of the finest coffee in town. The family-run hacienda from Yauco is known for its handpicked coffee, grown more than 3,000 feet above sea level. **Known for:** locally grown coffee; light bites; historic location. *Average main: $5 ✉ Cuartel de Ballajá, Calle Norzagaray at Calle Beneficiencia, Old San Juan ☎ 787/723–1462 🌐 www.cafedonruiz.com ⏲ No dinner.*

Café 4 Estaciones

$ | CAFÉ | At Café 4 Estaciones, tables and chairs sit under a canvas canopy surrounded by potted plants. This tiny kiosk-café is the perfect spot to put down your shopping bags and rest your tired feet. **Known for:** café con leche; mallorcas; quesitos. *Average main: $2 ✉ Plaza de Armas, Old San Juan ▭ No credit cards.*

Cafetería Mallorca

$ | CAFÉ | The specialty at this old-fashioned, 1950s-style diner is the *mallorca,* a sweet pastry that's buttered, grilled, and then sprinkled with powdered sugar. Wash one down with a cup of café con leche. **Known for:** old-school diner feel; mallorcas; café con leche. *Average main: $10 ✉ 300 Calle San Francisco, Old San Juan ☎ 787/724–4607 ⏲ No dinner.*

Caficultura

$$ | CAFÉ | Caficultura prides itself both on its full coffee-bar menu and its delicious *cocina de mercado.* For breakfast, which is served all day, try coconut-milk French toast with pineapple jam and coconut shavings. **Known for:** coconut-milk French toast with pineapple jam; beautifully presented lattes; outside seating. *Average main: $15 ✉ 401 Calle San Francisco, Old San Juan ☎ 787/723–7731 ⏲ No dinner.*

Carli's Fine Bistro & Piano

$$$ | INTERNATIONAL | As you might guess from the name, the music is as much of a draw as the food at Carli's. The genial owner and host, Carli Muñoz, toured for a number of years with the Beach Boys (note the gold album on the wall) and plays nightly with his jazz trio, often accompanied by singers and musicians who happen to drop in. **Known for:** live jazz; Caribbean-style tapas; classy ambience. *Average main: $25 ✉ Plazoleta Rafael Carrión, Calle Recinto Sur at Calle San Justo, Old San Juan ☎ 787/725–4927 🌐 www.carlisworld.com ⏲ No lunch. Closed Sun.*

Casa Cortés ChocoBar

$ | CONTEMPORARY | The Cortés family has been making bean-to-bar chocolate for more than 85 years. In 2013 they opened Puerto Rico's first "chocobar" to share their passion. **Known for:** chocolate incorporated into many dishes; breakfast specialties and pastries; locally made chocolates and soaps. *Average main: $10 ✉ 210 Calle San Francisco, Old San Juan ☎ 787/722–0499 🌐 www.casa-cortespr.com.*

El Jibarito

$$ | PUERTO RICAN | The menus are handwritten and the tables wobble, but locals in the know have favored this no-frills, family-run restaurant—tucked away on a quiet cobblestone street—for years. The *bistec encebollado,* goat fricassee, and shredded beef stew stand out on the comida criolla menu. **Known for:** traditional Puerto Rican comfort food; casual

Continued on page 76

WALKING OLD SAN JUAN

Old San Juan is Puerto Rico's quintessential colonial neighborhood. Narrow streets and plazas are still enclosed by thick fortress walls, and bougainvillea bowers spill over exquisite facades. A walk along streets paved with slate-blue cobblestones leads past colonial mansions, ancient churches, and intriguing museums and galleries. Vivacious restaurants and bars that teem with life young and old are always nearby, making it easy to refuel and reinvigorate anytime during your stroll.

by Christopher P. Baker

left, strolling down Calle del Cristo; top right, a view from El Morro; bottom right, dancers in front of Castillo San Cristóbal

A STROLL THROUGH OLD SAN JUAN

La Fortaleza

This walk is best done in the morning to avoid the afternoon heat and cruise-ship crowds. The route is 2 mi (3 km); it will take half a day at a leisurely pace, with plenty of stops along the way.

❶ **Start at Plaza del Inmigrante.** This cobbled square facing the cruise port has impressive neoclassical and art deco buildings. From here, the **Paseo de la Princesa** promenade unfurls west beneath the ancient city wall, **La Muralla**. Artisans set up stalls under the palms on weekends. Midway along the brick-paved walkway, stop to admire the **Fuente Raíces** monument and fountain: dolphins cavort at the feet of figures representing Puerto Rico's indigenous, Spanish, and African peoples.

Puerta de San Juan

❷ **Pass through the Puerta de San Juan.** This fortified entrance in La Muralla was built in 1520 and still retains its massive wooden gates, creaky on their ancient hinges. Immediately beyond, turn left and ascend to **Plazuela de la Rogativa**, a tiny plaza where a contemporary statue recalls the torch-lit procession that thwarted an English invasion in 1797. The harbor views are fantastic. Then, walk east one block to reach the **Catedral de San Juan Bautista,** the neoclassical 19th-century cathedral containing the mausoleum of Ponce de León.

❸ **Head south on Calle del Cristo.** Sloping gradually, this lovely street is lined with beautifully restored colonial mansions housing cafés, galleries, and boutiques. Passing Calle Fortaleza, note **La Fortaleza,** the official residence of the Puerto Rican Governor at the end of the street. Calle del Cristo ends at **Capilla**

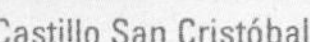
Castillo San Cristóbal

Calle del Cristo

Catedral de San Juan Bautista

Castillo San Felipe del Morro

del Cristo, a chapel adorned within by silver *milagros* (token requests).

❹ **Return via Calle del Cristo and continue to Plaza de San José.** Catercorner to the cathedral you'll find **El Convento**, a former convent turned hotel, with an excellent tapas bar. At **Plaza de San José** visit the **Iglesia de San José**, a simple church dating from 1532 that is one of the oldest churches in the Western Hemisphere.

❺ **Walk west on Calle San Sebastián.** This narrow street with colonial mansions painted in vibrant pastels ends at the gleaming white **Casa Blanca**. The oldest continually occupied residence in the Americas was originally the home of Ponce de León. Today it's a delightful museum furnished with period pieces. The garden is a tranquil spot for contemplation.

❻ **Follow Calle del Morro north.** One block from Casa Blanca you'll emerge upon a broad grassy headland—the Campo del Morro—popular with kite-flying families. It's skewered by an arrow-straight gravel path that aims at the imposing **Castillo San Felipe del Morro (El Morro)**, guarding the harbor entrance. Allow one-hour to roam the small museum, turrets, labyrinthine tunnels, and six levels of ramparts soaring 140 feet above the ocean.

❼ **Retrace your steps and turn left on Calle Norzagaray.** This street runs atop the Atlantic shoreline, offering sweeping ocean vistas. On your right you'll pass the **Plaza del Quinto Centenario**, pinned by an impressive statue: the *Tótem Telúrico*. Beyond, stroll past the Galería Nacional (Convento de los Domínicos) to reach the **Museo de San Juan**. Housed in a former market, it traces the city's history and displays works by Puerto Rico's master painters.

❽ **Continue east to Castillo San Cristóbal.** Spanning 27 acres, this multitiered fortress was completed in 1771 with mighty bulwarks that protected the city from eastern attack by land. It features superb historical exhibits and reenactments by soldiers in period costumes.

❾ **Exit the castle, turn south and walk one block to Plaza de Colón.** This leafy square is lined with excellent cafés and restaurants where you can rest your feet and enjoy a great meal.

The statues of the 19th-century fountain in the Plaza de Armas represent the four seasons.

atmosphere; gentle prices. *Average main: $14* ✉ *280 Calle Sol, Old San Juan* ☎ *787/725–8375.*

El Patio de Sam

$$ | **PUERTO RICAN** | This local restaurant serving comida criolla is a come-as-you-are spot, whether it's the end of the workweek or a long day of sight-seeing. Especially appealing is the airy courtyard with a skylight that gives the place its name. **Known for:** typical Puerto Rican specialties; homemade flan; local beers. *Average main: $16* ✉ *102 Calle San Sebastián, Old San Juan* ☎ *787/723–1149.*

La Bombonera

$$ | **CAFÉ** | You can't miss the stained glass and gorgeous Moorish-style tilework on the facade of this café, established in 1902. A local landmark famous for its *mallorca,* a sweet pastry that's grilled and buttered, La Bombonera is extremely popular in the morning—particularly on Sunday. **Known for:** mallorcas and other baked goods; old-school diner feel; asopao. *Average main: $14* ✉ *259 Calle San Francisco, Old San Juan* ☎ *787/705–3370* *Closed Mon. No dinner.*

La Madre

$$ | **MEXICAN** | La Madre is a hip Mexican restaurant, with a stylish, young clientele to match. Yes, it covers the standards, including some very tasty fish tacos, but you'll also find innovative, modern, international interpretations of Mexican cuisine. **Known for:** popular weekend brunch; outdoor seating; large variety of margaritas. *Average main: $18* ✉ *351 Calle San Francisco, Old San Juan* ☎ *787/647–5392.*

La Mallorquina

$$$ | **PUERTO RICAN** | Dating from 1848, La Mallorquina is thought to be the island's oldest restaurant. It specializes in various versions of *asopao,* a soupy rice dish with chicken or seafood, as well as other Puerto Rican and Spanish-inspired favorites. **Known for:** varieties of asopao; old-fashioned atmosphere; slow service. *Average main: $25* ✉ *207 Calle San Justo, Old San Juan* ☎ *787/722–3261* *Closed Mon.*

Great Itineraries

If You Have 1 Day

Many people find themselves with a single day (or even less) to explore the city, and there should be no question about your destination: Old San Juan. Spend the entire day rambling around the cobblestone streets and ducking into the many shops, and leave plenty of time for exploring the turrets, towers, and dungeons of **Castillo San Felipe del Morro**, the original fortress on a rocky promontory at the islet's northwestern tip.

If You Have 3 Days

It's only fitting that you spend the first day on a walking tour of Old San Juan. What to see? **Castillo San Felipe del Morro** should be at the top of your list, but you may want to explore the equally enthralling **Castillo San Cristóbal**, which has underground tunnels and hidden passages, plus cannon and a more impressive museum than El Morro's. **La Fortaleza**, the city's original fortress, wasn't much protection from marauding pirates, but it does a great job sheltering the governor and can be toured. And **Casa Blanca**, a home built for Juan Ponce de León, is a wonderful place to explore how the Spanish lived in colonial days. Reserve Day 2 for lounging on a *playa* (beach). Choose from the city's finest at Condado, Ocean Park, or Isla Verde, then park yourself in a rented chair with a good book, a cold drink, and plenty of sunscreen. In the evening, make sure you enjoy the warm weather by dining alfresco. On Day 3, hop the ferry across the bay to Cataño for a tour of the **Casa Bacardí Visitor Center.** Return in time for some shopping in the shops and delightful arts-and-crafts galleries along Calles Cristo and Fortaleza, followed by dinner—there are lots of great restaurants to choose from.

If You Have 5 Days

Follow the itinerary above for your first three days in San Juan. On Day 4, head for the Santurce district. You can immerse yourself in island art at the **Museo de Arte de Puerto Rico** and, nearby, the **Museo de Arte Contemporáneo de Puerto Rico.** Afterward, wander through the produce stalls at the Plaza del Mercado in Santurce, with a fresh papaya or soursop shake in hand. Be sure to note the giant bronze sculptures of avocados by artist Annex Burgos. If hunger strikes, head to José Enrique or Santaella, both favorites among locals. On the morning of Day 5, hit the beach once more; then head to Avenida Ashford in Condado for an afternoon of shopping in its ritzy boutiques.

★ Marmalade

$$$$ | ECLECTIC | Peter Schintler, the U.S.-born owner-chef of Old San Juan's hippest—and finest—restaurant, apprenticed with Raymond Blanc and Gordon Ramsay. Diners can build their own four- to six-course tasting menu from a list of dishes using primariliy local and organic ingredients. **Known for:** varying prix-fixe menus; exceptional service; excellent wine list. *Average main: $32* ✉ *317 Calle Fortaleza, Old San Juan* ☎ *787/724–3969* 🌐 *www.marmaladepr.com* ⏲ *No lunch.*

Pirilo Pizza Rustica

$$ | PIZZA | Day and night, locals flock to Pirilo to indulge in San Juan's finest pizza. Owner Eduardo Rubio makes everything from scratch, most notably the pizza

Plucky pontiff: the bronze bishop of Plazuela de la Rogativa is a monument to the religious procession that, according to legend, repelled a British invasion.

crust, which uses a 300-year-old starter as its base. **Known for:** pizza, both traditional and not; late-night eats; 50 craft beers. Ⓢ *Average main: $12* ✉ *207 Calle Tanca, Old San Juan* ☎ *787/721–3322.*

Raíces

$$$ | **PUERTO RICAN** | You can't miss this lively restaurant, thanks to its waitresses in all-white *campesina* (peasant) dresses. Themed as a country venue, with artsy re-creations of rustic life, the whole atmosphere feels a bit Disneyfied, but that doesn't stop the locals and tourists—who may have seen it featured on various TV shows—from packing in for comida criolla. **Known for:** Kan Kan pork chop and churrasco; garlic shrimp mofongo; long waits. Ⓢ *Average main: $21* ✉ *315 Calle Recinto Sur, Old San Juan* ☎ *787/289–2121* 🌐 *www.restauranteraices.com.*

★ **Señor Paleta**

$ | **CAFÉ** | **FAMILY** | There's nothing more refreshing on a hot day than an ice pop from Señor Paleta. All the ingredients used to make these artisanal *paletas* are fresh and many use local fruits. **Known for:** fruity ice pops on a stick; long waits on weekends; cash only. Ⓢ *Average main: $3* ✉ *153 Calle Tetuan, Old San Juan* ☎ *787/724–2337* ⏲ *Closed Mon.* ▭ *No credit cards.*

St. Germain Bistro & Café

$ | **INTERNATIONAL** | This charming French-inspired café-restaurant stands on a quiet cobblestone corner. The interior is inviting, with rustic white wooden tables and benches—the perfect setting for exceptionally fresh food and friendly service. **Known for:** vegetarian focus; aguas frescas; Sunday brunch. Ⓢ *Average main: $10* ✉ *156 Calle Sol, Old San Juan* ☎ *787/725–5830* ⏲ *No dinner Sun.–Wed.*

Trois Cent Onze *(311)*

$$$ | **FRENCH** | The perfectly lighted dining room—with crystal chandeliers, colonial arches, Moorish tiles, long drapes, and checkered marble floors—is a true example of Old San Juan charm. The menu is a mix of classic French with nouveau interpretations. **Known for:** romantic atmosphere; honey-roasted duck breast with foie gras; small but well-chosen wine list. *Average main: $30* *311 Calle Fortaleza, Old San Juan* *787/725–7959* *www.311restaurantpr.com* *Closed Sun. and Mon. No lunch.*

★ Verde Mesa

$$$ | VEGETARIAN | With punched-tin ceilings, mason-jar light fixtures, and eclectic decor inspired by Petit Trianon in Versailles, this pescatarian restaurant focuses on pleasing the senses. Executive Chef Gabriel Hernandez sources most of the organic produce from local farms, creating a menu that changes seasonally. **Known for:** strictly vegetarian and pescatarian menu; romantic atmosphere; no reservations. *Average main: $22* *107 Calle Tetuán, at Calle San José, Old San Juan* *787/390–4662* *Closed Sun. and Mon.*

Waffle-era Tea Room

$ | CAFÉ | The only tearoom in Puerto Rico is hugely popular. You can choose from nearly 30 loose teas—including white and fruity blends as well as black—or a thoughtful cocktail menu. **Known for:** creative waffles, both sweet and savory; large selection of teas; made-to-order siphon-brewed coffee. *Average main: $9* *250 Calle San José, Old San Juan* *787/721–1512* *www.waffle-era.com* *No dinner.*

Hotels

CasaBlanca Hotel

$ | HOTEL | Mere steps from some of the best dining in town, this boutique hotel in the heart of SoFo adds Moroccan-themed panache to Old San Juan and offers real value. **Pros:** exotic decor; close to restaurants and nightclubs; new elevator. **Cons:** some rooms are dark; noise from street can be an issue; smallish rooms. *Rooms from: $139* *316 Calle Fortaleza, Old San Juan* *787/725–3436* *www.hotelcasablancapr.com* *32 rooms* *No meals.*

Da House Hotel

$ | B&B/INN | This popular property is part art gallery, part hotel. **Pros:** hip, artsy vibe in a historic setting; friendly staff; rooftop terrace. **Cons:** noise from nearby bars; simple accommodations. *Rooms from: $120* *312 Calle San Francisco, Old San Juan* *787/977–1180* *www.dahouse-hotel.com* *27 rooms* *No meals.*

Decanter Hotel

$$ | HOTEL | Tucked away behind the cathedral, this restored 19th-century colonial mansion is the newest hotel to open up in Old San Juan. **Pros:** excellent location; rooftop terrace; good restaurant. **Cons:** some street noise; no pool; unassuming lobby. *Rooms from: $150* *106 Calle San José, Old San Juan* *787/305–3320* *www.decanterhotel.com* *20 rooms* *No meals.*

The Gallery Inn

$$ | B&B/INN | No two rooms in this 200-year-old mansion are alike, but all have four-poster beds, handwoven tapestries, and quirky antiques in every nook and cranny. **Pros:** one-of-a-kind lodging; ocean views; wonderful classical music concerts. **Cons:** several narrow, winding staircases; an uphill walk from the rest of Old San Juan; sometimes-raucous pet macaws and cockatoos. *Rooms from: $160* *204–206 Calle Norzagaray, Old San Juan* *787/722–1808* *www.thegalleryinn.com* *25 rooms* *Free Breakfast.*

★ Hotel El Convento

$$$ | HOTEL | There's no longer anything austere about this 350-year-old former convent. **Pros:** lovely historic building; atmosphere to spare; plenty of nearby dining options. **Cons:** near some noisy bars; small pool; small bathrooms. *Rooms from: $285* *100 Calle Cristo, Old San Juan* *787/723–9020* *www.elconvento.com* *58 rooms* *No meals.*

The narrow streets and sloping hills of Old San Juan are fantastic for walking. Driving? Not so much.

La Terraza de San Juan

$$ | HOTEL | This charming colonial-era boutique hotel on a quiet, residential street is the perfect way to experience Old San Juan like a local. **Pros:** rooftop pool and bar; elevator; 24-hour concierge. **Cons:** noise from rooftop terrace; some rooms have no windows; far from the beach. *$ Rooms from: $160 ⊠ 262 Calle Sol, Old San Juan ☎ 787/722–2014 ⊕ www.laterrazahotelsanjuan.com ⇨ 24 rooms 🍽 No meals.*

Sheraton Old San Juan Hotel

$$$ | HOTEL | FAMILY | Rooms facing the water at this triangular-shaped hotel have spectacular views of the mammoth cruise ships that sail in and out of the nearby harbor. **Pros:** harbor views; near many dining options; great pre-cruise option. **Cons:** chain-hotel feel to guest rooms; uphill walk to the rest of Old San Juan; casino has closed. *$ Rooms from: $259 ⊠ 100 Calle Brumbaugh, Old San Juan ☎ 787/289–1914 ⊕ www.sheratonoldsanjuan.com ⇨ 240 rooms 🍽 No meals.*

Villa Herencia Hotel

$$ | B&B/INN | The same owners as Da House transport guests back to the 19th century in this exquisitely restored former mansion with timeworn bare walls, original floral tile floors, and beamed ceilings. **Pros:** delightful furnishings; close to shops and cafés of Old San Juan; rooftop terraces with baths. **Cons:** no in-room phone; no elevator; smallish rooms. *$ Rooms from: $180 ⊠ 23 Caleta de las Monjas, Old San Juan ☎ 787/722–0989 ⊕ www.villaherencia.com ⇨ 8 rooms 🍽 Free Breakfast.*

Nightlife

BARS

El Batey

BARS/PUBS | This legendary dive bar won't win any prizes for decor, but it has an irresistibly artsy and welcoming vibe. Add your own message to the graffiti-covered walls—they have a "B.Y.O.S." policy (Bring Your Own Sharpie)—or hang your business card alongside the hundreds that cover the light fixtures. The jukebox has the best selection of oldies in town, and locals crowd the back room for billiards. ✉ *101 Calle Cristo, Old San Juan* ☎ *No phone.*

★ La Factoría

BARS/PUBS | La Factoría, the former Hijos de Borinquen, is hands-down the best cocktail bar in San Juan. Here, artisanal drinks are crafted with the highest-quality ingredients. Many bitters are homemade, as is the ginger beer, which is used in their popular Lavender Mule. Whether it's sweet, spicy, bitter, or something completely out of the box, these drinks will blow your mind. Behind the bar, there is a secret wooden door that leads to VINO Wine Bar, which has a great speakeasy feel. Tasty tapas are available and can be enjoyed in the adjacent room. These bars stay open till sunup, and a DJ spins in the back room on weekends. Salsa is played on Sunday and Monday. There's no sign on the door, so just look for the terra-cotta building at the corner of San Sebastián and San José. ✉ *148 Calle San Sebastián, Old San Juan* ☎ *787/594–5698.*

La Taberna Lúpulo

BARS/PUBS | If you love beer, don't leave Puerto Rico Rico without visiting Lúpulo. At the island's largest craft beer bar you'll find 25+ beers on tap and more than 100 bottles of the finest European and American brews. This casual hipster bar is open late and a great option for night bites. Weekend brunch is very popular among locals; try the "beermosa" and French toast with pineapple and rum compote. ✉ *151 Calle San Sebastián, Old San Juan* ☎ *787/721–3772.*

The Mezzanine

BARS/PUBS | In the former headquarters of the Nationalist Party, The Mezzanine is a contemporary take on the 1920s speakeasy. The chic space is conducive to sipping a creative cocktail and very refreshing after walking the hills of Old San Juan. Tapas are served all day. The Mezzanine also hosts one of the best happy hours in town (Tuesday–Friday 4–8); enjoy select tapas and cocktails for half off. You can't beat that in San Juan! Their brunch is very popular on weekends. It's typically closed on Monday. ✉ *St. Germain Bistro & Café, 156 Calle Sol, 2nd fl., Old San Juan* ☎ *787/724–4657.*

Señor Frog's

BARS/PUBS | Latin America's answer to the Hard Rock Cafe, Señor Frog's attracts both hard-partying tourists and the cruise-ship crowd—no surprise, as it's located directly in front of the dock. (Look for the giant inflatable frog.) The just-okay menu is a nod to Mexico, with south-of-the-border favorites like nachos and quesadillas. When it comes to drinks, expect quantity over quality; their signature is the Yard, a tall plastic cup filled with your favorite adult beverage. There's often live music, a ladies' night, or other special events. ✉ *102 Calle Marina, corner of Brumbaugh, Old San Juan* ☎ *787/977–4142* 🌐 *www.senorfrogs.com.*

Performing Arts

MAJOR VENUES

Fundación Nacional Para la Cultura Popular

ARTS CENTERS | This multifaceted foundation hosts a variety of events, including Latin music and dance performances and classes. Check the schedule online or call ahead. ✉ *56 Calle Fortaleza, Old San Juan* ☎ *787/724–7165* 🌐 *www.prpop.org.*

Teatro Tapia

THEATER | Named for Puerto Rican playwright Alejandro Tapia y Rivera, this is the oldest theater in Puerto Rico. It hosts traveling and locally produced theatrical and musical productions. Matinees for families are also held, especially around the holidays. ✉ *Plaza Colón, Calle Fortaleza, Old San Juan* ☎ *787/480–5004.*

The Piña Colada Wars

This mixture of pineapple juice, coconut cream, and liberal amounts of rum, always garnished with a wedge of pineapple and a maraschino cherry, was invented either by Ramón "Monchito" Marrero at the Caribe Hilton in 1954 or by Ramón Portas Mingot at the Barrachina Bar in 1963, depending on who you talk to. Was it Marrero, a young bartender who is said to have spent three months on a concoction that would appeal to patrons at the Beachcomber's Bar? (His secret? Using only fresh pineapple juice.) Or was it Mingot, an elderly bartender meeting the whims of his Old San Juan patrons? (He said his were so frothy because he froze the pineapple juice and coconut cream mixture instead of simply adding crushed ice.)

The two venues have fought over bragging rights for decades. The Caribe Hilton issues press release after press release reminding people that the drink was born in its seaside bar. (If what its public relations department says is true, the drink celebrated its 50th anniversary in 2004.) The Barrachina Bar put up a plaque that tells passersby that it is the true birthplace of the beverage. It seems the Caribe Hilton has a slight edge: local bartenders insist Marrero was the one who invented the famous drink. And Coco López, the company that makes the coconut cream most often used in the drink, honored him in 1978. In gratitude for his contribution to the "bartending arts," they presented him with a color TV. But the origins of the piña colada—which means "strained pineapple"—remain as cloudy as the cocktail itself. You may have to sample several before making up your own mind.

Shopping

ANTIQUES

El Alcázar

ANTIQUES/COLLECTIBLES | For nearly three decades, Robert and Sharon Bartos have been selling antiques and objets d'art from all over the world, much of it from Europe. ✉ *103 Calle San José, Old San Juan* ☎ *787/723–1229* 🌐 *www.elalcazar.com.*

ART GALLERIES

Galería Botello

ART GALLERIES | This influential gallery displays art by the late Angel Botello, who was hailed as the Caribbean Gauguin as far back as 1943. (His works also hang in the Museo de Arte de Puerto Rico.) His paintings often feature the bright colors of the tropics and usually depict island scenes. Also on display here are works by other prominent local artists, Puerto Rican santos, and sculptures by Botello. ✉ *208 Calle Cristo, Old San Juan* ☎ *787/723–9987* 🌐 *www.botello.com.*

Haitian Gallery

CRAFTS | The shop carries Haitian masks, statues, paintings, and wooden works of art. The second floor houses a large selection of paintings from the Caribbean. ✉ *367 Calle Fortaleza, Old San Juan* ☎ *787/725–0986.*

CIGARS

Cigar House

TOBACCO | The Cigar House has an eclectic selection of local and imported cigars from Nicaragua, Honduras, and the Dominican Republic. At the lounge and bar, you can enjoy your purchase with a glass of your favorite spirit. ✉ *257 Calle Fortaleza, Old San Juan* ☎ *787/723–5223.*

CLOTHING

Cappalli

CLOTHING | Noted local designer Lisa Cappalli sells her feminine, sensuous designs in this elegant boutique, which specializes in ready-to-wear and custom fashions including a small collection of whimsical, lacy wedding gowns. ✉ *206 Calle O'Donnell, Old San Juan* ☎ *787/289–6565.*

Collective Request

CLOTHING | This gorgeous boutique set in a restored colonial buidling caters to the stylish young woman. Owners Joel and Ashley are frequently on-site to help with any shopping needs. A menswear line was recently introduced. ✉ *159 Calle Luna, Old San Juan* ☎ *787/977–7707.*

Concalma

CLOTHING | Designer Matilsha Marxuach, who has an eye toward sustainable fashion, has her hip line of fair-trade handbags, messenger bags, bathing suits, vintage clothing, and other items made by local designers. ✉ *207 Calle San Francisco, Old San Juan* ☎ *787/421–4212* 🌐 *shopconcalma.com.*

Pure Soul

CLOTHING | Sylma Cabrera sells chic resort wear made of natural fabrics by local artists and under her own label, Pure Soul. You'll also find stunning handmade jewelry with semiprecious stones like quartz and lapis lazuli. ✉ *258 Calle San Justo, corner Tetuán, Old San Juan* ☎ *787/723–2800* 🌐 *www.puresoulboutique.com.*

CRAFTS

El Galpón

CRAFTS | At El Galpón, knowledgeable owners Betsy and Gustavo will fit you with a Panama hat ($65–$900), and you'll learn that the genuine article is actually made in Ecuador. They also carry a large selection of Puerto Rican *santos*, hand-carved wooden saints. ✉ *154 Calle Cristo, Old San Juan* ☎ *787/725–3945* 🌐 *www.elgalpon.net.*

Magia

CRAFTS | This clever shop carries what appear to be traditional crafts but warrants a closer look. Each one, likely made by artist-owner Manolo Díaz, is quite unique—a little wooden shrine, for example, may shelter an image of Marilyn Monroe. You can also find vintage costume jewelry and Puerto Rican santos. The store is closed on Sunday. ✉ *99 Calle Cristo, Old San Juan* ☎ *787/368–6164.*

Mi Pequeño San Juan

CRAFTS | You might find a reproduction of your hotel at this shop, which specializes in tiny ceramic versions of San Juan doorways. The works are created by hand in the shop, which also carries fine art prints. ✉ *152 Calle Fortaleza, Old San Juan* ☎ *787/721–5040* 🌐 *www.mipequenosanjuan.com.*

Mundo Taíno

CRAFTS | Near Plaza de Armas Square, Mundo Taíno sells high-quality folk art from around the island. ✉ *151 San José, Old San Juan* ☎ *787/724–2005.*

Olé

CRAFTS | Aficionados of the famous Panama hat, made from delicately handwoven straw, should stop at Olé. The shop sells top-of-the-line hats for as much as $1,000 as well as more affordable hats that can be custom-fit. Take a few moments to browse the other goods for sale like decades-old *santos* (hand-carved wood figurines of saints) and used books. ✉ *105 Calle Fortaleza, Old San Juan* ☎ *787/724–2445.*

Puerto Rican Arts & Crafts

CRAFTS | For one-of-a-kind santos, art, ceramics, and festival masks, head to Puerto Rican Arts & Crafts. All artwork is made by local artists. ✉ *204 Calle Fortaleza, Old San Juan* ☎ *787/725–6596* 🌐 *www.puertoricanart-crafts.com.*

GIFTS

Butterfly People

GIFTS/SOUVENIRS | Exotic *mariposas* cover the walls of Butterfly People. Clear plastic cases hold common species as well as many rarer specimens. The butterflies come from certified farms and are gathered only once they "have completed their short life spans," as the store puts it. It's closed on Friday. ✉ *257 Calle de la Cruz, Old San Juan* ☎ *787/723–2432* 🌐 *www.butterflypeople.com.*

Eclectika

GIFTS/SOUVENIRS | This boutique carries a variety of items, mostly from Indonesia, from bedspreads to beaded and wooden jewelry, furnishings to hand fans. ✉ *204 Calle O'Donnell, Plaza Colón, Old San Juan* ☎ *787/721–7236.*

Spicy Caribbee

GIFTS/SOUVENIRS | Kitchen items, cookbooks, jams, spices, and sauces from around the Caribbean are on offer. ✉ *154 Calle Cristo, Old San Juan* ☎ *888/725–7259* 🌐 *www.spicycaribbee.com.*

JEWELRY

Bared Jewelers

JEWELRY/ACCESSORIES | The store carries Rolex, Cartier, Bulgari, and Breitling watches, as well as a large selection of fine jewelry. Look for the massive clock face on the corner. ✉ *206 San Justo, Old San Juan* ☎ *787/724–4811.*

Catalá Joyeros

JEWELRY/ACCESSORIES | Family-run since the 1930s, the store is known for its large selection of pearls and precious stones, and for its jewelry design. ✉ *Plaza de Armas, 152 Calle Rafael Cordero, Old San Juan* ☎ *787/722–3231* 🌐 *www.catalajoyeros.com.*

Club Jibarito

JEWELRY/ACCESSORIES | Club Jibarito has a fantastic collection of high-end watches by Audemars Piguet, Chopard, H.Stern, Harry Winston, Panerai, and other designers. ✉ *202 Calle Cristo, Old San Juan* ☎ *787/724–7797* 🌐 *www.clubjibarito.com.*

N. Barquet Joyero

JEWELRY/ACCESSORIES | One of the bigger jewelry stores in Old San Juan, N. Barquet Joyero carries pieces in 18-karat gold and is the exclusive vendor of Italian designer, Nanis. Their Coquí el Original brand, depicting the local tree frog, has become a popular souvenir. If you're looking for unique and high-end jewels, ask to browse the private back room. ✉ *201 Calle Fortaleza, Old San Juan* ☎ *787/721–3366.*

Portofino

JEWELRY/ACCESSORIES | Portofino has an especially good selection of watches. ✉ *250 Calle San Francisco, Old San Juan* ☎ *787/723–5113.*

OUTLETS

Old San Juan has turned into an open-air duty-free shop for people pouring off the cruise ships. Because they have only a few hours in port, they often pass by more interesting shops and head directly for the factory outlets on and around Calle Cristo. The prices aren't particularly good, but nobody seems to mind.

Coach

OUTLET/DISCOUNT STORES | Stylish, upscale handbags for men and women can be purchased at Coach for a discounted price. ✉ *158 Calle Cristo, Old San Juan* ☎ *787/722–6830.*

Ralph Lauren

OUTLET/DISCOUNT STORES | Ralph Lauren's shop in front of the piers has some of the best deals around. Stop here toward the end of your trip, as there are plenty of items (e.g., peacoats and scarves) that you won't be wearing until you get home. ✉ *105 Paseo Gilberto Concepcinó de Gracia, Harbor Plaza Bldg., Old San Juan* ☎ *787/724–1020.*

Tommy Hilfiger

OUTLET/DISCOUNT STORES | There's signature Tommy gear for men and women at the Tommy Hilfiger in Old San Juan, and their staff are very friendly. ✉ *206 Calle Cristo, Old San Juan* ☎ *787/729–2230.*

San Juan's well-equipped *balnearios* (public beaches) are among the best on the island.

Puerta de Tierra

Just east of the Old City, Puerta de Tierra is home to a few notable hotels, a nice public beach, and several parks.

Sights

El Capitolio

GOVERNMENT BUILDING | The white-marble Capitol, a fine example of Italian Renaissance style, dates from 1929. The grand rotunda, which can be seen from all over San Juan, was completed in the late 1990s. Fronted by eight Corinthian columns, it's a dignified home for the commonwealth's constitution. Although the Senate and House of Representatives have offices in the more modern buildings on either side, the Capitol is where the legislators meet. Guided tours, which last about an hour and include the rotunda, are by appointment only. ✉ *Av. Constitución, Puerta de Tierra* ☎ *787/724–2030, 787/721–5200 for guided tours* 🎟 *Free* ⏲ *Closed weekends.*

Beaches

Balneario El Escambrón

BEACH—SIGHT | **FAMILY** | In Puerta de Tierra, this government-run beach has a patch of honey-color sand shaded by coconut palms. An offshore reef generally makes surf gentle, so it's favored by families. Nearby restaurants make picnicking easy. **Amenities:** food and drink; lifeguards; parking (fee); showers; toilets. **Best for:** swimming; walking. ✉ *Av. Muñoz Rivera, Puerta de Tierra* 🎟 *Parking $5.*

Shopping

ART GALLERIES

Walter Otero Contemporary Art

ART GALLERIES | This gorgeous 5,000-square-foot gallery showcases contemporary artwork by local and international artists. ✉ *402 Hwy. 25, Puerta de Tierra* ☎ *787/998–9622.*

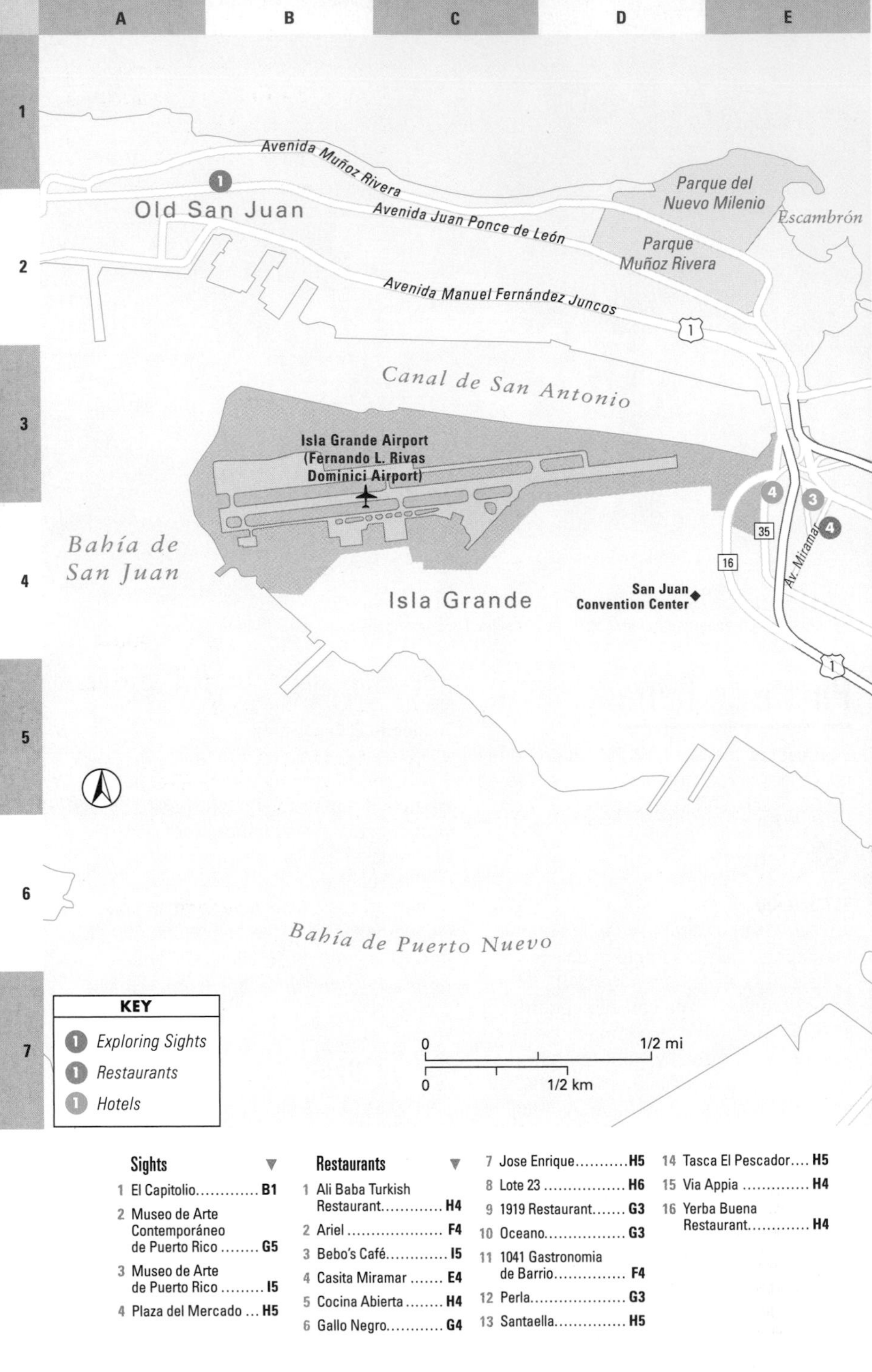

Sights

1 El Capitolio............. B1

2 Museo de Arte Contemporáneo de Puerto Rico G5

3 Museo de Arte de Puerto Rico I5

4 Plaza del Mercado ... H5

Restaurants

1 Ali Baba Turkish Restaurant............ H4

2 Ariel F4

3 Bebo's Café............. I5

4 Casita Miramar E4

5 Cocina Abierta H4

6 Gallo Negro........... G4

7 Jose Enrique........... H5

8 Lote 23 .... H6

9 1919 Restaurant....... G3

10 Oceano................. G3

11 1041 Gastronomia de Barrio............... F4

12 Perla.................... G3

13 Santaella............... H5

14 Tasca El Pescador.... H5

15 Via Appia H4

16 Yerba Buena Restaurant............ H4

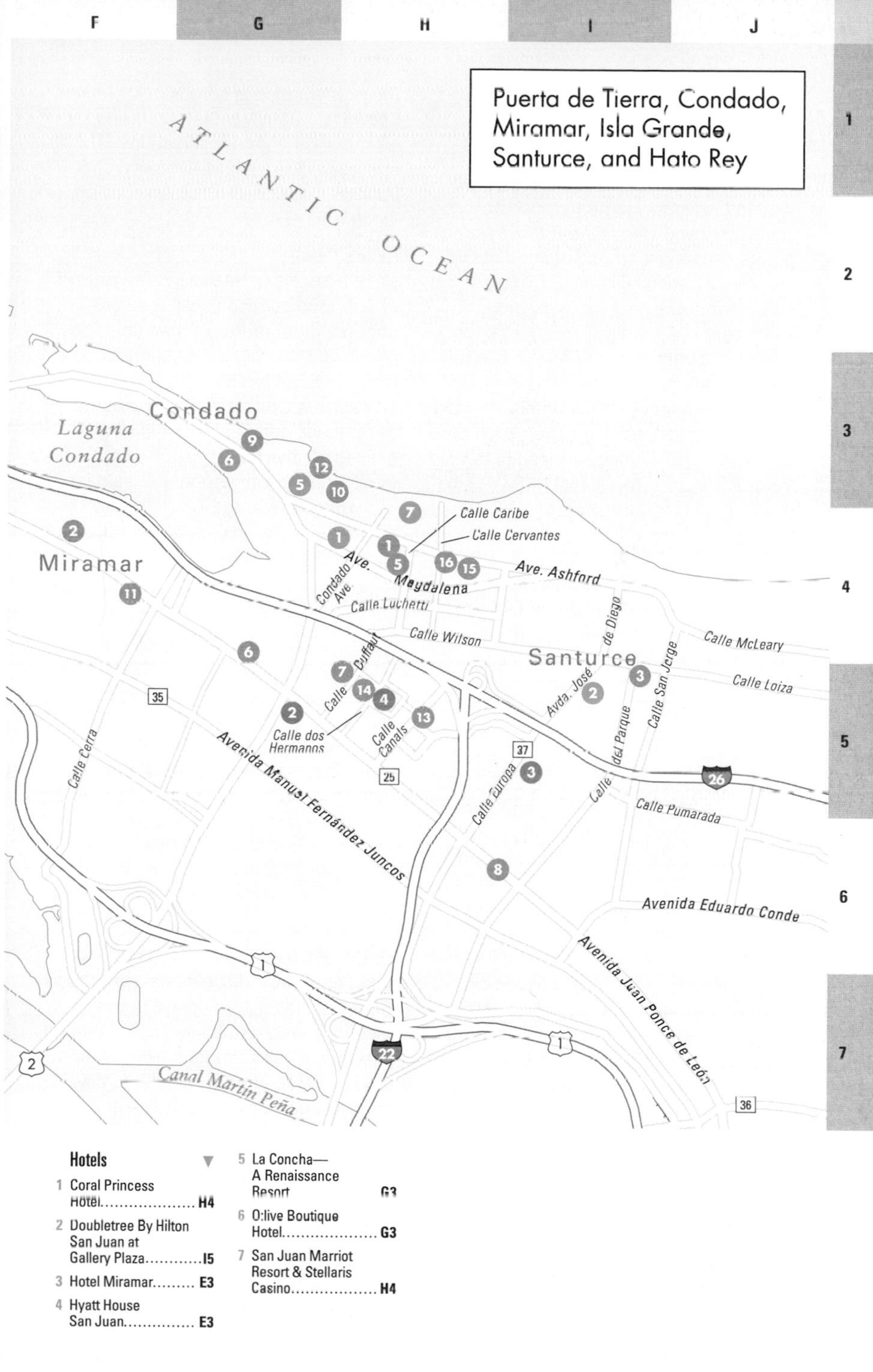

F
G
H
I
J
1
2
3
4
5
6
7
Puerta de Tierra, Condado, Miramar, Isla Grande, Santurce, and Hato Rey
ATLANTIC OCEAN
Condado
Laguna Condado
Miramar
Santurce
Calle Caribe
Calle Cervantes
Ave. Ashford
Ave. Magdalena
Condado Ave
Calle Luchetti
Calle Wilson
Calle McLeary
Calle Loiza
Calle Duffaut
Calle dos Hermanos
Calle Canals
Avda. José de Diego
Calle San Jorge
Calle del Parque
Calle Europa
Calle Pumarada
Calle Cerra
Avenida Manuel Fernández Juncos
Avenida Eduardo Conde
Avenida Juan Ponce de León
Canal Martín Peña
35
37
25
26
22
1
2
36
Hotels
1 Coral Princess Hotel.................... H4
2 Doubletree By Hilton San Juan at Gallery Plaza............I5
3 Hotel Miramar......... E3
4 Hyatt House San Juan............... E3
5 La Concha— A Renaissance Resort G3
6 O:live Boutique Hotel..................... G3
7 San Juan Marriot Resort & Stellaris Casino.................. H4

Condado

For multiple shopping and dining options within walking distance of one another, look to Condado. Home to much of the city's moneyed elite, it's the most vibrant pedestrian neighborhood outside of Old San Juan. Here you'll find old Spanish-style homes next to sleek, modern apartment buildings and designer shops. The main street, Avenida Ashford, is fun to stroll, but quieter residential areas are also very attractive. Many hotels situated along the ocean, although the beach here is not as big or alluring as those in Isla Verde.

Beaches

Playa del Condado

BEACH—SIGHT | **FAMILY** | East of Old San Juan and west of Ocean Park, this long, wide beach is overshadowed by an unbroken string of hotels and apartment buildings. Beach bars, water-sports outfitters, and chair-rental places abound. You can access the beach from several roads off Avenida Ashford, including Calles Cervantes, Vendig, Condado, and Candina. The protected water at the small stretch of beach west of the Condado Plaza Hilton hotel is particularly calm and popular with families; surf elsewhere in Condado can be a bit strong. The stretch of sand near Calle Vendig (behind the Atlantic Beach Hotel) is especially popular with the gay community. If you're driving, street parking is your only option. **Amenities:** none. **Best for:** partiers; people-watching. ✉ *Av. Ashford, San Juan.*

Restaurants

Ali Baba Turkish Restaurant

$$ | **MIDDLE EASTERN** | Standing discreetly just off Avenida Ashford, Ali Baba turns out delicious, meticulously prepared Middle Eastern and Mediterranean food, thanks to its Turkish chef-owner. Given how unpretentious this small place is, the presentation is surprisingly elegant. **Known for:** tangy, smooth hummus; iskender kebab; no reservations. [$] *Average main: $15* ✉ *1214 Av. Ashford, San Juan* ☎ *787/722–1176* ⏲ *Closed Mon. No lunch Tues.–Fri.*

Bebo's Café

$$ | **PUERTO RICAN** |**FAMILY** | Huge platters of delicious comida criolla are constantly streaming out of the kitchen here. Low prices and a family atmosphere ensure that this longtime local favorite—located near the DoubleTree on the border of Condado and Santurce—is always packed. **Known for:** large portions; family-friendly atmosphere; breakfast. [$] *Average main: $12* ✉ *1600 Calle Loíza, San Juan* ☎ *787/726–5700* 🌐 *beboscafe.touchmenuusa.com.*

Cocina Abierta

$$$ | **ECLECTIC** | Modern light fixtures, exposed walls, and repurposed decorative accents give Cocina Abierta one of the coolest decors in Condado. Chef Martin Louzao's eclectic menu is divided into five acts and crescendoes as you move from course to course. **Known for:** do-it-yourself tasting menus; octopus terrine and mofongo with duck confit; great wine list. [$] *Average main: $21* ✉ *58 Calle Caribe, San Juan* ☎ *787/946–1333* 🌐 *www.cocinaabierta.com* 💳 *No credit cards.*

★ 1919 Restaurant

$$$$ | **ECLECTIC** | Michelin-starred, Puerto Rico–born chef Juan José Cuevas operates this successful fine-dining restaurant in San Juan's most striking hotel, built in 1919 by the Vanderbilt family. The international cuisine—prix fixe or à la carte—changes seasonally and focuses on local ingredients. **Known for:** focus on organic, locally grown ingredients; prix-fixe and tasting menus; elegant setting. [$] *Average main: $36* ✉ *Condado Vanderbilt Hotel, 1055 Av. Ashford, San Juan* ☎ *787/724–1919* 🌐 *www.1919restaurant.com* ⏲ *Closed Sun. and Mon. No lunch.*

Oceano

$$$ | **CARIBBEAN** | This trendy restaurant in the heart of Condado has one of the best locations in town. Tucked off Avenida Ashford, Oceano is the place to dine alfresco and sip a cocktail while savoring the ocean breeze. **Known for:** beachfront dining room; seafood-heavy menu; Sunday jazz brunch. *Average main: $30* *2 Calle Vendig, San Juan* *787/724–6300* *www.oceanopr.com* *No lunch Mon.–Thurs.*

Perla

$$$$ | **SEAFOOD** | This shell-shape restaurant is an architectural wonder, one of the most striking buildings in San Juan. Illuminated by artichoke lamps made from Murano glass, the dining room makes you feel as if you've entered a luxurious ocean liner. **Known for:** seafood-focused menu; spectacular setting; baked lobster tail with lobster beurre blanc. *Average main: $43* *La Concha—A Renaissance Resort, 1077 Av. Ashford, San Juan* *787/977–3285* *perlarestaurant.com* *No lunch.*

Via Appia

$$ | **ITALIAN** | **FAMILY** | Popular for decades with everyone from local politicians and families to sunburned tourists who just dragged themselves off the beach, the bustling Via Appia is a no-frills restaurant known for serving simple Italian dishes. During lunch, however, they ladle out some delicious comida criolla, with specials changing daily. **Known for:** Italian food; casual, no-frills dining; outside terrace overlooking Avenida Ashford. *Average main: $12* *1350 Av. Ashford, San Juan* *787/725–8711.*

Yerba Buena Restaurant

$$$ | **CUBAN** | Tables on the terrace are hard to come by at this Cuban restaurant, one of the busier spots in Condado. Cuban classics such as *ropa vieja* (literally, "old clothes"—meat cooked so slowly that it becomes tender shreds) seamlessly complement local dishes served with imaginative presentation. **Known for:** welcoming service, even with large crowds; "original recipe" mojitos; big-band music on Monday night. *Average main: $25* *1350 Av. Ashford, San Juan* *787/721–5700* *www.yerbabuenapr.com* *No lunch.*

Hotels

Coral Princess Hotel

$ | **HOTEL** | This affordable boutique hotel is a good choice for a quiet, romantic getaway: the hotel is only a block from the neighborhood's main drag, and the beach is a three-minute walk away. **Pros:** comfortable common areas; Wi-Fi in rooms; friendly staff. **Cons:** not directly on the beach; small pool; limited parking. *Rooms from: $129* *1159 Av. Magdalena, San Juan* *787/977–7700* *www.coralpr.com* *25 rooms* *Free Breakfast.*

DoubleTree by Hilton San Juan at Gallery Plaza

$$ | **HOTEL** | Slightly geared to business travelers, the DoubleTree offers attractive rooms and an excellent value for anyone who doesn't need to be in central Condado or on the beach. **Pros:** excellent value for the neighborhood; good on-site dining options; free shuttle to beach. **Cons:** a bit of a walk to the beach and the main drag in Condado; chain-hotel feel; random location. *Rooms from: $249* *105 Av. de Diego, San Juan* *787/721–1200* *www.sanjuandoubletree.com* *184 rooms* *No meals.*

★ **La Concha—A Renaissance Resort**

$$$ | **RESORT** | Every stunning detail feels tropical and sexy, from the undulating ceiling in the sprawling lobby to Perla, the shell-shape signature restaurant and an architectural marvel. **Pros:** numerous on-site social activities; beautiful guest rooms; beachfront location. **Cons:** noisy bar/lobby, particularly when there's live music; beach can be narrow at high tide; pricey bar. *Rooms from: $299* *1077 Av. Ashford, San Juan* *787/721–7500*

www.laconcharesort.com 483 rooms No meals.

★ Olive Boutique Hotel
$$ | **HOTEL** | This luxurious all-suites boutique hotel may remind you of something from the south of France, but it's tucked away on a quiet street in Condado overlooking the lagoon. **Pros:** beautiful decor; close to shops and restaurants; rooftop terrace. **Cons:** small pool; see-through bathrooms not for everyone; no parking lot. *$ Rooms from: $249 55 Calle Aguadilla, San Juan 787/705–9994 www.oliveboutiquehotel.com 15 rooms Free Breakfast.*

San Juan Marriott Resort & Stellaris Casino
$$$ | **RESORT** | **FAMILY** | The shape and color of a cardboard box, this lively, popular hotel doesn't add much to the skyline of Condado, but step inside the impressive lobby—with its stunning coral sculpture carved from wood, chic spots for lounging, and welcoming bar—and you'll feel you've arrived in the Caribbean. **Pros:** on one of the area's best beaches; near dozens of dining options; lots of amenities. **Cons:** uninspired architecture; lots of conventions; noise from lobby. *$ Rooms from: $300 1309 Av. Ashford, San Juan 787/722–7000, 787/631–0595 www.marriottsanjuan.com 527 rooms No meals.*

Nightlife

BARS

Hard Rock Cafe
CAFES—NIGHTLIFE | Are you really surprised to find that there's a Hard Rock in San Juan? This one attracts a surprising number of locals for its well-versed upscale ambience, musicians' memorabilia, and eclectic menu. And it's at a new location in Condado. *1214 Av. Ashford, San Juan 787/977–4142 www.hardrock.com.*

CASINOS

By law, all casinos are in hotels, and the government keeps a close eye on them. They're allowed to operate 24 hours a day, but individual casinos set their own hours. That said, an easing of gaming regulations has set a more relaxed tone and made such perks as free drinks and live music more common. The range of available games has also greatly expanded. Typical games include blackjack, roulette, craps, Caribbean stud poker (a five-card stud game), and *pai gow* poker (a combination of American poker and the ancient Chinese game of *pai gow*, which employs cards and dice), in addition to the usual slot machines. The minimum age is 18. Dress for the larger casinos in San Juan tends to be on the formal side, and the atmosphere is refined; tank tops or shorts are usually not acceptable attire.

San Juan Marriott Resort & Stellaris Casino
CASINOS | The crowd is casual and the decor tropical and bubbly at this spacious gaming room. Right outside, there's a huge bar, where Latin musicians perform on weekends, and an adjacent café. *1309 Av. Ashford, Condado 787/722–7000.*

Shopping

CLOTHING

Monsieur
CLOTHING | The quality clothing at Monsieur is very sleek and stylish—everything for the well-dressed man. *1126 Av. Ashford, San Juan 787/722–0918 www.monsieurpuertorico.com.*

Nativa
CLOTHING | The window displays are almost as daring as the clothes at this shop, which caters to trendy young ladies looking for party dresses, jumpers, accessories, and shoes. The store is closed on Sunday. *55 Calle Cervantes, San Juan 787/724–1396.*

Design Lions

Puerto Rico's young fashion designers have opened many a boutique and atelier in metropolitan San Juan over the past few years. Their styles may differ, but these young lions all share an island heritage—complete with a tradition of true craftsmanship—and a level of sophistication acquired after studying and traveling abroad. The result is a fascinating assortment of original, exclusive, high-quality designs.

With all the warmth and sun, it goes without saying that Puerto Rico's designers are most inspired when it comes to creations for the spring and summer seasons. Lacy, flowing creations and lightweight, if not sheer, fabrics dominate designs for women. For men the trend is toward updated linen classics in tropical whites and creams. Whatever you find will be one of a kind, with stylish—if not playful or downright sexy—lines. Some of these designers have their own shops in San Juan.

Which designers should you check out? Lisa Cappalli, a graduate of New York City's Parsons School of Design, favors lace, as lace making is a tradition in her family. David Antonio uses upbeat colors—bold reds and vibrant oranges—in his updated classics. Harry Robles is a bit more established than his peers; he specializes in gowns for women, and his draping designs are often dramatic and always elegant. Each of these young designers has a shop in San Juan.

To see their collections, consider visiting during San Juan Fashion Week, which takes place each year in March and September. The events are full of shows and cocktail parties, all organized by the Puerto Rico Fashion Designers Group under the leadership of island-fashion icons Nono Maldonado and Mirtha Rubio.

—Isabel Abislaimán

Nono Maldonado

CLOTHING | Known for high-end, elegant men's and women's clothes, particularly in linen, Nono Maldonado worked for many years as the fashion editor of *Esquire* and presents a periodic couture collection. This second-floor store also serves as the designer's studio. ✉ *1112 Av. Ashford, 2nd fl., San Juan* ☎ *787/721–0456* 🌐 *www.nonomaldonado.com.*

Otto

CLOTHING | Otto Bauzá stocks international lines of casual and formal wear for younger men. His shop is closed Sunday and Monday. ✉ *69 Av. Condado, San Juan* ☎ *787/722–4609.*

Suola

SHOES/LUGGAGE/LEATHER GOODS | Fittingly for a shop named after the Italian word for "sole," the boot-shape country is the origin of most of the mile-high heels here, including designs by Alexander McQueen, Christian Louboutin, YSL, and Sergio Rossi. Like most Condado stores, it's closed on Sunday. ✉ *1124 Av. Ashford, San Juan* ☎ *787/723–6653.*

SPAS

Zen Spa

SPA/BEAUTY | This family-run spa focuses on wellness—with staff trained in Western, Chinese, and Ayurvedic techniques—but all kinds of treatments are available. One facial uses silk fibers to firm and tone skin. You can also get a green tea clay wrap or a lymphatic drainage massage. An attached shop sells Kiehl's and Eminence Organics products, as well the house line, Zendera. ✉ *1054 Av. Ashford, San Juan* ☎ *787/722–8433, 866/936–7720* 🌐 *www.zen-spa.com.*

Activities

KAYAKING

The Laguna del Condado is popular for kayaking, especially on weekends. You can simply paddle around it or head out under the Puente Dos Hermanos to the San Gerónimo fort right behind the Caribe Hilton and across from the Conrad San Juan Condado Plaza. Kayak rentals cost $25–$35 per hour.

Miramar and Isla Grande

Across the bay from Condado, is **Miramar,** a quiet, mostly residential neighborhood. Recently, many young professionals have been moving to the area, resulting in a new wave of great bars and restaurants. It's the home to the Convention District and the Puerto Rico Conservatory of Music. Home to the Puerto Rico Convention Center, the San Juan Marina, and Isla Grande airport, the once-industrial area of **Isla Grande** is rapidly developing along the waterfront. There are plans to create a shopping, dining, and entertainment destination in the area, but it's still relatively isolated from the rest of San Juan.

Restaurants

Ariel

$$$$ | EUROPEAN | Under the direction of noted chef Ariel Rodríguez, this restaurant is one of the more celebrated in the San Juan area, popular with the city's elite. One of the few old-school fine-dining restaurants left in San Juan, Ariel serves well-executed international cuisine with strong French influences. **Known for:** classic dishes like Muscovy duck breast and potato-crusted salmon; Sunday brunch; superb and extensive wine list. *$ Average main: $32* ✉ *Courtyard Marriott Miramar, 801 Av. Ponce de León, Miramar* ☎ *787/725–7700* ⏲ *Closed Mon. No lunch Sat.; no dinner Sun.*

★ Casita Miramar

$$ | PUERTO RICAN | This family-run restaurant in the heart of residential Miramar is known for its traditional comida criolla. It feels more like a home than a restaurant, which is what makes it such a great place to just sit back, relax, and enjoy your meal. **Known for:** old-fashioned dishes like crab-stuffed avocado; great drinks and sangria; friendly service. *$ Average main: $15* ✉ *605 Av. Miramar, Miramar* ☎ *787/200–8227* ⏲ *Closed Tues. No lunch Mon. and Wed.–Fri.*

1041 Gastronomia de Barrio

$$ | ARGENTINE | Inspired by the chef's childhood in Argentina, the restaurant is named after his family's house number on the outskirts of Buenos Aires. The menu has a strong focus on seasonal ingredients, and there's a good chance you'll see farmers delivering fresh produce. **Known for:** popularity among locals; half portions of some dishes for lighter eaters; excellent pastas. *$ Average main: $18* ✉ *Miramar Plaza, 954 Av. Ponce de León, Miramar* ☎ *939/337–0770* ⏲ *No dinner Sun.*

Hotels

Hotel Miramar

$ | HOTEL | Catering mostly to cruise-ship passengers, this hotel sits in the middle of Miramar, an up-and-coming neighborhood that is a short ride to both Condado and Old San Juan. **Pros:** walking distance to excellent restaurants; rooftop terrace with great views; close to Pan American Pier. **Cons:** simple rooms; no parking lot; no pool. *$ Rooms from: $149* ✉ *606 Av. Ponce de León, Miramar*

787/977–1000 www.hotelmiramarpr.com 50 rooms No meals.

Hyatt House San Juan

$ | HOTEL | This new all-suites hotel is a great option for longer stays—particularly if you are attending an event at the nearby convention center—but it's also convenient to the Pan American pier. **Pros:** great complimentary breakfast; rooms have full kitchens; friendly staff **Cons:** long walk to restaurants and bars; chain-hotel feel; not on or near a beach. *$ Rooms from: $125 615 Av. Fernandez Juncos, Isla Grande 787/977–5000 sanjuan.house.hyatt.com 126 rooms Free Breakfast.*

Shopping

ART GALLERIES

Galería Petrus

ART GALLERIES | Among those who have displayed their works at Galería Petrus are Dafne Elvira, whose surreal oils and acrylics tease and seduce (witness a woman emerging from a banana peel); Marta Pérez, another surrealist, whose bewitching paintings examine such themes as how life on a coffee plantation might have been; and Elizam Escobar, a former political prisoner whose oils depict typically dark subjects. Exhibitions change frequently and focus on local artists. *726 Calle Hoare, Miramar 787/289–0505 www.petrusgallery.com.*

Santurce and Hato Rey

Venture into **Santurce** to explore a mostly commercial district with a growing artistic community, thanks to the Museo de Arte de Puerto Rico and the Museo de Arte Contemporáneo. You'll also find a thriving nightlife scene there on weekends. Nearby, **Hato Rey** is a busy financial district, where you'll find the large Plaza Las Américas Mall.

Sights

Museo de Arte Contemporáneo de Puerto Rico

MUSEUM | This Georgian-style structure, once a public school, displays a dynamic range of works by established and up-and-coming Latin American artists. Many works have strong political messages, including pointed commentaries on Puerto Rico's status as a commonwealth. Only part of the permanent collection's more than 900 works is on display at a time, but it might be anything from ceramics to videos. *1220 Av. Ponce de León, at Av. R. H. Todd, Santurce 787/977–4030 www.mac-pr.org $5 Closed Sun. and Mon.*

★ **Museo de Arte de Puerto Rico**

MUSEUM | One of the Caribbean's biggest museums, this beautiful Neoclassical building was once the San Juan Municipal Hospital. The collection of Puerto Rican art starts with the colonial era, when most art was commissioned for churches. Works by José Campeche, the island's first great painter, include his masterpiece, *Immaculate Conception*, finished in 1794. Also well represented is Francisco Oller, who was the first to move beyond religious subjects to paint local scenes; another room has works by artists inspired by him. The original building, built in the 1920s, proved too small to house the collection; a newer east wing is dominated by a five-story stained glass window by local artist Eric Tabales. The museum also has a beautiful garden with native flora and a 400-seat theater with a remarkable hand-crocheted lace curtain. *299 Av. José de Diego, Santurce 787/977–6277 www.mapr.org $6 (free Wed. 2–8) Closed Mon. and Tues.*

Plaza del Mercado (*La Placita*)

MARKET | Though mostly overlooked by tourists, La Placita (as it's known by locals) is one of the most charming corners of San Juan. At its center is a market hall dating from 1910. Inside you'll find bushels of fruits and vegetables, many of which you probably haven't seen before such as *guanábana* and *caimito*; many chefs from the top city restaurants come here to find their produce. If all this food makes you hungry, dozens of storefront restaurants and bars face the central square. These places, mostly serving seafood, are quiet during the week but bustling on the weekends, especially in the evening. The area also has many *botánicas*—small shops that sell herbs, candles, and religious items. There may even be an in-house card or palm reader ready to show you your future. The square is between the Museo de Arte de Puerto Rico and the Museo de Arte Contemporáneo de Puerto Rico, making it a good place to stop for lunch if you are museum hopping. If you're looking for a party atmosphere, come here at night to sip rum cocktails alfresco and mingle with locals. ✉ *Calle Dos Hermanos at Calle Capital, Santurce.*

Restaurants

Gallo Negro
$$$ | MODERN AMERICAN | Chef María Mercedes's menu has wide-ranging international influences—from Spain to Turkey to Korea—and includes small plates with flavors that can be difficult to find in San Juan. The menu changes frequently, but you will always find signature dishes like her Korean barbecue with daikon and kimchi, or duck breast in a ginger-and-acerola glaze on a bed of mushroom risotto. **Known for:** taco Tuesday; popular Sunday brunch; large selection of whiskey. $ *Average main: $25* ✉ *1107 Av. Ponce de León, Santurce* ☎ *787/554–5445* ⏲ *Closed Mon. No lunch. No dinner Sun.*

★ Jose Enrique
$$$ | PUERTO RICAN | Since 2007, Chef Jose Enrique's eponymous restaurant has been popular with both locals and visitors for its elevated Puerto Rican cuisine served in a casual setting. The menu is ever-changing but always includes crab fritters, as well as fried whole yellowtail snapper served over a root mash with avocado and papaya salsa. **Known for:** focus on locally grown produce and other ingredients; ever-changing menu; no-reservations policy. $ *Average main: $30* ✉ *La Placita de Santurce, 176 Calle Duffaut, Santurce* ☎ *787/725–3518* 🌐 *www.joseenriquepr.com* ⏲ *Closed Sun. and Mon. No lunch Sat.*

Lote 23
$ | ECLECTIC | FAMILY | This outdoor food space with over a dozen kiosks offers an array of dining options. You'll find roast-pork sandwiches, poké bowls, thin-crust pizzas cooked in a stone oven, artisanal ice cream pops, fried chicken, Peruvian anticuchos, and more. **Known for:** wildly varied food offerings; reasonable prices; live music some nights. $ *Average main: $10* ✉ *1552 Av. Ponce de León, Santurce* 🌐 *lote23.com* ⏲ *Closed Mon.*

★ Santaella
$$$ | PUERTO RICAN | A career working with top chefs and a successful catering business prefaced chef José Santaella's namesake restaurant in La Placita Marketplace. The menu is dominated by tapas, which you can easily make into a meal. **Known for:** small plates of nouveau Puerto Rican specialties; trendy ambience; great cocktails. $ *Average main: $29* ✉ *La Placita de Santurce, 219 Calle Canals, Santurce* ☎ *787/725–1611* 🌐 *www.santaellapr.com* ⏲ *Closed Sun. and Mon. No lunch Sat.*

Tasca El Pescador
$$ | SEAFOOD | If you want Spanish-style seafood dishes, head to this restaurant, one of a dozen surround the Plaza del Mercado, which dates to 1910. The *chillo entero frito* (fried whole red snapper) and *camarones al ajillo* (shrimp with garlic) are tasty, but the standout is the *arroz con calamari*: this dramatic inky-black rice dish draws "oohs" and "aahs" from surrounding customers when it arrives

at your table. **Known for:** local popularity; squid-ink rice; outdoor dining. *Average main: $19* ✉ *178 Calle Dos Hermanos, Santurce* ☎ *787/721–0995* ⊙ *Closed Mon.*

Nightlife

BARS

La Penúltima

BARS/PUBS | After a night of drinking at La Placita, head to La Penúltima for a nightcap and late-night bites. Don't miss the carbonated Negroni or the food, which is surprisingly good! ✉ *1359 Av. Ponce de León, Santurce* ☎ *787/523–6538.*

GAY AND LESBIAN BARS AND CLUBS

With its sophisticated nightlife, San Juan has become a popular destination for gay tourists. Each June, the annual pride march, full of music and dancing, rivals those in similar cities around the world. Condado Beach has a strong gay following, while Santurce, just south of Condado, is known for nightlife. Most spots are located on or near Avenida Ponce de León. Parts of this neighborhood can be dangerous at night, so stay alert; consider taking a taxi to your destination rather than walking after dark.

Circo Bar

BARS/PUBS | This popular, late-night gay bar and club in Santurce offers a different themed event every night of the week—including karaoke, DJs, and dance parties—but it's mostly popular on weekends. If you're coming from Condado, you may want to take a taxi even though it's not that far by foot: the area around the bar can be rough. ✉ *650 Calle Condado, Santurce.*

Performing Arts

MAJOR VENUES

Centro de Bellas Artes Luis A. Ferré (*Luis A. Ferré Center for the Performing Arts*)

ARTS CENTERS | With four different theaters, the largest of which holds up to 1,900 people, this is the largest venue of its kind in the Caribbean. There's something going on nearly every night, from pop or jazz concerts to plays, operas, and ballets. It's also the home of the Puerto Rico Symphony Orchestra. ✉ *22 Av. Ponce de León, Santurce* ☎ *787/724–4747, 787/620–4444* 🌐 *www.cba.gobierno.pr.*

Coliseo de Puerto Rico José Miguel Agrelot

CONCERTS | Seating up to 18,000 people, this relatively new arena, affectionately known as "El Choliseo," is the top venue for international musical events on the island. Previous perfomers have included Ozzy Osbourne, Paul McCartney, Shakira, Beyoncé, and, of course, hometown favorite Ricky Martin. ✉ *50 Calle Arterial B, Hato Rey* ☎ *787/777–0800* 🌐 *www.coliseodepuertorico.com.*

Coliseo Roberto Clemente

ARTS CENTERS | Named after the baseball hall-of-famer, this arena has become an important island venue for concerts and fairs in addition to its status as a sports facility. Rap, reggae, salsa, jazz, and pop musicians play to crowds of up to 8,000 people. ✉ *500 Av. Roosevelt, across from Plaza Las Américas, Hato Rey* ☎ *787/781–2586.*

Estadio Hiram Bithorn (*Hiram Bithorn Stadium*)

ARTS CENTERS | Particularly big acts often use this outdoor stadium (adjacent to the Coliseo Roberto Clemente), which hosts baseball games and large concerts. There's seating capacity for at least 18,000, more when the infield is used to accommodate fans. ✉ *Av. Roosevelt at Plaza Las Américas, Hato Rey* ☎ *787/725–2110.*

CLASSICAL MUSIC

Orquesta Sinfónica de Puerto Rico (*Puerto Rico Symphony Orchestra*)

MUSIC | Under the direction of conductor Maximiano Valdés, this 80-member orchestra performs a 52-week season that includes classical music, operas, ballets, and popular music. The orchestra mainly play the Centro de Bellas Artes Luis A. Ferré, but they also do outdoor concerts at museums and universities around the island, in addition to educational outreach in island schools. Pablo Casals helped create the group in 1956. ✉ *San Juan* ☎ *787/918–1107* 🌐 *www.cba.gobierno.pr.*

Shopping

CLOTHING

Stella Nolasco

CLOTHING | Celebrated local designer Stella Nolasco has showcased her designs in both New York and Paris. You'll find bold colors, lace, and intricate beading in her luxurious pieces. Stella also deseigns one-of-a-kind wedding gowns. ✉ *Condominio Plaza de Diego, 305 Av. de Diego, Santurce* ☎ *787/723–2897* 🌐 *www.stellanolasco-collection.com.*

JEWELRY

Reinhold Jewelers

JEWELRY/ACCESSORIES | Reinhold Jewelers sells designs by Stephen Dweck, David Yurman, Tiffany & Co., and others. ✉ *Plaza Las Américas, 525 Av. Franklin Delano Roosevelt, Hato Rey* ☎ *787/754–0528* 🌐 *www.reinholdjewelers.com.*

MARKETS AND MALLS

Plaza Las Américas

SHOPPING CENTERS/MALLS | For a complete shopping experience, head to the massive Plaza Las Américas, which has more than 300 retailers, including the world's largest JCPenney store, Build-A-Bear Workshop, Carolina Herrera, Zara, Gap, Sears, Macy's, Sephora, Coach, Forever 21, L'Occitane, and Armani Exchange, as well as multiple restaurants and movie theaters. ✉ *525 Av. Franklin Delano Roosevelt, Hato Rey* ☎ *787/767–1525* 🌐 *www.plazalasamericas.com.*

Activities

BASEBALL

Does the name Roberto Clemente ring a bell? The late, great Pittsburgh Pirate, who died in a 1972 plane crash en route to deliver supplies to Nicaraguan earthquake victims, was born near San Juan and got his start in the Puerto Rican professional league. Many other Puerto Rican stars have gone on to play for Major League Baseball, including the brothers Roberto Alomar and Sandy Alomar Jr. and their father, Sandy Alomar. Three players have been inducted into the National Baseball Hall of Fame: Clemente, Orlando Cepeda, and Roberto Alomar.

Estadio Hiram Bithorn

BASEBALL/SOFTBALL | Baseball games in the San Juan area are played at Estadio Hiram Bithorn, named for the first Puerto Rican to play in the major leagues. It's the home of the Cangrejeros de Santurce (Santurce Crabbers). ✉ *Hato Rey* ☎ *787/725–2110.*

TENNIS

Parque Central Municipio de San Juan

TENNIS | The Parque Central Municipio de San Juan has several lighted courts. Fees are minimal for one hour of tennis. You can also bike, walk, or run throughout the park's trails, or exercise on the popular racetrack. There is a $2 fee to access the park by car; it's free for pedestrians. ✉ *Calle Cerra, exit on Rte. 2, Santurce* ☎ *787/480–2980.*

Ocean Park

Ocean Park is a partially gated residential community with a laid-back feel. If you dream of staying in a quiet guesthouse on a more secluded beach—away from the crowds—this might be the spot for you.

Beaches

Playa de Ocean Park

BEACH—SIGHT | The residential neighborhood east of Condado and west of Isla Verde is home to this 1½-km-long (1-mile-long) stretch of golden sand. The waters are often choppy but still swimmable—take care, however, as there are no lifeguards on duty. Windsurfers say the conditions here are nearly perfect. The tranquil beach is popular with young people as well as gay men—particularly on weekends. Parking is a bit difficult, as many of the streets are gated and restricted to residents. **Amenities:** none. **Best for:** partiers; windsurfing. ✉ *Calle Santa Ana, San Juan.*

Restaurants

Acapulco Taquería Mexicana

$ | **MEXICAN** | Located behind a pawn shop, Acapulco doesn't have the most inspiring location, but you should make a point to seek out this tiny restaurant to try some of the best Mexican food in Puerto Rico. The tacos and guacamole are always made from scratch, and the owners pride themselves on authenticity. **Known for:** delicious tacos and guacamole; friendly service; excellent margaritas made with fresh juices. *Average main: $8* ✉ *2021 Calle Loíza, San Juan* ☎ *787/727–5568* ⏲ *Closed Mon. No dinner.*

Kasalta

$$ | **CAFÉ** | Those who think coffee can never be too strong should make a beeline to Kasalta and its pitch-black brew. Display cases are full of luscious pastries, including the *quesito* (cream cheese–filled puff pastry), and sandwiches include the *medianoche,* made famous when President Obama ordered one while campaigning. **Known for:** great baked goods, including cream cheese–filled quesitos; medianoche sandwiches; sometimes curt service. *Average main: $18* ✉ *1966 Calle McLeary, San Juan* ☎ *787/727–7340* 🌐 *www.kasalta.com.*

La Cueva del Mar

$$ | **SEAFOOD** | **FAMILY** | For the freshest seafood and best value, head to La Cueva del Mar on Calle Loíza. This casual, marine-themed restaurant is a local favorite, often packed with an eclectic crowd. **Known for:** fish tacos; conch in season; homemade hot sauce. *Average main: $13* ✉ *1857 Calle Loíza, San Juan* ☎ *787/726–8700.*

Nonna

$$ | **ITALIAN** | There's great dining now in Ocean Park, on or near Calle Loíza, including this cozy spot that does a wonderful job with traditional Italian dishes your *nonna* (grandmother) might have made. Pastas are made from scratch, as is the mozzarella di bufala. **Known for:** all house-made pastas and mozzarella di bufala; popular weekend brunch; creative cocktails. *Average main: $19* ✉ *103 Calle San Jorge, San Juan* ☎ *787/998–0555* 🌐 *www.nonnapr.com.*

Pinky's

$ | **CAFÉ** | **FAMILY** | Tourists and locals alike pack this playful café, where bustling servers wear cheeky "Eat Me!" T-shirts, to enjoy some of the freshest wraps and sandwiches in town. Pinky's is also well known for salads, *batidas* (fruit smoothies), and coffee. **Known for:** a variety of batidas; the Surfer sandwich with turkey, mozzarella, basil, tomato, and pesto mayo; all-day breakfast. *Average main: $8* ✉ *1902 Calle Loíza, San Juan* ☎ *787/222–5222* ⏲ *No dinner.*

Tresbé

$ | **CARIBBEAN** | It's hard to miss this bright yellow container on Calle Loíza. The three B's here are *bueno, bonito, y barato,* a common saying that means "good, pretty, and affordable." Delicious and inexpensive—no wonder it's a hit with everyone from beachgoers and artists to young professionals. **Known for:** alfresco dining; grouper ceviche and beef sliders; cocktails at night. *$ Average main: $8 ✉ 1765 Calle Loíza, San Juan ☎ 787/294–9604.*

Hotels

Andalucía Guest House

$ | **B&B/INN** | In a Spanish-style house, this friendly little inn evokes its namesake region with such details as hand-painted tiles and ceramic pots filled with greenery. **Pros:** terrific value; helpful hosts; gorgeous courtyard. **Cons:** not right on the beach; some rooms smaller than others; could use an update. *$ Rooms from: $99 ✉ 2011 Calle McLeary, Ocean Park ☎ 787/309–3373 ⊕ www.andalucia-puertorico.com 11 rooms No meals.*

★ The Dreamcatcher

$$ | **B&B/INN** | In the heart of Ocean Park, the Dreamcatcher guesthouse provides the escape you've been longing for. **Pros:** house chef on-site; yoga offered daily; two blocks from beach. **Cons:** no pool; some rooms share bathrooms; no in-room TVs. *$ Rooms from: $159 ✉ 2009 Calle España, Ocean Park ☎ 787/455–8259 ⊕ www.dreamcatcherpr.com 18 rooms No meals.*

Hostería del Mar

$ | **B&B/INN** | Located right on the beach in a gated community, this small secluded inn has an unbeatable location and ocean views from its second-floor rooms. **Pros:** plasma TVs; right on the beach; good on-site dining. **Cons:** long walk to other restaurants; needs a face-lift; hot water can be inconsistent. *$ Rooms from: $139 ✉ 1 Calle Tapia, Ocean Park ☎ 787/727–3302 ⊕ www.hosteriadelmarpr.com 25 rooms No meals.*

Numero Uno Guest House

$$ | **HOTEL** | This relaxing inn is located in a residential section of San Juan, so close to the beach that you can hear the crashing waves. **Pros:** friendly atmosphere; good restaurant; on the beach. **Cons:** in a residential neighborhood far from other tourist areas; small pool; rooms are fairly basic. *$ Rooms from: $150 ✉ 1 Calle Santa Ana, Ocean Park ☎ 787/726–5010, 866/726–5010 ⊕ www.numero1guesthouse.com 11 rooms Free Breakfast.*

Shopping

CLOTHING

Harry Robles

CLOTHING | Puerto Rican couture designer Harry Robles specializes in elegant evening and bridal gowns. *✉ 1752 Calle Loíza, San Juan ☎ 787/727–3885 ⊕ www.harryrobles.com.*

JEWELRY AND ACCESSORIES

Luca

CLOTHING | This small shop sells modern clothing and jewelry by independant artists from Puerto Rico and abroad. *✉ 59 Calle Taft, San Juan ☎ 787/398–3468 ⊕ www.lucabyluca.com.*

Activities

SURFING

Tres Palmas Surf Shop

SURFING | At Ocean Park beach, famous surfer and proprietor Carlos Cabrero rents boards, repairs equipment, and sells all sorts of hip beach and surfing gear. *✉ 1911 Av. McLeary, San Juan ☎ 787/728–3377 ⊕ www.trespalmaspr.com.*

WINDSURFING AND PADDLEBOARDING

The waves can be strong and the surf choppy, but the constant wind makes for good sailing, windsurfing, or paddleboarding, particularly in Ocean Park and Punta Las Marías (between Ocean Park and Isla Verde). In general, you can rent a windsurfer for about $75 per hour, including a lesson.

YOGA

Ashtanga Yoga

AEROBICS/YOGA | Husband and wife team David Kyle and Elizabeth Sallaberry found the hot, humid climate of Puerto Rico perfect for practicing and teaching ashtanga vinyasa yoga, one of the more vigorous styles. Their friendly studio, which has a large local following, offers classes ranging from beginner to advanced (most are held in English) as well as workshops from internationally renowned instructors. Be prepared to sweat, as the studio is intentionally not air-conditioned, although there are ceiling fans. The rate is around $19 for a drop-in class, which includes mat rental. ✉ *1950 Av. McLeary, San Juan* ☎ *787/677–7585* 🌐 *www.ashtangayogapuertorico.com.*

Isla Verde and Carolina

If you came to work on your tan—and you came to do it on a big, beautiful Caribbean beach—then Isla Verde, home to the nicest beach in the metropolitan area, is your place. The main commercial strip is not especially attractive: it's filled with fast-food restaurants and other businesses. You'll also need a car or taxi to get anywhere. That said, the resort-style hotels (many of them beachfront) offer so many amenities and so many restaurants on-site, you may not want—or need—to leave very often.

Beaches

★ Balneario de Carolina

BEACH—SIGHT | **FAMILY** | When people talk about a "beautiful Isla Verde beach," this Blue Flag beach is the one, located so close to the airport that leaves rustle when planes take off. Thanks to an offshore reef, the surf here is not as strong as at other nearby beaches, so it's good for families. There's plenty of room to spread out underneath the palm and almond trees, and there are picnic tables and grills. Although there's a charge for parking, there's not always someone to take the money. On weekends, the beach is crowded; get here early to nab parking. The newly opened Vivo Beach Club offers lounge chairs and beautiful facilities for food and drink. **Amenities:** lifeguards; parking (fee); showers; toilets. **Best for:** swimming; walking. ✉ *Av. Los Gobernadores, Carolina* *Parking $4.*

Restaurants

Metropol Restaurant and Bar

$$ | **CARIBBEAN** | Across the street from a string of major hotels, this casual restaurant doesn't look like much from the outside, but inside it's decorated in warm, tropical colors. The kitchen turns out delicious versions of Cuban and Puerto Rican favorites at reasonable prices. **Known for:** local vibe; large portions of typical dishes like churrasco and ropa vieja; family-friendly atmosphere. $ *Average main: $15* ✉ *Av. Isla Verde, Anexo Club Gallistico, San Juan* ☎ *787/791–5585* 🌐 *www.metropolrestaurant.com.*

Zest Grill Room

$$$ | **PUERTO RICAN** | A lounge atmosphere, accented with white fixtures and blue lighting, makes dining at this modern steak house an unforgettable experience. The restaurant recently revamped its menu to include a premium selection of dry-aged beef, fresh seafood (try the grilled octopus), and a variety of side dishes made with local ingredients. Even if you are staying in Condado or Old San Juan, Zest is worth a trip to Isla Verde. **Known for:** molecular gastronomy; modernist interpretations of Puerto Rican classics; popcorn soup with truffle butter and rosemary. $ *Average main: $25* ✉ *San Juan Water Beach Club Hotel, 2 Calle Tartak, San Juan* ☎ *787/728–3666* ⏲ *Closed Mon. and Tues. No lunch.*

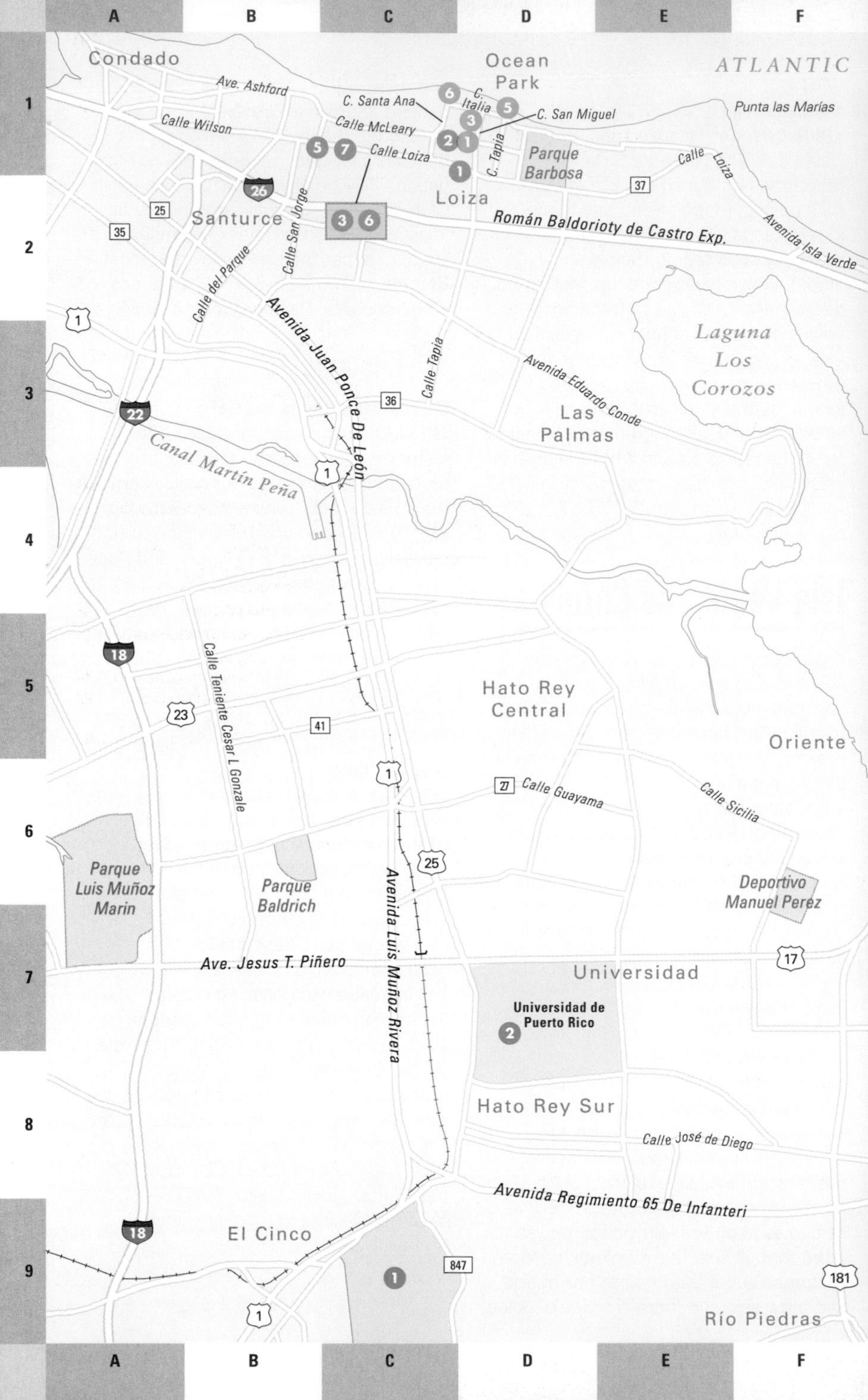

A
B
C
D
E
F
1
2
3
4
5
6
7
8
9
Condado
Ocean Park
ATLANTIC
Ave. Ashford
C. Santa Ana
C. Italia
C. San Miguel
Punta las Marías
Calle Wilson
Calle McLeary
Calle Loiza
C. Tapia
Parque Barbosa
Calle Loiza
26
37
25
Santurce
Loiza
35
Román Baldorioty de Castro Exp.
Avenida Isla Verde
Calle San Jorge
Calle del Parque
Avenida Juan Ponce De León
1
Calle Tapia
Laguna Los Corozos
Avenida Eduardo Conde
36
22
Las Palmas
Canal Martín Peña
18
Hato Rey Central
Calle Teniente Cesar L Gonzale
23
41
Oriente
1
27
Calle Guayama
Calle Sicilia
Parque Luis Muñoz Marin
Parque Baldrich
Avenida Luis Muñoz Rivera
25
Deportivo Manuel Perez
Ave. Jesus T. Piñero
17
Universidad
Universidad de Puerto Rico
Hato Rey Sur
Calle José de Diego
Avenida Regimiento 65 De Infanteri
18
El Cinco
847
181
1
Río Piedras

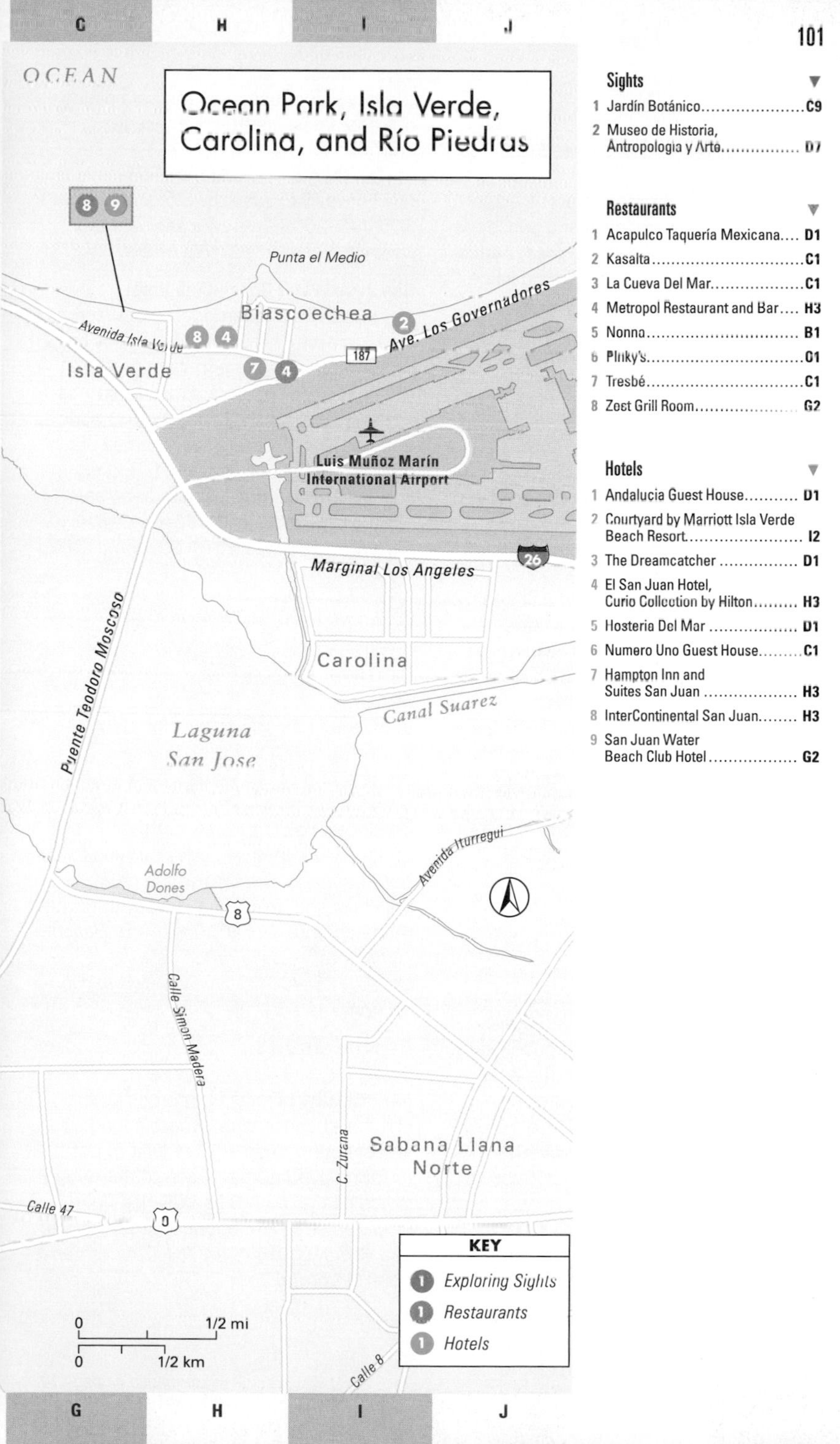

Sights

1 Jardín Botánico C9
2 Museo de Historia, Antropologia y Arte D7

Restaurants

1 Acapulco Taquería Mexicana D1
2 Kasalta C1
3 La Cueva Del Mar C1
4 Metropol Restaurant and Bar H3
5 Nonna B1
6 Pinky's C1
7 Tresbé C1
8 Zest Grill Room G2

Hotels

1 Andalucia Guest House D1
2 Courtyard by Marriott Isla Verde Beach Resort I2
3 The Dreamcatcher D1
4 El San Juan Hotel, Curio Collection by Hilton H3
5 Hosteria Del Mar D1
6 Numero Uno Guest House C1
7 Hampton Inn and Suites San Juan H3
8 InterContinental San Juan H3
9 San Juan Water Beach Club Hotel G2

Hotels

Courtyard by Marriott Isla Verde Beach Resort

$$ | **RESORT** | This 12-story resort tries to be all things to all people—and succeeds to a great degree. **Pros:** on a great beach; family-friendly environment; good value. **Cons:** you can hear airport noise from some rooms; lobby is busy and noisy; far from Condado and Old San Juan. *Rooms from: $235 7012 Av. Boca de Cangrejos, San Juan 787/791–0404, 787/999–6300 www.sjcourtyard.com 281 rooms No meals.*

★ El San Juan Hotel, Curio Collection by Hilton

$$$ | **RESORT** | **FAMILY** | After a much-anticipated renovation of both the rooms and public areas, the hotel's classic appeal remains, including the lobby's intricately carved mahogany walls and ceiling that date to 1955, while the rooms have been given a more modern look. **Pros:** beautiful pool; recently renovated; fantastic beach. **Cons:** noise in lobby from bars; parking lot a long walk from hotel entrance; small bathrooms. *Rooms from: $269 6063 Av. Isla Verde, San Juan 787/791–1000 curiocollection.hilton.com 388 rooms No meals.*

Hampton Inn and Suites San Juan

$$ | **HOTEL** | If you don't mind a short walk to the beach, you can get a room at this friendly hotel for much less than its competitors across the road. **Pros:** helpful staff; close to airport; good value. **Cons:** 5–10-minute walk from the beach; chain-hotel feel; some highway noise in pool area. *Rooms from: $189 6530 Av. Isla Verde, San Juan 787/791–8777 www.hamptoninn.com 200 rooms Free Breakfast.*

InterContinental San Juan

$$$ | **RESORT** | **FAMILY** | Somewhat dowdy on the outside, though modern on the inside, the InterContinental's main draws are its pool and spectacular beachfront location. **Pros:** lovely pool; on one of the city's best beaches; multiple dining options. **Cons:** unattractive facade; cramped lobby; no longer has a casino. *Rooms from: $319 5961 Av. Isla Verde, San Juan 787/791–6100, 800/443–2009 www.icsanjuanresort.com 398 rooms No meals.*

San Juan Water Beach Club Hotel

$$ | **HOTEL** | This ultramodern hotel across from beautiful Isla Verde Beach has great restaurants and is a popular nighttime destination for partiers. **Pros:** fun atmosphere; interesting design; rooftop pool and bar. **Cons:** dark hallways; small pool; beach is across the street. *Rooms from: $219 2 Calle Tartak, San Juan 787/728–3666, 888/265–6699 www.waterbeachhotel.com 80 rooms No meals.*

Nightlife

BARS

Mist

BARS/PUBS | On the roof of the San Juan Water Beach Club Hotel, this sexy spot offers some of Isla Verde's best ocean views. On the weekends there's a DJ, and locals pack in to relax at the bar or on the white leather beds reserved for bottle service. Don't miss the creative cocktails and delicious pizzas with homemade cheese. *San Juan Water Beach Club Hotel, 2 Calle Tartak, Isla Verde 787/725–4664 www.waterbeachhotel.com.*

DANCE CLUBS

Brava

DANCE CLUBS | Dress to impress at this chic hotel dance club, where a long line of young people (21+) wait to get in Thursday–Saturday. Each of the two levels has its own DJ and dance floor. *El San Juan Hotel, 6063 Av. Isla Verde, Isla Verde 787/791–2781 bravamanagementgroup.com.*

Continued on page 107

Salsa

A Guide to Puerto Rico's Favorite Music and Dance

Salsa: its hip-shaking rhythms and sensual moves embody the spirit of the Caribbean and Latin America. The songs and the steps create a language all their own—one that's spoken by passionate dancers and musicians the world over. But it's the Puerto Ricans who are the most fluent. Welcome to the home of salsa! Are you ready to dance?

by Julie Schwietert Collazo

As the first notes of the song sound, dancers come alive, eager to take their place on the floor with a partner whose skill matches their own. These are the most daring salsa devotees who are found in every corner of the island, dancers who won't quit moving until the music stops. Even as a bystander, it's impossible to stand still.

Salsa isn't a passive rhythm: it's animated, hot, and sensual, a metaphor for the Caribbean itself. In general, the themes of the songs mirror the moves of the dance, with choruses alluding to love, both forbidden and open. In the music and the movement, there's occasional improvisation among those who know the genre. Hips shake to the clave, which marks the basic rhythm, and shoulders shake from one side to the other, fanning the air. It's a democratic form, where experimentation is encouraged . . . you just have to be willing to get out there.

SALSA HISTORY

Timbale master Tito Puente

Though salsa has its roots outside Puerto Rico, the island is directly responsible for the rhythm known by this name. As a musical form, the components of salsa can be traced back to Europe and Africa. During the colonial period, Spanish conquistadores arriving from the West Indies brought island rhythms along with them. They also brought the complex, multi-rhythmic riffs of Arabic music, an artifact of the Muslim conquest of the Iberian Peninsula that had become embedded in the music of Spain and Portugal. In Puerto Rico, all of these musical strands came together to create a new rhythm known as bomba.

The emergence of salsa was deeply influenced by musical forms from Cuba and other parts of the Caribbean, as well as musical experimentation by diaspora Puerto Ricans living in New York. Among the most important of these mainland musicians was the late percussionist and band leader Tito Puente.

The history of salsa is the history of the new world. In salsa, there's evidence of rhythms from past ages, as well as the musical history of our own time. Salsa isn't a "pure" musical form, but represents—like Puerto Rico itself—a mixture of rhythmic elements, adapted by the inhabitants of the new world.

DID YOU KNOW?

- The first use of the word "salsa" related to music was in 1937 by Cuban composer Igancio Pineiro in his popular song, "Echale Salsita." It continues to be a frequently recorded song today by artists in and outside Cuba.
- The song "Oye Como Va" was originally composed by Tito Puente in 1963 and later recorded by Carlos Santana, who made it a number-one hit.
- The contribution of salsa to jazz music dates from 1940, when Dizzie Gillespie and Stan Kenton incorporated salsa in their tunes, giving birth to "Latin jazz."
- More than 30 countries celebrate salsa with annual festivals, among them, Poland, Israel, France, Serbia, and Japan.

SALSA SPEAK

ABRAZO: The *abrazo* is the positioning of the partners' hands and arms. The woman's left hand rests lightly on her partner's shoulder, while his right hand is placed on the small of her back to guide her. The abrazo establishes the space each partner maintains during turns.

Abrazo

Vueltas

VUELTAS: *Vueltas*, turns, are an important component of salsa. There are numerous styles, and they can occur in both directions, but all are determined and initiated by the male partner. Turns are spontaneous; their complexity depends upon the skill and experience of the dancers.

SOLOS: Solos—a favorite move of experienced dancers—are moments when the partners separate to move independently though still in response to each other. These are often synchronized with the solos of percussion musicians. Solos are also used as a means of rest after a series of complex turns before the pair comes together again for even more intricate turns.

Solos

SALSA STYLE

Two elements define salsa fashion: comfort and sensuality. Men and women both draw from the best of their wardrobes, with men often dressed in guayabera shirts, linen pants, and two-toned dance shoes. Suede shoes permit optimal movement for men and add a touch of elegance. Women typically wear dresses—often knee length or shorter—and open-toed, medium-heeled dance shoes with ankle support. For both men and women, freedom of movement and maximum ventilation are important elements of a salsa wardrobe.

The dance is an opportunity to show off your elegance and your sensuality, but your clothing should also honor the significance of the event and venue. Many dance organizers impose dress policies, prohibiting running shoes, sleeveless shirts, and overly informal or provocative clothing. Dress to impress.

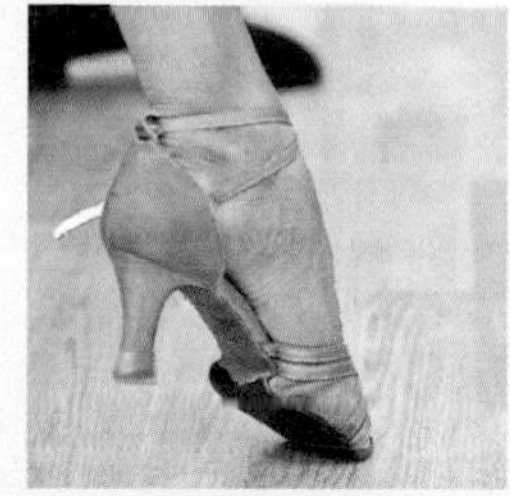

Salsa dance shoes

NEXT STEPS

If you're ready to take to the dance floor, here are some of the best places to learn—and then show off—your moves.

LESSONS

The Academia de Baile Julie Mayoral. On the Plaza de las Delicias in Ponce, Mayoral's second floor studio is steaming hot, and her young, enthusiastic instructors will have you doing proper vueltas in no time. For a bit more than $5 for an hour lesson, Mayoral probably offers the best deal in Puerto Rico. Mayoral also has studios in Coamo and Yauco. Call her Ponce studio (☎ 787/843–2830) for information about lessons at any of the three studios.

In San Juan, dancer Paulette Beauchamp offers salsa classes for children and adults on Tuesday. Her studio, **DanzActiva** (☎ 787/775–9438 🌐 www.danzactiva.com), is in the historic Cuartel de Ballaja building in Old San Juan.

HOTELS

Locals and tourists alike take to the dance floor at the **San Juan Marriott Resort** and **Stellaris Casino** on weekends, when homegrown musicians provide a soundtrack for the salsa experience. Entry is free, but you'll need to purchase drinks if you decide to rest at one of the tables circling the dance floor.

CLUBS

Old San Juan's **Nuyorican Café** looks like a dive—and it is—but it's the heart of Puerto Rico's salsa scene. Though the café also hosts jazz and rock groups as well as poetry readings and experimental theatre, its reputation for world-class salsa has expanded far beyond the island. Call ahead for the current schedule (☎ 787/977–1276).

FESTIVALS

As the home of salsa, Puerto Rico hosts an annual **International Salsa Congress.** It's held in San Juan each July, though the site changes each year. The congress attracts thousands of aficionados from the island and from surprisingly far-flung places, including Japan, Korea, and Norway.

(left) A couple prepares for competition at the International Salsa Congress held in San Juan. (right) Young dancers performing at the International Salsa Congress.

Shopping

MARKETS AND MALLS

Plaza Carolina

SHOPPING CENTERS/MALLS | About 15 minutes east of San Juan, you'll find Plaza Carolina, whose anchor stores are JCPenney, Best Buy, Sears, Forever 21, and Victoria's Secret. Get there via Route 26. ✉ *Av. Jesús M. Fragoso, Carolina* ☎ *787/768–0514* 🌐 *www.simon.com/mall/plaza-carolina.*

OUTLETS

The Outlet 66 Mall

OUTLET/DISCOUNT STORES | This outlet has more than 50 factory outlet stores, including Nautica, Nike, Guess, Gap, and Calvin Klein. A new entertainment center just opened and includes kart racing, virtual reality, bowling, an arcade, and more. It's in Canóvanas, about 20 minutes east of San Juan. ✉ *18400 Rte. 3, Km 18.4, Carolina* ☎ *787/256–7040* 🌐 *www.theoutlet66mall.com.*

Activities

DIVING AND SNORKELING

The waters off San Juan aren't the best places to scuba dive, but several outfitters conduct short excursions to where tropical fish, coral, and seahorses are visible at depths of 30–60 feet. Escorted half-day dives start around $70 for one or two tanks, including all equipment; in general, double those prices for night dives. Packages that include lunch and other extras start at $100; others that include accommodations are also available.

Snorkeling excursions, which include transportation, equipment rental, and sometimes lunch, start at $55–$60. Equipment rental runs about $10 at beaches. Avoid unsupervised areas, as rough waters and strong undertows make some places dangerous.

Ocean Sports

SCUBA DIVING | Ocean Sports offers certified scuba courses; snorkeling excursions; specialty courses in nitrox diving; diving trips; air-tank fill-ups; and equipment repairs, sales, and rentals. ✉ *3086 Av. Isla Verde, Isla Verde* ☎ *787/723–8513* 🌐 *www.osdivers.com.*

TENNIS

If you'd like to use the tennis courts at a property where you aren't a guest, call in advance for information about reservations and fees.

Club Tennis de Isla Verde

TENNIS | These four lighted courts are open to nonmembers at $20 per hour for up to four people (daily 8 am–10 pm). Reservations are required. ✉ *Isla Verde Park, Calles Ema at Delta Rodriguez, San Juan* ☎ *787/727–6490, 787/642–3208.*

Río Piedras

The mostly residential Río Piedras area is home to the Universidad de Puerto Rico and a few notable sights.

Sights

Jardín Botánico (*Botanical Garden*)

GARDEN | This 75-acre forest of more than 200 species of tropical and subtropical vegetation is the Universidad de Puerto Rico's main attraction. Gravel footpaths lead to a graceful lotus lagoon and a bamboo promenade, as well as orchid and palm gardens. Not all plants and trees are labeled, so the garden is more of a tranquil retreat than an opportunity to learn about the vegetation. Trail maps are available at the entrance gate; the $5 tour is well worth it. ✉ *Universidad de Puerto Rico, Rte. 1 at Rte. 847, at entrance to Barrio Venezuela, San Juan* ☎ *787/758–9957* 🌐 *www.upr.edu* *Free.*

Museo de Historia, Antropología y Arte

MUSEUM | The Universidad de Puerto Rico's small Museum of History,

Anthropology and Art offers rotating exhibitions in three areas. Its archaeological and historical collection covers the Native American influence on the island and the Caribbean, the colonial era, and the history of slavery. There's also a small collection of Egyptian antiquities. Art holdings include a range of Puerto Rican popular, graphic, folk, and fine art; the museum's prize exhibit is the painting *El Velorio* (*The Wake*), by the 19th-century artist Francisco Oller. If you're looking to see something in particular, call before you go, as only a small portion of the collection is on display at a time. Guided tours in English are available; call for reservations. ✉ *Universidad de Puerto Rico, Av. Ponce de León, San Juan* ☎ *787/763–3939* 🎫 *Free* ⏲ *Closed Sat.*

Shopping

MARKETS AND MALLS

The Mall of San Juan

SHOPPING CENTERS/MALLS | This upscale mall is the most luxurious in the Caribbean. Shops include Saks Fifth Avenue, Nordstrom, Jimmy Choo, Williams-Sonoma, Louis Vuitton, and more. The top floor houses Il Nuovo Mercato, an Italian food court where you can sample fresh pastas and brick-oven pizzas—don't miss the gelato stand. ✉ *1000 Mall of San Juan Blvd., Ramon Antonini, San Juan* ☎ *787/759–6310* 🌐 *themallofsanjuan.com.*

Cataño

Cataño, bordered by the Bahía de San Juan in the north, is an industrial suburb, perhaps most noted for its distillery belonging to Bacardí. Bayamón can be reached in 15–30 minutes from central San Juan; if you come by car, stop by the attractive central park, bordered by historic buildings.

A Golf Great

Juan "Chi Chi" Rodriguez, who was born in Río Piedras in 1935, was the first Puerto Rican golfer to be inducted into the World Golf Hall of Fame. During his career, he won 8 PGA Tour events and 37 tournaments over all. He continued playing on the Senior PGA Tour, winning 22 additional victories between 1986 and 1993. He founded the Chi Chi Rodriguez Youth Foundation in 1979 to help at-risk youth. He has designed two Puerto Rico golf courses: El Legado golf Resort in Guayama and the course at the Embassy Suites Dorado del Mar Beach & Golf Resort.

Sights

Casa Bacardí Visitor Center

INFO CENTER | Exiled from Cuba, the Bacardí family built a small rum distillery here in the 1950s. Today it's the world's largest, able to produce 100,000 gallons of spirits a day and 21 million cases a year. A basic tour of the visitor center includes one free drink, or you can opt for a mixology class or rum tasting. If you don't want to drive, you can take a ferry from Pier 2 for 50¢ and then a *público* (public van service) from the ferry pier to the factory for about $3 per person. ✉ *Bay View Industrial Park, Rte. 165, Km 2.6, at Rte. 888, Cataño* ☎ *787/788–8400* 🌐 *www.visitcasabacardi.com* 🎫 *Tour $15; mixology class or rum tasting $50.*

Guaynabo

Guaynabo is a mix of residential and industrial areas and is worth visiting for its historical importance—Juan Ponce de León established the island's first

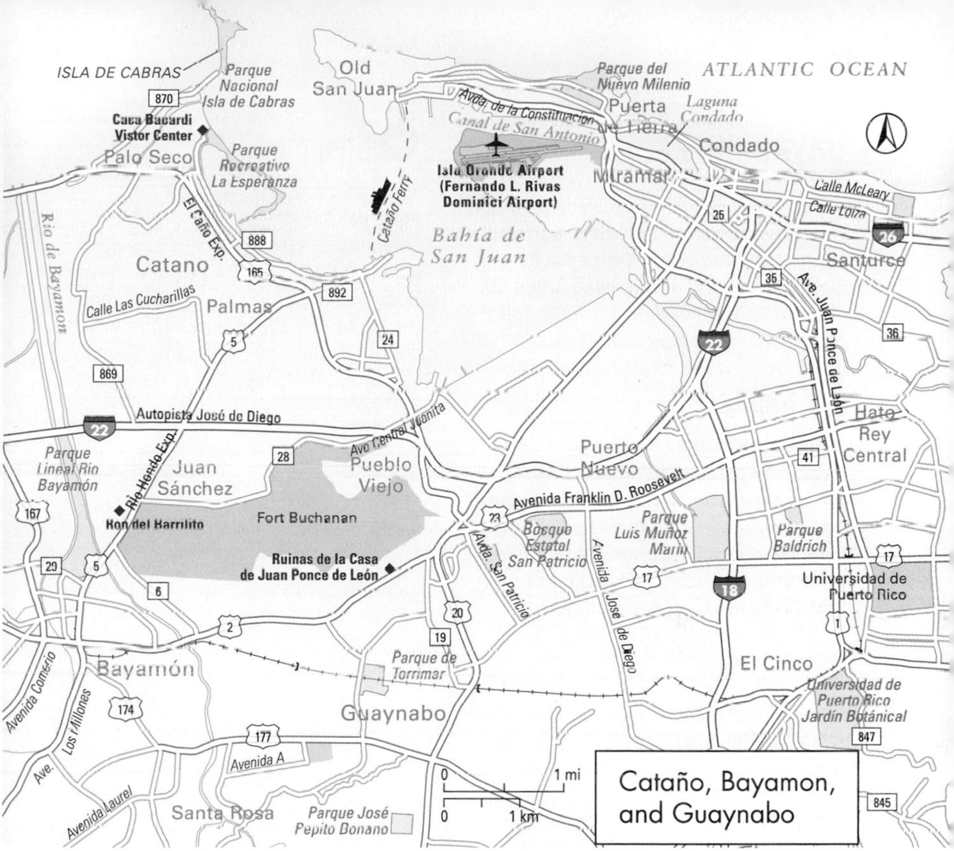

Cataño, Bayamon, and Guaynabo

settlement here in Caparra, and you can visit the ruins of the original fortification.

Sights

Ruinas de la Casa de Juan Ponce de León (*Caparra Archaeological Site*)
ARCHAEOLOGICAL SITE | In 1508 Ponce de León established the island's first settlement here. The Caparra Ruins—just a few crumbling walls—are all that remain of an ancient fort. The small **Museo de la Conquista y Colonización de Puerto Rico** (Museum of the Conquest and Colonization of Puerto Rico) contains historical documents, exhibits, and excavated artifacts, although you can see the museum's contents in less time than it takes to say its name. Both the ruins and the museum are maintained by the Puerto Rican Institute of Culture. ✉ *Rte. 2, Km 6.4, Guaynabo* ☎ *787/781–4795* 🎫 *Free* ⏲ *Closed weekends.*

Shopping

MARKETS AND MALLS

San Patricio Plaza
SHOPPING CENTERS/MALLS | Off Avenida John F. Kennedy, about 15 minutes south of San Juan, San Patricio Plaza has a T.J. Maxx and a Bed Bath & Beyond, a movie theater, and several restaurants. For the best dining in the area, head to Bottles or Avocado. ✉ *100 Av. San Patricio, at Av. Franklin Delano Roosevelt, Guaynabo* ☎ *787/792–5328* 🌐 *www.sanpatricio.com.*

Bayamón

Just to the west of Guaynabo, Bayamón is a busy, sprawling suburb of San Juan (it's actually the second-largest city in Puerto Rico). If tourists make it this far, it's usually for shopping at one of the area's giant shopping malls.

Sights

★ Ron del Barrilito

WINERY/DISTILLERY | Ron del Barrilito is handcrafted Puerto Rican rum that isn't often seen outside the island, but it is a well-aged local favorite. This rum has been around since 1880 and comes in three varieties: 2 stars, 3 stars, and the rare 5 stars. The varieties are differentiated by the amount of time they have spent in the barrel. Most places only carry the 2- and 3-star bottles, because the 5-star variety, which spends 35 years in oak casks, is extremely limited. Although a visitor center is under construction, there's no formal tour (nor samples). The factory only accepts visitors by appointment, so make sure you contact them ahead of time. Ron de Barrilito only produces about 14,000 cases of rum each year, so a visit is a great way to ensure you take home a truly special Puerto Rican souvenir, and it's a much more local experience than at a large, commercial distillery. ✉ *Hacienda Santa Ana, Carretera 5, Km. 5.5, Bayamón* ☎ *787/785–3490* 🌐 *rondelbarrilito.com* 🎫 *Free* 🕒 *Closed weekends.*

Shopping

MARKETS AND MALLS

Plaza del Sol

SHOPPING CENTERS/MALLS | Plaza del Sol includes Old Navy, Bed Bath & Beyond, Sunglass Hut, the Home Depot, and the Children's Place, among others. It's about 30 minutes west of San Juan. ✉ *725 Av. Principal Oeste, Bayamón* ☎ *787/778–8724.*

Chapter 4

EL YUNQUE AND THE NORTHEAST

Updated by Julie Schwietert Collazo

Sights ★★★★★ | Restaurants ★★★★☆ | Hotels ★★★★☆ | Shopping ★☆☆☆☆ | Nightlife ★☆☆☆☆

WELCOME TO EL YUNQUE AND THE NORTHEAST

TOP REASONS TO GO

★ **Take a hike:** Take in the spectacular waterfalls of El Yunque, the only rain forest within the U.S. National Forest system.

★ **Take a dip:** Relax at Luquillo Beach, one of the prettiest beaches in Puerto Rico and a family favorite.

★ **Take a seat:** Hang with locals at one of the dozens of outdoor seafood kiosks on the highway before you get to Luquillo Beach. There are dozens to choose from.

★ **Hit the links:** Tee off on the tree-lined fairways of one of the area's golf courses, especially at the St. Regis Bahia Beach.

If you seek an alternative to the hectic urban environs of San Juan, head to the pristine coastal towns and charming inland locales along Puerto Rico's northeast corridor. Easily reached by car, El Yunque and northeast Puerto Rico are convenient enough for a quick day trip, but offer enough exploration for at least two days. Kayak the lagoon in Piñones, take a surf lesson in Luquillo, horseback ride in the foothills of El Yunque, or tee off in Humacao—the list of exciting and relaxing activities in this region goes on and on.

1 **Piñones.** A popular destination among locals, this coastal town located between Isla Verde and Río Grande comes alive on the weekends, when food kiosks and roadside stands sell all manner of fried Puerto Rican snacks, many of them stuffed with freshly caught seafood. Grab one for yourself and sit along the shore, contemplating the vast Atlantic.

2 **Río Grande.** Río Grande is home to Puerto Rico's most popular attraction, El Yunque, North America's only tropical rain forest. There's not much in the town beyond that, but its proximity to Luquillo Beach and Ceiba, the departure point for ferries to Vieques and Culebra, make it a bustling town.

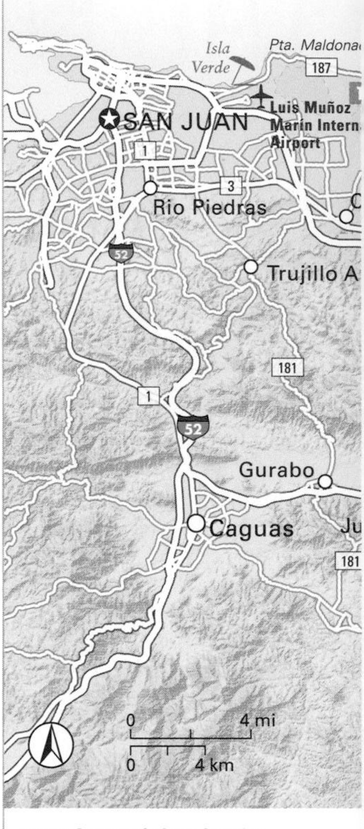

3 **El Yunque.** Puerto Rico's most visited point of interest is this tropical rain forest, a lush green palette. It was heavily damaged by Hurricane Maria, so check before making a day trip to ask about current conditions

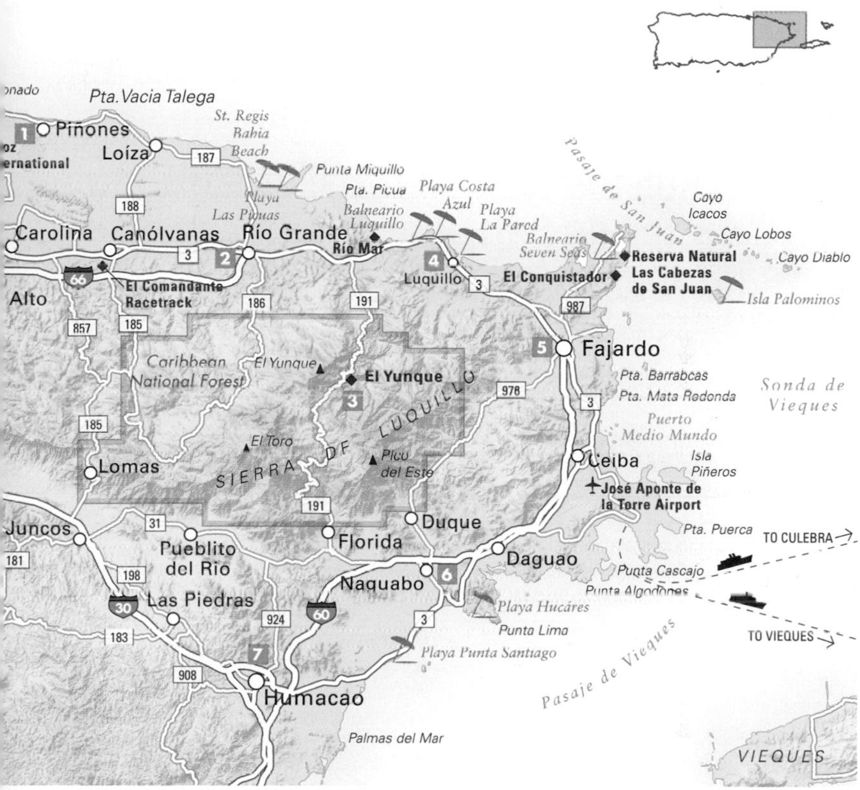

and accessibility of the specific parts of the forest you want to visit.

4 Luquillo. Luquillo is a lively town that attracts people from all over the island because of its expansive beach, which is postcard perfect thanks to its neat row of coconut palms.

5 Fajardo. While Fajardo has more development, nearby Ceiba (just to the south) is now the point of departure for ferries that make daily trips to the outlying islands of Vieques and Culebra.

6 Naguabo. The main reason to visit Naguabo is to use it as a launching point to take a boat ride around Monkey Island, where rhesus monkey research is conducted.

7 Humacao. Golfers won't want to skip this coastal town, which is where you'll find some of the island's best greens.

Tree frogs, rare parrots, and wild horses only start the list of northeastern Puerto Rico's offerings. The backdrops for encounters with an array of flora and fauna include the 28,000 acres of El Yunque tropical rain forest, the seven ecosystems in the Reserva Natural Las Cabezas de San Juan, and Laguna Grande, where tiny sea creatures appear to light up the waters.

As the ocean bends around the northeastern coast, it laps onto beaches of soft sand and palm trees, crashes against high bluffs, and almost magically creates an amazing roster of ecosystems. The beautiful beaches at Luquillo are complemented by more rugged southeastern shores. Inland, green hills roll down toward plains that once held expanses of coconut trees, such as those still surrounding the town of Piñones, or sugarcane, as evidenced by a few surviving plantations near Naguabo and Humacao.

The natural beauty and varied terrain continue in the area's other towns as well: Río Grande, which once attracted immigrants from Austria, Spain, and Italy; Naguabo, which overlooks what were once immense cane fields; and Cayo Santiago, where the only residents are monkeys.

You can golf, ride horses, hike marked trails, and plunge into water sports throughout the region. In many places along the coast, green hills cascade down to the ocean. On the edge of the Atlantic, Fajardo serves as a jumping-off point for diving, fishing, and catamaran excursions. Luquillo is the site of a family beach so well equipped that there are even facilities enabling wheelchair users to enter the sea.

MAJOR REGIONS

The Northeastern Coast. As you head east from San Juan to escape the city crowds, you'll first come to Piñones and its popular open-air eateries. Next you'll come to Río Grande, which is the closest developed area to the rain forest and home to several restaurants and popular resorts, as well as long strips of pristine beach. Its closest neighbor is the region's magnificent natural wonder, El Yunque, a park you can explore in the air-conditioned comfort of a car in a matter of hours, or hike for days without seeing all the greenery, waterfalls, and views. Nearby in Luquillo, Balneario de Luquillo (Luquillo Beach) beckons. At the island's eastern end, the Reserva Natural Las Cabezas de San Juan and Fajardo are worth exploring.

The Eastern Coast. Puerto Rico's southeastern coast is home to some of the island's most popular attractions. Be sure to check out the beautiful beaches and crystal-clear snorkeling before heading south to Naguabo. This town is said to be the birthplace of the *pastelillo de chapín,* a popular dish that consists of trunkfish wrapped inside a deep-fried flour dough. Farther south and west, travelers will discover Humacao, home of the island's exceptional Wyndham Garden at Palmas del Mar.

Planning

WHEN TO GO

In general, the island's northeast coast—preferred by those seeking abandoned beaches and nature reserves rather than casinos and urban glitz—tends to be less popular than San Juan. Exceptions include Easter and Christmas, when Luquillo and Fajardo become crowded with local sun worshippers, merrymakers, and campers. Island festivals also draw crowds, but planning a trip around one of them will give you a true sense of the region's culture. Be sure to make reservations well in advance if you're visiting during high season (December 15–April 15).

GETTING HERE AND AROUND

AIR TRAVEL

Air Flamenco, Cape Air, and Vieques Air Link offer flights between San Juan, Vieques, and Culebra. Flights are also offered from Ceiba, and are even shorter than flights departing from San Juan.

CONTACTS Air Flamenco. ☎ *787/724–1818* 🌐 *www.airflamenco.net.* **Cape Air.** ☎ *800/227–3247* 🌐 *www.capeair.com.* **Vieques Air Link.** ☎ *787/741–8331, 888/901–9247* 🌐 *www.viequesairlink.com.*

BUS TRAVEL

Públicos (a cross between a privately owned taxi and a small van or bus) travel between San Juan and Fajardo, stopping en route at the ferry terminal in Ceiba. The full journey can take up to four hours, depending on where you board, frequency of stops, traffic, and where you are dropped off. However, the fare is a huge bargain at about $26 (pay the driver as you board). To get to Fajardo or Ceiba, simply flag down a público anywhere along Route 3.

Within cities and towns local buses (35¢–50¢) pick up and discharge at marked stops. Enter and pay at the front (exact fare required), and exit at the front or the back.

CAR TRAVEL

Unless you are planning to hop directly onto a ferry to Vieques or Culebra, you should consider renting a car in eastern Puerto Rico. Even the destination resorts are fairly isolated, and you may appreciate the mobility if you want to get out and have a meal away from the resort or explore El Yunque or some of the great beaches. Rates start at about $40 per day, but it may be possible to rent directly from your hotel, so ask about packages. And keep in mind that most of these resorts do charge a daily fee for parking.

From San Juan the east coast is accessible via Route 3, or Route 187 if you want to visit Piñones and Loíza. At Fajardo the road intersects with Route 53, which continues down the coast. Route 3 also continues along the coast, providing a more scenic, if slower, trip.

TAXI TRAVEL

You can flag cabs down on the street, but it's faster and safer to have your hotel call one for you. Make sure it's clear whether you'll pay a flat rate or a meter will determine the fare. Instead of renting a car, consider taking a taxi to Fajardo; the cost from the San Juan area should be about $80 for up to five people.

CONTACTS Humacao Taxi. ☎ *787/852–6880.*

HOTELS

The east coast has a wide variety of lodgings, from small inns and guesthouses in the mountains to large, lavish resorts along the coast. Government-approved *paradores* are also available. A kind of country inn, paradores offer affordable Puerto Rican hospitality and the cozy comforts of home outside the San Juan metro area. These small, privately owned properties are usually quite picturesque and can be found throughout the interior and at more remote coastal towns. If you wish to get away from it all with a neatly packaged trip, eastern Puerto Rico has some of the island's top resorts: the St. Regis Bahia Beach Resort and El Conquistador, a Waldorf Astoria Resort, where the resort fee is being waived until all facilities are up and running after Hurricane Maria. You'll also find extensive facilities and services at large, self-contained complexes like the Wyndham Grand Río Mar and the Meliá Coco Beach, making the list of regional offerings more than complete.

RESTAURANTS

Some restaurants carry the tourism board's *mesón gastronómico* designation. Such establishments specialize in typical island food. The eastern region has both formal restaurants, where reservations are necessary, and casual beachside eateries, where you can walk in unannounced in beach attire and have a fine meal of fresh fish. The bill generally doesn't include a service charge, so a 15% tip is customary and expected. Most restaurants are open for dinner from late afternoon until about 10 pm.

HOTEL AND RESTAURANT PRICES

Restaurant and hotel reviews have been shortened. For full information, visit Fodors.com.

What It Costs in U.S. Dollars

	$	$$	$$$	$$$$
RESTAURANTS	under $12	$12–$20	$21–$30	over $30
HOTELS	under $150	$150–$250	$251–$350	over $350

PACKING FOR EL YUNQUE

When you come to El Yunque, bring binoculars, a camera (preferably with a good zoom function), bottled water, and sunscreen; wear a hat or visor, good walking shoes, and comfortable clothes. Although daytime temperatures rise as high as 80°F (27°C), wear long pants, because some plants can cause skin irritations. There are no poisonous snakes in the forest (or on the island as a whole), but bugs can be ferocious, so a strong repellent is a must. And remember: this is a rain forest, so bring a poncho and be prepared for frequent showers.

SAFETY

Although crime isn't as high in the island's eastern areas as it is in San Juan, use prudence. Avoid bringing valuables with you to the beach; if you must do so, be sure not to leave them in view in your car. It's best to keep your car locked while driving, and steer clear of out-of-the-way beaches after sunset.

VISITOR INFORMATION

Cities usually maintain information offices connected to the city hall, and most are open on weekdays during regular business hours.

CONTACTS Fajardo Tourism Office. ✉ *6 Calle Dr. Lopez, Fajardo* ☎ *787/863–4013* 🌐 *www.fajardopr.org.* **Naguabo Tourism Office.** ✉ *Playa Húcares Malecón, Naguabo* ☎ *787/874–5904.* **Río Grande Office of Tourism and Culture.** ✉ *Calle San José, Plaza de Recreo, Río Grande* ☎ *787/887–2370.*

If You Like

Great Food

In the east you'll find fine fare of all types. On the traditional side, look for the deep-fried snacks (often stuffed with meat or fish) known as *frituras*, as well as numerous dishes laced with coconut. Plantains are the star ingredient in the hearty *mofongo*, a seafood-stuffed dish, and also appear as *tostones* (fried plantain chips). Fresh fish is commonly prepared with tomatoes, onions, and garlic, or some combination of the three. These days, island chefs are experimenting with flavor and texture, putting modern spins on classic dishes. Throughout the island, you'll find a blend of old and new cooking styles and techniques that will suit all palates.

Golf

There's something to be said for facing a rolling, palm-tree-lined fairway with the distant ocean at your back. And then there are the ducks, iguanas, and pelicans that congregate in mangroves near some holes. That's what golf in eastern Puerto Rico is all about. The Arthur Hills–designed course at El Conquistador is one of the island's best. The Flamboyán course, a Rees Jones creation at Palmas del Mar Country Club, consistently gets raves, as do the courses at Wyndham Grand Río Mar and at St. Regis Bahia Beach Resort, where Robert Trent Jones Jr. oversaw construction of an eco-friendly green that overlooks the meeting place of the Espíritu Santo River and the Atlantic Ocean.

Piñones

16 km (10 miles) east of San Juan.

Funky Piñones is little more than a collection of open-air seaside eateries. Sand floors, barefoot patrons, and tantalizing seafood—traditionally washed down with icy beer—have made it popular with locals, especially on weekend evenings. Chilled *agua de coco* is served right from the coconut. During the day you can rent a bike and follow the marked seaside trail that meanders 11 km (7 miles) through the mangrove forest and along the northern coastline. It takes about two hours to bike from one end and back, but allow some time to stop and take pictures, grab something to eat, and explore the scenic beach areas.

The area has grown as a nightlife destination, too, as fancier establishments, some with live music, have opened up. As mid-afternoon turns into evening and people begin to leave the beach for refreshments, the air is thick with smoke from grilled fish, beef and chicken kebabs (called *pinchos* here), and the kettles of oil used to fry codfish and crab fritters. When the giant orange Caribbean sun starts to fall behind the San Juan skyline, salsa and merengue—not to mention reggae and Latin pop—start to blare from jukeboxes and sound systems at dozens of ramshackle establishments dotting Route 187, the main drag. Traffic on the two-lane road into and out of the area is daunting on Friday and Saturday nights, when many of these open-air bars host merengue combos, Brazilian jazz trios, or reggae bands.

GETTING HERE AND AROUND

The approach to Piñones from San Juan is simple. Take Route 26 east or Route 37 east, follow signs for the Balneario de Carolina, then go straight on Route 187 and cross Punta Cangrejos. Door to door, the trip should take about 15 minutes.

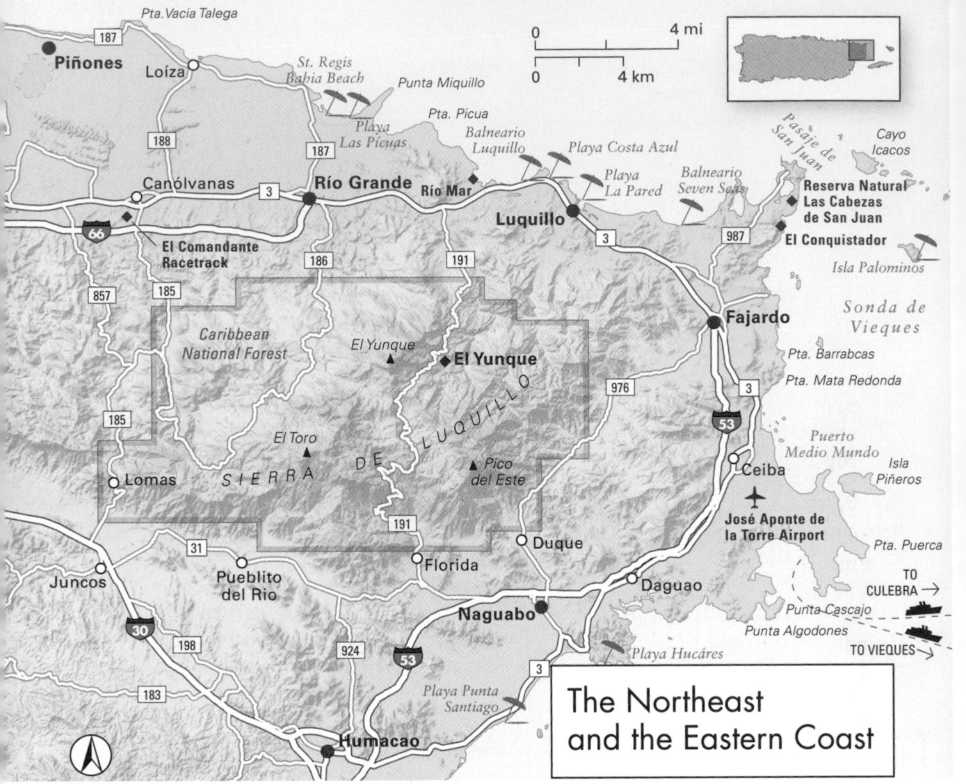

The Northeast and the Eastern Coast

You can also get a taxi to Piñones, or take the bus for about 75¢ (via C45)—but the latter can take more than an hour. To avoid getting stranded, prearrange a pickup time for your taxi driver to return.

TAXI CONTACTS AA American Taxi, Inc. ☎ *787/982–3466.* **Astro Taxi.** ☎ *787/727–8888.*

Sights

Paseo Piñones

PROMENADE | One of the most pleasant ways to pass the time in Piñones is walking along the Paseo Piñones. This 10½-km (6½-mile) boardwalk passes through sand dunes and crosses lagoons and mangrove forests. All the while, a line of coconut palms shades you from the sun. You'll share the path with bikers, joggers, and in-line skaters. Food kiosks abound. ✉ *Rte. 187.*

Beaches

Playa de Piñones

BEACH—SIGHT | You'll find Playa de Piñones right in front of the cluster of food kiosks built by the government for resident cooks. A large barrier reef blocks the strong currents and serves as the foundation for the large bathing pools in front of a sandy beach. **Amenities:** food and drink; parking. **Best for:** swimming. ✉ *Route 187, Km 8.*

Restaurants

El Kiosko Boricua

$ | **PUERTO RICAN** | **FAMILY** | Forget McDonald's and Taco Bell; in Puerto Rico, a beachside kiosk like this one is *the* place

Great Itineraries

If You Have 1 Day

If you have only a day (or even less) to visit eastern Puerto Rico, make a beeline for **El Yunque.** (Route 3 is the quickest way.) This rain forest has hiking trails of various lengths leading to secluded waterfalls and mountaintop towers with spectacular views. It's wonderful to explore even if you never get out of your car. If you are staying overnight, your best bet is nearby **Río Grande.**

If You Have 3 Days

If you have a bit more time, you can see much more of the region. To avoid the unrelenting string of strip malls along Route 3, take Route 187, which winds along the coast. Stop for lunch at one of the seafood kiosks that line the beach at **Piñones.** Spend the night in or near **Río Grande,** a town that makes a good base for exploring the region. On your second day, get up early to beat the crowds to **El Yunque.** Make sure to bring binoculars and watch for the rare Puerto Rican green parrot. On Day 3 you should head to **Luquillo,** which has one of the prettiest beaches on the island. Make sure to stop for lunch in one of the food kiosks on Route 3 just before you reach the town.

If You Have 5 Days

If you have five days, follow the three-day itinerary above. On Day 4 head east along Route 3 to the coastal city of **Fajardo,** which has plenty of accommodations in every price range. Make sure you have called ahead to reserve a spot on a tour of Reserva Natural Las Cabezas de San Juan. If there's no moon, sign up for a nighttime excursion to the reserve's bioluminescent bay. On Day 5, take a snorkeling trip to some of the nearby coral reefs.

to go for fast food. El Kiosko Boricua ticks all the boxes for fried Puerto Rican goodies, with *alcapurrias, arepas,* and *bacalaítos* among the items on offer. **Known for:** fast food, Puerto Rican–style; ultracasual setting; cash only. [$] *Average main: $8* ✉ *Rte. 187* ☎ *787/596–1684* ⏲ *Closed Mon.* ▭ *No credit cards.*

El Nuevo Acuario

$$ | PUERTO RICAN | One among the ever-changing cast of restaurants along Route 187, The New Aquarium, like its neighbors, won't win any awards for decor and design. The setting here is decidedly laid-back, with plastic tables and chairs serving as the humble backdrop for some stellar seafood. **Known for:** fresh seafood; ultracasual setting; good service. [$] *Average main: $12* ✉ *Punta Cangrejos, off Rte. 187* ☎ *787/662–8258.*

El Parrilla

$$ | PUERTO RICAN | Like its neighbors along Route 187, which fronts the Atlantic, El Parrilla specializes in seafood. Trunkfish fritters and seafood empanadillas are tasty starters, while the hearty seafood stew called *asopao* is the main event, and flan with fresh coconut can't be missed. **Known for:** the freshest seafood; traditional Puerto Rican–style asopao; cash only. [$] *Average main: $12* ✉ *Rte. 187, Loíza* ☎ *787/876–3191* ⏲ *Closed Mon.–Thurs.* ▭ *No credit cards.*

Nightlife

Nearly all the restaurants and cafés in Piñones have bands on weekends, most playing jazz and island rhythms, and locals go as much for the drinks and live entertainment as for the food. A largely

Soft sand and leaning palm trees are hallmarks of Luquillo beaches.

Dominican clientele frequent many of these beachfront dance halls, and you're likely to see some smokin' merengue steps. Couples also twirl to salsa, bounce to *bomba,* or move to the grittier beats of local *reggaetón.* You'll easily find several open-air establishments drawing weekend crowds to steamy dance floors inside and smoking barbecue pits outside.

Shopping

ART

Artesanías Castor Ayala
GIFTS/SOUVENIRS | Just east of Piñones is the town of Loíza, where you can find authentic coconut *vejigante* masks, dubbed "Mona Lisas" because of their elongated smiles. Craftsman Raúl Ayala Carrasquillo has been making these pieces for nearly half a century, following in the footsteps of his late father. Collectors prize these wild masks, most with tentaclelike horns. His one-room shop, in a shack that was painted yellow many years ago, is on the road between Loíza and Río Grande. ✉ *Rte. 187, Km 6.6, Loíza* ☎ *787/564–6403.*

Estúdio de Arte Samuel Lind
ART GALLERIES | At his studio on a short, dusty lane across the street from the Artesanías Castor Ayala, artist Samuel Lind sculpts, paints, and silk-screens images that are quintessentially Loízano. Lind's work is displayed in the two floors of his latticework studio. Of special note are his colorful folk-art posters inspired by everyday Puerto Rican life. ✉ *Rte. 187, Km 6.6, Loíza* ☎ *787/876–1494.*

Activities

Piñones is bordered by a 16-km (10-mile) strip of beaches along the coast, which winds to a bluff called Vacía Talega, a once infamous lovers' lane with a wonderful view of an unspoiled coast lined with dense palm groves and towering sea grapes. The area has some fine surf, and several spots have become favorites of local and visiting surfers. You'll also find good fishing, snorkeling, and scuba opportunities. Away from the coast is Torrecilla Baja, one of the largest mangrove swamps on the island.

BICYCLING

The area's big outdoor attraction is a bike path that follows swaying coconut palms on a quiet, breezy stretch, sometimes crossing the main roadway but mostly running parallel to it. Along most of its 11 km (7 miles), it's a wooden boardwalk for bicycles.

DIVING AND FISHING TRIPS

Locals go fishing and crabbing right off the coast, and it's likely the crab fritters you eat in any beachfront shack are local as well.

Cangrejos Yacht Club

FISHING | Charter-operated boating, deep-sea fishing, and scuba-diving trips are run out of the marina right below the bridge from Isla Verde. Call the yacht club to be referred to a captain who is appropriate for your trip. ✉ *Rte. 187, Km 3.8* ☎ *787/791–1015* 🌐 *www.cangrejosyacht-club.com.*

Puerto Rico Angling

FISHING | At Puerto Rico Angling, José Campos and his son run full- and half-day deep-sea fishing trips for up to six people for catch like tuna, wahoo, and dorado. They also offer fishing trips through the area's lagoon system. All charters practice tag and release. ✉ *Piñones* ☎ *787/209–6926* 🌐 *www.puertoricofishing.com.*

It's da Bomb(a)

The *bomba*—a musical and dance style for which the northeastern coast is famous—can be traced to the Kongo people of West Africa. Sometimes wearing a flouncy white dress, the woman of a dancing couple moves in a relatively fixed pattern of steps while her partner improvises to the drumbeat. A lead singer and a choir perform a call-and-response song—recounting a local story or event—while percussionists play maracas, *fuás* (wooden sticks that are smacked against a hard surface), *buleadores* (low-timbre, barrel-shape drums), and *subidores* (higher-pitch drums).

Río Grande

35 km (21 miles) southeast of San Juan.

This urban cluster of about 54,000 residents proudly calls itself "The City of El Yunque," as it's the closest community to the rain forest and most of the reserve falls within its municipal borders. Two images of the rare green parrot, which makes its home in El Yunque, are found on the city's coat of arms; another parrot peeks out at you from the town's flag.

Río Espíritu Santo, which runs through Río Grande, begins in El Yunque's highest elevations. It was once used to transport lumber, sugar, and coffee from plantations, and immigrants flocked to the region to take advantage of the employment opportunities.

GETTING HERE

Only 30 minutes from San Juan, Río Grande is easy to get to. From San Juan, take Route 26 toward Carolina until you reach Route 3. Then take Route 3 toward Fajardo for approximately 20 minutes until you see signs for Río Grande.

Restaurants

Antojitos Puertorriqueños

$$ | **PUERTO RICAN** | "*Buen provecho,*" says owner Jorge Martínez as you sit down to an authentic meal at this no-frills spot serving Puerto Rican favorites. Whether you're stopping for breakfast en route to the rain forest, catching the unbeatably cheap lunch special—which changes daily and offers choices like fried pork with plantains, grouper in creole sauce, and roasted chicken with beans and rice—or relaxing with a cocktail before dinner, the joint delivers. **Known for:** creole grouper; budget prices; very casual setting with plastic tables and chairs. *Average main: $13 160 Río Mar Blvd./Rte. 968, Km 0.4.*

Palio

$$$$ | ITALIAN | Northern Italian dishes—such as veal marsala, fettuccine with lobster, shrimp, mussels, and scallops, and fillet of beef with a caramelized shallot Barolo reduction—are the star attractions at this top-notch restaurant, where the staff are attentive and amiable. The dining room, with its black-and-white checkerboard floor and dark-wood paneling, is elegant and refined. **Known for:** Caesar salad prepared tableside; great ocean views, particularly at sunset; attentive service. *Average main: $35 Wyndham Grand Río Mar Beach Resort & Spa, 6000 Río Mar Blvd. 787/888–6000 www.wyndhamriomar.com No lunch.*

Richie's Café

$$$ | SEAFOOD | Perched on a mountaintop, this restaurant—a convenient option for Wyndham Grand Río Mar guests who don't want to dine on-site but are willing to pay resort prices—has a pair of open-air dining rooms with views to Vieques on a clear day. The atmosphere is festive; there's often a game playing on one of the big screens or a local band jamming on the weekend. **Known for:** fresh seafood, especially whole red snapper; fried plantains stuffed with seafood; ocean views. *Average main: $25 Rte. 968, Km 2.0 787/887–1435.*

Hotels

Meliá Coco Beach

$$$ | RESORT | This massive resort on a stretch of pristine coastline does a decent job of being all things to all people. **Pros:** beautiful setting; lovely pool area; short walk to beach. **Cons:** scarce parking; blank and uninviting facade; iguanas near pool bother some guests. *Rooms from: $319 200 Coco Beach Blvd. 787/809–1770, 877/476–3542 www.melia.com 550 rooms No meals.*

★ St. Regis Bahia Beach Resort

$$$$ | RESORT | Between El Yunque National Forest and the Río Espíritu Santo is this luxurious, environmentally aware property with 3 km (2 miles) of pristine private beach, an oasis of calm that hums with local wildlife. **Pros:** privacy; impeccable service; luxurious amenities. **Cons:** isolated location; slim off-property restaurant selection; very, very expensive. *Rooms from: $800 Rte. 187, Km 4.2 787/809–8000 www.stregisbahiabeach.com 174 rooms No meals.*

Wyndham Grand Río Mar Beach Resort & Spa

$$$ | RESORT |FAMILY | This sprawling resort offers a host of outdoor activities, including championship golf and tennis as well as hiking in the nearby rain forest. **Pros:** expansive beachfront; good restaurants; casino. **Cons:** dark and depressing parking garage; occasionally long lines at check-in; far from off-site restaurants. *Rooms from: $305 6000 Río Mar Blvd. 787/888–6000 www.wyndhamriomar.com 440 rooms No meals.*

Nightlife

Wyndham Grand Río Mar Resort & Spa

CASINOS | Pick a game—Caribbean stud poker, blackjack, slot machines—and then head to the Las Vegas–style casino at the Wyndham Grand Río Mar Resort & Spa. If all that betting makes you thirsty, step into the Players Club Bar, which is connected to the gaming room. *Wyndham Grand Río Mar Resort & Spa, 6000 Río Mar Blvd. 787/888–6000.*

Water recreation options abound in the enormous pools of the Wyndham Grand Río Mar Beach Resort & Spa.

Activities

Activities in the Río Grande region are mostly oriented around the area's resorts, Wyndham Grand Río Mar Resort & Spa and Meliá Coco Beach, as well as St. Regis Bahia Beach Resort.

GOLF

★ St. Regis Bahia Beach Resort Golf Course

GOLF | Designed by Robert Trent Jones Jr., this tranquil 18-hole course meanders alongside the island's Río Espíritu Santo and overlooks the Atlantic Ocean. Environmentally respectful, this challenging course traipses past scenic lakes, deep-rooted mangroves, and spectacular residences, blending into the area's rain-forest surroundings, while ocean breezes add a degree of difficulty to lush, rolling fairways. Greens fees vary seasonally; rates and times are available on request. ✉ *Rte. 187, Km 4.2* ☎ *787/957–1510* 🌐 *www.stregisbahiabeach.com* 🎫 *From $165* ⛳ *18 holes, 7014 yards, par 72.*

The Wyndham Grand Río Mar Beach Resort & Spa

GOLF | The Río Mar Country Club portion of the resort features two of the region's more luxurious golf courses. The **Ocean Course,** designed by Tom and George Fazio has slightly wider fairways than its sister course. Iguanas can usually be spotted sunning themselves near the 4th hole, but contrary to its name it has only one isolated ocean hole: the par-three 16th. **River Course,** designed by Greg Norman, has challenging fairways that skirt the Mamoyoc River. Either way, at the end of a round you can enjoy the spacious modern clubhouse with a pro-shop and two restaurants, so you can grab a sit-down lunch or a quick beverage and a bite. If you're not a resort guest, be sure to reserve tee times at least 24 hours in advance. Fees include discounts for resort guests and twilight times with club and shoe rentals available. ✉ *6000 Río Mar Blvd.* ☎ *787/888–6000* 🌐 *www.wyndhamriomar.com* 🎫 *9 holes from $130; 18 holes from $195* ⛳ *Ocean Course: 18 holes, 6782 yards, par 72;*

River Course: 18 holes, 6945 yards, par 72.

HORSEBACK RIDING

Carabalí Rainforest Park

HORSEBACK RIDING | A family-run operation, this hacienda is a good place to jump in the saddle and ride one of Puerto Rico's Paso Fino horses. Hour-long rides take you around the 600-acre ranch, while two-hour treks take you to a river where you and your horse can take a dip. If you prefer something more high-tech, rent a four-wheeler for an excursion through the foothills of El Yunque. ✉ *Rte. 3, Km 31.6, Luquillo* ☎ *787/889–4954* 🌐 *www.carabalirainforestpark.com.*

TENNIS

International Tennis Center

TENNIS | These tennis facilities are the best in the area. In addition to 13 courts with spectacular views, the center offers lessons for everyone from novices to old pros. ✉ *Wyndham Grand Rio Mar Resort & Spa, 6000 Río Mar Blvd.* ☎ *787/888–7066* 🌐 *www.wyndhamriomar.com* 🎫 *Court rentals from $25 per hr; half-hr private lessons from $45.*

El Yunque

11 km (7 miles) southeast of Río Grande; 43 km (26 miles) southeast of San Juan.

For more information on El Yunque, see the special feature at the beginning of this chapter.

The more than 100 billion gallons of precipitation that El Yunque receives annually spawn rushing streams and cascades, outsize impatiens and ferns, and 240 tree species. In the evening, millions of inch-long *coquís* (tree frogs) begin their calls. El Yunque is also home to the *cotorra,* Puerto Rico's endangered green parrot, as well as 67 other types of birds.

El Yunque is the only tropical rain forest in the U.S. National Forest system, spanning 28,000 acres, reaching an elevation of more than 3,500 feet and receiving an estimated average of 200–240 inches of rain each year. Prior to Hurricane Maria, the forest's 13 hiking trails were extremely well maintained. The hurricane damaged much of the forest, and work crews are still clearing trails; not all are open to the public as of this writing. Check with your hotel concierge or an El Yunque tour operator about the current status of trails. When open and clear of hurricane debris, most trails in the park are easy to navigate and less than 1.6 km (1 mile) long. If you prefer to see the sights from a car, as many people do, simply follow Route 191 as it winds into the mountains, and stop at several observation points along the way.

The forest itself is an easy and popular day-trip destination from San Juan. If you are driving yourself, arrive early for easier parking. If you are taking a guided tour that includes El Yunque, a morning departure will have you meeting fewer crowds.

On a leisurely drive through the forest you'll encounter beautiful waterfalls, hibiscus, banana, and orchid plants, geckos, and the occasional vista over the forest and out to the Atlantic Ocean.

GETTING HERE AND AROUND

You can take a taxi from San Juan to El Yunque (metered rates outside the city run about $36 per hour), but to get the most out of the rain forest it's best to rent a car, even if you have only a few hours to explore. From the greater San Juan area, take the Airport Expressway, Highway 26 (Baldorioty de Castro Avenue) and follow signs east to Carolina; once you are on the expressway, follow it approximately 22½ km (14 miles) to the end. At the final exit (Carolina), stay in the left-hand lane until you merge with Route 3, a multilane highway dotted with places to stop for cold drinks and typical Puerto Rican snacks. Continue on Route 3 approximately 21 km (13 miles) until you see the signs for Palmer–El Yunque.

Look closely at the small tree branches along El Yunque's nature trails and you may spot creatures such as the mountain garden lizard.

Turn right at the traffic signal and follow the road through the village of Palmer. There, you might want to stop at El Portalito HUB in Palmer. This is El Yunque's temporary visitors' center, and it's where you can pick up maps and get updated information about the current condition of the rain forest. Back in the car, drive until you see the sign for Route 191, the only road through the forest. Turn left on Route 191 and follow it approximately 3 km (2 miles) until you see the El Yunque National Forest sign. When mud slides haven't caused portions of the road to be closed, you can drive straight from the entrance to the base of Pico El Yunque (Km 13). Be sure to make a quick stop to climb the winding stairs of Yokahú Tower for breathtaking views of the rain forest and the island. Take note that drivers don't always recognize common road courtesies, such as slow cars to the right, stop signs, and signals. Obey the speed limit, as rental cars are frequently pulled over.

TOUR OPERATORS

Many companies in San Juan and Río Grande offer excursions to El Yunque, an alternative if you don't want to drive yourself. Check with your hotel concierge about which companies are currently offering tours.

ESSENTIALS

Admission Fees. There is no entrance fee for the El Yunque National Forest itself.

Admission Hours. The road into El Yunque opens daily at 7:30 am and closes at 6 pm.

Emergencies. If you witness an accident or an unlawful act or felony, or if you see something happening that looks wrong or suspicious, please contact the Law Enforcement and Investigation Patrol, at ☎ *787/888–5675 (office), 787/888–1880 (VHF radio paging), or 787/549–0075 (mobile).*

Restrooms. There are picnic areas with sheltered tables and bathrooms as well as several basic eateries along the road through the rain forest.

Sights

El Portalito HUB

INFO CENTER | FAMILY | El Portalito HUB, located in the town of Palmer, at the foot of the rain forest, is the temporary visitors' center for El Yunque. Here, you can pick up maps and ask for information about current conditions in the rain forest. ✉ *54 Calle Principal, Río Grande* ☎ *787/888–1880* 🌐 *www.fs.usda.gov/detail/elyunque*.

★ El Yunque

FOREST | FAMILY | The more than 100 billion gallons of precipitation that El Yunque receives annually spawn rushing streams and cascades, outsize impatiens and ferns, and 240 tree species. In the evening, millions of inch-long coquís begin their calls. El Yunque is also home to the cotorra, Puerto Rico's endangered green parrot, as well as 67 other types of birds.

El Yunque is the only tropical rain forest in the U.S. National Forest system, spanning 28,000 acres, reaching an elevation of more than 3,500 feet and receiving an estimated average of 200–240 inches of rain each year. Many of the forest's 13 hiking trails were damaged by Hurricane Maria and are only being reopened slowly; a full recovery is expected to be lengthy since fallen trees need to be removed and landslides dealt with. If you prefer to see the sights from a car, as many people do, simply follow Route 191 as it winds into the mountains and stop at several observation points along the way.

The temperature is about 73°F year-round, so weather isn't much of a factor for seasonal planning. For easy parking and fewer crowds, be sure to arrive early in the day, although the park rarely gets crowded by U.S. National Park standards. Expect rain nearly every day, but keep eyes peeled post-showers for the best bird-watching.

When the forest was fully operational, more than a million visitors from all over the world came to El Yunque to experience the rain forest's ecological treasures; it can still be crowded, particularly since only limited areas are open. Rivers and streams provide aquatic habitats for freshwater snails, shrimp, and crabs, while approximately 35 species of migratory birds either winter or pass through El Yunque. Sonorous coquí frogs, 14 different lizard species, and more than 1,200 insect species ranging from ants to beetles to flies all inhabit the forest.

Four major forest types, roughly stratified by elevation, are home to thousands of native plants, including 150 fern species, 240 tree species (88 of these are endemic or rare and 23 are exclusively found in this forest). Two of the island's highest peaks rise out of the forest: El Toro and El Yunque, both more than 3,500 feet (1,070 m).

El Yunque doesn't have bigger wildlife species like monkeys, large cats, and poisonous snakes, but there are hundreds of small creatures that find ecological niches. Many of these species exist nowhere else on the planet, such as the endangered Puerto Rican parrot, Puerto Rican Boa, and Puerto Rican Sharp-Shinned Hawk. If you're interested in bird-watching, pack your binoculars, because the Puerto Rican Tody, Puerto Rican Lizard Cuckoo, five species of hummingbirds, flycatchers, and warblers are commonly spotted.

The forest has 13 official trails, but only a few are open after damage by Hurricane Maria. Roughly 65% of the forest is currently accessible, with more opening all the time. El Portalito HUB is acting as a temporary visitor center while the permanent El Portal Visitor Center is being rebuilt.

A leisurely drive-through may not be as immersive as a hike, but you'll still encounter beautiful waterfalls, hibiscus, banana, and orchid plants, geckos, and the occasional vista over the forest and out to the Atlantic Ocean. The main and most direct route to El Yunque, Route 3, is a multilane highway dotted with places to stop for cold drinks and typical Puerto Rican snacks. Obey the speed limit, as rental cars are frequently pulled over. From the highway, hop onto Route 191, the only road through the preserve. When mudslides haven't caused portions of the road to be closed, you can drive straight from the entrance to Km 13, the base of Pico El Yunque. Be sure to make a quick stop to climb the winding stairs of Yokahu Tower for breathtaking views of the rain forest and the island. Take note that drivers don't always recognize common road courtesies, such as slow cars to the right, stop signs, and signals. ✉ *Rte. 191, Km 4, off Rte. 3, Río Grande* ☎ *787/888–1880* 🌐 *www.fs.usda.gov/main/elyunque/home* 🎫 *Free.*

Restaurants

La Muralla

$ | **PUERTO RICAN** | The rangers at El Yunque swear by this place, a cement-block building just past Cascada La Coca. You won't find a cheaper meal anywhere in Puerto Rico, that's for sure. **Known for:** rock-bottom prices; excellent fruit shakes; early closing. 💲 *Average main: $4* ✉ *Rte. 191, Km 7.4, El Yunque, Río Grande* 💳 *No credit cards* 🕑 *Closed Thurs.*

Activities

HIKING

Most of El Yunque's 13 trails are closed due to damage by Hurricane Maria; those that remain are all fairly easy and suitable for both beginning adult hikers and children. Most are short and paved.

HORSE RACING

Hípodromo Camarero

HORSE RACING/SHOW | Try your luck with *exactas* and *quinielas* at this large thoroughbred racetrack about 20 minutes east of San Juan. Post time is at 2:30 pm every day except Tuesday and Thursday. There's an air-conditioned clubhouse and restaurant (open at 12:30 pm on race day), as well as a bar where people occasionally dance to live rumba music. Parking and admission to the grandstand and clubhouse are free. ✉ *Rte. 3, Km 15.3, Canóvanas* ☎ *787/641–6060* 🌐 *www.hipodromo-camarero.com.*

Luquillo

13 km (8 miles) northeast of Río Grande; 45 km (28 miles) east of San Juan.

Known as the Sun Capital of Puerto Rico, Luquillo has one of the island's best-equipped family beaches. It's also a community where fishing traditions are respected. On the east end of Balneario de Luquillo, past the guarded swimming area, fishermen launch small boats and drop nets in open stretches between coral reefs.

Like many other Puerto Rican towns, Luquillo has its own signature festival—in this case, the Festival de Platos Típicos (Festival of Typical Dishes), a late-November or early December culinary event that revolves around one ingredient: coconut. During the festivities, many of the community's 20,000 residents gather in the Plaza de Recreo to sample treats rich with coconut or coconut milk. There's also plenty of free entertainment, including folk shows, troubadour contests, and salsa bands.

GETTING HERE AND AROUND

Públicos run between San Juan and Fajardo and will let travelers off at Luquillo (about a 45-minute ride). Driving takes about the same amount of time. From San Juan, head out Route 3, get off at Route 193, and follow signs for Luquillo. If you want to explore the town (it's small but well worth the time), a car is helpful. Take note not to park in places where the curb is painted yellow—it's a parking violation.

Did You Know?

El Yunque is divided into four forest types according to their elevations. At 2,500 feet (762 m) above sea level, cloud forest is the highest and receives nearly constant rainfall.

Beaches

Luquillo Beach (*Balneario La Monserrate*)
BEACH—SIGHT | FAMILY | Signs refer to this gentle beach off Route 3 as "Balneario La Monserrate," but everyone simply calls it Luquillo Beach. Lined with colorful lifeguard stations and shaded by soaring palm trees, it's a magnet for families and has picnic areas and 60-plus kiosks serving fritters and drinks—a local hangout. Lounge chairs and umbrellas are available to rent, as are kayaks and Jet Skis. Its most distinctive facility is the Mar Sin Barreras (Sea Without Barriers), a gradual ramp into the water that allows wheelchair users to take a dip. On busy days, the beach can be crowded and littered with a party atmosphere. **■ TIP→ There is a nominal fee for using the shower facilities, so bring small bills for this purpose.** **Amenities:** food and drink; lifeguards; parking (fee); showers; toilets; water sports. **Best for:** partiers; swimming; walking. ☒ *Off Rte. 3* ☎ *787/889–5871* *$5.40 per car (cash only).*

Playa Costa Azul
BEACH—SIGHT | Waving palm trees and fishing boats add charm to the small Playa Costa Azul, although the ugly residential buildings along the water make an unattractive backdrop. The water here is good for swimming, and the crowds are thinner than elsewhere, but there are no facilities. **Amenities:** none. **Best for:** swimming. ☒ *Off Rte. 193, near Rte. 3.*

Playa La Pared
BEACH—SIGHT | Playa La Pared (literally, "The Wall Beach") is a surfer haunt. Numerous local competitions are held here throughout the year, and several surfing shops are close by in case you need a wet suit or wax for your board. The waves here are medium-range. It's very close to Luquillo Beach, but has a separate entrance. There are no facilities. **Amenities:** none. **Best for:** partiers; surfing. ☒ *Off Rte. 3.*

Restaurants

Brass Cactus
$$ | STEAKHOUSE | This steak-and-chop eatery attracts so many English-speaking tourists that management doesn't bother printing a Spanish menu. Nearly every dish on the expansive menu is made to be washed down with beer. **Known for:** great steaks and burgers; fun sports-bar atmosphere; reasonably priced cocktails and beer. *$ Average main: $13* ☒ *Off Rte. 3, near main entrance to Luquillo* ☎ *787/980–9659.*

La Parrilla
$$$ | SEAFOOD | There are dozens of *kioskos,* or food stands, along Route 3 on the way to Luquillo Beach, most offering humble local fare, much of it fried. This full-service restaurant raises the bar for its culinary counterparts. **Known for:** good grilled seafood; alfresco dining; steaks for the non-fish eaters. *$ Average main: $25* ☒ *Luquillo Beach, Rte. 3, Kiosk 2.*

Lolita's
$$ | MEXICAN | When it comes to Mexican food, this place is the real deal. For lunch, grab a few tacos (soft or crispy), or try one of the classic Mexican entrées. **Known for:** authentic Mexican cuisine; generous portions; good (and large) margaritas. *$ Average main: $15* ☒ *Rte. 3, Km 41.3.*

Hotels

The Yunque Mar Hotel & Parador
$ | HOTEL | This cute little hotel is just west of the popular Luquillo Beach, but the hotel's own strand is nearly as nice and almost always deserted. **Pros:** on a lovely beach; friendly owners; nice pool. **Cons:** building is on a crowded street; bland decor; no in-room safe; no elevator. *$ Rooms from: $120* ☒ *Playa Fortuna, 6 Calle 1* ☎ *787/889–5555,* *www.hotelyunquemar.com* *15 rooms, 2 suites* *No meals.*

Best Luquillo Food Kiosks

Off Route 3, just before the exit for pristine Luquillo Beach, something of a culinary renaissance is occurring. Here you'll find dozens of food shacks or *kioskos*, some with CIA-trained (Culinary Institute of America) chefs, offering everything from burgers to ceviche to stuffed lobster. Stop in for breakfast, lunch, dinner, or cocktails. Take some time to weigh your options at establishments ranging from no-frills takeout counters to full-service restaurants. Once you've made your decision, pull up a seat and get ready to feast—these kioskos are turning out some of the island's best eats.

Each kiosk is numbered. Here are a couple of our favorites:

No. 2, La Parrilla. Head here for the original kiosko experience and indulge in a lobster or steak as big as your head.

No. 38, Ceviche Hut. Fresh ceviches and classics like *pescado a lo macho* (fish in Peruvian seafood sauce) are all solid choices.

Fajardo

11 km (7 miles) southeast of Luquillo; 55 km (34 miles) southeast of San Juan.

Fajardo, founded in 1772, was once notorious as a piratical pit stop. It later developed into a fishing community and an area where sugarcane flourished. Today it's a hub for yachts that use its marinas, divers who head to its good offshore sites, and day-trippers who travel by catamaran, ferry, or plane to the islands of Culebra and Vieques from nearby Ceiba. With the most significant docking facilities on the island's eastern side, Fajardo is a bustling city of 37,000—so bustling, in fact, that its unremarkable and somewhat battered downtown is often congested and difficult to navigate. Much of the tourist activity in Fajardo centers on the northern reaches of Las Croabas, near the gigantic Conquistador Resort.

GETTING HERE AND AROUND

Getting around Fajardo is tricky without a car, especially if you plan on visiting several of the sights. Thrifty has an office on-site at the Fajardo Inn. Ferries to Vieques and Ceiba now leave from a new terminal in Ceiba, about 8 km (5 miles) south of Fajardo. Tickets must be purchased in person at the ferry, and the early departures on weekends are particularly popular, so you are advised to arrive more than an hour ahead of the scheduled departure (several hours might be best on a busy weekend).

CAR RENTAL Thrifty Car Rental. ✉ *Parcelas Beltrán 52, Puerto Real* ☎ *787/860–2030* 🌐 *www.thrifty.com.*

FERRY CONTACTS Ceiba Ferry Terminal. ✉ *Marina Dr., Roosevelt Roads, Ceiba.*

Sights

Las Croabas

NEIGHBORHOOD | A few miles north of Fajardo is this fishing area, where seafood is sold in open-air restaurants along the ocean. A small park in the middle of town has a lovely waterfront walk, and it's easy to find outfitters for any kind of ocean adventure, from kayaking to sailing trips. ✉ *Rte. 3, Km 51.2.*

Marina Puerto Chico

MARINA | This lively marina off Route 987 is home to a cadre of glistening

The calm waters of Luquillo Beach are a draw for families and beachgoers looking for a relaxing ocean dip.

fishing boats, the offices of Kayaking Adventures, and one of the most popular restaurants on the east coast, El Varadero Seaside Grill. ✉ *Rte. 987* ☎ *787/863–0834, 787/860–3721* 🌐 *www.marinapuertochico.com.*

Marina Puerto del Rey

MARINA | Home to 1,000 slips, Puerto del Rey claims to be the Caribbean's largest marina. This is the place to hook up with a scuba-diving group, arrange an excursion to one of the bioluminescent bays, or charter a fishing boat. The marina, located south of Fajardo, also has several restaurants and boating-supply stores. ✉ *Rte. 3, Km 51.4* ☎ *787/860–1000* 🌐 *www.puertodelrey.com.*

★ Reserva Natural Las Cabezas de San Juan

NATURE PRESERVE | The 316-acre reserve on a headland north of Fajardo is owned by the nonprofit Conservation Trust of Puerto Rico. You ride in open-air trolleys and wander down boardwalks through seven ecosystems, including lagoons, mangrove swamps, and dry-forest areas. Green iguanas skitter across paths, and guides identify other endangered species. A half-hour hike down a wooden walkway brings you to the mangrove-lined **Laguna Grande,** where bioluminescent microorganisms glow at night. The restored **Fajardo Lighthouse** is the final stop on the tour; its Spanish-colonial tower has been in operation since 1882, making it Puerto Rico's second-oldest lighthouse. The first floor houses ecological displays, and a winding staircase leads to an observation deck. The only way to see the reserve is on a guided tour; reservations are required and can be made through the trust's website. ✉ *Rte. 987, Km 6* ☎ *787/722–5882* 🌐 *www.paralanaturaleza.org* 🎫 *$12.*

Villa Marina

MARINA | The second-largest marina in Fajardo, it's home to charter-fishing boats as well as several catamaran operators who give day tours for swimming and snorkeling to the deserted islands right off Puerto Rico's northeast coast. ✉ *Rte. 987, Km 1.3, Playa Sardinera*

☎ 787/863–5131 🌐 www.villamarinapr.com.

Beaches

Balneario Seven Seas

BEACH—SIGHT | FAMILY | One of Puerto Rico's prized Blue Flag beaches, this long stretch of powdery sand near the Reserva Natural Las Cabezas de San Juan has calm, clear waters that are perfect for swimming. There are plenty of picnic tables, as well as restaurants just outside the gates. **Amenities:** food and drink; parking (fee); showers (fee); toilets. **Best for:** swimming. ✉ *Rte. 195, Km 4.8, Las Croabas* ☎ *787/863–8180* *Parking $5.*

★ Cayo Icacos

BEACH—SIGHT | Cayo Icacos is one of about 10 small islands that make up the Cordillera Nature Reserve just off the coast of Puerto Rico. It's a beautiful beach with good snorkeling offfshore. Icacos can only be reached by boat, and the ride is a short 15–20 minutes, but it has no facilities, so you'll need to bring along whatever you might need for the day. Several tour operators in Fajardo offer day-trips here, or you can hire a boat in Las Croabas to take you there. **Amenities:** none. **Best for:** snorkeling, solitude, swimming, walking. ✉ *La Cordillera Nature Reserve, Las Croabas* ✣ *Off the coast about 10 minutes by boat from Las Croabas.*

Restaurants

Blossoms

$$$$ | ASIAN | This dining room brings the Far East to Puerto Rico. The first thing you'll notice is the sound of meats and vegetables sizzling on the large teppanyaki tables. **Known for:** good sushi; both Japanese and Chinese food; teppanyaki grill. $ *Average main: $35* ✉ *El Conquistador Resort, Rte. 987, Km 3.4* ☎ *787/863–1000* 🌐 *www.elconresort.com.*

Calizo

$$$ | SEAFOOD | There's a string of seafood shacks in the village of Las Croabas, all serving delicious fried fish. This open-air eatery, with tables covered with straw umbrellas and anchored by a bustling square bar, takes things up a notch or two. **Known for:** good fresh seafood; alfresco dining; rather high prices. $ *Average main: $29* ✉ *Rte. 987, Km 4.6, Las Croabas* ☎ *787/863–3664.*

El Varadero Seaside Grill

$$ | SEAFOOD | At this no-frills seaside spot perched on the docks of pretty Marina Puerto Chico, San Juan native Charlie Barrett has created a recipe for success. Simple yet cozy nautical touches serve as the backdrop for grilled fresh tuna, mahimahi, and snapper, as diners while away the hours watching the boats bob along the water. **Known for:** great grilled seafood; excellent sea views; house-made hot sauce. $ *Average main: $18* ✉ *Marina Puerto Chico, Rte. 987* ☎ *787/860–2662* ⏲ *Closed Mon. and Tues.*

★ La Estación

$$ | PUERTO RICAN | This laid back spot has elevated Puerto Rican street food to an art form, thanks to two New Yorkers (one Puerto Rican) with restaurant pedigree who decided to leave the big city and open a new spot dedicated to barbecue in an old gas station outside the Conquistador Resort. Highlighting products obtained from local fishermen and farmers, and smoking their own meats in an outdoor kitchen, Idalia García and Kevin Roth's awesome joint is one of Puerto Rico's don't-miss culinary treats. **Known for:** locally sourced produce and meats; delicious barbecue; friendly service. $ *Average main: $18* ✉ *Rte. 987, Km 4, Las Croabas* ☎ *787/863–4481* ⏲ *Closed Tues. and Wed.*

Pasión por el Fogón

$$$ | CARIBBEAN | At this beloved Fajardo restaurant, Chef Myrta Pérez Toledo transforms traditional dishes into something special. Succulent cuts of meat and fish are presented in unexpected ways. **Known for:** contemporary Caribbean cuisine; fresh seafood; great desserts. *Average main: $28 ✉ Rte. 987, Km 2.3 ☎ 787/863–3502 🌐 www.pasionporelfogon.net ⏲ No lunch weekdays.*

Stingray Cafe

$$$$ | **SEAFOOD** | To call this quiet restaurant, inside the Conquistador Resort at the bottom of the funicular, a "café" is misleading; it's an elegant dining room offering an impressive wine list heavy on New World and California reds. The menu features seafood and fish, cooked and garnished with local ingredients. **Known for:** seafood-focused menu; sophisticated dining room; great wine list. *Average main: $35 ✉ El Conquistador Resort, 1000 Conquistador Ave., Las Croabas ☎ 787/863–6616 🌐 www.elconresort.com.*

Hotels

El Conquistador, A Waldorf Astoria Resort & Spa

$$$$ | **RESORT** | Perched on a bluff overlooking the ocean, this sprawling complex on the northern tip of the island, with a beach just offshore on Palomina Island (reached by an eight-minute shuttle ride), is one of its most popular destination resorts, but it is still in the process of being fully renovated after Hurricane Maria. **Pros:** bright, spacious rooms; unbeatable views of nearby islands; good dining options. **Cons:** large-scale, post-hurricane renovation in progress; long waits at funicular running between levels; hidden fees including parking and kids club (and you need a car). *Rooms from: $400 ✉ 1000 Av. El Conquistador ☎ 787/863–1000, 888/543–1282 🌐 www.elconresort.com 999 rooms Free Breakfast.*

Fajardo Inn

$ | **HOTEL** | **FAMILY** | The buildings that make up this hilltop hotel offer lovely views of islands poking out of the Atlantic Ocean. **Pros:** pretty grounds; family-friendly environment; good value. **Cons:** not on the beach; motel-like rooms; lacks amenities. *Rooms from: $120 ✉ 52 Parcelas Beltrán, Rte. 195, Beltrán Sector ☎ 787/860–6000, 888/860–6006 🌐 www.fajardoinn.com 125 rooms No meals.*

Activities

DAY SAILS

Several reputable catamaran and yacht operators in Fajardo make excursions to the reefs and sparkling blue waters surrounding a handful of small islets just off the coast. Two of the most popular of these are Cayo Icacos and Isla Palominos, both of which are in La Cordillera Nature Reserve. Many of the trips include transportation to and from San Juan–area hotels. Whether or not you're staying in Fajardo, if you take a day trip on the water you'll see classic Caribbean scenes of coral reefs rife with sea life, breathtakingly clear water, and palm-fringed, deserted beaches. The day sails, with stops for snorkeling, include swimming breaks at deserted beaches and picnic lunches. Most of the craft are outfitted for comfort, with quality stereo systems, bathrooms, deck showers, and full-service bars. Many competent operators offer nearly identical experiences, so your selection will probably be based on price and which operators serve your San Juan hotel, or which operate out of the marina in Fajardo that you are visiting. Prices run $55–$95 per person, depending on whether you join a trip in San Juan or in Fajardo, and on what is included in the cost. Although they are often standard features, ask if picnic lunches and a full-service bar are included.

East Island Excursions

SAILING | This outfit operates 45- to 65-foot catamarans, three of which are powered to cut down on travel time to outlying islands. Trips may include offshore snorkeling, stops at isolated beaches, and a lunch buffet. Trips are offered to Cayo Icacos and Isla Palominos, within La Cordillera Nature Reserve. An evening excursion to Vieques to see the bioluminescent bay includes dinner at a local restaurant. All of the plush craft are outfitted with swimming decks, freshwater showers, and full-service bars. ✉ *Marina Puerto del Rey, Rte. 3, Km 51.4* ☎ *787/860–3434, 877/937–4386* 🌐 *www.eastislandpr.com.*

Erin Go Bragh III

SAILING | The *Erin Go Bragh III* is a 50-foot sailing yacht based in Fajardo that takes groups of up to six on tours of the islands and glistening waters nearby. Known for delicious barbecue picnic lunches, the outfitter also provides snorkel and fishing equipment. Overnight and longer charters are available for groups. Call for rates. ✉ *Marina Puerto del Rey, Rte. 3, Km 51.4* ☎ *787/231–3901* 🌐 *www.egbc.net.*

Spread Eagle II

SAILING | The *Spread Eagle II* is a 51-foot catamaran that heads out to isolated beaches on the islands off Fajardo. The trip includes an all-you-can-eat buffet, as well as unlimited piña coladas and tropical fruit punch. To top it off, you get a free snorkel to bring home. The boat is comfortable and well equipped with a bathroom and freshwater deck shower so you can rinse off salt and sand. Sunset and moonlight cruises are also available. ✉ *Dock J, Villa Marina Harbor, Rte. 987* ☎ *787/887–8821, 888/523–4511* 🌐 *www.snorkelpr.com.*

DIVING

Aqua Adventure

SCUBA DIVING | Aqua Adventure focuses its scuba and snorkeling activity on the islets of Palomino, Lobos, and Diablo in Fajardo, but also offers trips to Vieques and Culebra, as well as charters to Vieques's wondrous Puerto Mosquito bioluminescent bay. Full-day St. Thomas (U.S. Virgin Islands) dives are also available, as are PADI certification courses. ✉ *El Conquistador Resort, 1000 Av. El Conquistador* ☎ *787/860–3483* 🌐 *www.scubapuertorico.net* 🎫 *Diving from $99; snorkeling from $69.*

Sea Ventures Dive Center

SCUBA DIVING | Here you can get diving certification, arrange dive trips to 20 offshore sites, including Culebra and Vieques, and organize boating and sailing excursions. ✉ *Marina Puerto del Rey, Rte. 3, Km 51.2* ☎ *787/863–3483, 800/739–3483* 🌐 *www.divepuertorico.com.*

FISHING

787 Fishing Puerto Rico

FISHING | Sail away on one of Captain Marcos Hanke's 22- or 26-foot sportfishing boats for deep-sea, light-tackle, or fly-fishing excursions. Tarpon, snook, bonefish, and kingfish can be caught inland year-round, while game fish like marlin, sailfish, wahoo, tuna, and mahimahi await just offshore. Half-day charters are typically for four hours, full-day charters for eight hours (the latter on the 26-foot boat). Sunset fishing charters are also available. ✉ *Marina Puerto Chico, Slips 4 and 6* ☎ *787/646–2585* 🌐 *www.787fishing.com* 🎫 *Half-day charters from $450; full-day charters from $950.*

GOLF

Arthur Hills Golf Course at El Conquistador, A Waldorf Astoria Resort

GOLF | Named for its designer, this 18-hole course is famous for mountainous terrain with elevation changes of more than 200 feet—a rarity in the Caribbean. From the highest spot, on the 15th hole, you have great views of the surrounding mountains and rain forest. Trade winds challenge every shot—as if the gorgeous views, strategic bunkering, and many water hazards aren't distracting enough. You are also likely to spot the harmless and generally timid iguana that populate the area. ✉ *El Conquistador Resort, 1000*

Av. El Conquistador ☎ 787/863–6784 🌐 www.elconresort.com From $60 for non–hotel guests 18 holes, 6746 yards, par 72.

KAYAKING

Kayaking Puerto Rico

WATER SPORTS | This adventure outfitter has an excursion for all types of water (and kayak) lovers. They offer a host of day and night trips—such as kayaking the glowing waters of Fajardo's bioluminescent lagoon, paddling along Culebra's reefs, snorkeling with local turtles, and piloting an eco-friendly, inflatable speedboat across crystal clear waters. Group rates and specials can be found online. ✉ *Fajardo ☎ 787/435–1665, 787/245–4545 🌐 www.kayakingpuertorico.com From $48.*

Naguabo

18 km (11 miles) southwest of Fajardo.

In this municipality's downtown, pastel buildings give the main plaza the look of a child's nursery: a golden-yellow church on one side faces a butter-yellow city hall, and a pink-and-blue amphitheater anchors one corner. It's a good spot for people-watching until the heat drives you to the beach.

Offshore, Cayo Santiago (aka Monkey Island) is the site of some of the world's most important rhesus monkey research. A small colony of monkeys was introduced to the island in the late 1930s, and since then scientists have been studying their habits and health, especially as they pertain to the study of diabetes and arthritis. You can't land at Cayo Santiago, but Captain Frank López sails a small tour boat, *La Paseadora,* around it.

GETTING HERE AND AROUND

Naguabo is about an hour's drive from San Juan, just south of Fajardo along Route 31, off Route 53. From Route 31, turn down Calle Garzot to reach the town square. Although públicos run to and from Naguabo, public transportation within Naguabo is extremely limited, so a rental car is your best option.

Playa Húcares

BEACH—SIGHT | Playa Húcares is *the* place to be. Although the strip is a little rundown and the beach itself can be a bit messy, an authentic vibe permeates the casual outdoor eateries and funky little shops that vie with the water for your attention. Locals sell ice out of trucks, and the heavy bass of reggaetón music thumps from the windows of passing cars. Two Victorian-style houses anchor one end of the waterfront promenade, a dock with excursion boats anchors the other, and a red-green-and-blue-painted bridge connects both sides of the town. **Amenities:** food and drink. **Best for:** sunset. ✉ *Off Rte. 3, south of Naguabo.*

Casa Cubuy Ecolodge

$ | **B&B/INN** | El Yunque's southern edge is the setting for this eco-friendly hotel where guest rooms are simple (no phones or TVs) but comfortable, with tile floors, rattan furniture, and windows that show off one of the island's best views. **Pros:** spectacular setting; close to some of the island's best hiking trails; doting staff. **Cons:** basic rooms; access roads are often affected by landslides; lower-level rooms are small. *Rooms from: $110* ✉ *Rte. 191, Km 22 ☎ 787/874–6221 🌐 www.casacubuy.com 10 rooms Free breakfast.*

WATER TOURS

La Paseadora

TOUR—SPORTS | For more than 20 years, Captain Frank López has been sailing visitors from Naguabo's Malecón around

The Palmas Athletic Club features the Rees Jones–designed Flamboyán course.

Cayo Santiago aboard his boat, *La Paseadora.* López, a charming, well-informed guide, tailors outings to the group, and over the course of three hours you'll motor around and watch the monkeys at Monkey Island—one of the world's oldest primate colonies. Plan to make some fishing and snorkeling stops in local waters using onboard gear. ✉ *Playa Húcares, Rte. 3, Km 66.6* ☎ *787/850–7881, 787/316–0441.*

Humacao

15 km (9 miles) southwest of Naguabo; 55 km (34 miles) southeast of San Juan.

Travelers flock to the Humacao area for one reason: the sprawling resort community called Palmas del Mar and its two world-class golf courses, the Flamboyán and the Palm. Although it's not thought of as a tourist destination, Humacao does have a handful of interesting neocolonial buildings along its traffic-clogged downtown streets. These are worth a peek if you're stuck here on a rainy day.

GETTING HERE AND AROUND

Humacao is served by two highways and one toll expressway. Route 30 serves as the main highway coming from points west (Caguas and Las Piedras), while Route 53 serves origins to the north (Fajardo and Naguabo). Route 3, the main highway following the eastern coastline from San Juan, passes through Humacao.

Sights

Plaza de Recreo de Humacao

HISTORIC SITE | Plaza de Humacao, downtown's broad square, is anchored by **Concatedral Dulce Nombre de Jesús** (Sweet Name of Jesus Cathedral), which dates from 1869. It has a castlelike facade, and even when its grille door is locked, you get a peek at the sleek altar, polished floors, and stained-glass windows dominated by blues. Across the plaza, four fountains splash under the shade of old trees. People pass through feeding the pigeons, children race down the promenade, and retirees congregate on benches to chat. *Calle Font Martelo at Calle Ulises Martinez.*

Reserva Natural de Humacao

NATURE PRESERVE | As you travel from Naguabo to Humacao, you'll pass stretches of beach and swaths of undeveloped land, including the swamps, lagoons, and forested areas of the Reserva Natural de Humacao. This nature reserve has an information office, restrooms, and campsites. *Rte. 3, Km 74.3* *787/852–4440* *www.paralanaturaleza.org.*

Restaurants

Chez Daniel

$$$$ | **FRENCH** | Chef Daniel Vasse's French country-style dishes are some of the island's best. The Marseille-style bouillabaisse is full of fresh fish and bursts with the flavor of a white garlic sauce. **Known for:** French country cuisine; extensive wine cellar; upscale setting and experience. *Average main: $33* *Palmas del Mar, 1 Country Club Dr.* *787/850–3838* *www.chezdanielpr.com* *Closed Tues. No lunch.*

Pura Vida

$$ | **PUERTO RICAN** | Humacao and its neighboring towns have plenty of humble spots where you can pull up at a table and order traditional Puerto Rican fare. While the name is more evocative of Costa Rica than Puerto Rico, the menu's heavy emphasis on all things plantain will reassure you of your Caribbean location. **Known for:** fresh fish; any kind of mofongo; casual setting. *Average main: $20* *295 Palmas Inn Way* *787/914–0316* *Closed Mon.*

Hotels

Candelero Beach Resort

$ | **HOTEL** | Amid acres and acres of condo developments and golf courses, the Candelero (formerly a Wyndham Garden) is surprisingly modest in scale, given its opulent surroundings, but it does have a beautiful pool area. **Pros:** access to all the amenities at Palmas del Mar; outgoing staff; free Wi-Fi. **Cons:** uninspired architecture; some ongoing construction; no sea views from any rooms. *Rooms from: $140* *170 Candelero Dr.* *787/247–7979* *www.candelerobeachresort.com* *107 rooms* *No meals.*

Activities

FISHING

Maragata Charters

FISHING | This company takes anglers out from Palmas del Mar on a 38-foot power catamaran. Snorkeling and combination trips to Monkey Island, Vieques, and Culebra are also available. *Palmas del Mar, Anchor's Village Marina, Slip 14* *787/850–7548, 787/637–1802 (mobile)* *www.maragatacharters.com* *4-hr tours from $70; 8-hr tours from $200.*

GOLF

Palmas Athletic Club

GOLF | Palmas Athletic Club has two good golf courses. The Rees Jones–designed **Flamboyán** course was named for the nearly six dozen flamboyants (aka flame trees) that pepper its fairway. You begin play among villas, but the back nine ventures into forest and hills. It is considered one of the tougher courses in Puerto Rico. The older Gary Player–designed **Palm** course is a bit shorter in more of a resort style of play, with the 14th and 16th holes affording some wonderful Caribbean vistas. *Palmas del Mar, Rte. 906* *787/656–3000* *talgracefeeds.com/palmas/index.html* *From $100* *Flamboyán: 18 holes, 7117 yards, par 70; Palm: 18 holes, 6675 yards, par 71.*

Chapter 5

VIEQUES AND CULEBRA

Updated by
Julie Schwietert Collazo

Sights ★★★★★ | Restaurants ★★☆☆☆ | Hotels ★★☆☆☆ | Shopping ★☆☆☆☆ | Nightlife ★☆☆☆☆

WELCOME TO VIEQUES AND CULEBRA

TOP REASONS TO GO

★ **Puerto Mosquito:** Kayak after dark on the astounding bioluminescent bay of Vieques.

★ **Playa Flamenco:** Catch some rays on this Culebra bay, consistently ranked as one of the world's best white-sand beaches.

★ **Refugio Nacional de Vida Silvestre de Culebra:** Bird-watch and hike in one of Puerto Rico's oldest nature refuges.

★ **Comida Criolla:** Sample traditional Puerto Rican fare with the locals at colorful roadside restaurants, seafood shacks, and other nontouristy spots.

★ **Playa Carlos Rosario:** Stroll right into the waters off this deserted Culebra beach to snorkel a fabulous coral reef.

Vieques is 33½ km (21 miles) long and 6½ km (4 miles) wide, and has two small communities. On the northern shore is Isabel Segunda, the main town, where the ferry docks. On the southern shore is the village of Esperanza, a string of low-cost bars, restaurants, and hotels along a burgeoning waterfront promenade. Nearby is the world-famous bioluminescent bay, Puerto Mosquito. The bulk of the island consists of the Vieques National Wildlife Refuge. Within you'll find dozens of beaches with names such as Caracas, Pata Prieta, and Chiva, as well as many more that have no official names, found off unpaved side roads.

At 11 km (7 miles) long and 6½ km (4 miles) wide, Culebra is much smaller and less developed than Vieques. There's only one community: the tiny town of Dewey.

1 Vieques. Two-thirds of this island is a wildlife refuge, and it's a fabulous destination for active travelers who like bicycling, kayaking, and fishing. It is fringed by gorgeous beaches, and a visit to the bioluminescent bay is an awesome experience visitors will never forget. The island has several boutique hotels, trendy restaurants, and upscale resorts.

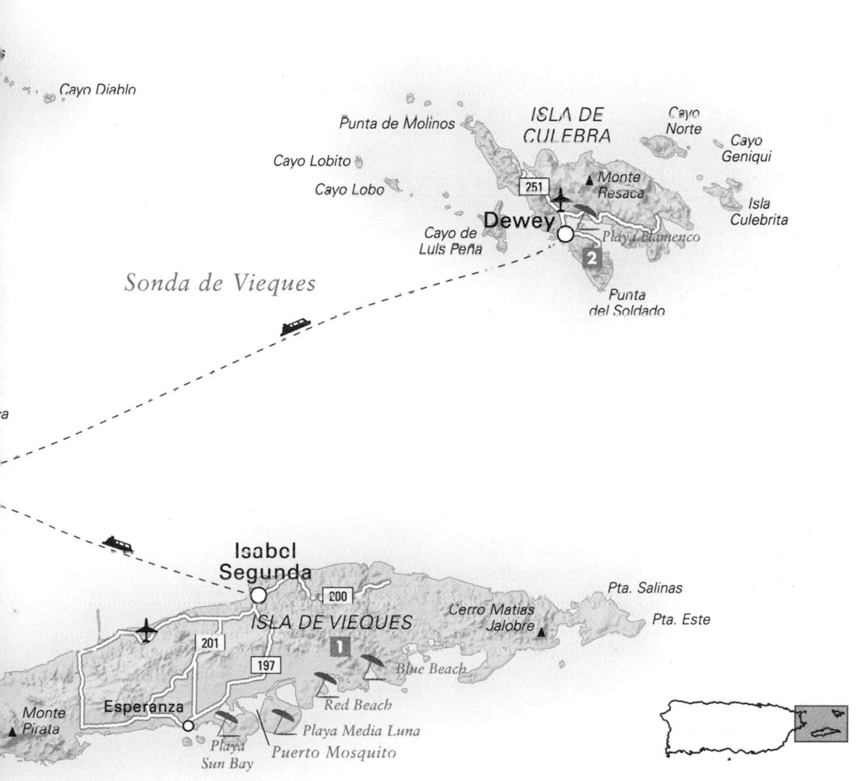

2 Culebra. The island is mostly unspoiled, a quality that brings many people back year after year. People come to Culebra to laze on Playa Flamenco, consistently rated one of the top 10 most beautiful beaches in the world, as well as lesser-known but sensational expanses of sand. Snorkeling and diving on the cays surrounding Culebra are rated world-class.

Although the islands of Vieques and Culebra (known as the "Spanish Virgins") are only a few miles off the coast of Puerto Rico, they feel like another world. While the mainland rings with the adrenaline rush of Latin America, this pair of palm-fringed islands has the laid-back vibe of the Caribbean—indeed, St. Thomas and St. Croix are clearly visible from the eastern edges of Culebra.

Vieques and Culebra are alike in many ways. Neither has much traffic—in fact, you won't find a single traffic light on either island; high-rise hotels haven't cast a shadow on the beaches; and there are no casinos, fast-food chains, strip malls, or most other trappings of modern life. "Barefoot" is often part of the dress code at casual restaurants, and the hum you hear in your room is more likely to come from a ceiling fan than an air conditioner. Things happen here *poco a poco*: slowly, at an islander's easy pace.

Beautiful beaches abound on both islands. Many of the best stretches of sand on Vieques—Chiva, Caracas, and Punta Arenas, to name a few—are on land that was once part of a U.S. naval base. This means that resort development hasn't reared its ugly head. It also means there are few, if any, amenities, so bring plenty of water and a picnic lunch. Most accommodations provide guests with beach chairs, towels, and coolers for the day; some will even pack guests' lunches to take to the beach. The beaches on Culebra are just as unspoiled; marine turtles are perfectly comfortable coming ashore to lay eggs.

Wild horses roam Vieques, where two-thirds of the island is a wildlife refuge protecting coastal lagoons, mangrove wetlands, subtropical dry forest, and islands—ecotourism is a key draw. Fishing in the turquoise flats just offshore is fantastic. And the island seems tailor-made for exploring by bicycle and/or kayak. Off Culebra, several cays delight birders with their colonies of boobies and other seabirds.

Some of the best snorkeling and diving in the Caribbean can be found in the waters surrounding Vieques and Culebra. You can sign up for a half-day or full-day excursion to nearby coral reefs, which teem with colorful fish. It's also possible to grab a mask and snorkel, and then simply wade out a few yards to see what you can see. Playa Esperanza, on the southern coast of Vieques, is a good place for beginners. More experienced snorkelers will prefer La Chiva (Blue Beach) or Punta Arenas (Green Beach).

MAJOR REGIONS

Vieques is 26 km (16 miles) southeast of the ferry port of Ceiba. **Isabel Segunda** is the major town, on the north shore. The other town is **Esperanza**, on the south shore. **Elsewhere on Vieques** are most of the best beaches, as well as the island's bioluminiescent bay, popular restaurants, and a scattering of hotels.

Culebra is 38 km (24 miles) east of Ceiba. It's also considerably smaller (less than half the size of Vieques). Many of the island's restaurants and small guest houses are concentrated in **Dewey,** but there are places all over the island.

Planning

WHEN TO GO

High season runs roughly December 15–April 15. Puerto Ricans flock here at Christmas and Easter, when Vieques and Culebra are packed with families enjoying the sun and sand. Be sure to make reservations well in advance if you're visiting during the holidays. The shoulder season, when prices are a bit lower, is a good option, but keep in mind that both islands are popular weekend getaways for mainland Puerto Ricans, so reservations are always advisable. And do note that some restaurants and hotels are closed during low season. The only time you might want to avoid is late August–late October, when hurricanes can strike the area.

GETTING HERE AND AROUND

AIR TRAVEL

Most international travelers fly from San Juan's Aeropuerto Internacional Luis Muñoz Marín (SJU), or from nearby Aeropuerto Fernando L. Ribas-Dominicci (SIG; more commonly known as Aeropuerto Isla Grande), which is cheaper. You can also fly from Ceiba's Aeropuerto José Aponte de la Torre (RVR), about 13 km (8 miles) south of Fajardo.

Air Flamenco flies daily from San Juan's Isla Grande Airport to Vieques and Culebra, and offers scheduled flights and charters to both islands from San Juan's international airport (SJU). The airline also services Vieques and Culebra with daily flights from the municipal airport in the town of Ceiba, which is about 13 km (8 miles) south of Fajardo.

Cape Air offers daily flights year-round between San Juan's international airport (SJU) and Vieques, as well as Culebra.

Taxi Aereo is essentially an air-taxi service. Missed your flight to Culebra or Vieques? Don't want to be limited by Air Flamenco's or Vieques Air Link's schedules? As long as you have a maximum of three passengers, you can walk into Ceiba airport and request on-the-spot service for $180 (up to three passengers, one-way; add $100 surcharge for night flights); the price for a six-seater is $360. The service is also available out of San Juan's Isla Grande Airport at considerably higher rates.

Vieques Air Link flies daily from San Juan's Luis Muñoz Marín International Airport and its Isla Grande Airport, as well as Ceiba's municipal airport to Vieques and Culebra. Charters are also available. Flights from San Juan take 20–30 minutes, and one-way fares are $75–$135; flights from Ceiba are about 10 minutes, and one-way fares $36–$46. Small propeller planes that hold up to nine passengers are used.

CONTACTS Air Flamenco. ☎ *787/724–1818* 🌐 *www.airflamenco.net* . **Cape Air.** ☎ *800/227–3247* 🌐 *www.capeair.com* . **Taxi Aereo.** ✉ *Aeropuerto José Aponte de la Torre, Ceiba* ☎ *787/602–7605* 🌐 *www.taxiaereopr.travel* **Vieques Air Link.** ☎ *888/901–9247* 🌐 *www.viequesairlink.com.*

CAR TRAVEL

It's nearly impossible to see either island without renting a car. You cannot rent a car on mainland Puerto Rico and ferry it across; you'll need to rent from a local agency, all of which specialize in SUVs.

Most agencies also rent golf carts, although they're not an ideal way of getting around if you want to explore the beaches. Road conditions and local driving habits are spotty. Rates are expensive ($50–$95 per day), so it's often cheaper to book a hotel–rental car package. Be sure to read Culebra and Vieques rental car companies' rules, as off-pavement driving is prohibited by many companies, and violations will result in a fine. Both islands' rental car companies also impose fees for excessive sand and/or water inside the vehicle.

FERRY TRAVEL

Ferries all depart from Ceiba, about 90 minutes by car west of San Juan. Some of these ferries carry cars, but rental agencies won't let you take their vehicles between the mainland and islands. A municipal parking lot next to the ferry costs $5–$7 per day. Fares are cheap: $2 per person from Fajardo to Vieques, $2.25 to Cuelbra; there are discounts for children and seniors, and passengers over 75 are free. They are also faster than they used to be, with travel to Vieques taking only 30 minutes, Culebra 45 minutes on the fast ferries. No ferries link Vieques and Culebra at present. There's limited seating, so arrive at least an hour ahead of the departure time (more on busy weekends, particularly for the early morning departures and mid-afternoon returns). You cannot reserve or pay for the ferries online; everything must be done in person.

CONTACTS Ceiba Ferry Terminal. ☎ *787/497–7740* 🌐 *www.dtop.gov.pr/transporte_maritimo/index.asp.* **Puerto Rico Ports Authority.** ☎ *787/494–0934* 🌐 *dtop.gov.pr/transporte_maritimo/index.asp.*

BEACHES

Vieques and Culebra are where you'll find Puerto Rico's most serene shores. Ideal for romantic strolls or family swims, the calm waters and long unspoiled stretches here are what you probably had in mind when you envisioned a Caribbean beach paradise.

Many of the beaches around Vieques were once named by the U.S. Navy, which assigned them random colors: Red Beach, Blue Beach, and Green Beach—most have since been renamed in Spanish by locals. Islanders know Sun Bay as Sombé. Those within the Vieques National Wildlife Refuge are open from 6 am to sunset. Of more than three-dozen beaches on Vieques, Sun Bay east of Esperanza is easily the most popular. Although the island's beaches are favored for their comparative isolation, crowds can gather on weekends at the most popular spots. On weekdays, however, it's not uncommon for large swaths of shore to be sparsely populated.

HOTELS

Vieques has a wide variety of lodgings, from surf shacks across from the beach to boutique hotels high up on secluded hillsides. There's something here for everyone. Looking for tropical splendor? Try Hacienda Tamarindo. Interesting architecture? There's El Blok or Hix Island House. An intimate inn where you'll meet fellow travelers? Head to Casa de Amistad.

Culebra has fewer options. Dewey, the island's only town, has a handful of small inns that are easy on the wallet. Scattered around the island are a couple of more luxurious lodgings plus villa rentals. Nothing remotely resembles a chain hotel, and that's how the locals like it.

PRIVATE VILLA RENTALS

One good way to visit Vieques is to rent one of the beautiful vacation homes that have been built in the hilly interior or along the coasts. These are concentrated in three major areas: Bravos de Boston, Esperanza, and Pilón. Several local real-estate agents deal in short-term rentals of at least a week. While you can always use AirBnB or Homeaway to find a rental, the services of an experienced management company with broad local knowledge are always helpful.

Rainbow Realty
A list of rental properties is available from this gay-friendly company. ✉ *278 Calle Flamboyán, Esperanza* ☎ *787/741–4312* 🌐 *www.viequesrainbowrealty.com.*

RESTAURANTS

Most of the restaurants on Vieques and Culebra are casual. Because even the most formal restaurants on the islands are on covered terraces or in open-air dining rooms, there's not a single establishment where you'll be frowned upon for wearing shorts. Pack a couple of nice shirts and you'll be set.

Seafood is on the menu at almost every eatery on both islands. The fish is as fresh as you'll find anywhere—your red snapper supper was probably splashing around in the Caribbean that very morning—and you can order it any number of ways. Many chefs are experimenting with European and Asian cooking techniques, so you may find your fish smoked or in a sushi roll.

Even if a restaurant focuses on a different type of food, you can be sure that mangoes, papayas, and other tropical fruits will make an appearance. Bills often include service; if not, a 15% tip is customary. Most restaurants are open for dinner from about 6 until about 10.

HOTEL AND RESTAURANT PRICES

Restaurant and hotel reviews have been shortened. For full information, visit Fodors.com.

What It Costs in U.S. Dollars

	$	$$	$$$	$$$$
RESTAURANTS				
	under $12	$12–$20	$21–$30	over $30
HOTELS				
	under $150	$150–$250	$251–$350	over $350

PACKING

Vieques has a pharmacy and a hospital, and Culebra's small hospital has a prescription-only pharmacy. Stock up on all supplies—allergy medications, contact-lens solution, or feminine supplies—before heading to the islands, and don't forget to bring insect repellent.

SAFETY

Drug-related violent crime has recently increased on Vieques. Tourists are largely unaffected, but it pays to be on your guard. Avoid bringing valuables to the beach, and don't leave any personal items in your car. Rental agencies advise that you leave your car unlocked when parked at a beach so thieves won't break the windows to get inside. There's very little crime on Culebra, but again, don't leave valuables in your car.

VISITOR INFORMATION

The islands' tourism offices are hit-and-miss when it comes to office hours and offering helpful material; however, local maps for both islands are available at most hotels and restaurants.

CONTACTS Culebra Tourism Office. ✉ *250 Calle Pedro Marquez, Dewey* ☎ *787/742–1033.* **Vieques Tourism Office.** ✉ *449 Calle Carlos Lebrón, Isabel Segunda.*

Vieques

13 km (8 miles) southeast of Fajardo.

Looking for a place to play Robinson Crusoe? Look no further than Vieques, where you can wander along almost any stretch of sand and rarely see another soul. You can while away the hours underneath coconut palms, wade in the warm water, or get a mask and snorkel and explore coral reefs that ring the island.

For many years the island was known mostly for the conflict between angry islanders and aloof federal officials. Over the course of six decades the U.S. Navy used two-thirds of Vieques, mostly on the island's eastern end, as a bombing range, and the western tip as an ammunition dump. After an April 1999 bombing accident took the life of one resident, waves of protests brought the maneuvers to a standstill, and political pressure from the island's governor helped force the military to leave on May 1, 2003.

Ironically, the military presence helped keep the island pristine by keeping resort developers away. Today the military's former holdings have been turned into Vieques National Wildlife Refuge. The woodsy western end of the island is laced by trails that offer fabulous cycling around the base of Monte Pirata, the island's highest peak. More and more of the eastern part of the island is being opened every year, granting access to stupendous beaches shelving into calm turquoise waters. The park also protects Puerto Mosquito, a flask-shape bay populated by microscopic organisms that glow when disturbed at night—a thrilling experience for kayakers.

Just because Vieques is sleepy doesn't mean there's nothing to do besides hit the beach. There are two communities—Isabel Segunda and Esperanza—where you can dine at a variety of excellent restaurants, stock up on supplies, or book a trip to the astonishing Puerto Mosquito, perhaps the world's most luminous bioluminescent bay.

GETTING HERE AND AROUND

Isabel Segunda is the transportation hub of Vieques. The ferry drops off passengers at the town's dock, and propeller planes deposit passengers at Aeropuerto Antonio Rivera Rodríguez (VQS), a 10-minute cab ride from Isabel Segunda, 15 minutes from Esperanza. Route 200 leads from the airport to Isabel Segunda, and Route 997 leads from Isabel Segunda to Esperanza. For a longer, more scenic drive, take Route 200 west from Isabel Segunda to Route 201 south; then, after about 1½ km (1 mile), take Route 996 to Esperanza.

If you want to rent or gas up a car, you need to make a trip to Isabel Segunda. Try Vieques Car Rental or Maritza's Car Rental.

You can flag down taxis on the street, but it's faster and safer to have your hotel call one for you. Either way, agree on the cost of the trip before you climb inside, as many drivers are prone to charge tourists exorbitant fares. **■ TIP→ If you plan to rent a car, make sure you reserve it in advance, especially during high season. Rental agencies have limited stock, and when they're out of cars, you're out of luck.**

AIRPORT CONTACTS Aeropuerto Antonio Rivera Rodríguez. ✉ *Rte. 200, Km 2.6* ☎ *787/741–0515.*

CAR RENTAL CONTACTS Avis. ✉ *Rte. 200, Km 5* ☎ *787/741–0284* 🌐 *www.avis.com.* **Maritza's Car Rental.** ✉ *Rte. 201* ☎ *787/741–0078* 🌐 *www.maritzascarrental.com.* **Vieques Car Rental.** ✉ *Rte. 200, Km 0.8, Monte Santo* ☎ *787/412–8540* 🌐 *www.viequescarrental.com.*

FERRY CONTACTS Vieques Terminal. ✉ *Calle Morropo* ☎ *787/494–0934* 🌐 *dtop.gov.pr/transporte_maritimo/index.asp.*

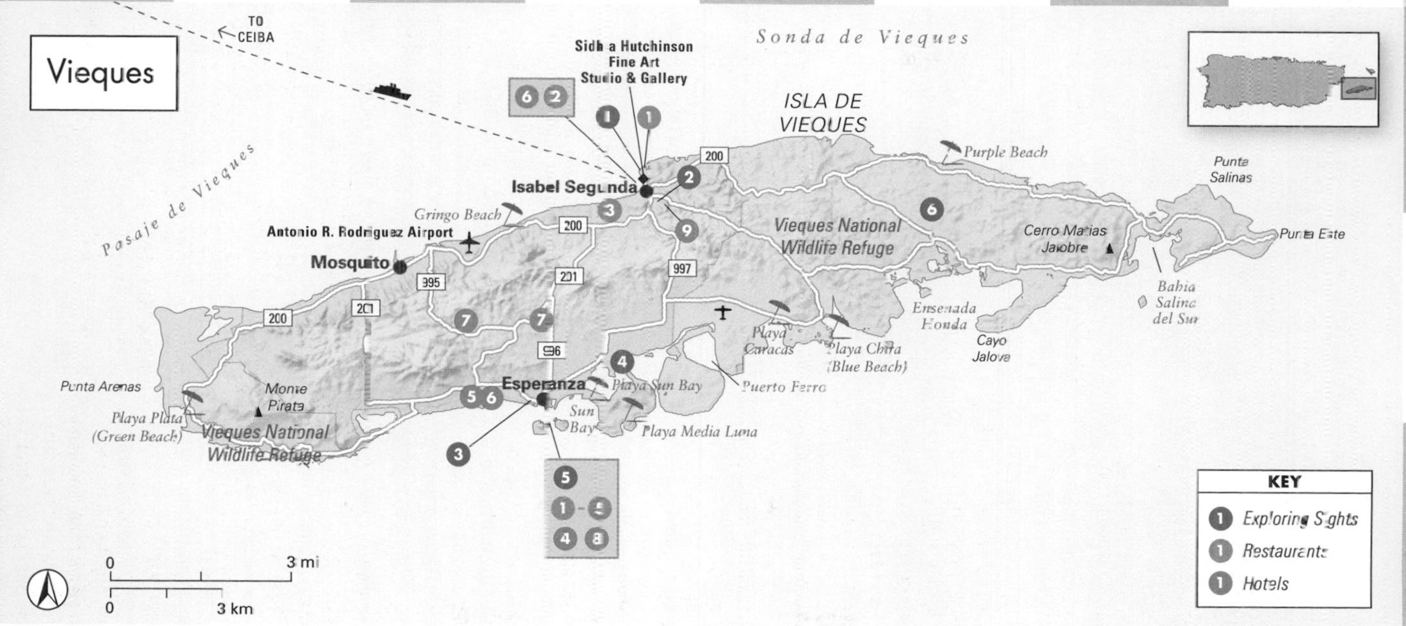

Vieques

Sights

1 El Faro Punta Mulas D1
2 El Fortín Conde de Mirasol D1
3 Malecón D2
4 Puerto Mosquito Bioluminescent Bay D2
5 Vieques Conservation & Historical Trust D2
6 Vieques National Wildlife Refuge F1

Restaurants

1 Bananas D2
2 Duffy's D2
3 El Blok Hotel Restaurant . D2
4 El Guayacan D2
5 El Quenapo D2
6 Rising Roost D1
7 Tin Box D2

Hotels

1 Bravo Beach Hotel D1
2 Casa de Amistad D1
3 Casa Ladera D2
4 El Blok Hotel D2
5 Hacienda Tamarindo C2
6 Hector's By the Sea C2
7 Hix Island House C2
8 Malecón House D2
9 Sea Gate Hotel D1

Great Itineraries

If You Have 1 Day

If you are headed to one of the islands for an overnight excursion, your best bet is **Vieques.** Get here by plane, either from San Juan or Ceiba, to maximize your time on the island. Spend the day exploring the beaches, especially the half moon–shape **Sun Bay.** In the evening you can dine at one of the oceanfront restaurants in Esperanza, then head off for an excursion to **Puerto Mosquito,** a bay filled with glow-in-the-dark dinoflagellates. Spend the night in Esperanza or Isabel Segunda.

If You Have 3 Days

If you have a few days, you can see most of Vieques. Start your first day in Isabel Segunda, where you can take a few snapshots of **El Faro Punta Mulas,** then explore the hilltop **Fortín Conde de Mirasol.** Head off for an afternoon by the ocean, perhaps at **Punta Arenas** (aka Green Beach) or one of the delightfully deserted beaches on the northern part of the island. Enjoy happy hour at **Duffy's,** by far the most popular bar in Esperanza. In the cool of the evening, have dinner in one of the chic eateries nearby. On your second day, go for an early-morning mountain-bike ride in the western portion of **Vieques National Wildlife Refuge,** a swath of wilderness that was once a naval base. Pack a picnic and head off to **Playa Media Luna** or another of the beautiful beaches along the southern coast. After dinner, make sure to book a tour of **Puerto Mosquito.** Spend your third day kayaking, snorkeling, and/or fishing.

If You Have 5 Days

If you have a few more days, you can see both Vieques and Culebra. After following the itinerary above, head to Culebra on your fourth day. (A 10-minute flight between the islands is the only way to travel between them directly.) Your destination should be **Playa Flamenco,** a long, curving beach of talcum-white sand and turquoise water; the mountains beyond make a striking backdrop. Dine that evening at **Susie's** in the island's only town: diminutive Dewey. On your last day, try snorkeling in **Refugio Nacional de Vida Silvestre de Culebra,** the island's lovely nature preserve. One of the best places for a morning boat trip is **Isla Culebrita,** an islet dominated by a lighthouse built in 1882, abandoned in 2003, and slated for restoration.

Isabel Segunda

29 km (18 miles) southeast of Fajardo by ferry.

Isabel Segunda (or Isabel II, as it's often labeled on maps) has charms that are not immediately apparent. There's a lovely lighthouse on the coast just east of the ferry dock, and on the hill above town you'll find the last fort the Spanish constructed in the New World. You can also find some of the best restaurants and a great bar here, as well as lodgings ranging from funky to fancy.

Sights

El Faro Punta Mulas

LIGHTHOUSE | This Spanish-built lighthouse above the ferry dock in Isabel Segunda dates from 1895. It was built to guide vessels into the harbor, which is surrounded by a chain of dangerous reefs. Its red light is rumored to be visible from as far away as St. Croix and St. Thomas.

El Faro Punta Mulas, a lighthouse built in 1895, is now a small museum exhibiting Vieques historical items.

In 1992, the elegant structure was carefully restored and transformed into a maritime museum that traces much of the island's history, including the visit by South American liberation leader Simón Bolívar. The tiny museum is open weekdays, but the lighthouse itself is worth a look any day. ✉ *End of Rte. 200, Isabel Segunda* 🎫 *Free* ⏲ *Closed weekends.*

El Fortín Conde de Mirasol (*Count of Mirasol Fort*)
MILITARY SITE | On a hilltop overlooking Isabel Segunda is the last military structure built by the Spanish in the New World. It was erected on Vieques's northern coast in 1840 at the order of Count Mirasol, then governor of Puerto Rico. Although it's tiny, it took more than a decade to complete, which meant Mirasol had to repeatedly ask for more money. (Queen Isabel, on being petitioned yet again, asked Mirasol whether the walls were made of gold.) The fort helped solidify Spanish control of the area, keeping British, French, Dutch, and Danish colonists away and dissuading pirates from attacking Isabel Segunda. After sitting empty for several decades, it was transformed into a museum in 1991. The museum has an impressive collection of artifacts from the Taíno and other cultures that thrived on this and nearby islands before the arrival of the Spanish. It also has an impressive collection of small arms, plus exhibits on the island's years as a sugar plantation and its occupation by the U.S. Navy. On occasion, it presents temporary exhibitions of contemporary artists. ✉ *Calle El Fuerte, Isabel Segunda* 🎫 *$2* ⏲ *Closed Mon. and Tues.*

Restaurants

Rising Roost
$ | **AMERICAN** | Part café and part boutique, Rising Roost is where early risers can get their caffeine and green juice fix. With a cute back patio and two streetside tables that are great for people-watching, the café serves healthy breakfast options including oatmeal, açai bowls, and avocado toast in addition to cold-pressed

juices, smoothies, and espresso drinks. **Known for:** quirky souvenirs and gifts; omelets and eggs; vegan and vegetarian options. *$ Average main: $10 ✉ 110 Calle Muñoz Rivera, Isabel Segunda 🌐 www.facebook.com/risingroost ⏲ Closed Tues. and Wed.*

Hotels

Bravo Beach Hotel

$$ | **HOTEL** | **FAMILY** | Several blocks north of the ferry dock in Isabel Segunda, this simple but attractive hotel makes a good home base for island exploration. **Pros:** gorgeous building; beautiful pools; friendly management. **Cons:** out-of-the-way location in residential neighborhood; can't swim on property's beach; breakfast is fairly basic. *$ Rooms from: $160 ✉ 1 North Shore Rd., Isabel Segunda ☎ 787/741–1128 🌐 www.bravobeachhotel.com 11 rooms 🍽 Free Breakfast.*

Casa de Amistad

$ | **B&B/INN** | If you're looking for a budget-friendly property in the town center, this groovy little guesthouse not far from the ferry dock in Isabel Segunda is the place to be. **Pros:** gay-friendly; funky furnishings; access to common kitchen. **Cons:** drive to beaches; cheaper rooms lack en-suite bathrooms; no elevator. *$ Rooms from: $130 ✉ 27 Calle Benito Castaño, Isabel Segunda ☎ 787/247–1017 🌐 www.casadeamistad.com 9 rooms 🍽 No meals.*

Sea Gate Hotel

$ | **HOTEL** | This hilltop hotel—the island's oldest—overlooks the island's picturesque, historic fort about 10 minutes by foot (downhill) from Isabel Segunda. **Pros:** friendly and helpful owner-manager; complimentary pickup at ferry or airport; continental breakfast included. **Cons:** small rooms; animal presence; no restaurant. *$ Rooms from: $125 ✉ Barrio Fuerte, Isabel Segunda ☎ 787/741–4661 🌐 www.seagatehotel.com 15 rooms 🍽 Free Breakfast.*

Shopping

Most residents do their shopping on the mainland, so there are very few shops on Vieques. You'll find mostly clothing stores that lean toward beach attire, as well as a few art galleries.

Siddhia Hutchinson / Glen Wielgus Gallery Vieques

ART GALLERIES | Since the mid-1980s this gallery has showcased pastel watercolor prints of Caribbean scenes, as well as limited-edition ceramic dinnerware. The gallery is a hip, sophisticated place for Caribbean artists to see and be seen, hosting openings of local artists, and it features a number of island artworks. Shoppers looking for more affordable wares or smaller souvenirs and locally made jewelry won't be disappointed. It's closed on Sunday and in September and October. *✉ Hotel Carmen, Calle Muñoz Rivera, Isabel Segunda ☎ 787/741–1343 🌐 www.hutchinsonwielgusgallery.com.*

Activities

BOATING AND KAYAKING

Various outfitters offer trips to Puerto Mosquito, the island's celebrated bioluminescent bay. Most trips are made in single-person kayaks, which can be a challenge if you lack experience or endurance. A better option for most people is electric-powered boat—gas-powered engines harm the environment.

Black Beard Sports

WATER SPORTS | This five-star PADI dive center is a one-stop shop offering outdoor gear rentals as well as guided excursions on both land and water. *✉ 370 Calle Antonio Mellado, Isabel Segunda ☎ 787/308–4478 🌐 www.blackbeard-sports.com.*

DIVING AND SNORKELING

Black Beard Sports

SCUBA DIVING | If you want to get your own snorkeling or diving equipment, head to this water-sports shop in downtown Isabel Segunda. The team arranges diving trips and PADI certification courses, as well as kayaking, biking, snorkeling, and hiking ecotours. A second location of Black Beard Sports can be found at the W Retreat & Spa. ✉ *370 Calle Antonio Mellado, Isabel Segunda* ☎ *787/308–4478* 🌐 *www.blackbeard-sports.com.*

Esperanza

10 km (6 miles) south of Isabel Segunda.

The only time there's a traffic jam in Esperanza is when one of the wild horses frequently seen on the nearby beaches wanders into the road. This community, once a down-at-the-heels fishing village, now hosts a string of bars, restaurants, and small hotels on the waterfront drag. All of them overlook Playa Esperanza, a shallow stretch of sand made all the more picturesque by the presence of a tiny islet called Cayo Afuera.

Sights

Malecón
PROMENADE | In the evening, there's no better way to enjoy the sunset than a stroll along Esperanza's 200-yard-long Malecón, a waterfront walkway running the length of the beach. ✉ *Esperanza.*

Vieques Conservation & Historical Trust
MUSEUM | **FAMILY** | The Vieques Conservation & Historical Trust was established to help save Puerto Mosquito, one of the last remaining bioluminescent bays in the world. The small museum, located on the main drag in Esperanza, has interesting information about the bay, as well as the island's flora and fauna and history. A little pool lets kids get acquainted with starfish, sea urchins, and other denizens of the not-so-deep. There's also a tiny gift shop whose profits are funneled back into the foundation. Call ahead if you're coming at lunchtime, as the place is sometimes closed for an hour or more. If you're interested in history and architecture, ask about a guided tour of the Playa Grande sugar mill ruins. ✉ *138 Calle Flamboyán, Esperanza* ☎ *787/741–8850* 🌐 *www.vcht.org* 💵 *Suggested donation $3* ⏲ *Closed Mon.*

Beaches

Balneario Sun Bay
BEACH—SIGHT | Just east of Esperanza, this mile-long stretch of sand skirts a perfect crescent-shape bay. Dotted with picnic tables, this beach gets packed on holidays and weekends. On weekdays, when crowds are thin, you might see wild horses grazing among the palm trees. There is a small fee for parking, but often there is no one at the gate to take your money. **Amenities:** food and drink; parking (fee); showers; toilets. **Best for:** snorkeling; swimming; walking. ✉ *Rte. 997, Esperanza* ☎ *787/741–8198* 💵 *Parking $2* ⏲ *Closed Mon. and Tues. in low season.*

Playa Esperanza
BEACH—SIGHT | People staying in any of the inexpensive accommodations in Esperanza can simply walk across the road to this beach. There's good snorkeling across the bay around Cayo Afuera, an uninhabited islet, and by the derelict pier. Manatees are occasionally spotted here, as well as barracudas and nurse sharks. If you're looking for swimming or sunbathing, keep moving; there are much better beaches nearby. **Amenities:** none. **Best for:** snorkeling; walking. ✉ *Esperanza Malecón, Esperanza.*

Playa Media Luna
BEACH—SIGHT | Ideal for families because the water is calm and shallow, this is also a good spot to try snorkeling. There are no facilities. **Amenities:** none. **Best for:** families; snorkeling; swimming. ✉ *Off Rte. 997, east of Balneario Sun Bay.*

Playa Negra (Black Sand Beach)
BEACH—SIGHT | About 2½ km (1½ miles) east of Esperanza, Playa Negra is a narrow black sand beach backed by cliffs. Often deserted, it's one of the most ruggedly beautiful beaches on the island, with sparkling turquoise water and soft sand. There's no shade or facilities, so bring water and sunscreen. The beach is accessed by an easy 15-minute hike through a riverbed surrounded by jungle, so be sure to wear mosquito repellent and waterproof shoes (or go barefoot), as the trail is often muddy. **Amenities:** none. **Best for:** solitude; swimming; walking. ✉ *Rte. 201* ✣ *2½ km (1½ miles) east of Esperanza, next to Oro Vieques.*

Restaurants

Bananas
$$ | **CARIBBEAN** | This longtime open-air favorite with playful rain-forest murals climbing the walls in a prime spot in Esperanza overlooking the Caribbean is geared toward gringos. Claim a spot at one of the curvy teal-colored concrete tables or under an umbrella out front and order the red snapper sandwich (popular at lunchtime) or the jerk chicken. **Known for:** party atmosphere; excellent salads; deep-fried bananas with hot honey sauce. $ *Average main: $12* ✉ *142 Calle Flamboyán, Esperanza* ☎ *787/741–8700* 🌐 *www.bananasvieques.com.*

Duffy's
$$ | **CARIBBEAN** | At some point during your time in Vieques, you should end up at Duffy's, the island's most popular hangout. Customers cluster around the bar here, which might make you think the food is secondary—and you wouldn't be entirely wrong. **Known for:** good bar food; lively atmosphere; cheap drinks. $ *Average main: $12* ✉ *140 Calle Flamboyán, Esperanza* ☎ *787/741–7600.*

★ El Blok Hotel Restaurant
$$$ | **PUERTO RICAN** | The inviting bar and restaurant on the ground floor of the trendy Blok Hotel is one of the most sophisticated and design-forward restaurants on the island. The menu is simple and spectacular, full of carefully selected and internationally inspired dishes with a Puerto Rican twist, including grilled fish, ceviche, and steak. **Known for:** irresistible churros; fresh salads; local spiny lobster. $ *Average main: $25* ✉ *El Block Hotel, 158 Calle Flamboyan, Esperanza* ☎ *787/741–6020* 🌐 *www.elblok.com.*

El Guayacan
$$ | **PUERTO RICAN** | This casual restaurant is one of the best places on the island to try traditional Puerto Rican dishes like mofongo, tostones, and empanadillas made with fresh, local ingredients. Casual and fun, the restaurant and bar on Esperanza's lively Calle Flamboyan is one of the friendliest places on the island. **Known for:** grilled spiny lobster; rum drinks; local flavors. $ *Average main: $15* ✉ *134 Calle Flamboyan, Esperanza* ☎ *787/477–1694* ⏲ *Closed Mon. and Tues.*

★ El Quenepo
$$$ | **ECLECTIC** | This elegant yet unpretentious spot brings fine dining and a touch of class to the Esperanza waterfront. The menu features local herbs and fruits such as quenepas and breadfruit in artfully prepared dishes that owners Scott and Kate Cole call "fun, funky island food." Scott is the chef, known for seafood specials highlighting the daily catch; Kate is the consummate hostess. **Known for:** fresh fish and seafood; grilled Caesar salad; good choice of wine and sangria. $ *Average main: $28* ✉ *148 Calle Flamboyán, Esperanza* ☎ *787/741–1215* 🌐 *www.elquenepovieques.com* ⏲ *Closed Sun. No lunch.*

Hotels

El Blok Hotel
$$ | **HOTEL** | This boutique hotel opened to rave reviews in 2014, in part because of the unique architecture and

design—minimalist concrete, open-air common spaces—and in part because of José Enrique, the famous chef who wrote the restaurant's menu. **Pros:** continental breakfast included; rooftop plunge pool; world-famous chef. **Cons:** can be noisy; may be too minimalist for some tastes; no TVs or phones in rooms; poor Wi-Fi. *Rooms from: $220 158 Calle Flamboyán, Esperanza 787/741–6020 www.elblok.com 22 rooms No meals.*

★ Hacienda Tamarindo

$$ | **HOTEL** | This plantation-style house and former dance hall takes its name from the centuries-old tamarind tree rising more than three stories through the center of the main building. **Pros:** beautiful views; nicely designed rooms; excellent breakfast included. **Cons:** must drive to beaches; no full-service restaurant; no elevator. *Rooms from: $200 Rte. 997, Km 4.5, Esperanza 787/741–8525 www.haciendatamarindo.com 17 rooms Free Breakfast.*

Hector's By the Sea

$ | **RENTAL** | Reached by a steep and denuded dirt road, this tiny property perches on a bluff overlooking a lovely beach, its three studio-style *casitas* spread across a breeze-swept lawn. **Pros:** hot tub under the stars; truly marvelous ocean vistas; nice pool. **Cons:** no credit cards accepted; meager facilities; maid service every three to four days. *Rooms from: $130 Rte. 996, Km 4.3, Esperanza 787/741–1178 www.hectorsbythesea.com No credit cards 3 rooms No meals.*

Malecón House

$$ | **B&B/INN** | Posh boutique spots like this seaside escape in Esperanza are raising the bar for Vieques lodging. **Pros:** affordable waterfront property; tasty breakfast; welcoming hosts. **Cons:** in-town location not for those seeking seclusion; rather small pool; surrounding area can be noisy. *Rooms from: $180 105 Calle Flamboyán, Esperanza 787/741–0663 www.maleconhouse.com 13 rooms Free Breakfast.*

Nightlife

Bananas

BARS/PUBS | Bananas is the place for burgers and beer—and not necessarily in that order. There's occasional live music and dancing, and a Monday happy hour special on bottles of Medalla, the local brew. *142 Calle Flamboyán, Esperanza 787/741–8700 bananasvieques.com.*

Duffy's

BARS/PUBS | Hands-down, Duffy's is the most popular bar on the island, thanks to live music, daily specials, and a prime location on Esperanza's Malecón—not to mention the jawboning of owner Michael Duffy. *140 Calle Flamboyán, Esperanza 787/741–7600.*

La Nasa

BARS/PUBS | La Nasa is the only establishment on the waterfront side of the street in Esperanza. This simple wooden shack, decorated with strings of Christmas lights the entire year, serves up cheap beer and rum drinks and draws island-born locals, rather than expats. Congregants take their seats at plastic chairs out front to play cards, or stare off into the placid Caribbean from the open-air back room. On weekends, the place explodes into a street party of salsa and merengue dancing. It may be humble, but the venue has even hosted celebrities; Colombian pop singer Juanes performed here in 2015. *107 Calle Flamboyán, Esperanza Closed Mon.–Thurs.*

Activities

BIKING

Vieques Adventure Company

BICYCLING | Vieques Adventure Company can set you up with mountain bikes and all the equipment you need. They'll even bring the bikes to wherever you are staying. Customized half-day tours of the island—which range from easy rides on country roads to muddy treks into the hills—include drinks and snacks. ✉ *Calle Robles, Esperanza* ☎ *787/414–4101* 🌐 *www.viequesadventures.com* 💳 *Bike rentals from $30, tours from $100.*

BOATING AND KAYAKING

Various outfitters offer trips to Puerto Mosquito, the island's celebrated bioluminescent bay. Most trips are made in single-person kayaks, which can be a challenge if you lack experience or endurance. A better option for most people is electric-powered boat—gas-powered engines harm the environment.

Abe's Snorkeling and Bio-Bay Tours

BOATING | Abe is one of Vieques's most animated characters, so it's no surprise that his kayaking tours to Puerto Mosquito are the most popular. Over the course of two hours, guests kayak into the glowing bay for a once-in-a-lifetime experience. For an entire day on the water, Abe's All-in-One Tour involves kayaking through mangrove lagoons, snorkeling coral reefs, watching the sunset on a secluded beach, and visiting the bio-bay after dark. Lunch is provided. ✉ *Esperanza* ☎ *787/435–1362* 🌐 *www.abessnorkeling.com* 💳 *Night tours from $50, full-day tours from $150.*

Marauder Sailing Charters

TOUR—SPORTS | The *Marauder*, a 34-foot sailing yacht anchored off Esperanza, can accommodate up to six passengers on trips around the southern coast, allowing a close-up look at the pristine nature of the island. There's a midday stop at a secluded spot for swimming, snorkeling, and sunbathing, followed by a gourmet lunch with open bar. Half-day and full-day trips, sunset cruises, brunch cruises, and custom and private charters are available. All charters depart from Esperenza. ✉ *Esperanza* ☎ *787/435–4858* 🌐 *www.maraudersailingcharters.com.*

FISHING

Vieques Adventure Company

FISHING | If you just want to do some unguided fishing from a kayak, this is your go-to company. Vieques Adventure Company will rent you a kayak with a dry box along with rods and tackle for a day of fishing on your own. ✉ *261 Calle Robles, Esperanza* ☎ *787/414–4101* 🌐 *www.viequesadventures.com* 💳 *From $150.*

Vieques Sport Fishing

FISHING | Captain J. Ferguson has been a charter fisherman since 1989, and off Vieques's coast he navigates a 26-foot boat into waters laden with tuna, mahimahi, dorado, kingfish, and marlin. He offers four-hour deep-sea fishing trips. ✉ *103 Calle Hucar, Esperanza* ☎ *787/502–3839* 🌐 *www.viequessportfishing.com* 💳 *From $350.*

HORSEBACK RIDING

★ Esperanza Riding Company

HORSEBACK RIDING | If you've ever dreamed of riding a horse on the beach, splashing through waves and under palm trees, Esperanza Riding Company can make your dreams come true. Morning and afternoon rides are offered and typically include a route that takes riders into the hills and down to Playa Negra, sometimes even riding in the water. Group rides are $80 per person, or you can book a private ride for $125. Go online to make reservations. All experience levels are welcome. ✉ *Rte. 996 at Rte. 201* ☎ *787/435–0073* 🌐 *esperanzaridingcompany.com/vieques.*

Elsewhere on Vieques

Isabel Segunda and Esperanza are just a tiny portion of Vieques. Most of the island—more than two-thirds of it, in fact—was commandeered by the military until 2003. It's now a nature preserve that draws thousands of visitors each year.

Continued on page 159

BIOLUMINESCENT BAYS

Plankton Pyrotechnics in Puerto Rico

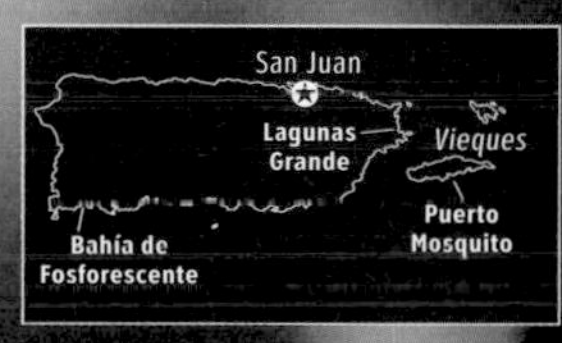

Puerto Rico's bioluminescent bays are beautiful. The slightest stirring of these waters, whether from the swish of a stick or droplets of rain, produces tiny bursts of teal-blue light. The darker the night, the better the bright; a moonless sky affords the most gorgeous marine moments in these wondrous bays.

by Francesca Drago

It's estimated that there are only 12 bio bays in the world, but it's difficult to determine exactly because the phenomenon occurs sporadically in warm seas. Puerto Rico has three. **Puerto Mosquito** in Vieques is the most spectacular bay. It won a Guinness World Record for most outstanding bioluminescent bay in the world. **Lagunas Grande** in Fajardo is not as bright, but convenient to see from San Juan. **Bahía de Fosforescente** in La Parguera's deserves an honorable mention even though water pollution, primarily from gas- and diesel-powered tourist boats, has darkened its luster.

Positively glowing! Puerto Rico's bio bays will literally have you beaming with joy.

Kayaks are an environmentally friendly way to explore the bays.

Seeing your oars glow as they blade through the water is a magical experience. Go with an operator that uses glow sticks to illuminate the stern of each kayak (for minimal light interference) and reviews safety practices at the start. Never book a tour with an operator who is unlicensed or uses gas- or diesel-powered boats. Ask your hotel concierge for assistance. On Vieques all hotels listed in our Where to Stay section will help arrange tours of Puerto Mosquito Bay.

RECOMMENDED OUTFITTERS IN VIEQUES

Island Adventures runs nightly bio bay tours and an educational tour aboard an open-air electric boat. (Prone to motion sickness? Be advised that a 45-minute cruise on a catamaran and 15-minute bus ride on a rough, unpaved road is part of this trip.) **Aqua Frenzy Kayaks** and **Abe's Snorkeling & Bio Bay Tours** both provide sturdy kayaks and knowledgeable guides for day and night trips to Puerto Mosquito.

IN FAJARDO

The two-hour night tour at Las Cabezas Nature Reserve (see Exploring, Fajardo, chapter 3) takes you on a winding boardwalk through mangroves to the water's edge. Strike the dark lagoon with a stick and marvel at the flashing wakes, or stir the water to "draw" with light.

For more information on recommended outfitters, see Boating & Kayaking in this chapter.

KNOW BEFORE YOU GLOW

- Paddling through the long, dark mangrove channel to reach Mosquito Bay is exciting but also challenging. Kayaking can be strenuous and requires teamwork; book with small groups, if possible, because crowds with varying experience and endurance can lead to exasperation and delay.
- People with little or no kayak experience, or with small children, may prefer a pontoon trip that provides an easy and safe way to swim in luminescent water.
- Puerto Mosquito is aptly named. Wear a hat, water shoes, and nylon pants as protection from bites. A lightweight, waterproof windbreaker worn over a bathing suit is ideal.
- Jellyfish are sometimes present but cannot be seen in the dark water. Look carefully.

NEW MOON

Bioluminescence is best experienced on a cloudy or moonless night. The darkest nights occur during the new moon phase, when its face is in shadow. Ask your tour guide what the moon phase will be and when it will rise, as a full moon may not appear in the sky until after your planned excursion.

PUERTO MOSQUITO: A BAY IN BALANCE

Dinoflagellates occur sporadically in tropical waters around the world, but the highest concentration on earth can be found in Puerto Mosquito Bay in Vieques. Billions of dinos dwell here because their habitat is balanced by a number of ecological features and protections.

"Channel surf:" A kayaker paddles the channel leading to Puerto Mosquito Bay

① Puerto Mosquito Bay is a **designated wildlife preserve.** This special zoning prevents rampant development, pollution, and destruction of the surrounding forest, which acts as a natural barrier against strong winds and rain.

② Salt-tolerant **mangrove trees** are vital for healthy coastal ecosystems. Their pronged roots stabilize the silt-rich shoreline, helping to filter sediments and reduce erosion, while leaves and bark fall into the water, where they rot and provide food and nutrients essential to the dinos' diet (e.g., vitamin B12). Moreover, the mangroves absorb carbon dioxide and store carbon in their sediments, which makes them a vital resource for reducing greenhouse gasses in the atmosphere.

③ The long, **narrow channel leading to the ocean** acts as a buffer that minimizes how much seawater flows into the bay daily and limits the amount of dinoflagellates (and nutrients) that are swept out with the tides. This enables the dinos to concentrate in the bay's shallow refuge.

④ The **channel exit** at the windward end of the bay allows sufficient water exchange with the sea to keep it from overheating or stagnating. The water in Puerto Mosquito remains calm and warm, creating the ideal environment for dinoflagellates to thrive in.

WHAT'S IN THE WATER?

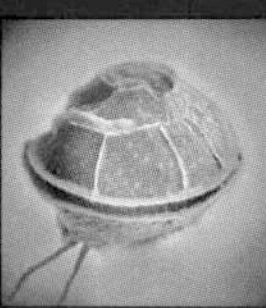

The undersea shooting stars are produced by microscopic algae called dinoflagellates, or "dinos." They convert chemical energy into light energy and emit tiny flashes when the water is disturbed. Scientists have theorized that their sudden sparks are a defense mechanism—a way to startle and disorient a predator and perhaps attract a larger predator to eat the first one.

A bio bay's brightness is a measure of its health. Dinoflagellates use the energy from sunlight to photosynthesize. Their luminescence is influenced by circadian rhythms, meaning their brightness depends on the light-dark conditions over a 24-hour period. One full day of sunshine and no clouds will result in two nights of plankton brilliance—with the second night brighter than the first. A cloudy day may still produce a bright night, but the following night won't be as spectacular. Artificial and ambient light will disrupt the fragile cycles of these "living lanterns" and erase their natural bioluminescence. Preservation of bio-bay brightness depends on public awareness about the harmful effects of light pollution and thoughtful planning for future land development.

The species of dinoflagellate Pyrodinium Bahamenese, found in Puerto Mosquito, is only 1/500 of an inch

PROTECTING THE BAYS

Destruction of mangroves, dredging, land development, and overuse of the bays' waters endanger the bio bays. Light pollution is especially harmful, since artificial and ambient light suppress the luminescence of the dinoflagellates. The Vieques Conservation and Historical Trust (VCHT) held its first symposium in the fall of 2008, convening expert scientific and technical authorities to discuss conservation of the bio bays. The goal, said Trust marine expert Mark Martin, was to "involve everybody," including government and the public, and rally commitments and resources to ensure the continuous scientific monitoring of Puerto Mosquito. The VCHT wants to name Puerto Mosquito a UNESCO World Biosphere Reserve to preserve it for future generations.

Here's what you can do to help maintain the pristine condition of this precious natural resource:

- Book with licensed operators who use kayaks or electric boats only.
- Swimming is banned in all the bio bays but Puerto Mosquito. Shun those operators who ignore the law.
- Dinoflagellates absorb basic chemicals directly from the water. Bug repellents containing DEET will kill them. Rinse off any remnants of suntan lotion, perfume, and deodorant before swimming.
- Do not throw any objects in the water or litter in any way.
- Support the conservation efforts of the VCHT.

Popular with local fisherman, the gentle waters of Esperanza Beach are ideal for small boats.

Sights

★ Puerto Mosquito Bioluminescent Bay

BODY OF WATER | East of Esperanza, Puerto Mosquito is one of the world's best spots for a glow-in-the-dark experience with undersea dinoflagellates—microorganisms that light up when the water around them is agitated. Local operators offer kayak trips or excursions on nonpolluting boats to see the bay's light show. Look behind your boat at the twinkling wake. Even the fish that swim through and jump from the water bear an eerie glow. The high concentration of dinoflagellates sets the bay apart from other spots (including in Puerto Rico) that are home to these microorganisms. The bay is at its best when there's little or no moonlight; rainy nights are beautiful, too, because raindrops hitting the water produce ricochets that shimmer like diamonds. Note that licensed operators are prohibited from leading tours on the day before, during, and after a full moon. ✉ *Unpaved roads off Rte. 997.*

Vieques National Wildlife Refuge

NATURE PRESERVE | A portion of the west and the entire eastern end of the island is administered by the U.S. Fish and Wildlife Service as the Vieques National Wildlife Refuge, comprising almost 18,000 acres, the biggest protected natural reserve in Puerto Rico. The 900-acre bombing range is permanently closed off, a consequence of its contamination by the ammunition shot over its 60-year existence. But most of the rest of eastern Vieques is pristine nature, astonishingly beautiful and well forested, with a hilly center region overlooking powder-white sandy beaches and a coral-ringed coastline; it served mainly as a buffer zone between the military maneuvers and civilian population. The vast majority of this acreage remains off-limits to visitors as authorities carry out a search for unexploded munitions and contaminants. Nonetheless, many of the beaches on the northern and southern coasts are open to the public; in 2009, a new asphalt road opened up six southern beaches. Hiking, biking, and horseback riding are allowed on designated trails. Fishing (both shore and from kayak), swimming, snorkeling, and diving are also permitted in designated zones. ✉ *Rte. 997, Km 3.2* ☎ *787/741–2138* 🌐 *www.fws.gov/refuge/vieques.*

★ **Pata Prieta** (*Secret Beach*)
BEACH—SIGHT | The not-so-secret Secret Beach is a heavenly cove for those seeking privacy. This tiny yet beautiful horseshoe-shape stretch of sand, reached via a rambling dirt road, is calm and secluded. You can find yourself completely alone, or one of a few couples embracing in the crystal clear water. **Amenities:** none. **Best for:** snorkeling; swimming. ✉ *Off Rte. 997, east of Playa Caracas.*

Playa Caracas (*Red Beach*)
BEACH—SIGHT | One of the first stretches of sand east of Esperanza, this well-maintained beach boasts covered cabañas for lounging. Less rustic than other nearby beaches, it is sheltered from waves. **Amenities:** parking (no fee); toilets. **Best for:** snorkeling; swimming; walking. ✉ *Off Rte. 997.*

Playa La Chiva (*Blue Beach*)
BEACH—SIGHT | Some consider this the most beautiful beach on Vieques. It has a handful of covered cabañas with individual parking spots, so guests can claim their own personal stretch of sand and survey an expansive, tranquil horizon. Beware of strong surf in some spots. **Amenities:** none. **Best for:** solitude; walking. ✉ *Off Rte. 997, 4 km (2½ miles) east of Esperanza.*

Punta Arenas (*Green Beach*)
BEACH—SIGHT | On the western edge of the island, at the end of a long unpaved road marred by potholes, this beach faces the Vieques Passage. Miles of coral reef just offshore attract snorkelers and divers, but caution is required due to strong currents. From the shore you can catch a glimpse of El Yunque on the mainland. **Amenities:** none. **Best for:** snorkeling; solitude. ✉ *Off Rte. 200, at western end of Rte. 994.*

★ **Tin Box**
$$ | **BARBECUE** | **FAMILY** | Tin Box is, quite literally, a tin box serving barbecue platters and po'boys piled high with smoked chicken, pork, fried shrimp, or ribs, served with classic sides like coleslaw, baked beans, and cornbread. A sushi bar rounds out the offerings—you can't go wrong with one of the rolls made with local spiny lobster. **Known for:** watermelon margaritas and martinis; house-cured bacon; best sushi and barbecue on the island. $ *Average main: $18* ✉ *Rte. 996 at Rte. 201* ☎ *787/741–7700* 🌐 *www.facebook.com/tinboxvqs* ⏲ *Closed Mon. and Tues.*

★ **Casa Ladera**
$$ | **RENTAL** | **FAMILY** | This group of apartment-style units with a separate villa is ideal for families and groups of friends who want a home-style accommodation for their island getaway. **Pros:** proximity to beach; spacious, sunny accommodations; pool and beach. **Cons:** three-night minimum stay; housekeeper viewed by some visitors as invasive; no owner on-site. $ *Rooms from: $150* ✉ *Off Rte. 200, Monte Santo* ☎ *240/515–4665* 🌐 *www.casa-ladera.com* *4 units* 🍽 *No meals.*

Hix Island House
$$ | **HOTEL** | Constructed entirely of concrete and set in a tropical forest, the four buildings of this luxurious hotel echo the granite boulders strewn around Vieques, blending with its surroundings. **Pros:** acclaimed eco-friendly architecture; very secluded setting; friendly staff. **Cons:** the lack of window screens means bugs get in; no a/c, TVs, or phones; no Wi-Fi in rooms (although it's free in public areas). $ *Rooms from: $225* ✉ *Rte. 995, Km 1.5* ☎ *787/435–4590* 🌐 *www.hixislandhouse.com* *19 rooms* 🍽 *Free Breakfast.*

Vieques Libre

For nearly six decades the U.S. Navy had a stranglehold on Vieques. It controlled the island's eastern half and western end and exerted enormous influence over the destiny of the civilian area in between. Though long protested, the bombing, shelling, and amphibious landings continued. When an off-target bomb killed a civilian on Navy land in April 1999, opposition transformed the island's placid beaches into political hotbeds.

Protesters camping out on the bombing range kept it shut down from 1999 to 2000. Hundreds of Puerto Rican residents were arrested for trespassing on Navy land during war games. They were joined by celebrity protesters from the United States, including environmental lawyer Robert F. Kennedy Jr. (who gave his baby daughteson Aiden the middle name Vieques), the wife of Reverend Jesse Jackson, and Reverend Al Sharpton, all of whom were arrested for trespassing on the bombing range. For much of 2000 and 2001 protests were so commonplace that there were semipermanent encampments of opponents. Songs such as "Paz Pa' Vieques" (Peace for Vieques) began to surface, as did bumper stickers and T-shirts with protest slogans. Latin pop celebrities like singer-songwriter Robi Draco Rosa (who wrote Ricky Martin's "Livin' la Vida Loca"), actor Edward James Olmos, singer Millie Corretjer, and protest singer Zoraida Santiago, as well as other actors, painters, doctors, and lawyers later added to the fanfare.

President Bill Clinton finally agreed that residents could vote on whether to continue to host the Navy. A nonbinding referendum held in 2001 found that 68% of the island's voters wanted the military to leave immediately. Although some members of Congress argued that the Navy should stay indefinitely—a faction whose cries grew louder after September 11, 2001, when even local protesters called for a moratorium on civil disobedience—the administration ultimately capitulated. The Navy finally withdrew from its Atlantic Fleet training grounds in May 2002, and in 2003 the installation was officially closed. By the end of 2005 much of the former military base was transformed into the Vieques National Wildlife Refuge. Today there are concerns that the sustained bombing activity produced high levels of contamination that are linked to health issues such as higher cancer rates among residents. Visitors who may be concerned about potential risks associated with travel to the area should check the Centers for Disease Control website (*www.cdc.gov*) for the latest information.

Shopping

★ Oro Vieques

ART GALLERIES | This art gallery, event space, and boutique is dedicated to Puerto Rican artists and designers, with monthly events and ongoing exhibits. Stop by before or after your visit to Playa Negra to browse affordable paintings and photographs by local artists, or check the calendar for upcoming artist dinners and other events while you're in town. ✉ *Rte. 997* ✣ *Next to Playa Negra* *www.orovieques.com* *Closed Sun. and Mon.*

Culebra

28 km (17 miles) east of Fajardo by ferry.

"Open some days, closed others," reads the sign on a food kiosk near the canal that cuts through a part of this island. It's a pretty good motto for most of Culebra, which—if you can imagine it—is even more laid-back than Vieques. Visitors don't come here for highbrow entertainment. They come for one thing: beaches. Culebra is known around the world for its curvaceous coastline. Playa Flamenco, the tiny island's most famous stretch of sand, is considered one of the top 10 best beaches in the world. If Playa Flamenco gets too crowded, as it often does around Easter or Christmas, many other neighboring beaches will still be nearly deserted. And if it's complete privacy you're after, hire a motorboat to take you to one of the nearby islets, such as Isla Culebrita or Cayo Luis Peña. It won't be difficult to find a little cove that you can have all to yourself.

Archaeological evidence shows that Taíno and Carib peoples lived on Culebra long before the arrival of the Spanish in the late 15th century. The Spanish didn't bother laying claim to it until 1886; a lack of freshwater made it an unattractive location for a settlement. The U.S. Navy and Marine Corps, however, thought it was a very valuable piece of real estate. Although President Theodore Roosevelt created a wildlife refuge here in 1909, the military later used this island, as well as nearby Vieques, for target practice and amphibious assault training, beginning in WWII. Despite having a smaller population than Vieques, the residents of Culebra staged a number of sit-ins and succeeded in ousting the military in 1975.

GETTING HERE AND AROUND

AIR TRAVEL

Culebra's airport is a no-frills affair, with bathrooms, airline counters, and a small café inside, and chickens pecking the ground outside. The airport is about three minutes from downtown Dewey. Route 250 leads east and south of the airport; Route 251 leads northeast to Playa Flamenco. Two car rental companies have facilities directly across the street from the airport, a two-minute walk at most.

CONTACTS Aeropuerto Benjamin Rivera Noriega (CPX). ✉ *Rte. 250 at Rte. 251.*

CAR TRAVEL

Renting a Jeep or at least a golf cart is imperative for getting around Culebra.

Carlos Jeep Rental, a quick walk from the airport, is a good place to choose your steed. Daily rates range from $27, for a four-passenger golf cart, to $50. Customers arriving by ferry can request courtesy round-trip shuttle service.

Directly across from Culebra's airport, Jerry's Jeep Rental is the most convenient car rental spot on the island, but advance reservations are recommended year-round and are imperative during high season. In addition to a fleet of Jeeps, Jerry's has golf carts; both types of vehicles are available for rentals as short as a few hours or as long as a month.

CONTACTS Carlos Jeep Rental. ✉ *Aeropuerto Benjamin Rivera Noriega* ☎ *787/742–3514* 🌐 *www.carlosjeeprental.com.* **Jerry's Jeep Rental.** ✉ *Rte. 251, directly across from the airport* ☎ *787/742–0526* 🌐 *www.jerrysjeeprental.com.*

TAXI TRAVEL

If you don't rent a Jeep or golf cart, then Willy's Taxi is your go-to full-service operator offering taxi service. The company also offeres Jeep rentals and water taxi trips to Isla Culebrita.

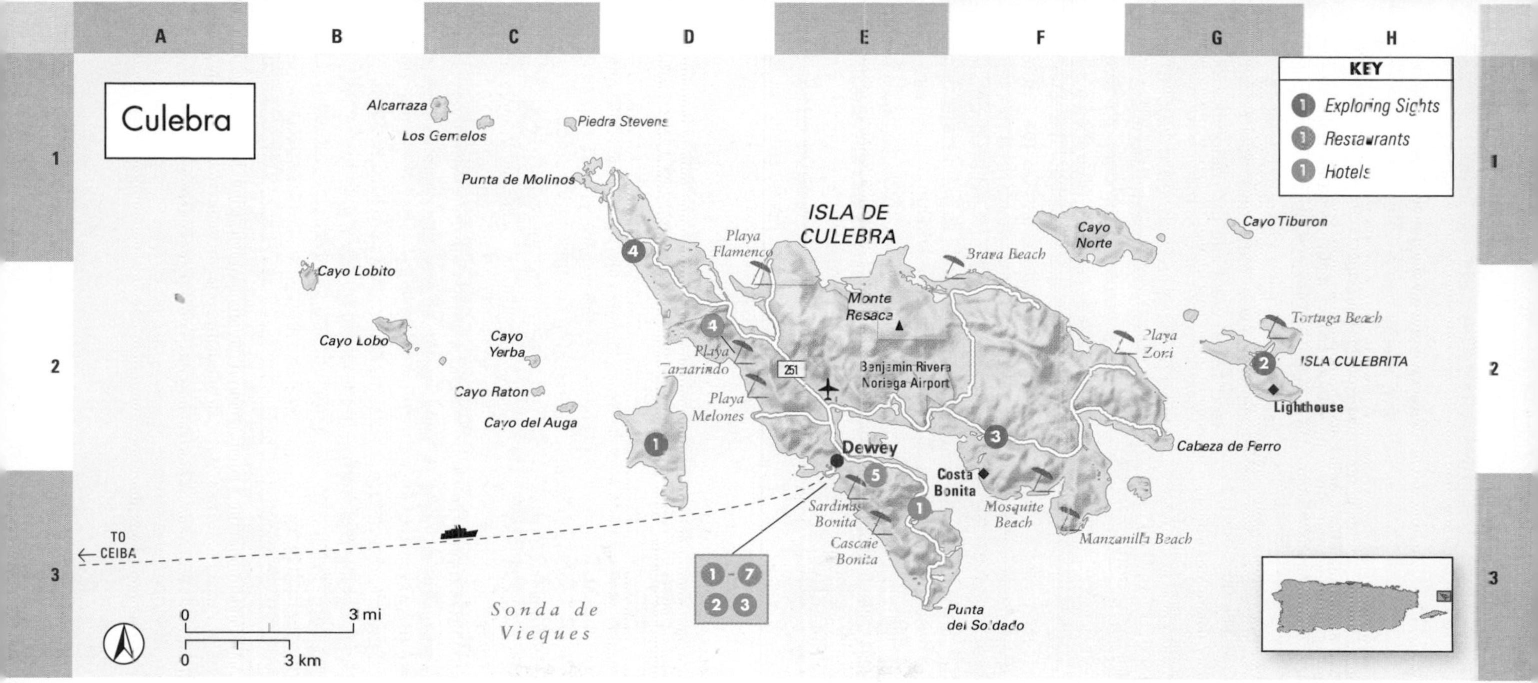

Culebra

A
B
C
D
E
F
G
H

KEY

1 *Exploring Sights*
1 *Restaurants*
1 *Hotels*

Alcarraza
Los Gemelos
Piedra Stevens
Punta de Molinos
Cayo Lobito
Cayo Lobo
Cayo Yerba
Cayo Raton
Cayo del Auga
ISLA DE CULEBRA
Playa Flamenco
Playa Tamarindo
Playa Melones
251
Monte Resaca
Benjamin Rivera Noriega Airport
Brava Beach
Cayo Norte
Cayo Tiburon
Playa Zoni
Tortuga Beach
ISLA CULEBRITA
Lighthouse
Cabeza de Ferro
Dewey
Costa Bonita
Mosquite Beach
Manzanilla Beach
Sardinas Bonita
Cascaie Bonita
Punta del Soldado
TO CEIBA
Sonda de Vieques
0 3 mi
0 3 km

Sights

1 Cayo Luis Peña........D2
2 Isla Culebrita........G2
3 Museo El Polvarín........F2
4 Refugio Nacional de Vida Silvestre de Culebra......D1

Restaurants

1 Dinghy Dock..............E3
2 El Eden....................E3
3 Heather's Pizza...........E3
4 Mamacita's..............E3
5 Susie's..................E3
6 Vibra Verde.............E3
7 Zaco's Tacos.............E3

Hotels

1 Club Seabourne...........F3
2 Mamacita's................E3
3 Posada La Hamaca.......E3
4 Tamarindo Estates........D2
5 Villa Boheme..............E2

Sights

Almost everything about Culebra is diminutive. The island's only community—named for U.S. Admiral George Dewey (locals resent the association, preferring to call it simply "el pueblo" instead)—is set along a single street leading from the ferry dock. You can explore the few shops along Calle Pedro Márquez in a half hour. The one-room airport is 1 km (½ mile) to the north. Except for one resort, few hotels have more than a dozen rooms.

Cayo Luis Peña

ISLAND | A kayak is a great way to reach Cayo Luis Peña, an islet just off the western edge of Culebra. There are a handful of protected beaches where you can soak up the sun and not run into a single soul. Cayo Luis Peña is also part of the Refugio Nacional de Vida Silvestre de Culebra (Culebra National Wildlife Refuge).

★ Isla Culebrita

ISLAND | Part of the Refugio Nacional de Vida Silvestre de Culebra, uninhabited Isla Culebrita is clearly visible from the northeast corner of Culebra. An essential day-trip excursion, this islet is a favorite destination for sunbathers and snorkelers who want to escape the crowds at Playa Flamenco. Isolation set against a palate of crystalline, turquoise waters and dewy, lush greens makes for a one-of-a-kind natural experience. On the northern shore there are several tidal pools; snuggling into one of them is like taking a warm bath. Snorkelers and divers love the fact that they can reach the reef from the shore and carouse with sea turtles, rays, and schools of colorful fish. Bring your sneakers; in about 20–30 minutes you can hike to the islet's peak, where the spectacular ruins of an old lighthouse await. Views of the surrounding Caribbean are sublime from the top of the structure, but you may not be able to climb its 54 steps; the lighthouse is currently being restored. To get to Culebrita, take a dive boat or hire a water taxi.

Museo El Polvorín

MILITARY SITE | If the collection of this museum underwhelms, take a close look at the photo album next to the visitor log to see how much community spirit and sweat went into the restoration of El Polvorín, a former U.S. military munitions building, constructed in 1905. It reopened in 2008 as a museum, but not without an enormous amount of effort; the structure was little more than a shell. Today, it houses a small but interesting collection of objects and photos that tell the island's history (don't miss the story of Puerto Rico's first female mayor), along with several TVs with interesting oral history–based documentaries on loop. ✉ *Rte. 250* ☎ *787/617–8517* 🎟 *$1.*

★ Refugio Nacional de Vida Silvestre de Culebra

NATURE PRESERVE | Commissioned by President Theodore Roosevelt in 1909, the Culebra National Wildlife Refuge is one of the nation's oldest. The total protected area comprises some 1,500 acres of the island. It's a lure for hikers and bird-watchers: Culebra teems with seabirds, from laughing gulls and roseate terns to red-billed tropic birds and sooty terns. Maps of trails in the refuge are hard to come by, but you can stop by the U.S. Fish and Wildlife Service office east of the airport to find out about trail conditions and determine whether you're headed to an area that requires a permit. The office also can tell you whether the leatherback turtles are nesting. From mid-April to mid-July, volunteers help monitor and tag these creatures, which nest on nearby beaches, especially Playa Resaca and Playa Brava. If you'd like to volunteer, you must agree to help out for at least three nights. ✉ *Rte. 250, north of Dewey* ☎ 🌐 *www.fws.gov.*

Beaches

★ Playa Flamenco

BEACH—SIGHT | FAMILY | Consistently ranked one of the most beautiful beaches in the world, this beach has snow-white sands, turquoise waters, and lush hills rising on all sides. During the week, it's pleasantly uncrowded; on weekends it fills up with day-trippers from the mainland. With kiosks selling simple dishes and vendors for lounge-chair and umbrella rentals, it's easy to make a day of it. There's great snorkeling past the old dock. Tanks on the northern end of the beach are a reminder that the area was once a military base. **Amenities:** food and drink; parking (no fee); showers; toilets. **Best for:** snorkeling; swimming; walking. ✉ *Rte. 251, west of the airport* ☎ *787/742–0700.*

Playa Melones

BEACH—SIGHT | Just west of Dewey, this is a favorite spot for snorkelers. The reef that runs around the rocky point is easy to reach from shore. Locals swear this is the best place for sunsets. To get here, head uphill on the unmarked road behind the church. **Amenities:** none. **Best for:** snorkeling; sunset; swimming. ✉ *Camino Vecinal, west of town, Dewey.*

Playa Zoni

BEACH—SIGHT | On the island's northeastern end, this beach is long and narrow—perfect for afternoon strolls. From the shore you can catch a glimpse of Isla Culebrita, as well as St. Thomas and St. Croix. Leatherback turtles nest here. Note that there is a gravel parking lot, but it's small; it won't fit more than a dozen Jeeps at a time. **Amenities:** parking (no fee). **Best for:** swimming; walking. ✉ *End of Rte. 250, 11 km (7 miles) northeast of Dewey.*

Restaurants

Dinghy Dock

$$ | SEAFOOD | This restaurant takes its name from the nearby site of Culebra's heaviest traffic—the arrival and departure of the water taxi. The menu leans toward grilled meats, from hamburgers and wraps to sirloin steaks. **Known for:** creole-style seafood; burgers and other bar food; laid-back atmosphere. $ *Average main: $18* ✉ *Calle Fulladoza, Dewey* ☎ *787/742–0233.*

El Eden

$$$ | ECLECTIC | Funky El Eden is a little bit of everything when it comes to eating and drinking on Culebra. What started as a deli serving sandwiches on freshly baked bread morphed into a liquor store, and now churns out soups, local catch, *churrasco* (skirt steak) platters, pastas, and a signature saffron lobster risotto. **Known for:** Caribbean lobster; fresh bread; friendly service. $ *Average main: $23* ✉ *836 Sardinas* ☎ *787/617–8517* 🌐 *www.eledenculebra.com.*

Heather's Pizza

$$ | PIZZA | Pizza on the tiny island of Culebra, you ask? Yep, and pretty good pizza at that. **Known for:** Pizza Boricua; spaghetti with meat sauce; casual setting. $ *Average main: $15* ✉ *14 Calle Pedro Márquez, Dewey* ☎ *939/731–4434.*

Mamacita's

$$ | CARIBBEAN | Pull your dinghy up to the dock and watch the resident iguanas plod past this simple open-air, tin-roofed restaurant on a rough-plank deck beside the Dewey canal. Tarpon cruise past, and the to-and-fro of boaters completes the show at Culebra's favorite watering hole and gringo hangout. **Known for:** grilled seafood; lunchtime burgers; casual setting. $ *Average main: $12* ✉ *66 Calle Castelar, Dewey* ☎ *787/742–0090* 🌐 *www.mamacitasguesthouse.com.*

Susie's

$$$ | **ECLECTIC** | *Sanjuanera* owner-chef Susie Hebert learned her culinary skills at San Juan's swank Caribe Hilton and Ritz-Carlton before settling on Culebra and opening her casual and unpretentious fine-dining restaurant, a soothing space filled with banquettes, pillows, and couches. A huge courtyard is perfect for dining under the stars. **Known for:** Caesar salad; fresh seafood and lobster; steaks, especially filet mignon and rib eye. *Average main: $25 ✉ Rte. 250, Las Delicias, Dewey ☎ 787/340–7058 Closed Wed. and Thurs. No lunch.*

Vibra Verde

$$ | **PUERTO RICAN** | This cash-only spot on Dewey's main drag is within walking distance to the ferry dock. It doubles as a health-food store, and the restaurant specializes in natural, organic meals served at breakfast and lunch. **Known for:** organic, locally sourced ingredients; fresh baked goods; breakfast. *Average main: $13 ✉ 3 Plaza Mercado, Dewey Closed Tues. and Wed. No credit cards.*

★ Zaco's Tacos

$ | **MEXICAN** | After years in the kitchen of popular hangout Mamacita's, chef Zach Sizer decided to open his own joint: a no-frills taco spot delivering fresh, flavorful, affordable grub. And a good thing he did—Zaco's Tacos is a runaway success. **Known for:** meat and fish tacos; great margaritas in many flavors; casual setting. *Average main: $7 ✉ 21 Calle Pedro Márquez, Dewey ☎ 787/742–0243 www.zacostacos.com.*

Hotels

★ Club Seabourne

$$ | **HOTEL** | The most sophisticated place in Culebra, this cluster of lovely plantation-style cottages creates a pretty assemblage on a picturesque hilltop overlooking Fulladoza Bay. Though just a five-minute drive south of Dewey, it feels completely isolated—in a good way. **Pros:** lush gardens; nice pool; airport or ferry transfers included. **Cons:** some steps to negotiate; service can be hit or miss; spotty Internet and mobile phone reception. *Rooms from: $249 ✉ Rte. 252, northwest of town ☎ 787/742–3169 www.clubseabourne.com 13 rooms Free Breakfast.*

Mamacita's

$ | **HOTEL** | The best rooms in Mamacita's venerable guesthouse have balconies overlooking the canal, but this is a decidedly no-frills establishment suitable for budget-minded travelers. **Pros:** friendly staff; pickup point for water taxis; popular restaurant and bar in guesthouse. **Cons:** basic rooms; no elevator; on a narrow street. *Rooms from: $89 ✉ 66 Calle Castelar, Dewey ☎ 787/742–0090 www.mamacitasguesthouse.com 11 rooms No meals.*

Posada La Hamaca

$ | **HOTEL** | This building, which shares Mamacita's mangrove-lined canal, has spick-and-span guest rooms—as simple as they come—with louvered windows and calming color schemes. **Pros:** walk to shops and restaurants; laid-back atmosphere; cheap rates. **Cons:** some rooms are small; constant clunking noises from adjacent bridge; no parking. *Rooms from: $90 ✉ 68 Calle Castelar, Dewey ☎ 787/742–3516 www.posada.com 12 rooms No meals.*

Tamarindo Estates

$$ | **RENTAL** | On a 60-acre estate hidden away on the western coast of Culebra, this string of one- and two-bedroom apartment cottages sits directly on a long, sandy beach, although most of the cottages are a bit farther inland. **Pros:** peaceful location; pretty pool area; all apartments have full kitchens. **Cons:** short walk to the beach; isolated, far from dining options; no housekeeping service. *Rooms from: $169 ✉ Off Rte. 251 ☎ 787/742–3343 www.tamarindoestates.com 12 cottages No meals.*

Villa Boheme

$ | **B&B/INN** | Colorful and breezy, this Spanish-style guesthouse is centrally located, next to popular Dinghy Dock. **Pros:** expansive view of the bay; walk to restaurants and shops; not on the beach. **Cons:** basic furnishings; no elevator; few on-site amenities. *Rooms from: $120 ✉ 368 Calle Fulladoza, Dewey ☎ 787/742–3508 🌐 villaboheme.com ⇨ 11 rooms 🍽 No meals.*

Dinghy Dock

BARS/PUBS | Watch the island's expat community pile into this bar around sunset—it can be a raucous scene, especially when there's a band. The party continues into the wee hours, even on weeknights. ✉ *Calle Fulladoza, Dewey* ☎ *787/742–0233.*

Mamacita's

BARS/PUBS | The island's favorite gringo watering hole is always jumping, with a weekday happy hour (4–6) and Saturday night's live music jam. Don't miss the bar's signature drink: the frozen Bushwhacker—a delicious but deadly mix of rum, vodka, Bailey's, amaretto, Kahlua, and coconut. ✉ *66 Calle Castelar* ☎ *787/742–0090* 🌐 *www.mamacitas-guesthouse.com.*

Shopping

Culebra is smaller than Vieques but has much better shopping. Dewey has several shops on its main drag that sell trendy jewelry, clothing, and a range of souvenirs from the tacky to the terrific.

Estudio Arte Fango

CRAFTS | The island's best place for gifts is located right above the popular Dinghy Dock restaurant. Local artist Jorge Acevedo paints scenes of island life and Culebra's natural tableaux of mangroves and seascapes. Make time to browse his one-of-a-kind works and original T-shirts, as well as his wife's handmade jewelry. If you happen to be around on a Saturday, follow him downstairs to Dinghy Dock, where he plays conga music. ✉ *Above Dinghy Dock restaurant, Dewey* ☎ *787/435–6654* 🌐 *www.artefango.com.*

Island Boutique

CRAFTS | Find local apparel like sarongs, handmade jewelry, and original souvenirs such as wind chimes at this store across from the ferry depot. ✉ *4 Calle Pedro Márquez, Dewey* ☎ *787/742–0439.*

La Cava

CLOTHING | Forgot your snorkel? Left your bathing suit at home? Need a new pair of flip-flops or a souvenir for your favorite cousin? La Cava is the perfect place to meet all of those needs. ✉ *138 Calle Escudero, Dewey* ☎ *787/742–0566.*

BOATING AND KAYAKING

Pez Vela Charters

SAILING | Operating out of Bahia Marina, Captain Bill Penfield offers a true island experience aboard his 33-foot catamaran. Most popular is the Picnic Sail, which includes a bit of everything Culebra is known for—visits to nearby Culebrita and Cayo Norte, snorkeling, swimming, plus a hot lunch. All regularly scheduled sailings include snorkeling gear. Custom charters and private excursions can also be arranged. ✉ *Bahia Marina, Fulladoza Bay* ☎ *787/215–3809* 🌐 *www.culebracatamaran.com* 🎫 *From $135.*

DIVING AND SNORKELING

Aquatic Adventures

BOATING | Captain Taz Hamrick takes guests out on snorkeling and PADI-certified scuba trips, as well as charters to the surrounding keys. ✉ *372 Sector Fulladoza, Dewey* ☎ *515/290–2310* 🌐 *www.diveculebra.com.*

Culebra Divers

SCUBA DIVING | The island's premier dive shop caters to scuba newbies and old hands alike. The company's 25-foot cabin cruisers travel to more than 50 local sites to see spotted eagle rays, octopus, moray eels, and turtles. You can also rent a mask and snorkel to explore on your own. ✉ *4 Calle Pedro Márquez, Dewey* ☎ *787/742–0803* 🌐 *www.culebradivers.com.*

Chapter 6

THE NORTH COAST AND THE CORDILLERA CENTRAL

Updated by Julie Schwietert Collazo

Sights ★★★★☆ Restaurants ★☆☆☆☆ Hotels ★★☆☆☆ Shopping ★☆☆☆☆ Nightlife ★☆☆☆☆

WELCOME TO THE NORTH COAST AND THE CORDILLERA CENTRAL

TOP REASONS TO GO

★ **Bosque Estatal de Toro Negro:** Hike to the island's highest lake and explore its tallest mountain.

★ **Arecibo Observatory:** Witness the world's largest radio telescope.

★ **Hacienda La Esperanza:** Tour a restored sugar plantation to learn more about the commodity's role in Puerto Rican history.

★ **Bosque Estatal de Maricao:** Go bird-watching in this forest, home to more species than anywhere else on the island.

The North Coast and Cordillera Central are two distinct regions, each with its own gorgeous geography (and, thus, its own road conditions). Highways 22 and 2 lead west out of San Juan, unspooling in a smooth, fast ribbon of road across the northern shore. Below the region's limestone (karst) formations sit Puerto Rico's famous caves. Head south on any secondary road to cut into the core of the island, through which the Cordillera Central runs east-to-west; these are typically two-lane roadways that wind through mountainous terrain. The region had vast damage from Hurricane Maria in 2017, so visitors should be especially cautious when traveling here. There are still few places to spend the night, and roads are undergoing repair. Always ask about conditions before heading out, and if you aren't planning to stay in one of the few available lodgings, give yourself sufficient time to return to your accommodations before dark.

1 Dorado and Environs. Just beyond the metropolitan San Juan area lies Dorado, a northern beach town that has a more laid-back vibe than San Juan. Though hard-hit by Hurricane Maria in 2017, the area has been recovering and many local services and attractions have reopened.

2 Arecibo. Best-known for being home to the world's largest radio

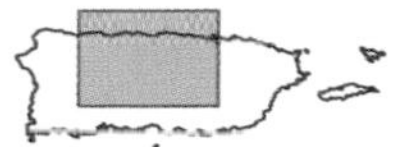

telescope, Arecibo is also the launching point for a day trip to Lago Dos Bocas.

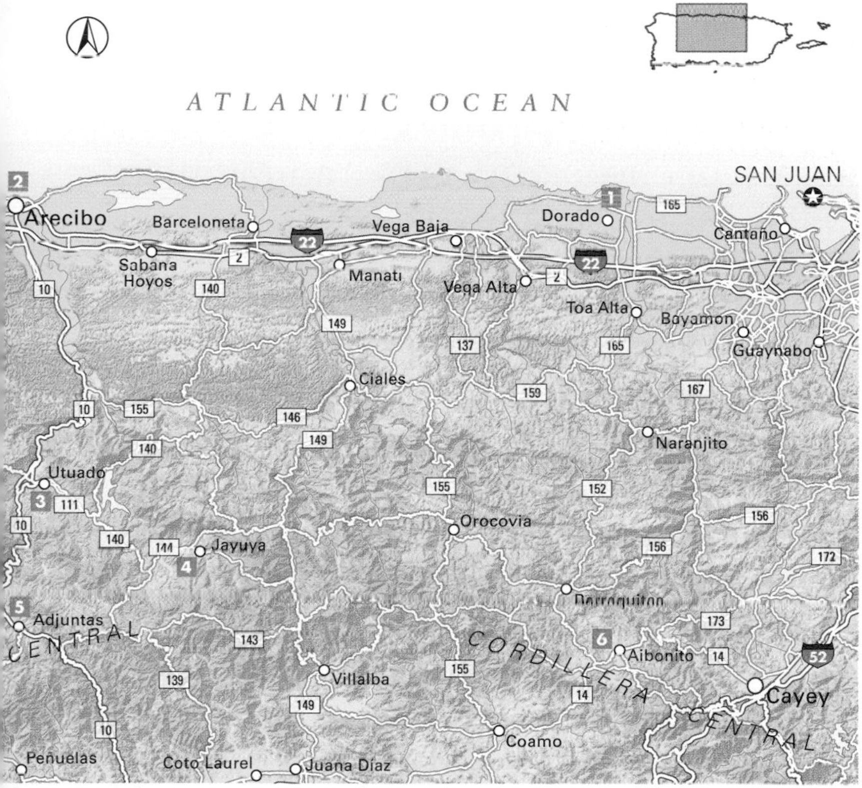

3 Utuado. This mountainous town was, like most of central Puerto Rico, battered by Hurricane Maria; however, it remains a beautiful home base for those who want to explore some of the lesser-known attractions in the island's interior.

4 Jayuya. Learn more about Taíno culture at Jayuya's Museo El Cemí, a uniquely shaped structure with symbolic significance.

5 Adjuntas. Adjuntas could be considered the gateway to Puerto Rico's coffee culture; be sure to visit Hacienda Buena Vista, a former coffee plantation that offers tours.

6 Aibonito. Several legends attempt to to explain the name of this town, but regardless of which one you choose to believe, Aibonito is "bonito" and is best-known for its annual flower festival.

There's more to Puerto Rico than beautiful beaches, as anyone who lives on the island will tell you. When islanders want to escape the heat, they head to the Cordillera Central. This mountain range, which runs most of the length of the island, is incredibly lush. Towering trees lean over the narrow roadways that crisscross the region, often brushing branches with those across the pavement. In the shade below, impatiens in shades of pink and purple bloom in profusion.

Agriculture is very important to the economy of the Cordillera Central. Bananas, pineapples, and plantains are grown throughout the region. Coffee was once a dominant crop along the hillsides between Utuado and Maricao, and it has enjoyed a resurgence of late. Travelers can now visit coffee plantations and a coffee museum; if they time their visit right, they might even catch one of the island's many coffee festivals. A few of the old plantation homes have become quaint country inns, all of them stocked with plenty of blankets for cool evenings, when temperatures—especially in higher elevations—can drop into the 40s.

In the east you'll find a number of attractive colonial towns, such as Aibonito and Barranquitas. Farther west is karst country—terrain built up by limestone deposits in which erosion has produced fissures, sinkholes, and underground streams and rivers. The peaks above are often astounding, and visitors love the kinds of photo ops provided by aboveground caves like the popular Cueva Ventana. Along the Cordillera Central, the road will thread in and out of the Bosque Estatal de Toro Negro, where the island's highest peak, Cerro de Punta, rises 4,398 feet above sea level. It may not measure up to many around the world, but on this island it seems as tall as Mt. Everest.

All too often, visitors to the Cordillera Central zoom right past the northern coast's many appealing attractions. In Dorado, there's the natural rock formation Ojo del Buey (Bull's Eye) right on the beach; it's believed to have held significance for the people who lived on the island before the arrival of Columbus, as quite a few artifacts have been found there. Many of them are displayed in the town's Museo de Arte e Historia (Museum of Art and History). West of Dorado, you'll find the Reserva Natural Laguna Tortuguero, a natural recreation area with diverse habitat and an array of birds and other wildlife. Just south of the reserve is the Hacienda Don Carmelo, home of the School of Equestrian Art. Its gardens and grounds make for a pleasant stroll; one highlight is a 130-year-old tree that is the setting for a magical tree house with cathedral-esque windows and a series of porches. Arecibo's main attraction is the world-famous (and world's largest) radio telescope, which is open to the public. Nearby is the world's third-largest underground cave system, the Parque de las Cavernas del Río Camuy, a fascinating and accessible landscape.

Planning

WHEN TO GO

The temperate climate of the mountainous central zone makes it a pleasure to visit year-round, and outdoor activities abound in any season. Locals especially like to head up to this area in summer, when Aibonito holds its flower festival (late June or July) and Barranquitas hosts its artisans' fair (July)—but there are fun local festivals nearly every month, celebrating everything from handmade lace to coffee. It gets hot in August and September, but north coast beaches help everyone stay cool. Note that during busy times some hotels require a two- or three-night minimum stay on weekends.

GETTING HERE AND AROUND

Highways 22 and 2 head west out of San Juan. These are frequently congested with commuters heading into and out of the capital. Local roads to Dorado, Arecibo, and other points west, north, and south, are accessible via exits off these two highways.

AIR TRAVEL

Arecibo has a small airport for charter planes but no regularly scheduled service. There are no airports in the Cordillera Central. Depending on your destination, you can fly into the airports in San Juan, Fajardo, Ponce, Mayagüez, or Aguadilla.

BUS TRAVEL

Bus service is all but nonexistent outside of metro San Juan and should not be considered a viable form of transportation for visitors, as service, when it exists at all, is unreliable. You'll have to depend on *públicos* (passenger vans), which make many stops. These vans usually stop near a town's main square.

CAR TRAVEL

A car is essential if you want to explore this area, and a road map is a must in the Cordillera Central—GPS systems are not always reliable. The well-maintained and scenic Route 10, which can be accessed in Arecibo, is one main link to the central mountain region. The Ruta Panorámica runs east–west across the island and near some of the central mountain towns; it's made up of a number of small roads, many of which can be hilly and curvy—navigating them takes patience. Most signs in the region give a route number, rather than the name of a town. You'll have to arrange for a rental car in one of the large cities on the coast or at your arrival airport (probably the easiest option).

HOTELS

High-class resorts aren't limited exclusively to San Juan and the eastern coast; on the north coast, for example, travelers who aren't constrained by a budget will find Dorado Beach, a Ritz-Carlton Reserve, sitting on 1,400 acres, much of it prime beachfront. For the most part, however, paradores and other modest lodgings are the norm in the small towns, especially in the Cordillera. In this part of the island there are seldom more than two or three options in any given town. Sometimes there's just one hotel, take it or leave it—and you'd better take it, especially if you're traveling on a weekend. The best lodgings, rustic retreats set beside a river or on acres of lush forest, are often booked solid. Make sure to call ahead, as it's a long way between towns.

RESTAURANTS

Traditional Puerto Rican cooking is the norm in this part of the island. Many of the ingredients on your plate—breadfruit, coconuts, plantains, mangoes, root vegetables, and the *ají* pepper, to name a few—are sold at roadside stands throughout the region, and they are served at humble eateries along the highways and secondary roads. With a couple of exceptions, don't expect upscale dining or international influences in these regions. Do expect down-home cooking and memorable meals, especially along Route 184, where you'll find a number of restaurants serving slow-roasted *lechón* (suckling pig), a local delicacy cooked outdoors over coals.

HOTEL AND RESTAURANT PRICES
Hotel and restaurant reviews have been shortened. For full information visit Fodors.com.

What It Costs in U.S. Dollars

$	$$	$$$	$$$$
RESTAURANTS			
under $12	$12–$20	$21–$30	over $30
HOTELS			
under $150	$150–$250	$251–$350	over $350

SAFETY

For the most part, visitors to towns on the northern coast and Cordillera will find that the biggest hazards are traffic and rough patches of road. Still, the same common sense you use anywhere else applies here, too. Don't leave valuables exposed in your rental car or left out in your hotel room. Be aware of your surroundings, especially if walking alone at night or using an ATM. And keep your receipts if you're using a credit or debit card, as fraud is an occasional (but not widespread) problem.

VISITOR INFORMATION

Arecibo, Jayuya, and Utuado have tourism offices in their town halls. All are open weekdays during normal business hours.

CONTACTS Arecibo City Hall. ✉ *100 Av. José de Diego, Arecibo* ☎ *787/333–1063.* **Jayuya.** ✉ *Plaza Principal de Jayuya, Jayuya* ☎ *787/828–0900.* **Utuado.** ✉ *8–26 Calle Dr. Betances, Utuado* ☎ *787/894–3505.*

Dorado and Environs

27 km (17 miles) west of San Juan.

This small and tidy town is one of the oldest vacation spots on the island, having gotten a boost in 1955, when Laurance Rockefeller bought the pineapple, coconut, and grapefruit plantation of Dr. Alfred Livingston and his daughter Clara and built a resort on the property. Sadly, the Hyatt Dorado Beach Resort & Country Club closed in 2005. Its excellent golf courses—among the best-known in Puerto Rico—are still open, however, and the property has been redeveloped as a private residential resort. Those looking for upscale accommodations evoking the erstwhile golden age still have an option here, thanks to the Dorado Beach, a Ritz-Carlton Reserve. The town of Dorado itself is fun to visit; its winding road leads across a bridge to a main square, with small bars, restaurants, and shops nearby. Most visitors, however, don't stray too far from the beach.

GETTING HERE AND AROUND

As is the case throughout most of Puerto Rico, the best means of getting to and around Dorado and the surrounding towns is by car. Public transportation is

Great Itineraries

If You Have 1 Day

If you feel like escaping San Juan for a day, head to one of the resorts in Dorado. Because so many *sanjuaneros* do just that, this pretty little town has some good restaurants. For a dose of history or culture, squeeze in a guided tour of Hacienda La Esperanza, a restored sugar plantation, or a visit to Hacienda Don Carmelo, either a short drive from Dorado.

If You Have 2 Days

Head to the town of Guavate via Route 184, where you'll find a string of open-air eateries serving lechón. On weekends the roads are jammed with people from San Juan and Ponce sampling Puerto Rican comfort food. Spend the night at Aibonito or Barranquitas; then, on Day 2, visit the Cañón de San Cristóbal and the Bosque Estatal de Toro Negro. Stop for photos along the way, pulling over at one of the *miradores*, or lookout points.

If You Have 3 Days

Set up base camp at one of the converted coffee plantations near Utuado. Make sure to explore the area's sights, like the Parque Ceremonial Indígena de Caguana. If it's a weekend, take a boat ride across Lago Dos Bocas. On Day 2, explore the trails that crisscross Bosque Estatal de Toro Negro, near Jayuya. On Day 3, head to Maricao, where you'll find the spectacular Bosque Estatal de Maricao; this state forest is one of the island's most important bird-watching destinations.

virtually nonexistent outside San Juan, and when it is available, it's rarely reliable. A map and a sense of adventure will be your greatest assets.

Sights

Hacienda Don Carmelo

FARM/RANCH | Hacienda Don Carmelo means different things to different people. To couples getting married, it's a gorgeous backdrop for a dream wedding. To jockeys and horse lovers, it's a school of equestrian art and a venue for the finest horse shows on the island (tours are offered on the first Saturday of the month). And to visitors who just happen to stop by on their travels along Puerto Rico's northern coast, it's a pleasant opportunity to take a break from the traffic and enjoy a walk through the 60-acre property, which yields to views of the Atlantic Ocean. The branches of a 130-year-old tree hold a beautiful tree house. If the property looks vaguely familiar, you might have seen it before: the hacienda appeared on Anthony Bourdain's *No Reservations.* ✉ *Rd. 670, Km. 8.2, Vega Baja, about 15 miles west of Dorado* ☎ *787/991–7044* 🎫 *Tours $15.*

Hacienda La Esperanza

FARM/RANCH | One of several Conservation Trust properties around the island is a restored sugar plantation with a functioning steam engine, which once powered the sugarcane press, increasing production fourfold. Listed on the National Register of Historic Places, the hacienda requires an appointment for tours, but visitors with a little time will find it a worthwhile opportunity to learn a great deal about the bittersweet role of sugar in Puerto Rican and Caribbean history. ✉ *616 Calle La Esperanza, Manatí, about 40 km (25 miles) west of Dorado* ☎ *787/854–2679, 787/722–5834* 🌐 *www.paralanaturaleza.org* 🎫 *Tours $12–$18*

⌚ *Tours not offered every day and must be booked ahead.*

Museo de Arte e Historia de Dorado (*Art and History Museum of Dorado*)
MUSEUM | Dorado isn't known as one of Puerto Rico's archaeological centers, but visitors to this museum learn that indigenous communities existed not just in the interior, but along the northern coast, too. This modest museum displays a group of artifacts that were discovered near a beachfront rock formation called El Ojo del Buey (still visible today); these include the skeletal remains of "La India," a young woman from the pre-Taíno period. ✉ *Calle Mendéz Vigo at Juan Francisco, Dorado* ☎ *787/796–5740* 🎫 *Free* ⌚ *Closed Sun. and Mon.*

Beaches

Playa Breñas
BEACH—SIGHT | This exceptional strand is known for surfing, but adventurous swimmers also enjoy the waves. The beach itself is crescent-shape, and its toast-color sands are a popular backdrop for local photo shoots. **Amenities:** none. **Best for:** surfing. ✉ *Rte. 693, Km 10.8.*

Playa Cerro Gordo
BEACH—SIGHT | The 2,500-foot-long beach, one of Puerto Rico's government-administered *balnearios,* is a crescent-shape stretch of groomed sand lined with cliffs. It's very popular and can get crowded on weekends. Take care if you intend to scramble around on the rocks; currents here are strong, and it's not uncommon for crashing waves to wash over the rocks unexpectedly. This beach also has a large camping area and some facilities, including food kiosks that tend to be open only on busy days. **Amenities:** food and drink; toilets. **Best for:** walking. ✉ *End of Rte. 90.*

Playa Los Tubos
BEACH—SIGHT | This beach is popular for both swimming and surfing, but take care with the strong current. There's a summer festival with live music and water-sports competitions here, normally the first week of July. Lots of local scuba instructors hold classes and do dive certifications here as well. **Amenities:** parking (no fee). **Best for:** snorkeling; surfing; swimming. ✉ *Rte. 687, Vega Baja.*

★ **Playa Mar Chiquita**
BEACH—SIGHT | The beaches along Puerto Rico's northern coast are unique in that many of them are formed from natural pools surrounded by limestone walls that protect these swimming holes from the rough waters of the Atlantic Ocean. Food trucks selling all of PR's fave fried goodies are always set up here, and arts vendors come out on the weekends when the beach is busier. The water gets rough in the winter months, and swimming may not always be a good idea. **Amenities:** food and drink; parking (no fee). **Best for:** snorkeling; swimming; walking ✉ *Rte. 684.*

Playa Sardinera
BEACH—SIGHT | This Dorado beach—not to be confused with a beach by the same name in the northwestern town of Isabela—is suitable for swimming and has shade trees, changing rooms, and restrooms, although it's certainly not top-of-class among northern coast beaches. **Amenities:** food and drink; lifeguards; parking (fee); showers; toilets. **Best for:** swimming. ✉ *End of Rte. 697.*

★ **Pozo de las Mujeres**
BEACH—SIGHT | Pozo de las Mujeres is another natural North Coast swimming hole protected by rock formations. This beach is almost split in two by the rock formations. On the left-hand side, the water is shallow, calm, and protected from the rougher waters outside the natural barricade. On the right-hand side, however, the rocks do not form a protective barrier and the water is much rougher year-round. **Amenities:** parking (no fee). **Best for:** snorkeling; swimming; walking. ✉ *Tierras Nuevas Poniente.*

Restaurants

★ El Ladrillo

$$$ | **STEAKHOUSE** | Original paintings cover brick walls (*ladrillo* means "brick") from floor to ceiling at this steak house, popular among locals for more than 40 years. It's known primarily for steaks—and offers an excellent filet mignon—but given its location on the northern coast, there's also a wide selection of fresh seafood. **Known for:** filet mignon; ample wine cellar; zarzuela. *Average main: $24 ✉ 334 Calle Mendéz Vigo, Dorado ☎ 787/796–2120 🌐 www.elladrillorest.com ⏲ Closed Mon.*

★ Grappa

$$$ | **ITALIAN** | Dorado's most charming restaurant—and perhaps the most appealing one on the northern coast—Grappa is spectacular, both in design and on the plate. Specializing in Italian fare, the kitchen staff make pasta by hand and serve it with fruits of the sea or delicious, tender beef. **Known for:** fresh seafood; housemade pastas; romantic setting. *Average main: $25 ✉ 247 Calle Mendéz Vigo, Dorado ☎ 787/796–2674 ⏲ Closed Mon. and Tues.*

Mi Casa

$$$ | **PUERTO RICAN** | The homey name of Chef José Andrés's first restaurant outside the continental U.S. belies its sophisticated fare, which, while drawing on local ingredients and ideas, is characterized by his many international influences. Take, for instance, the lechón appetizer: it's presented in a steamed bun, drizzled with mayonnaise made from chayote. **Known for:** lechón; fresh seafood; squid-ink pasta with shrimp and cuttlefish. *Average main: $30 ✉ Dorado Beach, a Ritz-Carlton Reserve, 100 Dorado Beach Dr., Dorado ☎ 787/278–7217 🌐 www.ritzcarlton.com.*

Hotels

★ Dorado Beach, A Ritz-Carlton Reserve

$$$$ | **RESORT** | This resort's big draws include a restaurant from Chef José Andrés and a setting along 5 km (3 miles) of Puerto Rican coastline. **Pros:** all rooms are beachfront; activities galore; excellent spa and gourmet dining. **Cons:** $95 daily resort fee; exceedingly expensive; occasional service lapses. *Rooms from: $1,399 ✉ 100 Dorado Beach Dr., Dorado ☎ 787/626–1100 🌐 www.ritzcarlton.com ⇨ 114 rooms 🍽 No meals.*

Embassy Suites by Hilton Dorado del Mar Beach Resort

$$$ | **HOTEL** |**FAMILY** | This resort, directly on the beach, is much like an Embassy Suites anywhere else in the world, offering a consistent, quality experience but little local flavor. **Pros:** on a gorgeous beach; breakfast and happy hour included; suites have kitchenettes. **Cons:** chain-hotel feel; noisy common areas; limited on-site food options. *Rooms from: $259 ✉ 201 Dorado del Mar Blvd., Dorado ☎ 787/796–6125 🌐 embassysuites3.hilton.com ⇨ 209 suites 🍽 Free Breakfast.*

Hyatt Residence Club Dorado, Hacienda del Mar

$$$ | **RENTAL** | This Hyatt-branded vacation club features studio, one-, and two-bedroom condos. **Pros:** lots of peace and quiet; beachfront setting; great golf. **Cons:** perhaps a bit too isolated; need to drive off-site for additional dining options; $20 resort fee added for each night's stay. *Rooms from: $259 ✉ 301 Rte. 693, Dorado ☎ 787/796–3000 🌐 www.hyattresidenceclub.com ⇨ 82 suites 🍽 No meals 💳 No credit cards.*

Shopping

Puerto Rico Premium Outlets

OUTLET/DISCOUNT STORES | About 20 minutes from Dorado via Highway 22 at Exit 55 in the town of Barceloneta is

The tony Dorado Beach, A Ritz-Carlton Reserve resort, was originally developed by Laurance Rockefeller, who opened it as the Caribbean's first eco-resort on an expansive 1,400-acre former plantation in 1958.

Puerto Rico's first factory-outlet mall. Puerto Rico Premium Outlets is a pastel village of more than 40 stores selling discounted merchandise from such familiar names as Polo, Calvin Klein, the Gap, Nautica, Perry Ellis, Puma, and Tommy Hilfiger. ✉ *Hwy. 2, Km 54.8, Barceloneta* ☎ *787/846–5300* 🌐 *www.premiumoutlets.com/outlet/puerto-rico.*

Activities

GOLF

TPC Dorado Beach

GOLF | Three 18-hole regulation courses blend Caribbean luxury and great golf at this iconic property with a storied tradition. Designed by Robert Trent Jones Sr., the famous **East** course, renovated by Robert Trent Jones Jr. in 2011, lies in seaside seclusion along 3 km (2 miles) of northeasterly shore within the former Rockefeller estate. Two Plantation Courses—the **Sugarcane** (more challenging) and **Pineapple** (easier)—complete the offerings. All three were purchased by the Tournament Players Club (TPC) in 2015. ✉ *5000 Plantation Dr., Dorado* ☎ *787/262–1010* 🌐 *www.tpc.com* *East Course $282, Plantation Courses $170* *East Course: 18 holes, 7200 yards, par 72; Sugarcane: 18 holes, 7119 yards, par 72; Pineapple: 18 holes, 6196 yards, par 72.*

Arecibo

60 km (38 miles) west of Dorado

The town of Arecibo was founded in 1515 and is known as the Villa of Capitán Correa because of a battle fought here by Captain Antonio Correa and a handful of Spanish soldiers to repel a British sea invasion in 1702. Today it's a busy manufacturing center, and serves as a link to two fascinating sights—the Parque de las Cavernas del Río Camuy (which is currently closed due to damage caused by Hurricane Maria) and the Arecibo Observatory, both south of the city—as well as deeper exploration of the central mountain region. For one of the best ocean drives on the island, get off the main road at Barceloneta and take Route 681 through Arecibo's waterfront district.

GETTING HERE AND AROUND

To get to Arecibo from San Juan, take Highway 2 or 22 west toward Arecibo. Exit at Arecibo, turn left off the ramp from the highway, and follow signs to the observatory. Note that the hike from the parking lot to the observatory, museum, and shop is a steep one; a free shuttle service is available if you feel you can't make the climb.

Sights

★ **Arecibo Observatory** (*Observatorio de Arecibo*)
OBSERVATORY | Hidden among pine-covered hills, this observatory is home to the world's largest radar radio telescope. Operated by the National Astronomy and Ionosphere Center of Cornell University, the 20-acre dish lies in a 563-foot-deep sinkhole in the karst landscape. If the 600-ton platform hovering eerily over the dish looks familiar, it may come from the movie *Contact*. You can walk around the viewing platform and explore two levels of interactive exhibits on planetary systems, meteors, and weather phenomena in the visitor center. There's also a gift shop. Note that the trail leading to the observatory is extremely steep. Those with difficulty walking or a medical condition can ask at the gate about a courtesy shuttle. ✉ *Rte. 625, Km 3, Arecibo* ☎ *787/878–2612* 🌐 *www.naic.edu* 🎫 *$12* 🕓 *Closed Mon. and Tues.*

Arecibo Water Park
AMUSEMENT PARK/WATER PARK | **FAMILY** | This water park is everything a playground in a hot climate should be: full of sprinklers and wet slides and buckets that drench excited kids with cool water. Its Atlantic Ocean view isn't too bad, either. Parents will want to keep a close eye on their children, as the park has a tendency to fill up quickly and staff are not quite as vigilant as they could be. And be sure to wear sunscreen; there's not a lot of shade here, although umbrellas can be rented for a fee. ✉ *Parque Garcia (aka Parque Julio Rodríguez Olmo), Av. Víctor Rojas, Arecibo* ☎ *787/597–5257* 🎫 *$7* 🕓 *Closed weekdays.*

Cueva Ventana
CAVE | For years this cave was known among locals only, but thanks to social media, their well-kept secret is out. The attraction has since become a bit commercialized, and now a local landowner charges admission. Still, many travelers find the the view worthwhile—it's not called "Window Cave" for nothing (be sure to bring your camera). It's possible to arrange nighttime visits, when the cave is lighted by torches, by calling ahead for reservations. If you purchase VIP tickets you can skip the line and get a bottle of water. ✉ *Rd. 10, Hato Viejo, Arecibo* ☎ *787/322–3554* 🌐 *www.cuevaventanapr.com* 🎫 *$19, VIP tickets $22*

Faro de Arecibo (*Arecibo Lighthouse*)
LIGHTHOUSE | **FAMILY** | A beautiful example of Spanish colonial architecture, the Faro de Arecibo is among the loveliest lighthouses on the island. Dating from 1897, it sits on a bluff high above Arecibo. Although the museum inside the lighthouse has maritime treasures that will interest everyone in your group, the rest of the park is strictly kid stuff. There are scaled-down replicas of Christopher Columbus's *Niña, Pinta,* and *Santa María,* as well as replicas of the huts used by the island's original inhabitants, the Taíno Indians. On weekends, groups in traditional costumes play live music; you can watch the revelry from the sitting area of the café. ✉ *End of Rte. 655, off Rte. 681, Arecibo* ✣ *Follow signs from Hwy. 2* ☎ *787/880–7540* 🌐 *www.arecibolighthouse.com* 🎫 *$12; $3 parking fee.*

Parque de las Cavernas del Río Camuy
CAVE | The 268-acre Parque de las Cavernas del Río Camuy contains one of the world's largest cave networks. A tram takes you down a trail shaded by bamboo

Today, anyone can visit the world's largest radar-radio telescope, the Arecibo Observatory, which includes a 20-acre dish built inside a giant sinkhole.

and banana trees to Cueva Clara, where stalactites and stalagmites turn the entrance into a toothy grin. Hour-long guided tours in English and Spanish lead you on foot through the 180-foot-high cave, which is teeming with wildlife. You're likely to see blue-eyed river crabs and long-legged tarantulas. More elusive are the more than 100,000 bats that make their home in the cave; they don't come out until dark, but you can feel the heat they generate at the cave's entrance (not to mention smell their presence). The visit ends with a tram ride to Tres Pueblos sinkhole, where you can see the third-longest underground river in the world pass from one cave to another. Tours are first-come, first-served; plan to arrive early on weekends, when local families join the crowds. Tours are sometimes canceled if it's raining, as the steep walkways can get slippery. There's a picnic area, cafeteria, and gift shop. ⚠ **The caverns have been closed due to heavy damage from Hurricane Maria in 2017; do not visit unless you have verified that they have reopened.** ✉ *Rte. 129, Km 18.9, Camuy* ☎ *787/898–3100* 🎫 *$18* 🕒 *Closed Mon. and Tues.*

Restaurants

El Buen Cafe

$$ | PUERTO RICAN | Often packed with locals, especially on weekends, this diner near Hatillo makes a good pit stop to refuel. You can sit at the curvy counter or at one of the cozy booths. **Known for:** carne mechada; red snapper with rice and beans; breakfast. $ *Average main: $15* ✉ *Parador El Buen, 381 Hwy. 2, Km 84, Hatillo* ☎ *787/898–1000* 🌐 *www.paradorelbuencafe.com.*

Gustitos Criollos

$ | PUERTO RICAN | This popular restaurant specializes in value-priced Puerto Rican favorites, including daily specials ranging from *sancocho* (root-vegetable stew) to pork chops with plantains and rice and beans. Portions are generous, service is attentive, and the atmosphere is ultra-casual. **Known for:** large portions; casual setting; great coffee. $ *Average main:*

$8 ✉ *Hwy. 2, Km 65.9* ☎ *787/815–0804*
⏲ *No dinner.*

Utuado

32 km (20 miles) south of Arecibo, 24 km (15 miles) northwest of Jayuya.

Utuado was named after a local Taíno chief, Otoao. Surrounded by mountains and dotted with blue lakes, the town of Utuado sits in the middle of lush, natural beauty. The drive along Route 10 between Arecibo and Utuado is an experience—imposing brown limestone cliffs flank the road, and clouds often hover around the tops of the surrounding hills. Utuado's narrow and sometimes busy streets lead to a double-steepled church on the main plaza. The best sights, however, are outside town along winding side roads.

■ TIP→ Give yourself plenty of time when navigating the Ruta Panorámica (Panoramic Route), which runs through the Cordillera Central. Almost all segments of the route are marked by hairpin curves and bridges originally built for horse-drawn carts. The area also sustained significant damage during Hurricane Maria.

GETTING HERE AND AROUND

As with almost everywhere in Puerto Rico, the best way to get to and around Utuado is by car. Public transportation is all but nonexistent, commonly difficult, and unreliable, especially for visitors.

Sights

Bosque Estatal de Río Abajo (*Río Abajo State Forest*)
NATURE SITE | In the middle of karst country, the Bosque Estatal de Río Abajo spans some 5,000 acres and includes huge bamboo stands and native silk-cotton trees. It also has several plantations of Asian teak, Dominican and Honduran mahogany, and Australian pine, which are part of a government tree management program that supplies wood for the local economy (primarily for artisans and fence builders). Walking trails wind through the forest, one of the habitats of the rare Puerto Rican parrot. An information office is near the entrance, and a recreation area with picnic tables is farther down the road. ✉ *Rte. 621, Km 4.4, Utuado* ☎ *787/817–0984* 🌐 *www.drna.pr.gov.*

Lago Dos Bocas
BODY OF WATER | East of Bosque Estatal de Río Abajo is Lago Dos Bocas, one of several man-made lakes near Utuado. Government-operated boats take you around the U-shape lake from a dock, called El Embarcadero, near the intersection of Routes 123 and 146. Although the boats are used primarily as public transit for residents, the 45-minute ride around the lake is pleasant and scenic, and gets you to a shoreline restaurant known for criollo cuisine and seafood. Boats are free and leave daily 7–5. Trips after 3 pm are usually reserved for residents and returning passengers. The lake is stocked with sunfish, bass, and catfish; you can also fish from the shore. ✉ *Off Rte. 10, accessed via Rtes. 621, 123, 146, and 612, Utuado* ☎ *787/879–1838 El Embarcadero.*

Parque Ceremonial Indígena de Caguana
ARCHAEOLOGICAL SITE | This 13-acre site was used more than 800 years ago by the Taíno tribes for worship and recreation, including a game—thought to have religious significance—that resembles modern-day soccer. Today you can see a dozen *bateyes* (ball courts) of various sizes, as well as some large stone monoliths carved with petroglyphs. Archaeologists believe this may have been one of the most important ceremonial sites for the Taíno people. ✉ *Rte. 111, Km 12.3, Utuado* ☎ *787/894–7325* 🎟 *$5.*

Activities

HIKING

Expediciones Tanamá
WATER SPORTS | This company leads half- and full-day excursions into the

Río Tanamá underground-cave system. Guides speak limited English but are friendly and eager. Lunch is included. There's a free camping site adjacent to the office, which provides electricity and bathrooms. ✉ *Rte. 111, Km 14.5, Barrio Angeles* ☎ *787/462–4121* 🌐 *www.tanamariveradventures.com.*

Jayuya

24 km (15 miles) southeast of Utuado.

Jayuya is a small town in the foothills of the Cordillera Central, Puerto Rico's tallest mountain range. Cerro de Punta, the island's highest peak, looms to the south of the town center. Named after the Taíno chief Hauyua, Jayuya is known for preserving its Indian heritage, drawing people from all over the island for its yearly Indigenous Festival in November, which features crafts, exhibits, parades, music, and dancing. Coffee is still grown in the area—look for the locally produced Tres Picachos.

GETTING HERE AND AROUND

As with other areas outside of metropolitan San Juan, it's best to get to and around Jayuya by car. The Puerto Rico Travel Map, free and available at most hotels, should be adequate to get you to the town.

Sights

Bosque Estatal de Toro Negro (*Toro Negro State Forest*)
NATIONAL/STATE PARK | The main attraction of the 7,000-acre "Black Bull" State Forest is the island's crowning glory: 4,398-foot Cerro de Punta. Toro Negro also has the island's highest lake, Lago Guineo, and one of the most impressive waterfalls, the 200-foot Salto de Doña Juana. The best place to start is at the ranger station on Route 143. Be sure to ask the friendly staffers for a map; the trails—like the one that leads from the ranger station to an observation tower with views of the northern and southern sides of the island—are not always well marked. There are more trails east of the ranger station, at the Area Recreacional Doña Juana. Keep an eye out for exotic birds, such as the Guadalupe woodpecker. The reserve also contains a huge swimming pool (often out-of-service) built into a mountainside. Note that some trails have not been fully cleared or restored following Hurricane Maria's devastation in 2017. ✉ *Rte. 143, Km 32.4* ☎ *787/867–3040* *Free.*

La Piedra Escrita (*Written Stone*)
ARCHAEOLOGICAL SITE | This huge boulder with a handful of highly visible Taíno petroglyphs is located in a stream among several other large rocks. There are several viewing areas and a shady spot for a picnic lunch. Don't worry: the boulder in the parking lot painted a lurid shade of blue is *not* La Piedra Escrita. ✉ *Rte. 144, Km 7.8.*

Museo El Cemí (*Cemí Museum*)
ARCHAEOLOGICAL SITE | This could be the oddest building in Puerto Rico. Named for a Taíno artifact believed to have religious significance, the tiny structure resembles the snail-like *cemí*—you enter through its mouth. The collection, however, is only mildly interesting; it consists of religious and ceremonial objects of the Taíno found on the island. ✉ *Rte. 144, Km 9.3* ☎ *787/828–1241* *$2.*

Hotels

Parador Hacienda Gripiñas
$ | **B&B/INN** | Built on the grounds of a coffee plantation, this 19th-century inn is surrounded on all sides by mountain peaks. **Pros:** set amid coffee fields; interesting, historic building; great meals included in rate. **Cons:** isolated location; Wi-Fi doesn't reach all rooms; accommodations are simple and rustic. *Rooms from: $98* ✉ *Rte. 152, Km 1.7* ☎ *787/828–1717* *19 rooms* *Free Breakfast.*

Did You Know?

The Toro Negro State Forest has the island's highest mountain, the 4,398-foot Cerro de Punta; the island's highest lake, Lago Guineo; and its most impressive waterfall, the 200-foot Doña Juana Falls.

Adjuntas

27 km (17 miles) southwest of Jayuya

The coffee-growing town of Adjuntas sits north of Puerto Rico's Ruta Panorámica. It's also the world's leading producer of citron, a fruit whose rind is processed here and then shipped for use in sweets. Few tourists do more than drive through the town itself, but it has a quaint central plaza and a sporadic trolley used mostly by locals and school children.

GETTING HERE AND AROUND

A rental car is really the only way to get to and around Adjuntas and neighboring towns. Town trolleys are great for getting a sense of the local landscape, but aren't viable modes of transportation.

Sights

Bosque Estatal de Guilarte (*Guilarte State Forest*)

NATIONAL/STATE PARK | Hiking trails surrounded by wild impatiens lead up to the 3,900-foot Pico Guilarte and elsewhere in this state forest. Bird-watchers have 26 different species to look for, including the carpenter bird. If your interest is botany, you can find a variety of trees, such as candlewood, trumpet, Honduran mahogany, and Honduran pine. ⚠ **Many trails are still being restored following 2017's Hurricane Maria, so hike with caution.** ✉ *Rte. 518 at Rte. 131, Adjuntas* ☎ *787/829–5767.*

Hotels

Parador Villas Sotomayor

$ | RESORT | If you're looking for a natural setting in which to relax and forget about the stress of city life, look no further than these cabinlike villas amid 14 lush acres of rolling hills. **Pros:** friendly staff; great for kids; gym offers Spin and dance classes. **Cons:** many bugs; noise from neighboring villas; rustic setting won't appeal to all guests. [$] *Rooms from: $122* ✉ *Carretera 123, Km 56, at Int. 522, Km 0.2, Adjuntas* ☎ *787/829–1717* 🌐 *www.paradorvillassotomayor.com* *35 villas* *No meals.*

Aibonito

78 km (48 miles) east of Adjuntas

Legend has it that Aibonito got its name when a Spaniard exclaimed, "*¡Ay, que bonito!*" (Oh, how pretty!) upon seeing the valley where the town now stands. At 1,896 feet above sea level, it's Puerto Rico's highest city. A double-steepled cathedral graces the charming town square. Local guides organize outings to the nearby Cañón de San Cristóbal. Aibonito is known as "The Queen of Flowers" because flowering plants thrive in its temperate climate. The city hosts a flower festival every year, usually in late June or July, and gives awards for blossoms and garden design.

GETTING HERE AND AROUND

Aibonito is best explored by car. Forgo any promises made by public transportation, and take the reins yourself.

Sights

Cañón de San Cristóbal

LOCAL INTEREST | The canyon may be difficult to find, but it's well worth the effort. Trails of tropical vegetation lead to a breathtaking waterfall. ✉ *Rte. 725, Km 5.1, Aibonito* ☎ *787/857–2065.*

Mirador Piedra Degetau (*Degetau Lookout Rock*)

VIEWPOINT | Degetau Lookout Rock is a scenic point near Aibonito. From the tower, use the telescope to get a closer look at the surrounding mountains. You'll find picnic tables under gazebos and a playground nearby. ✉ *Rte. 7718, Km 0.7, Aibonito* ☎ *787/735–3880.*

Chapter 7

RINCÓN AND THE PORTA DEL SOL

Updated by
Paulina Salach

Sights ★★★★★

Restaurants ★★★☆☆

Hotels ★★★★☆

Shopping ★☆☆☆☆

Nightlife ★★☆☆☆

WELCOME TO RINCÓN AND THE PORTA DEL SOL

TOP REASONS TO GO

★ **Visit El Combate:** Hike to the lighthouse at this peninsula, which juts out into the Caribbean Sea.

★ **Savor the area's delicious eatries:** From food trucks to farm-to-table restaurants to simple roadside stands, the west has great dining and snacking options.

★ **Delight your palate at the "Golden Mile":** Sample fresh seafood at any of the oceanfront eateries in Joyuda.

★ **Catch a wave at Playa Tres Palmas:** Challenge the waves here or at any of Rincón's world-famous surfing spots.

★ **Explore Desecheo Island or Mona Island:** Enjoy snorkeling, diving, or fishing around these spectacular islands.

The speedy Route 22 and the more meandering Route 2 head west from San Juan and swing around the northwestern part of the island. After Arecibo, Route 2 continues along the coast, where the ragged shoreline holds some of the island's best surfing beaches; a steady contingent of surfers in Aguadilla and Rincón gives the area a laid-back atmosphere. Past Mayagüez, Route 100 leads to an area known as Cabo Rojo, where you'll find seaside communities like Joyuda, Boquerón, and El Combate.

1 Rincón. The first World Surfing Championships in 1968 put Rincón on the map, and its laid-back vibe and epic waves have kept it there. Paddle out to one of the town's 15 surf spots, or experience horseback riding on the beach and fishing in the crystal Caribbean waters. One of Rincón's greatest attractions is the diving and snorkeling at nearby Desecheo Island.

2 Mayagüez. Stroll the marble-paved square of Plaza Colón, where a statue of Christopher Columbus commemorates the site where he allegedly disembarked. Experience an artistic performance at the Teatro Yagüez, which dates back to 1909. Savor the flavor of Mayagüez by sampling traditional *brazo gitano* (gypsy arm) jelly rolls baked at the century-old Ricomini Bakery.

3 Joyuda. This small fishing village is known for its fresh seafood and incredible ocean views. The sunsets are breathtaking.

4 Boquerón. Minutes away from Cabo Rojo, Boquerón is perfect for a relaxing getaway. Quiet during the week, this town comes alive on weekends; visit one of the many oceanfront dining options for fresh seafood after a day spent at Playa Buyé.

5 El Combate. Locals flock to the edge of the island's southwest coast to soak up the sun at beaches like Playa Sucia and El Combate.

6 Aguadilla. Surfers from all over the world fly to Aguadilla to surf some of the Island's best waves at Wilderness, Crashboat, and Gas Chamber beaches.

7 Isabela. You can surf, hike, golf, or just bake on the beach in this small town on the Island's northwest coast. The area is also home to the Guajataca Forest Reserve.

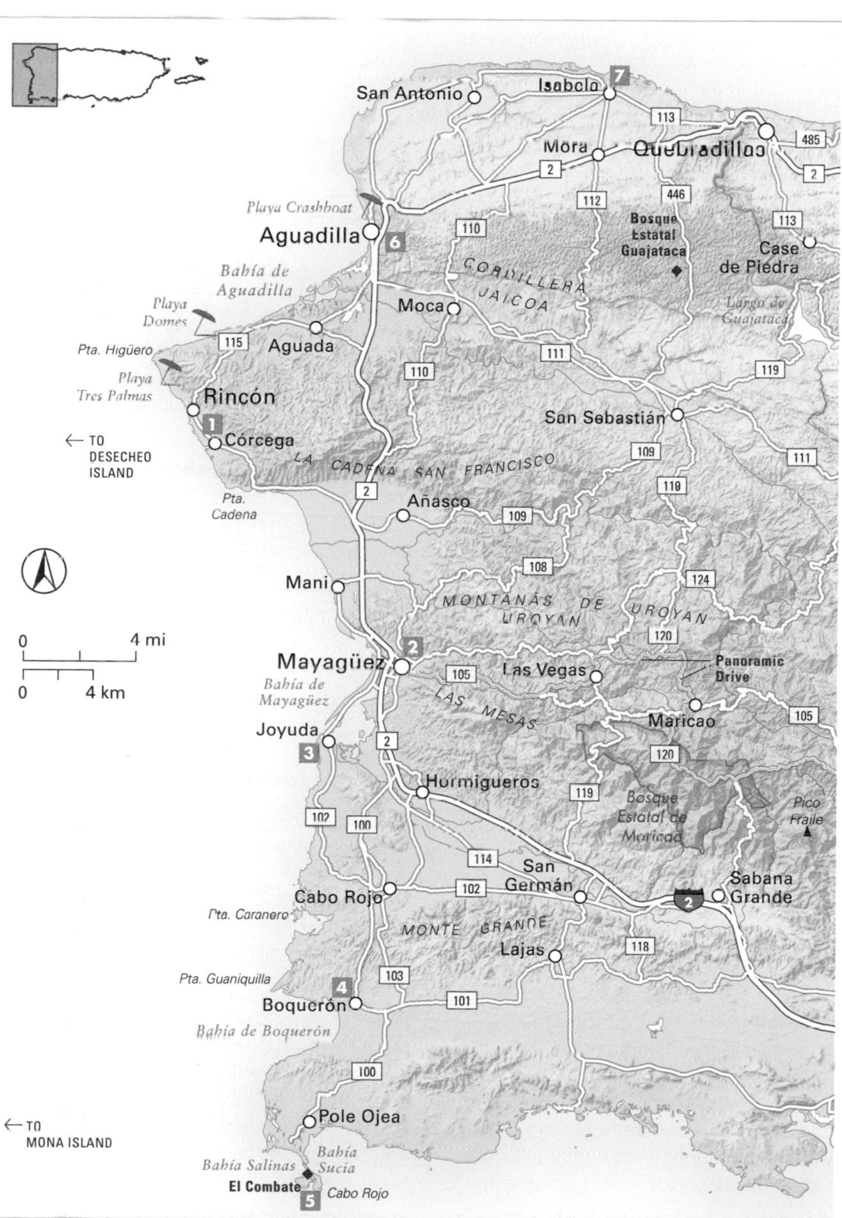
San Antonio
Isabela
Mora
Quebradillas
Playa Crashboat
Aguadilla
Bahía de Aguadilla
Playa Domes
Pta. Higüero
Playa Tres Palmas
Aguada
Moca
Bosque Estatal Guajataca
Case de Piedra
Lago de Guajataca
CORDILLERA JAICOA
Rincón
Córcega
TO DESECHEO ISLAND
San Sebastián
LA CADENA SAN FRANCISCO
Pta. Cadena
Añasco
Mani
MONTAÑAS DE UROYAN
Mayagüez
Bahía de Mayagüez
Las Vegas
Panoramic Drive
LAS MESAS
Maricao
Joyuda
Hormigueros
Bosque Estatal de Maricao
Pico Fraile
San Germán
Sabana Grande
Cabo Rojo
Pta. Caranero
MONTE GRANDE
Lajas
Pta. Guaniquilla
Boquerón
Bahía de Boquerón
Pole Ojea
TO MONA ISLAND
Bahía Salinas
Bahía Sucia
El Combate
Cabo Rojo
0 4 mi
0 4 km
1
2
3
4
5
6
7
113
485
2
446
112
110
113
115
111
119
110
109
111
110
109
108
124
120
105
105
120
119
102
100
114
102
118
103
101
100

"La Porta del Sol" is how tourism officials describe the island's western coast—but the Gateway to the Sun is still not nearly as well known as the area around San Juan. Even at Rincón, which has the lion's share of lodging, the beaches are delightfully deserted. And in places like Aguadilla and Isabela, two sleepy towns on the northwestern corner of the island, it's easy to find a stretch of shoreline all to yourself.

Since the time of Christopher Columbus, adventurers have been drawn to the jagged coastline of northwestern Puerto Rico. Columbus first stopped here on his second voyage to the Americas in 1493. His exact landing point is the subject of ongoing dispute: both Aguadilla, on the northernmost tip of the coast, and Aguada, just south of Aguadilla, claim the historic landing, and both have monuments honoring the explorer.

Less than a century ago western Puerto Rico was still overwhelmingly rural—a few larger fruit plantations dotting the coast, while farther inland coffee was grown on hillside *fincas* (farms). The slow pace of rural life began to change in the mid-20th century, as new roads brought development to once-isolated towns. They also brought international surfers, who were amazed to find some of the world's best waves in Rincón, Isabela, and Aguadilla. Now there are top-notch hotels, interesting natural areas to explore, and almost every kind of water sport imaginable.

MAJOR REGIONS

Rincón is Puerto Rico's surfing capital and attracts a wide range of travelers, from backpackers to families to honeymooners.

Mayagüez was once a textile and tuna-processing center, two industries that are long gone now, and the city is better known for its university and a handful of interesting historical sights.

The Cabo Rojo region at the island's southwestern corner is known for its low-key small towns (including Joyuda, Boquerón, and El Combate), inexpensive hotels, beautiful beaches, opportunities for outdoor activities, and waterfront restaurants.

North of Rincón along the island's Northwestern Coast are less developed beaches with modest hotels that have appealed historically to local families. Some say the waves here are better than south in Rincón itself. The major destinations are Aquadilla and Isabela.

Planning

WHEN TO GO

Winter brings the best weather—plus it's the height of the surfing season—so you'll need to book well in advance. Between December and March you may get a glimpse of the humpback whales off the coast. In summer the weather gets hot, especially in August and September, and many family-oriented hotels fill up with *sanjuaneros* escaping the city for the weekend. Some hotels require a two-night stay, and larger resorts normally drop their rates by at least 10% during this time of year.

GETTING HERE AND AROUND

AIR TRAVEL

Aguadilla is a convenient gateway to western Puerto Rico, thanks to several daily international flights. United Airlines flies from Newark (EWR) to Aguadilla, Spirit flies from Fort Lauderdale (FLL), and JetBlue has daily service from Orlando (MCO) or New York–JFK to Aguadilla. Cape Air flies between San Juan and Mayagüez.

Transfers: There are no airport shuttles in either Aguadilla or Mayagüez. A taxi from either airport into town is about $10, but if you are going any farther, you should rent a car.

AIRLINES Cape Air. ☎ *800/227–3247* 🌐 *www.flycapeair.com.* **JetBlue.** ☎ *800/538–2583* 🌐 *www.jetblue.com.* **Spirit Airlines.** ☎ *801/401–2200* 🌐 *www.spirit.com.* **United Airlines.** ☎ *800/525–0280* 🌐 *www.united.com.*

AIRPORTS Aeropuerto Eugenio María de Hostos (*MAZ*). ✉ *Rte. 2, Km 148.7, Mayagüez* ☎ *787/833–0148.* **Aeropuerto Internacional Rafael Hernández** (*BQN*). ✉ *Hangar Rd. between Rtes. 110 and 107, off Rte. 2, Km 148.7, Aguadilla* ☎ *787/891–2286, 787/890–6075.*

BUS AND VAN TRAVEL

There is no easy bus network linking the towns of the Porta del Sol region as there is in San Juan. Renting a car is easy and relatively inexpensive if booked in advance.

CAR TRAVEL

You really need a car to see northwestern Puerto Rico, especially the areas in the mountains. The toll road, Route 22, makes it easy to reach Arecibo from San Juan. Route 22 turns into Route 2 just after Arecibo, swings by the northwestern tip of the island, then heads south to Mayagüez. If you don't rent in San Juan, major agencies are represented at both of the area's main airports, in both Aguadilla and Mayagüez.

TAXI TRAVEL

Taxis can be hailed near the main plaza in Mayagüez, but they may be hard to come by in smaller towns. Check with your hotel or restaurant, and the staff may be able to call one for you.

HOTELS

The western part of the island near Rincón has a variety of hotels, from furnished villas geared toward families to beachfront hotels ideal for honeymooners. Interior design leaves much to be desired, however, as most rooms are decorated with faux wood, sun-bleached photographs, floral bedding, and white linoleum flooring. Fortunately, some of the newer accommodations resemble Spanish villas, a refreshing change from the typical 1970s decor. Few hotels provide Internet access, usually in common areas only, when they do. Smaller beach cottages, especially in Rincón, usually have "adopted" dogs or cats roaming the premises, so guests with allergies may want to inquire ahead of time.

VILLA RENTALS

Villa rentals are becoming more and more popular in Rincón. Because many people come here for a week or more to surf, find a secluded spot on the beach, or just hang out, renting a villa makes perfect sense. Guests can make the place their own, without worrying about their noisy kids bothering the people in the next room or leaving sandy shoes outside the door. In the long run, it might also be a money-saver for those who like to cook at home rather than dine out. There are several local chefs who will prepare gourmet dinners for large groups in private villas.

There are a few things to keep in mind, however. If you're looking for a secluded location, you won't find it on such a crowded part of the coast; it's likely that your neighbor will be within shouting distance. In addition, few villas are actually on the ocean, and those that are go for a premium price. Many are within walking distance of the water, but others require a drive to reach the shore—if a beachfront location is important to you, make that clear. Lastly, where you stay will depend on whether or not you're a surfer. Those who like to ride the waves favor the northern coast, while those who want to snorkel, scuba dive, or swim prefer the calmer southern shore.

Island West Properties
Around for years, this office rents villas in Rincón by the day, week, or month. ✉ *Rte. 413, Km 0.7, Rincón* ☎ *787/823–2323* 🌐 *www.rinconrealestateforsale.com.*

RESTAURANTS

If you like seafood, you're in the right place. Throughout northwestern Puerto Rico you'll find wonderful *comida criolla* (Puerto Rican creole) cuisine. Most local eateries serve deep-fried tapas, commonly called *frituras* (fritters). Dozens of foreign-owned eateries offer relief from the usual fried fare, serving everything from sushi and hamburgers to vegetarian and Thai. Farther south along the coast options are limited, so you may want to ask the chef to grill or sauté your fish.

A trip to Puerto Rico is not complete without sampling Puerto Rico's most iconic dish, *mofongo relleno,* made from fried, seasoned, and mashed plantain or yuca stuffed with your choice of seafood or meat. Simply head to where locals from all over the island go for fresh seafood: Joyuda. When it comes to beverages, locals usually drink rum and coke, or rum and fresh-squeezed orange or grapefruit juice. You'll also see people sipping on Medalla Light, Puerto Rico's most popular and affordable beer. All restaurants are no-smoking. Gratuity is not usually included in the bill, but it's always wise to double-check; unless it is, tip the customary 15%–20%.

HOTEL AND RESTAURANT PRICES

Hotel and restaurant reviews have been shortened. For full information visit Fodors.com.

What It Costs in U.S. Dollars

	$	$$	$$$	$$$$
RESTAURANTS	under $12	$12–$20	$21–$30	over $30
HOTELS	under $150	$150–$250	$251–$350	over $350

SAFETY

Unless you're camping in a recreational area, it's best to visit forest reserves during daylight hours only. Outside metro areas there's little crime, but you should take normal precautions: Remember to lock your car, and don't leave valuables unattended.

For Surfers: The waves near Rincón range from gentle, low waves suitable for novice surfers to expert-only breaks. It's a good idea to talk with other surfers about which beaches would be suitable for your skill level.

VISITOR INFORMATION

The Puerto Rico Tourism Company has an office at the airport in Aguadilla. The Cabo Rojo branch is open weekdays 8–4:30. Rincón's tourism office is open weekdays 8–4. Mayagüez has a tourism office in the city hall.

CONTACTS Cabo Rojo Tourism Office. ✉ *Galleria 100, Rte. 100, Km 7.6, Cabo Rojo* ☎ *787/851 7070.* **Isabela Tourism Office.** ☎ *787/872–2100* . **Mayagüez City Hall.** ✉ *Calle Peral, Mayagüez* ☎ *787/834–8585.* **Puerto Rico Tourism Company.** ✉ *Rafael Hernández Airport, 405 Hangar Rd., Aguadilla* ☎ *787/890–3090* 🌐 *www.seepuertorico.com.* **Rincón Tourism Office.** ✉ *Sunset Village, Calle Cambija, next to Balneario de Rincón, Rincón* ☎ *787/823–5024* 🌐 *www.rincon.org.*

Rincón

93 miles (150 km) southwest of San Juan.

Jutting out into the ocean along the rugged western coast, Rincón ("corner" in Spanish) may have gotten its name because it's tucked into a bend of the coastline. Some, however, trace the town's name to Gonzalo Rincón, a 16th-century landowner who let poor families live on his land. Whatever the history, the name suits the town, which is like a little world unto itself.

The most famous hotel in the region is the Horned Dorset Primavera. Although a couple of other larger hotels, including the Rincón of the Seas and Rincón Beach Resort, have been built, Rincón remains a laid-back place. The town is still a mecca for wave-seekers—particularly surfers from the East Coast of the United States, who often prefer the relatively quick New York–Aguadilla flight to the long Pacific haul. The town caters to all sorts of travelers, however, from budget-conscious surfers to families to honeymooners in search of romance.

The pace picks up October–April, when the waves are at their best, but tourists can be found here year-round, and many American mainlanders have settled here. Budget travelers will most likely find discount accommodations in August and September, when tourism is slow. Hurricane season runs June–November, bringing occasional swells for the surf crowd.

GETTING HERE AND AROUND

Rincón itself is a spread-out labyrinth of unmarked streets without any apparent logic to its layout. The city is built on a hillside, so most streets are narrow and steep, weaving erratically through the intermingled residential-business zones. There are three main highways to keep in mind; Route 115 cuts through the middle of "downtown" (the administrative center) and runs north to the Aguadilla airport and south to the Mayagüez airport. Route 413 snakes along the hillsides, past villas and local restaurants. The smaller Route 4413 follows the water, past Punta Higuero Lighthouse, and ends at the Bonus Thermonuclear Energy Plant.

AIR TRAVEL

San Juan's international airport is the most commonly used on the island and is approximately two hours from Rincón. The closest airports, however, are in Mayagüez and Aguadilla—only 20 minutes' drive in either direction. A taxi from either airport into town costs around $10, but the best option is to rent a car at the airport, since you'll need it for transportation during your trip.

BUS AND VAN TRAVEL

Amigos Tours & Travel has private transfers from Aguadilla's airport to Rincón and to most hotels in the Porta del Sol for $80 per van (limit five passengers).

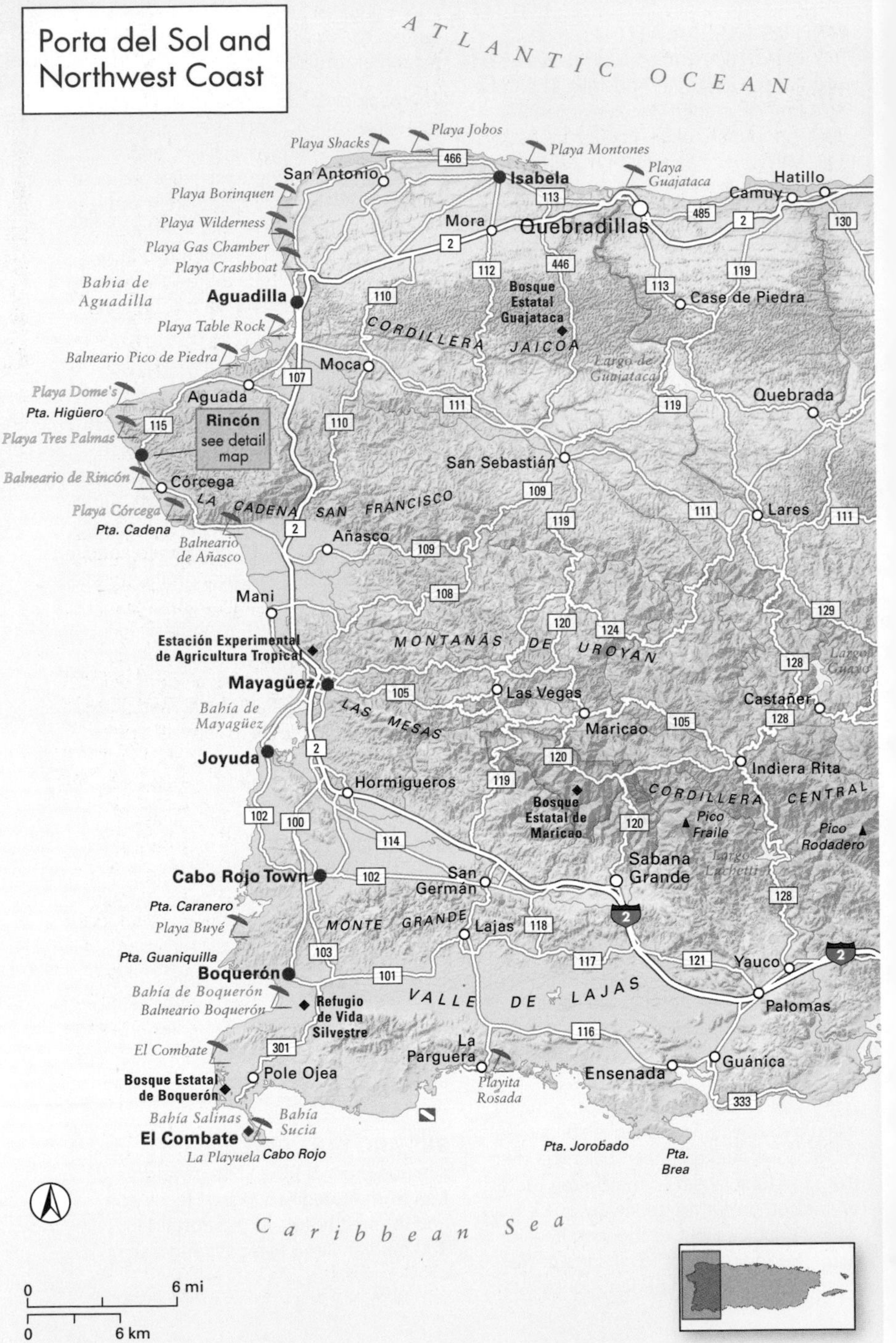

Porta del Sol and Northwest Coast

ATLANTIC OCEAN
Playa Jobos
Playa Shacks
466
Playa Montones
Playa Guajataca
San Antonio
Isabela
Hatillo
Playa Borinquen
113
Camuy
Playa Wilderness
Mora
Quebradillas
485
2
130
Playa Gas Chamber
2
Playa Crashboat
112
446
119
Bahia de Aguadilla
Aguadilla
110
Bosque Estatal Guajataca
113
Case de Piedra
Playa Table Rock
CORDILLERA JAICOA
Balneario Pico de Piedra
Moca
Largo de Guajataca
107
Playa Dome's
Aguada
111
119
Quebrada
Pta. Higüero
115
Rincón see detail map
110
Playa Tres Palmas
San Sebastián
Balneario de Rincón
Córcega
109
LA CADENA SAN FRANCISCO
Playa Córcega
111
Lares
111
119
Pta. Cadena
2
Añasco
Balneario de Añasco
109
108
Mani
129
120
124
Estación Experimental de Agricultura Tropical
MONTAÑAS DE UROYAN
Largo Guayo
128
Mayagüez
105
Las Vegas
Castañer
Bahía de Mayagüez
LAS MESAS
105
128
Maricao
Joyuda
2
120
Indiera Rita
Hormigueros
119
CORDILLERA CENTRAL
Bosque Estatal de Maricao
102
100
120
Pico Fraile
Pico Rodadero
114
Sabana Grande
Largo Luchetti
Cabo Rojo Town
102
San Germán
128
Pta. Caranero
2
Playa Buyé
MONTE GRANDE
Lajas
118
Pta. Guaniquilla
103
117
121
Yauco
2
Boquerón
101
Bahía de Boquerón
Refugio de Vida Silvestre
VALLE DE LAJAS
Palomas
Balneario Boquerón
116
El Combate
301
La Parguera
Guánica
Ensenada
Pole Ojea
Bosque Estatal de Boquerón
Playita Rosada
333
Bahía Salinas
Bahía Sucia
El Combate
Pta. Jorobado
Pta. Brea
La Playuela
Cabo Rojo
Caribbean Sea

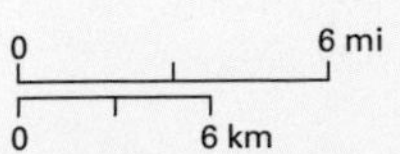

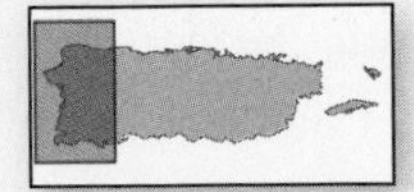

CAR TRAVEL

To reach Rincón from San Juan, take Route 22, which merges Route 2 after Arecibo. Follow it past the northwestern tip of the island, just beyond Aguadilla. Then take Route 115 southwest past Aguada until you reach Rincón's Route 413, "the Road to Happiness."

TIMING

Occupying a total area of 14 square miles (36 square km), Rincón is easily traversable in a single afternoon. Nevertheless, to fully embrace its laid-back surfer vibe you'll want to leave yourself three to five days for surfing, diving, fishing, or just relaxing at the beach.

Desecheo Island

ISLAND | Protected by the U.S. Fish and Wildlife Service, this uninhabited island—about 20 km (13 miles) off the coast of Rincón—is home to lizards, rats, and rhesus monkeys, first introduced in 1967 from Cayo Santiago. Among divers, it's known for abundant reef and fish life; the main draw here is "Candyland," a rocky bottom that rims the island and slopes to 120 feet. Long tunnels and caverns covered with purple hydrocoral distinguish one formation known as Yellow Reef. With visibility of 150 feet, this is also a popular snorkeling spot. Other sites have plentiful fish and coral in shallower water just off Rincón's shores. ✉ *Rincón.*

Parque Pasivo El Faro

LIGHTHOUSE | Surrounding the Faro de Punta Higuero (Rincón's lighthouse), Parque Pasivo El Faro has small kiosks at the water's edge. If you're lucky, you may spot a whale in the distance. (Have patience, though, as it could take days to see one.) You can also glimpse the rusty, mint-color dome of the defunct Bonus Thermonuclear Energy Plant from here; it has been closed since 1968. The park—complete with benches and a refreshment stand—is a nice place to take in sunsets. The lighthouse is closed to the public, but it's hard to walk away without taking a photo of the stately white structure. ✉ *End of Rte. 413* *Free.*

The waves of northwestern Puerto Rico have long played a siren song for traveling surfers. Spared the trade winds that limit surf in other areas, these northwest beaches boast some of the best waves in the world, especially in winter. But you don't have to be a big-wave rider to enjoy the beaches here.

The best beaches north of Rincón follow Route 413 and Route 4413 (the road to the lighthouse). South of town the only beach worth noting is Playa Córcega, off Route 115. As with many other beaches in the Caribbean, there are often urchins, riptides, undertows, and rocky reefs below the surface—never swim alone.

Balneario de Rincón

BEACH—SIGHT | Families enjoy the tranquil waters, playground, and shelters for seaside picnics. The beach is within walking distance to the center of town. **Amenities:** parking (no fee); showers; toilets. **Best for:** sunset; swimming. ✉ *Calle Cambija.*

Domes

BEACH—SIGHT | Named for the eerie green domes on a nearby power plant, this beach is extremely popular with surfers, with its consistent rights and occasional lefts. On a good surf day, arrive early if you want a spot on the sand. Though not recommended for swimmers because of the rocks, it's a great whale-watching spot in winter. The dirt road leading to the parking area is rather steep and difficult to exit. There are no facilities here, so plan accordingly. **Amenities:** none. **Best for:** surfing. ✉ *Rte. 4413, north of the lighthouse.*

Maria's

BEACH—SIGHT | This surf spot, south of Domes, can get crowded when the

The small park surrounding the Faro del Punta Higuero in Rincón is called the Parque Pasivo El Faro. It's a great place to take in the sunset, but you can't enter the lighthouse itself.

waves are high. When waves are small, it serves as a schoolhouse for surf lessons. It's popular with locals, as much for its breaks as for its proximity to the Calypso Café. To get here, look for the street sign reading "Surfer crossing." **Amenities:** none. **Best for:** sunsets; surfing. ✉ *Rte. 4413, south of the lighthouse.*

Playa Córcega

BEACH—SIGHT | The long stretch of yellow sand in front of Villa Cofresí is considered one of the best swimming beaches in Rincón. It's the perfect beach for relaxing and stand-up paddleboarding. **Amenities:** none. **Best for:** swimming; walking. ✉ *Rte. 115, Km 12.*

Steps (*Tres Palmas*)

BEACH—SIGHT | This beach takes its name from the mysterious concrete steps sitting by the water's edge. On calm days, it's an excellent snorkeling spot, home to the Tres Palmas Marine Reserve, and a good place to find sea glass. Waves here break on a shallow reef, and they can get huge. On a handful of days each year, the surf delivers one of the world's best, most epic rides, drawing surfers from around the globe. A small food truck serves coconut water, fish tacos, empanadas, and other treats. The beach is hard to find—look for the turnoff at a whale-shape sign reading "Playa Escalera." **Amenities:** none. **Best for:** snorkeling; sunsets. ✉ *Rte. 413, north of turnoff for Black Eagle Marina.*

Restaurants

Café 413

$$ | ECLECTIC | FAMILY | This multi-cuisine dining locale is coffee shop, restaurant, and bar all in one. Conveniently located right on the town square, it's a great place for a latte, smoothie, wrap, or even a full breakfast or dinner. **Known for:** breakfast; family-friendly dining; gluten-free and vegan choices. $ *Average main: $14* ✉ *157 Calle Progreso* ☎ *939/697–8188* ⏲ *Closed Wed.*

Cafe 2 Go

$ | CAFÉ | For the best coffee in town, make your way to this tiny food cart

Great Itineraries

If You Have 1 Day

If you have only a day for the Puerta del Sol, head to **Joyuda** for some of Puerto Rico's freshest seafood. You probably won't be the only one driving from San Juan for this feast.

If You Have 3 Days

If you have a few days to explore the region, start in **Rincón,** where you'll find accommodations for every taste, from compact inns to sprawling resorts. There isn't too much to see, other than the lighthouse at Parque Pasivo El Faro, but you will see plenty of beautiful beaches. The secret's out about many of them, but if you crave complete solitude, you're more likely to find it on beaches near **Aguadilla** or **Isabela.** On Day 2, drive south to the coastal communities in the Cabo Rojo. Your first stop should be **Joyuda,** where you can choose from dozens of seaside restaurants. After lunch, continue past **Boquerón** to **El Combate.** This is the end of the line, quite literally: the road ends at the lighthouse that once warned sea captains about the treacherous waters around the island's southwestern tip. On Day 3 you can explore more of this windswept landscape, or head offshore for a look at **Mona Island.**

If You Have 5 Days

After spending three days along the western coast, you may be tempted to set sail to one of the islands off the coast. On Day 4, head out on an overnight trip to **Mona Island,** a 14,000-acre paradise known as the "Galápagos of the Caribbean." You'll have to camp on this deserted island, but the view from the 200-foot cliffs on the northern shore makes it all worth it. Trips to Mona Island must be arranged weeks in advance.

off Route 413. Owner Aaron makes an awesome latte using local Puerto Rican coffee. **Known for:** Puerto Rican coffee; açaí bowls; made-to-order fruit smoothies. *Average main: $3* *Rte. 413, Km 0.5* *Closed June–Oct.*

Carta Buena

$ | **VEGETARIAN** | This bright-orange food truck sits on a beautiful green lot with a farm, plantain trees, and the ocean steps away. Fruit smoothies, kale salads, and fresh-pressed juices are served daily. **Known for:** fresh-pressed juices; vegan and vegetarian dishes; on-site garden for some ingredients. *Average main: $7* *Rte. 413, Km. 1.2* *787/679–2365* *www.cartabuena.com* *No credit cards.*

★ The English Rose

$ | **CAFÉ** | **FAMILY** | Open for breakfast only, this quaint bed-and-breakfast has a spectacular view of the valley spilling into the sea. If terrace seating is not available, indoor dining is equally charming, with walls colorfully adorned by the work of local artisans. **Known for:** eggs Benedict; house-baked breads and croissants; beautiful views. *Average main: $10* *Rte. 413, Km 2* *787/823–4032* *www.larosainglesa.com* *Closed Sept. and Oct. Closed Mon.–Wed. May–Aug.*

★ Estela

$$$ | **CARIBBEAN** | On weekends, patrons come from as far as San Juan to dine at this cozy farm-to-table restaurant. Operated by husband-and-wife team Juan and Nerylu, it's found a niche in Rincón offering locally sourced ingredients—you may even see a fisherman pull up with a giant yellowfin tuna. **Known for:** fresh seafood; good wine list; locally sourced

ingredients. $ *Average main: $22* ✉ *Rte. 115, Km 14* ☎ *787/823–1795* ⏲ *Closed Mon. and Tues. No lunch.*

Jack's Shack

$ | **VEGETARIAN** |**FAMILY** | This popular beachfront food cart is located right on Maria's beach, offering a healthy menu that focuses on seasonal ingredients and the catch of the day. Veggie burgers and quinoa salad are also on the menu, but the fish tacos remain a favorite. **Known for:** fish tacos; breakfast burritos; fresh-pressed juices. $ *Average main: $9* ✉ *Maria's Beach, Rte. 4413, Km. 0.5* ☎ *939/274–8066* ⏲ *No dinner.*

La Cambija

$ | **SEAFOOD** |**FAMILY** | This casual roadside restaurant serves the freshest fish in town. Order an assortment of grilled fish skewers, choosing from tuna, mahimahi, grouper, wahoo, and more. **Known for:** grilled fish skewers; housemade empanadas; happy-hour drink prices all day. $ *Average main: $8* ✉ *Calle Cambija, at Calle B* ☎ *787/823–1118.*

La Copa Llena at The Black Eagle

$$$ | **CARIBBEAN** | Right on the beach, La Copa Llena's location draws patrons from all over the island for spectacular sunset views. Whether you choose one of the small plates or an entrée, fresh seafood is always the focus here—and your best bet from the menu. **Known for:** fresh seafood; sunset drinks; great outdoor deck. $ *Average main: $25* ✉ *Black Eagle Rd., off Rte. 413, Km 1.0, Ensenada* ☎ *787/823–0896* 🌐 *www.attheblackeagle.com* ⏲ *Closed Sept. and Oct., and Mon. and Tues. No lunch.*

Mangia Mi

$$ | **ITALIAN** |**FAMILY** | Chef Rebecca White of Food Network's *Cooks vs. Cons* whips up Italian fare at her newest venture in Rincón. The open kitchen allows you to see the staff meticulously preparing each dish between strands of hanging fresh pasta. **Known for:** homemade pastas; good wine list by the bottle; pizza. $ *Average main: $15* ✉ *4 Muñoz Rivera St. E* ☎ *787/823–4812* ⏲ *Closed Wed. No lunch.*

The Pool Bar Sushi

$ | **SUSHI** | One of only a few sushi restaurants on the west coast, the open-air Pool Bar attracts visitors from as far away as San Juan. The menu rivals that of any high-end Japanese restaurant, with mango tuna rolls, eel maki, shumai, and wakame seaweed salads. **Known for:** sushi rolls; fish tacos for lunch; movie night. $ *Average main: $10* ✉ *Pools Beach Cabanas, Rte. 413* ☎ *787/823–2583* 🌐 *www.poolbarsushi.com* ⏲ *Closed Thurs. No lunch in low season.*

Shipwreck Bar & Grill

$$$ | **CARIBBEAN** |**FAMILY** | This pirate-themed restaurant has a laid-back vibe and a friendly staff who are always ready with a smile or a joke. Don't be surprised to see local fishermen making their way to the kitchen with their still-flapping catch. **Known for:** fresh seafood and steaks; kid-friendly dining environment; large portions. $ *Average main: $22* ✉ *Black Eagle Marina, Black Eagle Rd., off Rte. 413* ☎ *787/823–0578* 🌐 *www.rinconshipwreck.com* ⏲ *No lunch weekdays.*

Tamboo

$$ | **CARIBBEAN** | The best thing about this bar and grill is its beachfront location. The open-air venue serves a mean mojito, and the deck is a great place to watch novice surfers wipe out on the beach. **Known for:** guava barbecue ribs; fish sandwiches; drinks on the deck. $ *Average main: $16* ✉ *Beside the Pointe, Rte. 413, Km 4.4* ☎ *787/823–8550* 🌐 *www.besidethepointe.com* ⏲ *Closed Sept.*

Hotels

Beside the Pointe

$$ | **HOTEL** | This perennial favorite sits right on Sandy Beach, where the waves are big but not too large for novice surfers. **Pros:** social atmosphere; popular

restaurant; great views from some rooms. **Cons:** noise from restaurant, not all rooms have ocean views; no elevator. *Rooms from: $160* *Rte. 413, Km 4.4* *787/823-8550* *www.besidethepointe.com* *Closed Sept.* *8 rooms* *No meals.*

★ Blue Boy Inn

$$ | **B&B/INN** | A walled garden that surrounds this little inn makes you think you're miles away from civilization. **Pros:** gorgeous gardens and pool; use of common kitchen; extremely private. **Cons:** not on beach; some noise from nearby restaurant; a long walk to town. *Rooms from: $200* *556 Black Eagle Rd., off Rte. 413* *787/823-2593* *www.blueboyinn.com* *Closed Sept.* *8 rooms* *Free Breakfast.*

Casa Isleña

$$ | **B&B/INN** | With its barrel-tiled roofs, walled gardens, and open-air dining room, Casa Isleña might remind well-traveled souls of a villa on the coast of Mexico. **Pros:** beautiful beach; friendly staff; walking distance to great restaurants. **Cons:** books up quickly; somewhat dated decor; rooms are very basic. *Rooms from: $155* *Rte. 413, Km 4.8* *787/823-1525, 888/289-7750* *www.casaislena.com* *Closed Oct.* *9 rooms* *Free Breakfast.*

Dos Angeles del Mar Bed and Breakfast

$ | **B&B/INN** | On a quiet hillside overlooking the ocean, this no-frills guesthouse is about as clean and comfortable as it gets. **Pros:** friendly staff; great breakfast; peaceful haven. **Cons:** morning rooster crows; uphill climb from the beach; far from town. *Rooms from: $149* *Calle Vista del Mar* *787/823-1378, 787/431-6057* *www.dosangelesdelmar.com* *5 rooms* *Free Breakfast.*

The English Rose

$ | **B&B/INN** | Nestled in the hills of Rincón, this charming inn—with a pale blue exterior and white plantation shutters—has some of the best views of the Caribbean. **Pros:** excellent breakfast; all rooms have kitchens; friendly staff. **Cons:** somewhat isolated with a breakfast-only restaurant; not on the beach; reservations taken only online. *Rooms from: $140* *Rte. 413, Km 2* *www.larosainglesa.com* *Closed Sept. and Oct.* *3 apartments* *Free Breakfast.*

Horned Dorset Primavera

$$$$ | **RESORT** | Whitewashed villas scattered throughout tropical gardens are designed for privacy, whether you're relaxing in your plunge pool or admiring the sunset from one of your balconies. **Pros:** unabashed luxury; lovely setting; pet-friendly. **Cons:** very narrow beach; long staircase to some villas; some repairs needed. *Rooms from: $400* *Rte. 429, Km 3* *787/823-4030, 800/633-1857* *www.horneddorset.com* *14 villas* *No meals.*

Lazy Parrot Inn

$ | **HOTEL** | **FAMILY** | Painted in eye-popping tropical hues, this mountainside hotel doesn't take itself too seriously, but rooms are a bit more subdued. **Pros:** in-room microwaves; beautiful pool; great pizza at on-site restaurant. **Cons:** not on the beach; stairs to climb; some may consider the whimsical style tacky. *Rooms from: $100* *Rte. 413, Km 4.1* *787/823-5654, 800/294-1752* *www.lazyparrot.com* *22 rooms* *No meals.*

Lemontree Oceanfront Cottages

$ | **HOTEL** | Right on the beach, this pair of lemon-yellow buildings holds six apartments with names like Mango, Coco, Banana, and Piña. **Pros:** far from the crowds; on-call massage therapist; spacious balconies. **Cons:** very narrow beach; it's a drive to shops and restaurants; no elevator. *Rooms from: $130* *Rte. 429, Km 4.1* *787/823-6452* *www.lemontreepr.com* *6 apartments* *No meals.*

Mar Azul Villas

$ | **RENTAL** | Set in a tropical garden behind Mar Azul Surf Shop (the best in town),

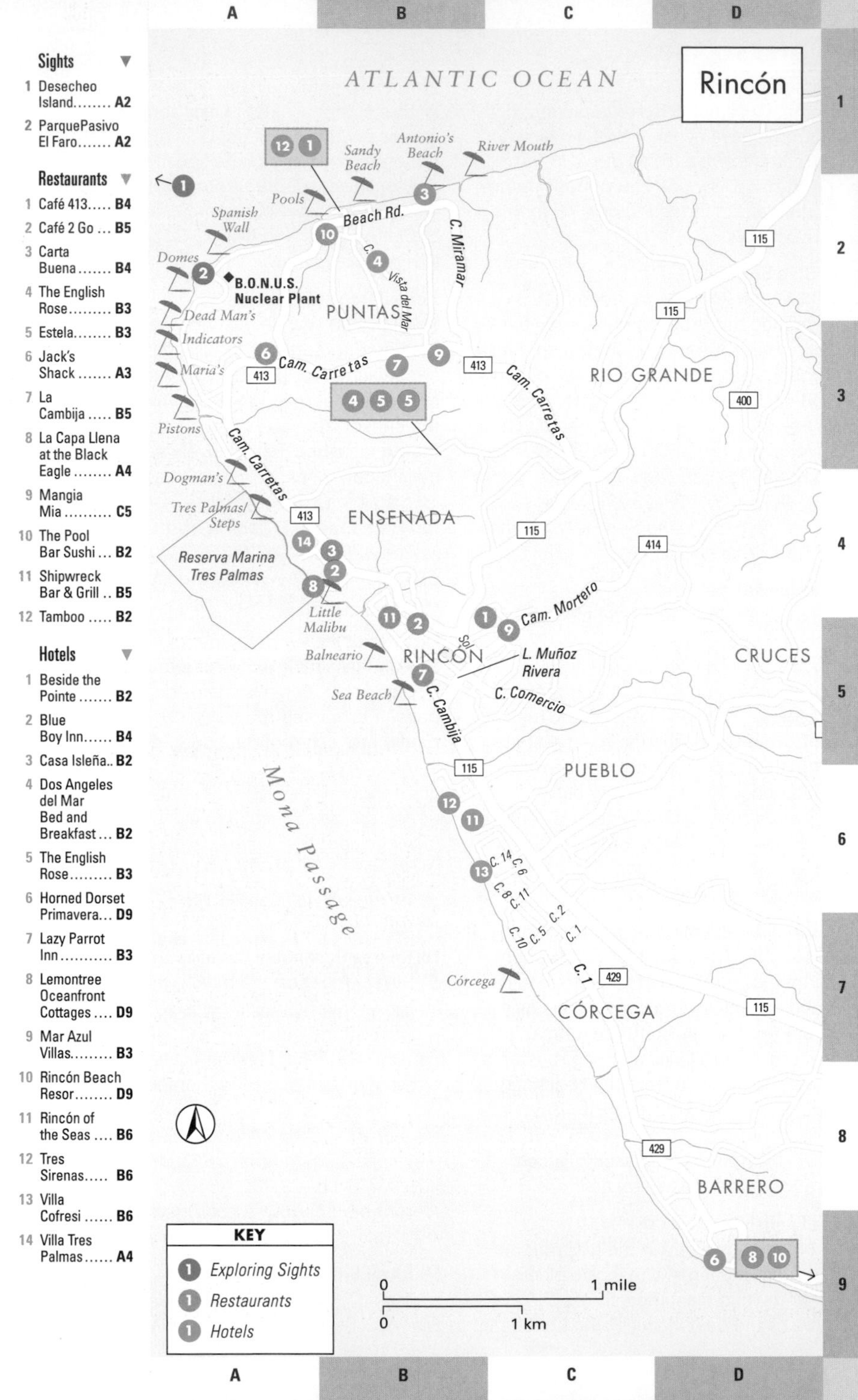
Rincón
Sights
1 Desecheo Island........ A2
2 ParquePasivo El Faro....... A2
Restaurants
1 Café 413..... B4
2 Café 2 Go ... B5
3 Carta Buena....... B4
4 The English Rose......... B3
5 Estela........ B3
6 Jack's Shack A3
7 La Cambija B5
8 La Capa Llena at the Black Eagle A4
9 Mangia Mia C5
10 The Pool Bar Sushi ... B2
11 Shipwreck Bar & Grill .. B5
12 Tamboo B2
Hotels
1 Beside the Pointe B2
2 Blue Boy Inn...... B4
3 Casa Isleña.. B2
4 Dos Angeles del Mar Bed and Breakfast ... B2
5 The English Rose......... B3
6 Horned Dorset Primavera... D9
7 Lazy Parrot Inn........... B3
8 Lemontree Oceanfront Cottages D9
9 Mar Azul Villas......... B3
10 Rincón Beach Resor........ D9
11 Rincón of the Seas B6
12 Tres Sirenas..... B6
13 Villa Cofresi B6
14 Villa Tres Palmas...... A4
ATLANTIC OCEAN
Sandy Beach
Antonio's Beach
River Mouth
Pools
Spanish Wall
Beach Rd.
Domes
B.O.N.U.S. Nuclear Plant
C. Vista del Mar
C. Miramar
PUNTAS
Dead Man's
Indicators
Maria's
Pistons
Cam. Carretas
RIO GRANDE
Dogman's
Tres Palmas/ Steps
Reserva Marina Tres Palmas
ENSENADA
Little Malibu
Cam. Mortero
Sol
Balneario
RINCÓN
L. Muñoz Rivera
CRUCES
Sea Beach
C. Comercio
C. Cambija
PUEBLO
Mona Passage
C. 14
C. 6
C. 8
C. 11
C. 2
C. 10
C. 5
C. 1
Córcega
CÓRCEGA
BARRERO
115
413
400
414
429
KEY
Exploring Sights
Restaurants
Hotels
0
1 mile
0
1 km
A
B
C
D
1
2
3
4
5
6
7
8
9

these charming little apartments have all the comforts of home. **Pros:** spotless rooms; friendly owners; walking distance to restaurants. **Cons:** limited ocean view; foot traffic from attached surf shop; not on the beach. *Rooms from: $95 Rte. 413, Km 4.4 787/214-7224, 787/823-5692 www.puertoricosurfinginfo.com 2 apartments No meals.*

Rincón Beach Resort

$$ | **RESORT** | **FAMILY** | It's a bit off the beaten path, but that's part of the allure of this oceanfront resort, which sits on a great swimming beach and offers bountiful activities. **Pros:** beautiful pool area; laid-back vibe; children's playground. **Cons:** far from restaurants; decor is slightly dated; halls echo. *Rooms from: $195 Rte. 115, Km 5.8, Añasco 787/589-9000 www.rinconbeach.com 112 rooms No meals.*

Rincón of the Seas

$$ | **RESORT** | **FAMILY** | Tucked away at the end of a palm-lined drive, this high-rise hotel feels as if it could be in Miami Beach. **Pros:** lush gardens; nice pool area; Wi-Fi in common areas. **Cons:** on a slender beach; loud music blares from pool area all day; rooms need a makeover. *Rooms from: $151 Rte. 115, Km 12.2 787/823-7500 www.rinconoftheseas.com 112 rooms No meals.*

★ **Tres Sirenas**

$$ | **B&B/INN** | Waves gently lap against the shore at this boutique inn named "Three Mermaids" for the owners' daughters. **Pros:** in-room massage; spotless; tastefully decorated. **Cons:** often fully booked far in advance; Wi-Fi occasionally drops; long walk to restaurants. *Rooms from: $230 26 Seabeach Dr. 787/823-0558 www.tressirenas.com 5 rooms Breakfast.*

Villa Cofresí

$$ | **HOTEL** | **FAMILY** | On one of the best swimming beaches in town, Villa Confresí is Rincón's oldest hotel, making it extremely popular with Puerto Rican families. **Pros:** good restaurant; family-friendly environment; some rooms have kitchenettes. **Cons:** standard rooms lack ocean views; not enough parking; lots of noise from pool area. *Rooms from: $155 Rte. 115, Km 12 787/823-2450 www.villacofresi.com 107 rooms Free Breakfast.*

Villa Tres Palmas

$$ | **RENTAL** | Not all beach houses are created equal, as Villas Tres Palmas makes clear. **Pros:** full kitchen; near many good restaurants; great location for surfers. **Cons:** only the bedrooms have air-conditioning; not on a bathing beach; two rooms share a bath. *Rooms from: $175 Off Rte. 413 787/539-3519 www.trespalmasvillas.com 6 rooms No meals.*

Nightlife

Rincón attracts a younger crowd, so there are plenty of options for fun after dark.

Calypso Café

BARS/PUBS | On weekends the Calypso Café often has live music. The open-air establishment has a daily sunset happy hour and is a good place to grab fresh ceviche, grilled fish, or a juicy burger after you've had your fill of the beach. *Maria's Beach, Rte. 4413 787/823-1626.*

Rincón Beer Company

BARS/PUBS | RBC serves a great selection of local and craft beers. The food is surprisingly good, especially the brussels sprouts and fish tacos. There's live music on Thursday nights during the Art Walk. *Town Square, 15 Calle Muñoz Rivera 787/823-2538.*

Tamboo Tavern

BARS/PUBS | A casual beachfront restaurant by day, Tamboo Tavern turns into a fun, loud hangout at night. A DJ spins every Friday night, and there is live music every Saturday. Stop in for happy hour (daily 5–9). ✉ *Beside the Pointe, Rte. 413, Km 4.4* ☎ *787/823–8550* 🌐 *www.besidethepointe.com.*

Shopping

CLOTHING

Ocean State of Mind

CLOTHING | This bohemian boutique sells women's swimsuits, jewelry, clothing, and other eclectic items, all inspired by nature. ✉ *4 Calle Progreso* ☎ *808/384–1950* ⏲ *Closed Oct.*

The Uncharted Studio

CLOTHING | This shop in the main town square makes eco-friendly screen-printed T-shirts using their own ocean-inspired designs. ✉ *Rincón Plaza, 6 Calle Sol* ☎ *939/697–8177* 🌐 *www.theuncharted-studio.com.*

GIFTS AND SOUVENIRS

Playa Oeste

ART GALLERIES | Playa Oeste has an eclectic collection of surf art, jewelry, clothing, and pottery. Paintings and photographs can be shipped directly to your home. ✉ *Rte. 413, Km 0.5* ☎ *787/823–4424* 🌐 *www.playaoestegallery.com.*

SURF GEAR

Desecheo Surf & Dive Shop

SPORTING GOODS | This shop sells swimwear, sandals, sunglasses, and surf gear, and rents body boards and a variety of short and long surfboards, as well as snorkeling equipment. They can also organize surfing lessons. ✉ *Rte. 413, Km 2.5, Maria's Beach* ☎ *787/823–0390.*

Activities

DIVING AND SNORKELING

Most of the region's dive operators also run fishing charters around Desecheo Island and whale-watching trips in season.

Taíno Divers

DIVING/SNORKELING | Taíno Divers has all-day snorkeling and diving trips that include lunch. It also offers daily trips to Desecheo Island, winter whale-watching trips, and scuba certification courses. ✉ *Black Eagle Marina, Black Eagle Rd., off Rte. 413* ☎ *787/823–6429* 🌐 *www.tainodivers.com* 💵 *From $89.*

HORSEBACK RIDING

Pintos R Us

HORSEBACK RIDING | Pintos R Us has two-hour horseback riding tours along the beach to the lighthouse, as well as full-moon tours and riding lessons. The horses are spirited but gentle enough for newcomers. Reservations are a must. ✉ *Rte. 413, Km 4.7* ☎ *787/516–7090* 🌐 *www.pintosrus.com.*

SAILING

Katarina Sail Charters

SAILING | Set sail in the morning for a day in the sun, or in the late afternoon for unobstructed sunset views. The catamaran sails from Black Eagle Marina, except mid-August–November 15 (hurricane season). ✉ *Black Eagle Marina, Black Eagle Rd., off Rte. 413* ☎ *787/823–7245* 🌐 *sailrinconpr.com.*

SURFING

After hosting the World Surfing Championship in 1968, Rincón became a popular surfing destination. Today, locals and tourists flock to this small, laid-back town every winter to catch the season's best waves. But you don't need to be a pro to vacation in Rincón. There are several surfing schools that offer lessons for beginners, and the town's chill vibe is the perfect place to unwind, relax, and soak up the sun.

Mar Azul

SURFING | One of the best surf shops on the entire island has Rincon's finest selection of performance surfboards and stand-up paddleboards to buy or rent. Inquire about surfing and paddleboard lessons. ✉ *Rte. 413, Km 4.4* ☎ *787/823–5692* 🌐 *www.puertoricosurfinginfo.com.*

Puntas Surf School

SURFING | With more than a decade of surf-coaching experience, Puntas is a great surf school for beginners and kids. ✉ *Rincón* ☎ *787/366–1689* 🌐 *www.puntassurfschool.com.*

Rincón Surf School

SURFING | This popular surf school offers private and group lessons. ✉ *Rte. 413, Km 4.4* ☎ *787/823–0610* 🌐 *www.rincon-surfschool.com.*

Surf Lessons Puerto Rico Adventure Company

SURFING | Ex–pro surfer Ramse Morales has been conducting high-quality surfing classes since 2000. ✉ *Rincón* ☎ *787/617–4731* 🌐 *www.surflessonspuertorico.com* 💲 *From $75 for private 2-hr lessons.*

YOGA

Barefoot Yoga PR

AEROBICS/YOGA | Enjoy a beachfront yoga session hosted under a canopy of almond trees. ✉ *Sandy Beach, Rte. 413 Interior, Km 4.8* ☎ *787/234–8124* 🌐 *www.barefootyogapr.com.*

Mayagüez

24 km (15 miles) southeast of Rincón.

"Me encanta" is what most people from Puerto Rico say when you ask them about Mayagüez. But you are likely to be less than enchanted with this grungy city, home to 12,000 university students and several casinos. With more charming communities in every direction, there's no real reason to stop in this traffic-clogged area. But if you have some spare time, the city known as the "Sultan of the West" has some worthwhile attractions. Its tree-lined main square, Plaza Colón, is dominated by a large statue of Christopher Columbus, and on the surrounding streets you'll find the domed Teatro Yagüez, which dates from 1902, as well as a mishmash of buildings that run the gamut from Neoclassical to Baroque to art deco. You'll also find the largest shopping mall on the west coast.

Mayagüez isn't famous for its beaches—you'll find better in Rincón, about 25 minutes north—but Balneario de Añasco (aka Tres Hermanos Beach) is 10 minutes north of town via Route 2 and Routes 115 and 401. Dotted with palm trees, it's good for swimming and has changing facilities and restrooms.

GETTING HERE AND AROUND

AIR TRAVEL

The small Aeropuerto Eugenio María de Hostos (MAZ), just north of Mayagüez on Route 2, has flights between San Juan and Mayagüez on Cape Air. If you are not stopping first in San Juan, you can rent a car at the airport; rates run $35–$65 per day.

CAR TRAVEL

Driving in Mayagüez can be complicated, especially in the high-trafficked town center, where the city grid is made up of one-way streets. Nevertheless, a rental car is your best option for getting around town. From Route 2 you can reach downtown by taking Route 105 (Calle McKinley) or Route 106 (Calle Méndez Vigo); either will take you to the heart of the city.

CAR RENTAL Avis. ✉ *975 Av. Eugenio Maria de Hostos* ☎ *787/805–5911* 🌐 *www.avis.com.* **Budget.** ✉ *Aeropuerto Eugenio María de Hostos, off Rte. 2* ☎ *800/527–0700* 🌐 *www.budget.com.* **Enterprise.** ✉ *13 Calle Los Velez* ☎ *844/794–8596* 🌐 *www.enterprise.com.* **Hertz.** ✉ *Aeropuerto Eugenio María de Hostos, off Rte. 2* ☎ *787/890–5650.* **Thrifty.** ✉ *Aeropuerto Eugenio María de Hostos, off Rte. 2* ☎ *787/834–1590 in Mayagüez* 🌐 *www.thrifty.com.*

TAXI TRAVEL

In Mayagüez taxis charge flat rates—no meters—by location. A one-way trip to or from San Juan costs about $120.

Yagüez Theatre

ARTS VENUE | The Teatro Yagüez is an extravagant yellow-and-white theater dating from 1902 that's famed throughout the island for its lavish, columned facade, impressive chandeliers, and domed roof. The structure, a little over the top, is still the main venue for theater in Mayagüez. ✉ *Calle McKinley, 1 block from Plaza Colón* 🎫 *Free* 🕒 *Closed weekends.*

Ricomini Bakery

$ | CAFÉ | This popular bakery, open daily 5 am–midnight, is a good spot to try one of the city's trademark delicacies, a *brazo gitano* (gypsy arm). These gigantic jelly rolls are filled with anything from guava to sweet cheese. **Known for:** brazo gitano jellyrolls; Fido's sangria; sandwiches for lunch. $ *Average main: $6* ✉ *101 Calle Méndez Vigo* ☎ *787/832–0565* 🌐 *www.ricominipr.com* 🕒 *No dinner.*

Holiday Inn Mayagüez & Tropical Casino

$ | HOTEL |FAMILY | They've managed to shoehorn nearly everything into this big box on the northern edge of Mayagüez—the sound of slot machines is impossible to escape in the extremely popular casino, which is adjacent to the lobby, as well as the bar and restaurant. **Pros:** great staff; pretty pool area; family-friendly. **Cons:** not on the beach; motel-style rooms; continental breakfast free for executive rooms only. $ *Rooms from: $125* ✉ *2701 Rte. 2, at Km 149.9* ☎ *787/833–1100* 🌐 *www.ihg.com* *141 rooms* 🍽 *No meals.*

Howard Johnson Downtown Mayagüez

$ | HOTEL |FAMILY | Housed in a former monastery, this downtown hotel still has stained-glass windows in some rooms and a stone cross on the roof. **Pros:** interesting building; rooms designed for families and businesspeople; central location. **Cons:** far from the beach; rooms and bathrooms need some updating; noise from nearby bars. $ *Rooms from: $100* ✉ *70 Calle Méndez Vigo* ☎ *787/832–9191* 🌐 *www.hojo.com* *50 rooms* 🍽 *Free breakfast.*

Small stores and pharmacies dot downtown Mayagüez.

Mayagüez Mall

SHOPPING CENTERS/MALLS | For heavy-duty shopping, the Mayagüez Mall has local stores, a food court, movie theaters, and stateside chains like JCPenney, Old Navy, Sears, Walmart, and Marshalls. ✉ *975 Av. Eugenio María de Hostos* ☎ *787/834–2760.*

MULTISPORT OUTFITTERS

AdvenTours

The Mayagüez-based AdvenTours offers bird-watching, biking, and kayaking trips. ✉ *1102 Calle Uroyán* ☎ *787/530–8311* 🌐 *www.adventourspr.com.*

Cabo Rojo Town

People often assume that the town of Cabo Rojo is at the southwestern tip of Puerto Rico, where there is a lighthouse by the same name. In fact, Cabo Rojo is located south of Mayagüez, east of Joyuda, and slightly northwest of Lajas.

GETTING HERE

The area is a good stopping point for those heading from Mayagüez south to El Combate. To get here, take Route 2 south to Route 100 south to Route 102 east. This road will take you directly into the center of Cabo Rojo, approximately 30 minutes from Mayagüez.

Joyuda

21 km (14 miles) south of Mayagüez.

Known as the Milla de Oro (Golden Mile) because of its string of more than 15 seaside restaurants, the community of Joyuda is a must for seafood lovers. The same can't be said for those in search of a beautiful beach, as erosion has taken a terrible toll, leaving in some places only a sliver of sand. But that doesn't stop hordes of local families from making a beeline to the bit of beach that's left.

GETTING HERE AND AROUND

From Mayagüez, take Route 2 south to Route 100 south toward Cabo Rojo. Head west on Route 102 until you hit the coastal town of Joyuda. Most of the area's restaurants and hotels are staggered along a 3-km (2-mile) stretch on Route 102, making this a convenient town to explore on foot.

Sights

Mona Island

ISLAND | About 80 km (50 miles) off the coast of Cabo Rojo, Mona Island sits brooding in the Atlantic Ocean. Known as the "Galápagos of the Caribbean," the 14,000-acre island has long been a destination for adventurous travelers. It's said to have been settled by the Taíno Indians and visited by both Christopher Columbus and Juan Ponce de León. Pirates were known to use the small island as a hideout, and legend has it that there is still buried treasure to be found here. Today, however, Mona's biggest lure is its distinctive ecosystem. It is home to a number of endangered species, such as the Mona iguana and the leatherback sea turtle, as well as a number of seabirds, including the red-footed booby. Off its coast are reefs filled with 270 species of tropical fish, black coral, and purple seafans. There are plenty of places to explore, such as the 200-foot cliffs on the north side of the island or the abandoned lighthouse that once warned ships off the southern coast. Travelers must reach the island by boat—planes aren't permitted to land. Several tour operators in Joyuda and Boquerón, as well as companies in Mayagüez and Rincón, offer overnight camping trips to the island; they will help you with the camping permits from the Puerto Rico Department of Natural and Environmental Resources. ⚠ **You need to reserve at least a few weeks ahead for an overnight stay.** ✉ *Joyuda* ☎ *787/722–1726 Departamento de Recursos Naturales y Ambientales (DRNA).*

Activities

DIVING AND SNORKELING

Several reef-fringed cays lie off the Cabo Rojo area near walls that drop to 100 feet. A mile-long reef along Las Coronas, better known as Cayo Ron, has a variety of hard and soft coral, reef fish, and lobsters.

Boquerón

5 km (3 miles) south of Joyuda.

Once a quiet fishing village, Boquerón still has its share of seaside shanties. Its narrow streets are quiet during the week but come alive on the weekend, when vendors appear with carts full of clams and oysters you can slurp down on the spot, and when bars and restaurants throw open their doors—if they have any, that is. Many of the establishments here are open to the breeze, making this a Puerto Rican party spot where the music (and the people) can be heard until 2 in the morning. Boquerón is also a water-sports center; many companies operate from or near the docks of the imposing Club Nautico de Boquerón, which is easy to find at the end of Route 100.

Surrounded by rugged coastline, the Cabo Rojo Lighthouse is best reached with four-wheel drive.

GETTING HERE AND AROUND

To reach Boquerón from Mayagüez, take Route 2 south to Route 100. After you pass Cabo Rojo heading south, take Route 101 and follow the signs southwest to Boquerón. The small town can easily be explored on foot.

Beaches

Balneario Boquerón

BEACH—SIGHT | The long stretch of sand at this beach off Route 101 is a favorite with islanders, especially on weekends. This is a Blue Flag beach, meaning it is recognized for its adherence to high environmental standards. ⚠ **This beach sustained significant damage from Hurricane Maria in 2017 and is still off-limits.** **Amenities:** lifeguards; parking (no fee); picnic tables; playground; showers; toilets. **Best for:** relaxing; swimming. ✉ *Off Rte. 101.*

Playa Buyé

BEACH—SIGHT | This white-sand beach has crystal clear water lined with swaying palm and almond trees for shade. The beach is a bit hard to find and very crowded on weekends, so visit during the week or in off-season. In high season, some kiosks with food and drink are open. Parking along Calle Buyé is free, but you'll pay $3 to park at the Buyé Beach Resort. **Amenities:** parking (no fee); showers; toilets. **Best for:** swimming; walking. ✉ *Rte. 307, Km 4.8, north of Boquerón.*

Restaurants

Galloway's

$$ | **SEAFOOD** | From a covered deck overlooking Bahía Boquerón, you can catch the sunset while enjoying some seafood—freshly caught in local waters, of course. Steak, ribs, chicken, and pasta are also available, but the red snapper and dorado—prepared breaded, sautéed, or grilled—are by far the best options. **Known for:** fresh red snapper and dorado; popular happy hour; free parking. *Average main: $20* ✉ *12 Calle José de Diego* ☎ *787/254–3302* 🌐 *www.gallowaysrestaurant.com* ⏲ *Closed Wed., and Oct.*

101 West Kitchen & Bar

$$ | AMERICAN | This casual restaurant serving New American cuisine is a must when visiting Boquerón. Sit on the patio, and indulge in their small but tasty menu that includes dishes like lobster mac 'n' cheese, pork sliders, and key lime pie. **Known for:** lobster mac 'n' cheese; good drinks from the bar; Sunday brunch. *$ Average main: $14 ✉ Rte. 101, Km 5.7 ☎ 787/649–4320 ⏲ Closed Mon.*

Hotels

Aquarius Vacation Club

$ | RESORT | FAMILY | As Boqueron's largest resort, this high-rise offers one-, two-, and three-bedroom suites, each with a private balcony. **Pros:** family friendly; calm beach; full kitchens and laundry in every unit. **Cons:** hotel is often full; congested lot with a lot of double parking; rooms need an update. *$ Rooms from: $135 ✉ Rte. 101, Km 18 ☎ 787/254–5400 ⊕ www.aquariusvacationclub.com 88 rooms No meals.*

Activities

FISHING

Light Tackle Adventure

FISHING | You can arrange fishing trips with Captain Francisco "Pochy" Rosario, whose specialty is tarpon—plentiful in these waters. *✉ Boquerón ☎ 787/547–7380 ⊕ lighttackleadventuretarponfishing.blogspot.com.*

El Combate

3 km (2 miles) south of Boquerón.

Welcome to the end of the Earth—or the end of the island, anyway: El Combate sits on the southwest corner of Puerto Rico, a bit removed from everything. The travel industry hasn't figured out how to market this place quite yet, so they've left it mostly to the locals, who have built small but elaborate weekend homes—some with grandiose touches like fountains—along the narrow streets. On the road closest to the beach (called Calle 3, for some reason) is a cluster of seafood shacks. The more prosperous among them have added second stories.

In case you're wondering about the town's odd name—which literally means "The Combat"—it seems that long ago some unscrupulous characters were eyeing the salt flats just outside town, but they were repelled by machete-wielding villagers, who were to live forever in local lore. Is it a true story? Residents of El Combate swear it is.

GETTING HERE AND AROUND

To reach the coastal town of El Combate from Route 101, head south on Route 301 to Km 7.8, where the road intersects with Route 3301. The five-minute drive west on Route 3301 ends at El Combate Beach, where a cluster of restaurants and hotels line the main strip (Calle 3). To reach Cabo Rojo Lighthouse and the salt flats, bypass Route 3301 and continue south on Route 301 until the road ends. This paved road soon turns into a bumpy one with potholes dotting the dusty course. The trek is well worth the effort, however, as jutting mangroves and crystal waters welcome travelers to Puerto Rico's southwestern tip.

It's a good idea to rent a four-wheel-drive vehicle if you are heading to Cabo Rojo Lighthouse, as it is reached via a truly terrible dirt road.

Sights

Cabo Rojo Lighthouse

LIGHTHOUSE | The area's most popular attraction is this Neoclassical lighthouse, dating from 1881. The magnificent structure, built on a limestone cliff, has amazing views of the Caribbean Sea. It is open to the public, and you are free to hike around the rugged terrain or relax on La Playuela or one of the other pink-sand beaches nearby. **■ TIP→ There are**

no facilities here, so bring water, food, and sunscreen. ✉ *End of Rte. 301* ☎ *787/255-1560* 🎫 *Free* ⏲ *Closed Wed.*

Centro Interpretativo Las Salinas de Cabo Rojo
INFO CENTER | The Cabo Rojo Salt Flats Interpretive Center has two-hour guided tours along the nature trails and a small display about the salt flats. (Remember that the name of the town comes from a battle over control of the salt flats.) The best part of the center is a massive observation tower that lets you scan the outline of Cabo Rojo itself. Next to the main building is an audiovisual center where presentations on marine ecosystems and bird migration are offered. ✉ *Rte. 301, Km 11* ☎ *787/254-0115* 🌐 *www.ccpsai.org* 🎫 *Center free, tours $6* ⏲ *Closed Mon.–Thurs.*

Beaches

El Combate
BEACH—SIGHT | This great beach draws large crowds on weekends to its rustic waterfront eateries and calm waters. You can rent small boats and kayaks here. **Amenities:** food and drink. **Best for:** partiers; swimming. ✉ *End of Rte. 3301.*

★ **Playa Sucia** (*La Playuela*)
BEACH—SIGHT | The crescent-shape strand is the most secluded, and beautiful, of the area's beaches. It's commonly referred to as "Playa Sucia" (Dirty Beach) by locals, because of the blankets of seaweed that drift to shore during winter months. The label is rather unfitting for the white sand and turquoise waters that mark the island's southwestern corner, reachable by way of a dirt road lined with mangroves. **Amenities:** none. **Best for:** hiking; swimming. ✉ *End of Rte. 301, past the vast salt flats, Cabo Rojo.*

Restaurants

Annie's Place
$$ | SEAFOOD | A dining room facing the ocean is a fitting place to try some of the southwest coast's best seafood. You can snack on *empanadillas* (fritters), then move on to red snapper with rice and beans or mofongo relleno. **Known for:** fresh red snapper; waterfront dining with great ocean views; empanadillas. 💲 *Average main: $15* ✉ *Rte. 3301, Km 3, at Calle 3, Cabo Rojo* ☎ *787/254-2553.*

Buena Vibra
$$ | PUERTO RICAN | Located right on Route 308, this no-frills Puerto Rican restaurant has an inviting, relaxed vibe. Friendly staff serve local specialties like stuffed avocado, churrasco, and mofongo. **Known for:** fresh seafood; stuffed avocado; family-friendly atmosphere. 💲 *Average main: $15* ✉ *Rte. 308, Km 7.1, Cabo Rojo* ☎ *787/718-0024* ⏲ *Closed Mon. and Tues.*

Los Chapines
$ | CARIBBEAN | This rustic seaside shack, painted orange and green, sells a variety of fish and Puerto Rican dishes. The deck in back is a perfect place to catch the breeze. 💲 *Average main: $8* ✉ *Rte. 3301, Km 3, at Calle 3* ☎ *787/254-5470* ⏲ *Closed Mon.–Thurs.*

Hotels

Parador Combate Beach
$ | HOTEL | FAMILY | On a quiet side street near the beach, this nicely renovated little hotel is one of the best in the area and is a good value. **Pros:** quiet neighborhood; recently remodeled; complimentary breakfast. **Cons:** isolated location; patios face the parking lot; not on the beach. 💲 *Rooms from: $115* ✉ *Rte. 3301, Km 2.7* ☎ *787/254-2358* 🌐 *www.combatebeachresort.com* 🛏 *18 rooms* 🍽 *Free Breakfast.*

Aguadilla

18 km (12 miles) north of Rincón.

Resembling a fishing village, downtown Aguadilla has narrow streets lined with small wooden homes. Weathered but lovely, the faded facades recall the city's long and turbulent past. Officially incorporated as a town in 1775, Aguadilla subsequently suffered a series of catastrophes, including a devastating earthquake in 1918 and strong hurricanes in 1928 and 1932. Determined to survive, the town rebuilt after each disaster, and by World War II it had become known for the sprawling Ramey Air Force Base. The base was an important link in the U.S. defense system throughout the Cold War. Ramey was decommissioned in 1973; today this area comprises some small businesses, a golf course, a university, and the region's most important airport. As a result of tourism, the north end of town is budding with international restaurants, surf shops, and even an outdoor mall. Additions such as a children's water park and ice-skating rink make Aguadilla a family-friendly destination, too.

Perhaps the town's greatest draw is its surfing at local spots like Playa Wilderness, Playa Crashboat, and Playa Gas Chamber. Famous for their right-hand barrels, these beaches have hosted a variety of amateur and professional surfing events, including the 1968 and 1988 International Surfing Association (ISA) World Championships and the 2010 Association of Surfing Professionals (ASP) World Tour.

GETTING HERE AND AROUND

Most people arrive in Aguadilla either by car from San Juan or by flying directly into Aguadilla's Aeropuerto Internacional Rafael Hernández. United Airlines offers daily flights from Newark to Aguadilla, and JetBlue has service from Orlando or New York. Rental cars ($35–$65 per day) are available from companies operating out of the Aguadilla airport. To reach Aguadilla by car from San Juan, head west on Route 22 (toll road), which turns into Route 2. Continue on Route 2 until it intersects with Route 111, leading to the center of town.

Sights

Aguadilla Ice Skating Arena

SPORTS VENUE | FAMILY | As you might imagine, this is the only year-round ice-skating complex in the Caribbean. ✉ *Rte. 442, Km 4.2, Paseo Colón, Plaza Plácido Acevedo* ☎ *787/819–5555* 🎫 *$10.*

La Ponderosa Ruins

LIGHTHOUSE | Along Route 107—an unmarked road crossing through Punta Borinquen Golf Club—you'll find the ruins of La Ponderosa, an old Spanish lighthouse, as well as its replacement, Punta Borinquen, at Puerto Rico's northwesternmost point. The original lighthouse was built in 1889, destroyed by an earthquake in 1918, and rebuilt in 1920 by the U.S. Coast Guard. Just beyond the ruins is a local surf spot, **Playa Wilderness.** ✉ *Rte. 107.*

Museo de Arte de Aguadilla

MUSEUM | Built in 1925, the building that houses this small museum was listed on the National Register of Historic Places in 1985. Inside you'll find a collection of oil paintings and sculptures by local artists. ✉ *Calle Betances 5, between Calle San Carlos and Calle Corchado* ☎ *787/882–4336* 🌐 *www.museodeartedeaguadilla.com* 🎫 *Free* 🕓 *Closed Sun.–Wed.*

Beaches

★ Playa Borínquen

BEACH—SIGHT | This big, beautiful stretch of white sand leads to large rocks and a cliff that juts into the sea. The water can be too rough and choppy for swimming in the winter, but the summer months are great for swimming and snorkeling. During low tide, you'll find a small cave at the far end. **Amenities:** parking (free). **Best for:** snorkeling; swimming; walking. ✉ *Av. Borínquen.*

Playa Crashboat

BEACH—SIGHT | Named for the rescue boats used when nearby Ramey Air Force Base was in operation, this beach has soft, sugary sand, water as smooth as glass, and the sort of colorful fishing boats picture on postcards. A food stand serves the catch of the day with cold beer. **Amenities:** food and drink; parking (no fee); showers; toilets. **Best for:** partiers; snorkeling; swimming. ✉ *End of Rte. 458, off Rte. 107.*

Playa Gas Chamber

BEACH—SIGHT | Just north of Playa Crashboat, this beach with big sucking barrels is favored by surfers. There is limited parking and no beach area, just coral. On a good surf day, this is where you come to watch the pros charge the waves. **Amenities:** none. **Best for:** surfing. ✉ *Rte. 107, north of Playa Crashboat.*

★ **Playa Peña Blanca**

BEACH—SIGHT | Swimming in the crystal clear waters of Peña Blanca is best in the summer months during low tide. In the winter months, the waters reach the rocks around the beach, eliminating the already fairly small shoreline. This also means it can get pretty crowded in the summer. Regardless, the views here are stunning and the beach warrants a visit. **Amenities:** parking (no fee in winter, fee in summer when it's busy). **Best for:** snorkeling; walking. ✉ *Calle Wishin Wells.*

Playa Wilderness

BEACH—SIGHT | This undeveloped beach near La Ponderosa ruins is recommended only for experienced surfers, as it can have dangerous breaks. The long rights, and difficulty in reaching the break, make it popular with locals. To get here, take Route 107 through the Punta Borinquen Golf Club. **Amenities:** none. **Best for:** surfing. ✉ *Rte. 107, north of Playa Gas Chamber.*

Restaurants

The Coffee Spot

$ | BAKERY | You'll love the chill vibe at this Aguadilla café, where you can sip on a latte, use Wi-Fi, and indulge in one of their creative sandwiches. Most dishes and drinks are named after famous composers and classical pieces. **Known for:** great coffee; good spot for breakfast; friendly service. [$] *Average main: $9* ✉ *Rte. 110, Km 4.6* ☎ *787/996–7340* ⊙ *No dinner.*

Levain Bakery

$ | BAKERY | This small bakery across the street from the airport makes the best breads and croissants on the island. They also serve lattes and breakfast items such as cinnamon buns, as well as sandwiches and quiche for lunch. **Known for:** great coffee; excellent fresh breads and croissants; weekend brunch. [$] *Average main: $9* ✉ *333 Wing Rd.* ☎ *787/658–6220* ⊙ *No dinner.*

Hotels

Courtyard by Marriott Aguadilla

$$ | HOTEL | This former military hospital has been transformed into a hotel attracting both business executives and vacationing families. **Pros:** near the airport; nice pool area. **Cons:** airplane and casino noise; not on the beach; Wi-Fi in lobby only. [$] *Rooms from: $177* ✉ *West Parade, off Cliff Rd.* ☎ *787/658–8000* 🌐 *www.marriott.com* *150 rooms* *No meals.*

Activities

DIVING AND SNORKELING

Aquatica Dive and Surf

DIVING/SNORKELING | Near Gate 5 of the old Ramey Air Force Base, Aquatica offers scuba-diving certification courses, as well as snorkeling, stand-up paddleboarding, and surfing trips. There's a great selection of surfboards and paddleboards for rent. For a memorable

Did You Know?

Playa Crashboat is named for the boats that were used for search and rescue of downed airmen when Ramey Air Force Base was in operation. Now brightly painted fishing boats line its shore.

adventure, try the two-hour stand-up paddleboard tour down the Río Guajataca. ✉ *Rte. 110, Km 10, Gate 5, Maleza Alta* ☎ *787/890–6071* 🌐 *www.aquaticapr.com.*

GOLF

Punta Borinquen Golf Club

GOLF | The 18-hole Punta Borinquen Golf Club, on the former Ramey Air Force Base, was a favorite of President Dwight D. Eisenhower. Now a public course, the beachfront course is known for its tough sand traps and strong crosswinds. Membership is not required to play, but some say the course needs better upkeep and repairs since Hurricane Maria. ✉ *Rte. 107, Km 2* ☎ *787/890–2987* 🌐 *www.puntaborinquengolfclub.org* *From $25, including cart* *18 holes, 6633 yards, par 72.*

Isabela

20 km (13 miles) east of Aguadilla.

Founded in 1819 and named for Spain's Queen Isabella, this small town on the northwestern tip of the island skirts tall cliffs that overlook the rocky shoreline. Locals have long known of the area's natural beauty, and lately more offshore tourists have begun coming to this niche, which offers secluded hotels, sprawling golf courses, fantastic beaches, excellent surf, and hiking through one of the island's forest reserves.

GETTING HERE AND AROUND

Flying into Aguadilla's airport (BQN) is the fastest way to reach Isabela and will eliminate the two-hour drive from San Juan. Direct flights to Aguadilla from Newark are available through United Airlines, and from Orlando or New York through JetBlue. Several rental-car companies are on-site at Aguadilla's Aeropuerto Internacional Rafael Hernández, only 15 minutes from Isabela. If you are driving to the town of Isabela from San Juan, take Route 2 west to Route 112 north to the intersection with Route 4466, Isabela's coastal road.

Sights

Guajataca Forest Reserve

NATURE PRESERVE | Explore karst topography and subtropical vegetation at the 2,357-acre Guajataca State Forest, between the towns of Quebradillas and Isabela. On more than 46 walking trails you can see 186 species of trees, like royal palm and ironwood, and 45 species of birds—watch for red-tailed hawks and Puerto Rican woodpeckers. Bring a flashlight and descend into the **Cueva del Viento** (Cave of the Wind) to find stalagmites, stalactites, and other strange formations. At the forest entrance there's a small ranger station where you can pick up a decent hiking map (get here early, as the rangers don't always stay until closing time). ✉ *Rte. 446, Km 10* ☎ *787/872–1045* *Free* *Ranger station closed weekends.*

Palacete Los Moreau

HOUSE | In the fields south of Isabela toward the town of Moca, a French family settled on a coffee and sugar plantation in the 1800s. The grand two-story house was immortalized in the novel *La Llamarada,* written in 1935 by Puerto Rican novelist Enrique A. Laguerre. In the novel, about conditions in the sugarcane industry, the house belonged to his fictional family, the Moreaus. Although it doesn't have many furnishings, you can walk through the house and also visit Laguerre's personal library in the mansion's basement. ✉ *Rte. 2, Km 115.9* ☎ *787/830–4475* *Free* *Closed Tues. and Wed.*

Beaches

Playa de Guajataca

BEACH—SIGHT | Nearby is El Tunel de Guajataca, part of an old tunnel used by a train that once connected the towns of Isabela and Quebradillas and transported sugarcane. Just before El Tunel is El Merendero de Guajataca, a picnic area with cliffside trails. This is not a swimming beach due to strong currents but it's a great place for walks and photo ops. **Amenities:** none. **Best for:** walking. ✉ *Off Rte. 113.*

Playa Jobos

BEACH—SIGHT | This beach is famous for surfing. On the same stretch of sand there are a couple of restaurants with oceanfront decks. Down the road, the dunes and long stretches of golden sand are gorgeous for walking or running. Route 466 runs parallel to it, and there's parking and beach access along the way. ⚠ **Next to the large rock formation is a strong riptide that drags people out to sea. The water is only about thigh high, but when the wind changes, the current is like a raging river.** There are no lifeguards, no signs, and no roped-off areas, so be sure to stay close to shore. **Amenities:** none. **Best for:** partiers; surfing; walking. ✉ *Rte. 466.*

Playa Montones

BEACH—SIGHT | Not far from Playa Jobos, this is a beautiful beach for swimming; it has a protected natural pool perfect for children. **Amenities:** none. **Best for:** swimming; walking. ✉ *Rte. 466, in front of Villas del Mar Hau.*

Playa Shacks

BEACH—SIGHT | Known for its surfing and horseback riding, this secluded spot has an area called the Blue Hole that's popular with divers. It is east of the Villa Montaña beach resort, where you can stop in for a great meal at their oceanfront restaurant, The Eclipse. **Amenities:** none. **Best for**: snorkeling; surfing; swimming; walking. ✉ *Rte. 4446.*

Restaurants

The Eclipse

$$$ | **ECLECTIC** | Beautiful beachfront dining, farm-to-table ingredients, and fantastic service are worth the drive from San Juan. The setting is rustic yet elegant, and the view is ideal. **Known for:** great pizza; weekend brunch; unbeatable beachfront location. [$] *Average main: $28* ✉ *Villa Montaña, Rte. 4466, Km 1.9* ☎ *787/872–9554* 🌐 *www.villamontana.com.*

Ocean Front Restaurant

$$ | **CARIBBEAN** | This seaside restaurant overlooks Playa Jobos, the area's most popular surf break. Outdoor seating is appropriately decorated with surfboards hanging from the rafters and a boat-shape bar in the center of a rough-hewn patio. **Known for:** magnificent sea views; fresh seafood; great ceviche. [$] *Average main: $20* ✉ *Playa Jobos, Rte. 4466, Km 0.1* ☎ *787/872–3339* 🌐 *www.oceanfront-pr.com* ⊙ *Closed Mon. and Tues.*

Restaurant at La Casa

$$$ | **ECLECTIC** | Many things stand out at this picturesque restaurant: the emerald-green golf course in the foreground, the majestic cliffs on the coast, and the roaring ocean in the background. All fruits and vegetables served are grown at Royal Isabela's River Farm and Gatehouse Garden; all the fish is caught off-shore. **Known for:** freshest seafood; Caribbean lobster specials; farm-to-table approach. [$] *Average main: $30* ✉ *Royal Isabela, 396 Av. Noel Estrada* ☎ *787/609–5888* 🌐 *royalisabela.com/restaurant-at-la-casa/menu.*

Uma's Playa Jobos

$$ | **EUROPEAN** | With one of the best beachfront locations on the Island, Uma's is the newest spot to open up in Playa Jobos. This Rockaway Beach (NYC) outpost serves Euro-Asian cuisine with a tropical twist. **Known for:** great dumplings; perfect beachfront location; live reggae on Saturday. [$] *Average main: $13* ✉ *Playa Jobos, Rte. 4466, Km 7.2* ☎ *917/865–6261.*

Hotels

★ Royal Isabela
$$$$ | **RESORT** | One of the area's newest luxury properties, this 2,200-acre paradise is a must for anyone remotely interested in golf—it definitely has the best course in Puerto Rico. **Pros:** great views; luxurious accommodations; access to a private beach. **Cons:** casitas are pricey; 15 minutes from other dining options; long walk to beach. *Rooms from: $899* *396 Av. Noel Estrada* *949/940–4150* *www.royalisabela.com* *20 casitas* *No meals.*

Villa Montaña
$$$ | **RESORT** |**FAMILY** | This cluster of villas, on a deserted stretch of beach between Isabela and Aguadilla, feels like its own little town. **Pros:** bikes and playground; secluded beach; great restaurant on-site. **Cons:** a bit pricey for some dated rooms; far from off-site restaurants; airplane noise. *Rooms from: $255* *Rte. 4466, Km 1.9* *787/872–9554* *www.villamontana.com* *71 rooms* *No meals.*

Villas del Mar Hau
$$ | **HOTEL** | One-, two-, and three-bedroom cottages—painted in cheery pastels and trimmed with gingerbread—are the heart of this simple beachfront hotel. **Pros:** laid-back vibe; protected swimming cove great for children; good restaurant. **Cons:** very basic rooms; may be too kitschy for some; late check-in (4 pm). *Rooms from: $150* *Rte. 466, Km 8.3* *787/872–2045* *www.hauhotelvillas.com* *46 cottages* *No meals.*

Activities

GOLF

★ Golf Links at Royal Isabela
GOLF | Mixing luxurious service, ecological sensitivity, and an incomparable setting, this 18-hole course, which opened in 2011, is already considered among the Caribbean's best. Designed and developed by Stanley and Charlie Pasarell with assistance from course architect David Pfaff, it can play to as much as 7,667 yards and a par of 72 or 73, depending upon how you play the fork-in-the-road 6th. The course has many signature moments—from the 6th to the island green at No. 9 to the carry over the sea at No. 12. Carts are available, although walking is encouraged and caddies are mandatory. *396 Av. Noel Estrada* *787/609–5888* *www.royalisabela.com* *$250 (guests $125); caddie $90 for 2 players* *18 holes, 7667 yards, par 73.*

HORSEBACK RIDING

Tropical Trail Rides
HORSEBACK RIDING | Group rides depart Playa Shacks, one of the region's prettiest beaches, for two-hour tours along the beach and through a forest of almond trees. At the end you have a chance to take a dip in the ocean. The company also offers hiking trips to the limestone caves at Survival Beach. *Rte. 4466, Km 1.9* *787/872–9256* *www.tropicaltrailrides.com.*

SURFING

Hang Loose Surf Shop
SURFING | For surf lessons, Hang Loose Surf Shop offers a two-hour basic course and has board rentals. Lessons are usually held at Playa Jobos, a great surfing spot where you can reward yourself with a refreshing drink from one of the beach shacks. *Rte. 446, Km 1.2* *787/560–0181.*

Wave Riding Vehicles
SURFING | Surfboard rentals and one-hour surfing lessons are offered through this surf shop and board factory. They also rent stand-up paddleboards and bodyboards. *Playa Jobos, Carretera 4466* *787/669–3840* *www.waveridingvehicles.com* *Rentals from $20 per hr, lessons from $35.*

Chapter 8

PONCE AND THE PORTA CARIBE

Updated by
Julie Schwietert Collazo

Sights	Restaurants	Hotels	Shopping	Nightlife
★★★★★	★★☆☆☆	★★☆☆☆	★☆☆☆☆	★☆☆☆☆

WELCOME TO PONCE AND THE PORTA CARIBE

TOP REASONS TO GO

★ **Parque de Bombas:** Marvel at a century-old firehouse whose red-and-black color scheme has inspired thousands of photographers.

★ **Bosque Estatal de Guánica:** Hike where the cactus may make you think you're in the American Southwest.

★ **Hacienda Buena Vista:** Sample a cup of the local brew on a tour of the historic, beautifully restored coffee plantation outside Ponce.

★ **San Germán:** Stroll cobblestone streets lined with architectural treasures, then dine on fine Puerto Rican cuisine high above the main plaza.

★ **Casa Cautiño:** Step back in time to a colonial-era residence in the community of Guayama.

Ponce is the region's dynamic center, with a surrounding metropolitan area that includes a slew of vibrant attractions and sophisticated restaurants and hotels rivaled only by San Juan. Southeast of dynamic Ponce, the shoreline is rugged and the villages more rural and isolated. Small seaside inns and some of the island's best seafood can be found here. Slightly inland are charming colonial towns and the beautiful historic city of San Germán, one of Puerto Rico's oldest settlements.

1 Ponce. Reminiscent of Old San Juan before cruise ships, Ponce has a yesteryear charm and an increasingly cosmopolitan vibe that delight many visitors.

2 Coamo. Puerto Ricans come from all over the island to Coamo, where thermal baths offer a promise of relaxation.

3 Salinas. Just off the main highway leading from San Juan to Ponce, Salinas is a destination for seafood lovers.

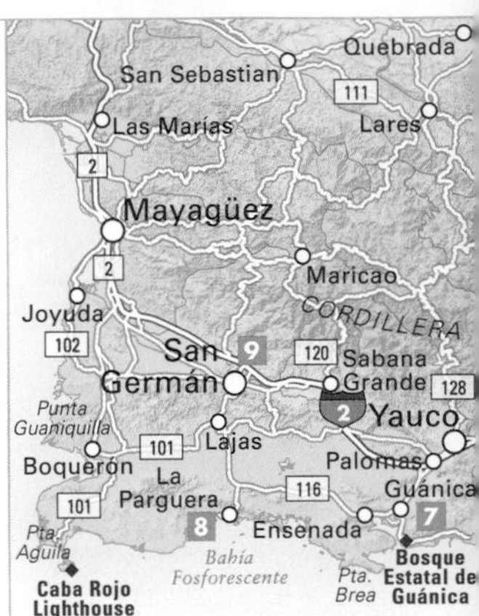

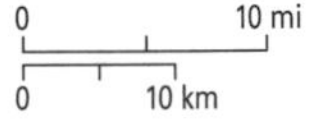

4 Guyama. A stop in Guayama should include Casa Cautiño, a 19th-century home that tells the story of the colonial period in Puerto Rico.

5 Juana Díaz. A small town that's worth at least a pit stop for its most famous drink, *maví*, a fermented beverage made from the ironwood tree.

6 Patillas. Puerto Rico's "emerald of the south" is so named because of its green mountains to the north. It is also, though, a beach town, and its sunsets are stellar, so time your visit accordingly.

7 Guánica. Even though most Americans have probably never heard of it, Guánica is believed to be the spot where Columbus landed when he arrived in 1493; it's also where U.S. troops arrived to wrest Puerto Rico from the Spanish in the Spanish-American War.

8 La Parguera. This unassuming southern coastal town is home to one of Puerto Rico's three bioluminescent bays, best seen when there's no moon.

9 San Germán. Architecture buffs won't want to bypass this town, whose squares and surrounding neighborhoods offer examples of every kind of architectural style.

THE MASKS OF PUERTO RICO

Puerto Rico's masks are one of the premier expressions of folk art on the island, a tradition that dates back to early 17th-century Spain.

During the Fiestas de Santiago Apóstol (Saint James Festivals), brightly dressed *vejigantes* (pronounced "veh-hee-GAN-tays") represented the Devil in a holy battle between good and evil. Their costumes consisted of long robes and grotesque masks, and they would wave cow bladders, or *vejigas,* on long sticks at anyone they passed. Parading as devils, their intention was to frighten sinners to compel them to return to church for Lent. Today balloons and plastic bottles have replaced the cow bladders, and the now more playful masks have become one of Puerto Rico's most distinguished forms of artistic expression. One week before Ash Wednesday, vejigantes—wearing long, colorful robes and brightly painted horned masks—turn the normally placid city of Ponce into a hotbed of rowdiness. The masked mischief-makers prowl city streets, scaring and fascinating anyone in their path.

ISLAND ART

The best hand-designed masks in Puerto Rico come from three parts of the island: Ponce, Loíza, and Hatillo. Mask making is a family tradition in these towns, and styles are passed down for generations. For a fine souvenir and a memorable experience, head to one of the local workshops. Small masks cost \$20–\$30; larger ones by well-known artisans may cost more than \$1,000.

PONCE

Ponce's vejigante masks are made of papier-mâché and are most prominent during the February carnival. Many have

African and Native American elements; it's even possible to detect influences from ancient Greece and Rome. All masks have at least two horns, but most have several protruding from the forehead, chin, and nose. Some antique masks have more than 100 horns. At the beginning of the 20th century, masks were usually painted red with yellow dots or vice versa; today, they come in every imaginable color and pattern.

Where to Go: One of the best-known mask-making families is the Caraballo family from Playa de Ponce near El Ancla restaurant *(see review in Restaurants)*. To purchase a mask, just show up at the door to their home; if someone is there, you'll be allowed to peruse the workshop. Your best chances for success are in February leading up to Ponce's carnival. **Caraballo family.** ✉ *24 San Tomas, Playa de Ponce.*

LOÍZA

Founded by freed and escaped African slaves, Loíza is known as the island's Capital of Traditions for its bomba and plena music and dance, and traditional Taíno and African cuisine. Loíza's masks are created from coconut husks, and the individual shape of each determines the face and placement of the nose and lips. The teeth are made of bamboo, and the tongue is made of coconut shell.

Where to Go: For generations the Ayala family, whose workshop sits just east of town, has been the most renowned of Loíza's mask makers. Their masks appear during the Saint James Festival of Loíza each July. **Artesanias Castor Ayala.** ✉ *Rte. 187, Km 6.6, Barrio Mediana Alta* ☎ *787/564–6403.*

HATILLO

Hatillo was founded in 1823 by settlers from the Canary Islands. These *isleños,* in honor of King Herod's soldiers, the first Christian martyrs or Holy Innocents, would dress head-to-toe in costumes with a cape, hat, and mask made of fine metallic screening meant to resemble the face of a Spaniard. Today the masked performers run through surrounding neighborhoods, joined by children, singing and dancing. The annual mask festival, Día de las Máscaras, is held every December 28.

Where to Go: Puerto Rico Flea Market. ✉ *Rte. 2, Km 86, Barrio Carrizales.*

Not as popular as San Juan or Vieques, the south is a region full of underrated attractions, fine food, and a laid-back, authentic vibe that is hard to come by elsewhere. From lush tropical mountains to arid seacoast plains, Puerto Rico's southern region lets you sample the island from a local's perspective.

Though rich in history, the area also provides ample opportunities for golf, swimming, hiking, and cave exploration. Snaking roads between major highways reveal a glimpse of how rural Puerto Ricans enjoy life. Every mile or so you'll see a café or bar, which is the local social center. The only traffic jams you'll likely encounter will be caused by slow-moving farmers taking their goods to the local market.

At the center of everything is Ponce, the "Pearl of the South," founded in 1692 by farmers attracted to the rich soil in the area, which was perfect for growing sugarcane. Evidence found at the Tibes Indian ceremonial site, just north of the city, suggests that people have inhabited this area since 400 BC. Many residents still carry the last names of the dozens of European pioneer families who settled here during the 19th century. The region's largest city, Ponce is home to some of the island's most interesting architecture, excellent restaurants, and one of its most important art museums. Nearby San Germán, the second-oldest city in Puerto Rico, is known for its two historic main squares, which exhibit well-preserved examples of a wide variety of architectural styles.

On the coast, Guayama and Patillas show off their splendor as little-known destinations for beachgoers. But the real party is at La Parguera, which attracts a young but noisy crowd. If you're willing to explore beyond the casinos, high-rises, and daily traffic congestion of the island's capital, the south is a great escape from Puerto Rico's usual tourist fare. Don't be surprised by the help many of its residents will offer, whether you ask for it or not—*puertorriqueños* in these parts are known for their friendliness in addition to their own brand of southern hospitality.

MAJOR REGIONS

Ponce, on the south coast of Puerto Rico, is the most populous city outside the greater San Juan region and has been an important city since Spanish colonial times.

The **Southeastern Coast** is one of the least-visited areas of Puerto Rico by tourists, but it's popular with locals, including such towns as Coamo, Salinas, Guyama, Juana Díaz, and Patillas.

The Southwestern Coast is where you'll find Guánica, home to a fascinating tropical dry forest as well as the spot where Columbus may have landed; La Parguera, one of Puerto Rico's three bioluminiscent bays; as well as San Germán, a university town famous for its architecture.

Planning

WHEN TO GO

The towns of Patillas, Guánica, and La Parguera are popular with Puerto Ricans during Easter and Christmas and during summer, when children are out of school, and Ponce's spirited pre-Lenten carnival, held the week before Ash Wednesday, draws many visitors. For the rest of the year, much of the south is quiet and receives only a fraction of the number of visitors as other parts of the island, though the weather is equally superb and most facilities remain open. It's not unusual for hotels to close for two to four weeks around October and November, when tourism is at its slowest. Hotels tend to lower their rates May–November, so do look around for any deals. Some *paradores* (small, government-sponsored inns) and hotels require a minimum two- or three-night stay on weekends.

GETTING HERE AND AROUND

AIR TRAVEL

The only international flights to Ponce, the region's only airport, are on JetBlue, which flies from New York (JFK) and Orlando (MCO).

Transfers: Taxis at the airport use meters; expect to pay about $10–$12 to get to downtown Ponce. Some hotels have shuttles to and from the airport, but you must make arrangements in advance.

AIRLINE CONTACTSS JetBlue. ☎ *800/538–2583* 🌐 *www.jetblue.com.*

AIRPORT CONTACTS Aeropuerto Mercedita. ✉ *Rte. 506, off Rte. 52, Ponce* ☎ *787/842–6292.*

BUS TRAVEL

There's no easy network of buses linking the towns in southern Puerto Rico with San Juan or with each other. Some municipalities and private companies operate buses or *públicos* (usually large vans) that make many stops. Be sure to call ahead; although reservations aren't usually required, you'll need to check schedules, which change frequently. The cost of a público from Ponce to San Juan is about $20–$25; agree on the price beforehand.

CAR TRAVEL

Getting around southern Puerto Rico without a car can be quite frustrating. You can rent cars at the Luis Muñoz Marín international airport and other San Juan locations. There are also car-rental agencies in some of the larger cities along the south coast. Rates run about $35–$65 per day. A road map is essential in southern Puerto Rico. So is patience: allow extra time for twisting mountain roads and wrong turns. Many roads, especially in rural areas, aren't plainly marked.

TAXI TRAVEL

In Ponce you can hail taxis in tourist areas and outside hotels. In smaller towns it's best to call a taxi. You can also hire a car service (make arrangements through your hotel); often you can negotiate a lower rate than with a taxi.

HOTELS

Modest, family-oriented establishments near beaches or in small towns and the occasional restored colonial hacienda or mansion are the most typical accommodations. Southern Puerto Rico doesn't have the abundance of luxury hotels and resorts found to the north and east; however, the Hilton Ponce Golf & Casino Resort and Copamarina Beach Resort and Spa are self contained complexes with a dizzying array of services.

RESTAURANTS

Not all the hot spots are in San Juan—in fact, people from the capital drive to Ponce or Guánica to see scan the culinary horizon. Some of the more ambitious restaurants in this part of Puerto Rico are experimenting with Asian and Latin fusion cuisines, which means you might find pork with tamarind glaze or guava sauce, or snapper in a plantain crust. But mostly what you'll find are open-air eateries serving simple, filling fare. The southern coast is known for seafood, particularly in Salinas and Ponce, both of which have a string of popular seaside restaurants. A 15%–20% tip is customary; most restaurants won't include it in the bill, but it's wise to check.

HOTEL AND RESTAURANT PRICES
Hotel and restaurant reviews have been shortened. For full information visit Fodors.com.

What It Costs in U.S. Dollars

	$	$$	$$$	$$$$
RESTAURANTS				
	under $12	$12–$20	$21–$30	over $30
HOTELS				
	under $150	$150–$250	$251–$350	over $350

SAFETY

For the most part, the south is safe. You won't encounter big-city crime, but you should take a few simple precautions. Don't wear flashy jewelry outside tourist areas. Keep an eye on your belongings at the beach; don't leave valuables locked in your car for all to see. And avoid out-of-the-way beach areas after dark.

TOURS

VIP Tours in Ponce offers city tours, horseback riding, and island-hopping adventures.

CONTACTS VIP Tours. ☎ *787/536–4683* 🌐 *www.viptourspr.com.*

VISITOR INFORMATION

In Ponce the municipal tourist office is open weekdays 8–4:30, as is the small information desk in the Parque de Bombas. Smaller cities generally have a tourism office in the city hall, open weekdays 8–noon and 1–4.

CONTACTS Ponce Municipal Tourist Office. ✉ *Located in City Hall (Alcaldía), Plaza de las Delicias, Ponce* ☎ *787/284–4141* 🌐 *www.visitponce.com.*

Ponce

34 km (21 miles) southwest of Coamo.

"Ponce is Ponce and the rest is parking" is the adage used by residents of Puerto Rico's second-largest city (population 166,000) to express their pride in being *ponceños*. The rivalry with the island's capital began in the 19th century, when European immigrants from England, France, and Spain settled here. Because the city limits extend from the Caribbean to the foothills of the Cordillera Central, it's a lot hotter in climate than San Juan. Another contrast is the Neoclassical architecture of the elegant homes and public buildings that surround the main square.

Many of the 19th-century buildings in Ponce Centro, the downtown area, have been renovated, and the Museo de Arte de Ponce—endowed by its late native son and former governor of Puerto Rico, Luis A. Ferré—is considered one of the Caribbean's finest art museums. Just as famous is Ponce's pre-Lenten carnival. The colorful costumes and *vejigante* (mischief-maker) masks worn during the festivities are famous throughout the world. The best dining in Ponce is just west of town. Seafood restaurants line the highway in an area known as Las Cucharas, named for the spoon-shape bay you'll overlook as you dine.

GETTING HERE AND AROUND

The fastest route through the region is the Luis A. Ferré Expressway (Route 52), a toll road that runs from San Juan to Ponce, crossing the island's central mountain range. The trip from Condado or Old San Juan takes about two hours. Route 2, also a toll road, connects to San Germán, Mayagüez, and the western part of the island.

Great Itineraries

If You Have 1 Day

Many residents of San Juan think nothing of a day trip to **Ponce.** If you head south on Route 52, you'll be there in less than two hours. There's plenty to do here, including a tour of the Museo de Arte de Ponce, one of the island's top art collections. The best way to spend an hour or two is to stroll around the lovely Plaza de las Delicias. Make sure to dine in one of the area's outstanding restaurants and have ice cream at King's Cream, which features tropical flavors.

If You Have 3 Days

From San Juan, head south on Route 52 until you reach **Ponce,** the "Pearl of the South." Spend the afternoon strolling around the Plaza de las Delicias, peeking into the beautiful Catedral de Nuestra Señora de Guadalupe and the striking Parque de Bombas. On the following day, visit some of the other attractions in and around the city, perhaps the Museo de Arte de Ponce, the Castillo Serrallés, or Hacienda Buena Vista. Dedicate your final day to **Guánica,** where you'll find wonderful beaches and deserted cays; spend the night here before heading back to San Juan. If you are in the mood for hiking, check out Bosque Estatal de Guánica, a dry forest.

If You Have 5 Days

Make a leisurely trip south from San Juan on Route 52, stopping for a half or full day at Albergue Olímpico, a massive sports complex that features, among other installations, two family-friendly water parks and Puerto Rico's Olympic Museum. Spend the night in **Coamo,** a town whose hot springs were thought by some to be Ponce de León's Fountain of Youth. Soak in them and feel the years melt away before continuing on your second day to **Ponce** for two days of exploring. Travel west along the coast and settle at a waterfront hotel in **Guánica.** In the evening you can take a boat trip to the bioluminescent bay in **La Parguera.** On your last day, explore the beautifully preserved colonial city of **San Germán**; don't miss the lovely colonial-era chapel known as the Capilla de Porta Coeli.

Car rental is typical for most visitors to Ponce and makes exploring the surrounding region considerably easier. Most hotels have parking lots, and metered parking is easy to come by in the center.

CAR RENTAL Avis. ✉ *Aeropuerto Mercedita, Rte. 506, off Rte. 52* ☎ *787/842–6154* 🌐 *www.avis.com.* **Budget.** ✉ *Aeropuerto Mercedita, Rte. 506, off Rte. 52* ☎ *787/848–0907* 🌐 *www.budget.com.* **Enterprise.** ✉ *1023 Av. La Ceiba* ☎ *844/794–8595.* **Thrifty Car Rental.** ✉ *Aeropuerto Mercedita, Rte. 506, off Rte. 52* ☎ *787/290–2525* 🌐 *www.thrifty.com.*

Ponce Centro

At the heart of Ponce Centro is Plaza de las Delicias, with trees, benches, and the famous lion fountain. Several interesting buildings are on this square and adjacent streets, making the area perfect for a leisurely morning or afternoon stroll.

Sights

Catedral de Nuestra Señora de Guadalupe
RELIGIOUS SITE | This pale blue cathedral has always been one of the city's jewels, but it regained much of its luster after a

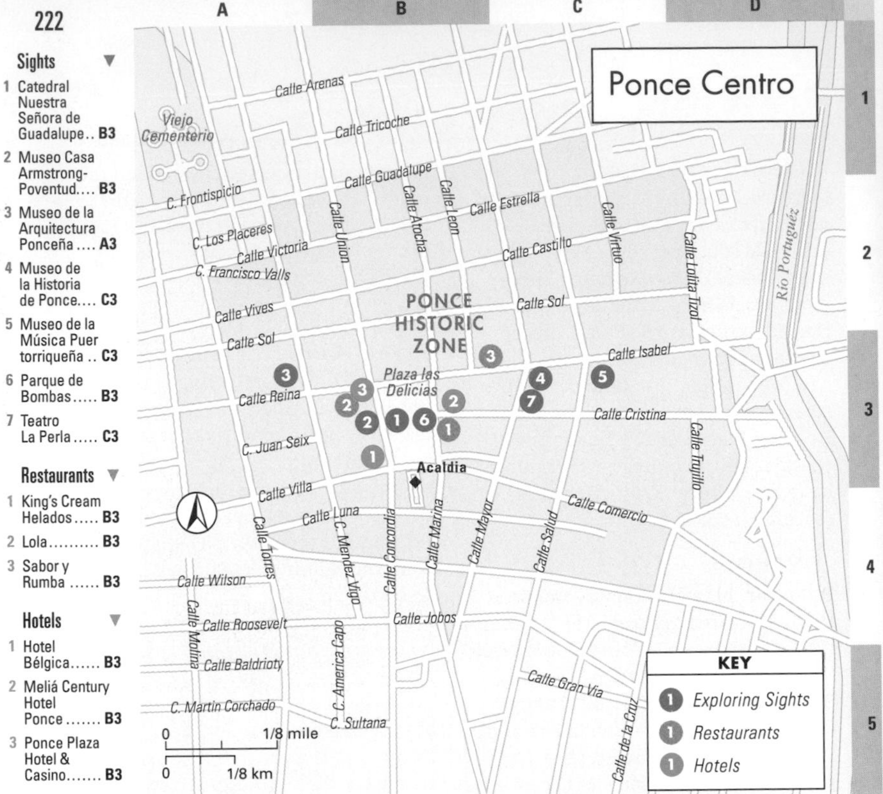

complete renovation in 2007. Dedicated to the Virgin of Guadalupe, it is built on the site of a 1670 chapel destroyed by earthquakes. Part of the current structure, where Mass is still held, dates from 1835. After another earthquake in 1918, new steeples and a roof were put on and Neoclassical embellishments were added to the facade. Inside, you'll see stained-glass windows and two alabaster altars. ✉ *Plaza de las Delicias, Ponce.*

Museo Casa Armstrong-Poventud
HOUSE | Banker and industrialist Carlos Armstrong and his wife, Eulalia Pou, lived in this Neoclassical house designed and built for them in 1901 by Manuel V. Domenech. The building recently underwent a top-to-bottom renovation, and now you can admire the ornate facade, which is chock-full of columns, statues, and intricate moldings. Original furnishings belonging to the family are on display. ✉ *Calle Unión, across from Catedral de Nuestra Señora de Guadalupe, Ponce* ☎ *787/290–1530* 🎫 *Free* ⏲ *Closed Mon. and Tues.*

★ **Museo de la Arquitectura Ponceña**
MUSEUM | In a city filled with Neoclassical confections, this is one of the most elaborate. Alfredo B. Wiechers, who returned to his native Ponce after studying architecture in Paris, designed the house. Though small in scale compared with some of its neighbors, it makes a big impression with details like huge arched windows and a massive rooftop gazebo. No wonder that soon after it was completed in 1911 the Villaronga-Mercado family decided to make it their own. Check out the stained-glass windows and other fanciful touches. Inside you'll find original furnishings and exhibits on

A Good Walk: Ponce Centro

Start on the tree-lined Plaza de las Delicias. (You'll find parking nearby on Calle Marina, Calle Isabel, and Calle Reina.) Dominating it is the **Catedral Nuestra Señora de Guadalupe,** dating from 1835. Across the street is **Casa Armstrong-Poventud,** home of the Institute of Culture's Ponce branch. Leaving Armstrong-Poventud, cross back to the plaza, circle south by the Alcaldia, and continue to the plaza's east side to visit the red-and-black-striped fire station, **Parque de Bombas.**

From the intersection of Calles Marina and Cristina, take Calle Cristina a block east to one of the city's first restoration projects, **Teatro La Perla,** at the corner of Calles Cristina and Mayor. One block north of the theater, at Calles Mayor and Isabel, is a former home that's now the **Museo de la Historia de Ponce.** A block east, at the corner of Calles Salud and Isabel, is the **Museo de la Música Puertorriqueña.** Four blocks west (you'll go by Plaza de las Delicias again; Calle Isabel will turn into Calle Reina) is the 1911 architectural masterpiece **Casa Wiechers-Villaronga.** For more early-20th-century architecture, continue west on Calle Reina, where you'll see examples of *casas criollas,* wooden homes with spacious front balconies that were popular in the Caribbean during the early 1900s.

Timing

Although it's possible to see Ponce Centro in a single morning or afternoon, it's best to devote a full day and evening. Explore the streets and museums during daylight, and then head for the plaza at night, when the lion fountain and streetlamps are illuminated and townspeople are out on a stroll. With police officers on nearly every corner, this area is very safe to explore. **TIP→ Two of the city's most popular museums—Casa Wiechers-Villaronga and the Museo de la Música Puertorriqueña—are not air-conditioned, so they close early when the weather is hot. If you want to see these sites, make sure to arrive before 11 am. Also note, most of the museums in Ponce are closed Monday and Tuesday.**

Wiechers and other Ponce architects of his era. The house, restored by the Institute of Puerto Rican Culture, now operates as the Museum of Puerto Rican Architecture. ✉ *106 Calle Reina, at Calle Méndez Vigo, Ponce* 🎫 *Free* ⏲ *Closed Mon. and Tues.*

Museo de la Historia de Ponce

MUSEUM | Housed in two adjoining Neoclassical mansions, this museum includes 10 rooms with exhibits covering the city's residents, from Taíno Indians to Spanish settlers to the mix of the present. Guided tours in English and Spanish give an overview of the city's history. Although descriptions are mostly in Spanish, displays of clothing from different eras are interesting. ✉ *53 Calle Isabel, at Calle Mayor, Ponce* ☎ *787/844-7071* 🎫 *Free* ⏲ *Closed Mon.*

Museo de la Música Puertorriqueña

MUSEUM | At this museum you'll learn how Puerto Rican music has been influenced by African, Spanish, and Native American cultures. On display are dozens of instruments, such as the *tres* (a small string instrument resembling a banjo), as well as memorabilia of local composers and musicians. The small museum takes up several rooms of a Neoclassical former residence, which alone is worth the trip. ✉ *Calle Isabel at Calle Salud, Ponce*

Today it's a museum, but for more than 100 years Parque de Bombas served as Ponce's main firehouse.

787/848–7016 *Free* *Closed Mon. and Tues.*

★ **Parque de Bombas**

BUILDING | **FAMILY** | After El Morro in Old San Juan, this distinctive red-and-black-striped building may be the second-most-photographed structure in Puerto Rico. Built in 1882 as a pavilion for an agricultural and industrial fair, it was converted the following year into a firehouse. In 1990, it took on new life as a small museum tracing the history—and glorious feats—of Ponce's fire brigade. Kids love the antique fire truck on the lower level. Short tours in English and Spanish are given on the hour starting at 10; if the trolley is running, you can sign up for free tours of the historic downtown here, too. Helpful tourism officials staff a small information desk inside. *Plaza de las Delicias, Ponce* *787/284–3338* *www.visitponce.com* *Free.*

Teatro La Perla

ARTS VENUE | This theater was restored in 1941 after an earthquake and fire damaged the original 1864 structure. The striking interior contains seats for 1,047 and has excellent acoustics. It's generally open for a quick peek on weekdays. *Calle Mayor at Calle Cristina, Ponce* *787/284–4141* *Free* *Closed weekends.*

Restaurants

★ **King's Cream Helados**

$ | **CAFÉ** | An institution since it opened in 1964, King's Cream Helados, across from Plaza de las Delicias, is *the* place for ice cream in Ponce. It serves 12 varieties—from tamarind, peanut, and passion fruit to classics like chocolate and vanilla. **Known for:** tropical fruit flavors; cash only; long hours. *Average main: $5* *9223 Calle Marina, Ponce* *787/843–8520* *No credit cards.*

Lola

$$$ | **ECLECTIC** | This trendy bistro in the heart of downtown has an eclectic menu to match the decor. Grab a seat in a red velvet booth and start with the sampler of mahimahi nuggets, bruschetta, fried plantains, and egg rolls. **Known for:** mahimahi in lobster sauce; Lola Martini (grapefruit, cranberry, Champagne, lime, and rum); showcase for local artists. *Average main: $27 Ponce Plaza Hotel & Casino, Calle Reina at Calle Union, Ponce 787/813–5033 www.lolacuisine.com.*

Sabor y Rumba

$$ | **PUERTO RICAN** | The short menu of this alfresco dining spot allows the kitchen to focus on its specialties, which include tostones, ceviche, and skirt steak. But even more than the food, many guests love the vibe of Sabor y Rumba, whose name alludes not only to its tasty flavors, but also its fun-loving spirit. **Known for:** churrasco; mofongo; live music and dancing on weekends. *Average main: $16 66 Calle Isabel, Ponce No credit cards.*

Hotel Bélgica

$ | **HOTEL** | Near the central square, this hotel dating from 1872 is both comfortable and economical, with worn yet clean rooms with hardwood floors, high ceilings, and wrought-iron beds. **Pros:** a taste of old Ponce; friendly staff; excellent rates. **Cons:** front-facing rooms are noisy; some rooms don't have windows; lots of steps and no elevator. *Rooms from: $75 122 Calle Villa, Ponce 787/844–3255 www.hotelbelgica.com 20 rooms Free Breakfast.*

Meliá Century Hotel Ponce

$ | **HOTEL** | In the heart of the city, this family-owned hotel has been a local landmark for more than 120 years; in fact, it claims to be the island's oldest hotel. **Pros:** great location on the main square; good dining options nearby; budget-friendly. **Cons:** somewhat dated decor; front rooms can be noisy; Internet service is often spotty. *Rooms from: $95 75 Calle Cristina, Ponce 787/842–0260 www.meliacentury-hotel.com 78 rooms No meals.*

Ponce Plaza Hotel & Casino

$ | **HOTEL** | In a stunningly restored building that dates back to 1882, Ponce Plaza Hotel & Casino sits right on the main square. **Pros:** excellent location; lively bar and restaurant; historic rooms are beautifully atmospheric. **Cons:** regular rooms lack charm; small pool gets foot traffic from attached restaurant; pool is small. *Rooms from: $119 Calles Reina at Calle Unión, Ponce 787/813–5050 www.ponceplazahotelandcasino.com 70 rooms No meals.*

Teatro La Perla

THEATER | Check for Spanish-language theater productions and concerts at the Teatro La Perla, a Neoclassical masterpiece in the center of Ponce. *Calle Mayor at Calle Cristina, Ponce.*

On holidays and during festivals, artisans sell wares from booths in Plaza de las Delicias. There are a few souvenir and gift shops in the area around the plaza, and Paseo Atocha, a pedestrian mall with shops geared to residents, runs north of it.

Mi Coquí

CRAFTS | Explore shelves filled with carnival masks, colorful hammocks, freshly ground coffee, and bottles and bottles of rum. *9227 Calle Marina, Ponce 787/841–0216.*

Utopia

CRAFTS | Utopia sells carnival masks, carved figurines, and other crafts. *78 Calle Isabel, Ponce 787/848–5441.*

The stately lobby of the Museo de Arte de Ponce

Greater Ponce

The greater Ponce area has some of Puerto Rico's most notable cultural attractions, including one of the island's finest art museums and its most important archaeological site.

Sights

Centro Ceremonial Indígena de Tibes (*Tibes Indian Ceremonial Center*)
ARCHAEOLOGICAL SITE | This archaeological site, discovered after flooding from a tropical storm in 1975, is the island's most important. Dating from AD 300–700, it includes nine playing fields used for a ritual ball game that some think was similar to soccer. The fields are bordered by smooth stones, some of which are engraved with petroglyphs that might have ceremonial or astronomical significance. In the eye-catching Plaza de Estrella (Plaza of the Star), stones are arranged in a pattern resembling a rising sun, perhaps used to chart the seasons. A village with thatched huts has been reconstructed. Visit the small museum before taking a walking tour of the site. "Last entry" varies from day to day, so call ahead to confirm. ✉ *Rte. 503, Km 2.5, Barrio Tibes* ☎ *787/840–2255, 787/840–5685* 🎫 *$3* ⏲ *Closed Mon.*

Cruceta El Vigía
VIEWPOINT | At the top of Cerro Vigía—a hill where the Spanish once watched for ships, including those of marauding pirates—is this colossal concrete cross. You can climb the stairs or take a glass elevator to the top of the 100-foot cross for a panoramic view across the city. Purchase tickets at nearby Castillo Serrallés. ✉ *17 El Vigía, across from Castillo Serrallés, El Vigía* ☎ *787/259–1770* 🌐 *www.museocastilloserralles.com* 🎫 *$5.73, includes admission to Japanese garden* ⏲ *Closed Mon.–Wed.*

Faro De Maunabo
VIEWPOINT | Route 3 going eastward intersects with Route 901, the eastern portion of the cross-island Ruta Panorámica. Along the way you'll pass animals grazing

in fields and cliffs that drop straight down to the ocean. If you turn off on Route 760 and take it to the end, you'll be rewarded by a dramatic view of the Faro de Maunabo (Maunabo Lighthouse) at Punta Tuna. While not open to the public, it's a must-stop spot for photos. ✉ *Maunabo.*

★ Hacienda Buena Vista

FARM/RANCH | FAMILY | Built by Salvador de Vives in 1838, this was one of the area's largest coffee plantations. It's a technological marvel: water from the nearby Río Canas was funneled into narrow brick channels that could be diverted to perform any number of tasks, like turning the waterwheel. (Seeing the two-story wheel slowly begin to turn is fascinating, especially for kids.) Nearby is the two-story manor house, with a kitchen dominated by a massive hearth and furniture that hints at life on a coffee plantation nearly 150 years ago. In 1987 the plantation was restored by the Puerto Rican Conservation Trust, which leads several tours each day (at least one in English; by reservation only, call several days in advance or reserve online). A gift shop sells coffee beans and other souvenirs. Allow an hour's drive on the winding road from Ponce. ✉ *Rte. 123, Km 17.3, Sector Corral Viejo* ☎ *787/284–7020 weekdays* 🌐 *www.paralanaturaleza.org* 🎟 *$12.*

La Guancha de Ponce

PROMENADE | FAMILY | Encircling the cove of a working harbor, the seaside boardwalk features a small lookout tower and kiosks where vendors sell local food and drink. The adjacent park has a large children's area filled with playground equipment and, on weekends, live music. The nearby public beach has restrooms, changing areas, a medical post, and plenty of free parking. On Sunday night, this place gets packed with locals strolling the boardwalk. Weekend visitors might want to take advantage of tour outfitters, including Island Venture, which lead day trips to Caja de Muertos from here, as well as evening bay rides. ✉ *End of Rte. 14, La Guancha* ☎ *787/844–3995.*

★ Museo Castillo Serrallés

HOUSE | This lovely Spanish-style villa—so massive that townspeople dubbed it a castle—was built in the 1930s for Ponce's wealthiest family, the makers of Don Q rum. Guided tours provide a glimpse into the lifestyle of a sugar baron, and a permanent exhibit explains the area's sugarcane and rum industries. Highlights include the dining room, with original hand-carved furnishings, and the extensive garden, with sculptured bushes and a shimmering reflection pool. A large cross looming over the house is an observatory; from the top, you can see the Caribbean. ✉ *17 El Vigía, El Vigía* ☎ *787/259–1774* 🌐 *www.museocastilloserralles.com* 🎟 *$8.86, includes gardens and butterfly garden; $13.34, also includes Japanese Garden and Cruceta* ⏲ *Closed Mon. and Tues.*

★ Museo de Arte de Ponce

MUSEUM | Designed by Edward Durell Stone, who also designed the original Museum of Modern Art in New York City and the Kennedy Center in Washington, D.C., Ponce's art museum is easily identified by the hexagonal galleries on the second story. The museum has one of the best art collections in Puerto Rico, which is why residents of San Juan frequently make the trip. The 4,500-piece collection includes works by famous Puerto Rican artists such as Francisco Oller, represented by a lovely landscape called *Hacienda Aurora*. European works include paintings by Peter Paul Rubens and Thomas Gainsborough as well as pre-Raphaelite paintings, particularly the mesmerizing *Flaming June*, by Frederick Leighton, which has become the museum's unofficial symbol. The museum also offers special exhibits, three sculpture gardens, and a café. ✉ *2325 Bul. Luis A. Ferré Aguayo (Hwy. 163), Sector Santa María* ☎ *787/840–1510* 🌐 *www.museoarteponce.org* 🎟 *$6* ⏲ *Closed Tues.*

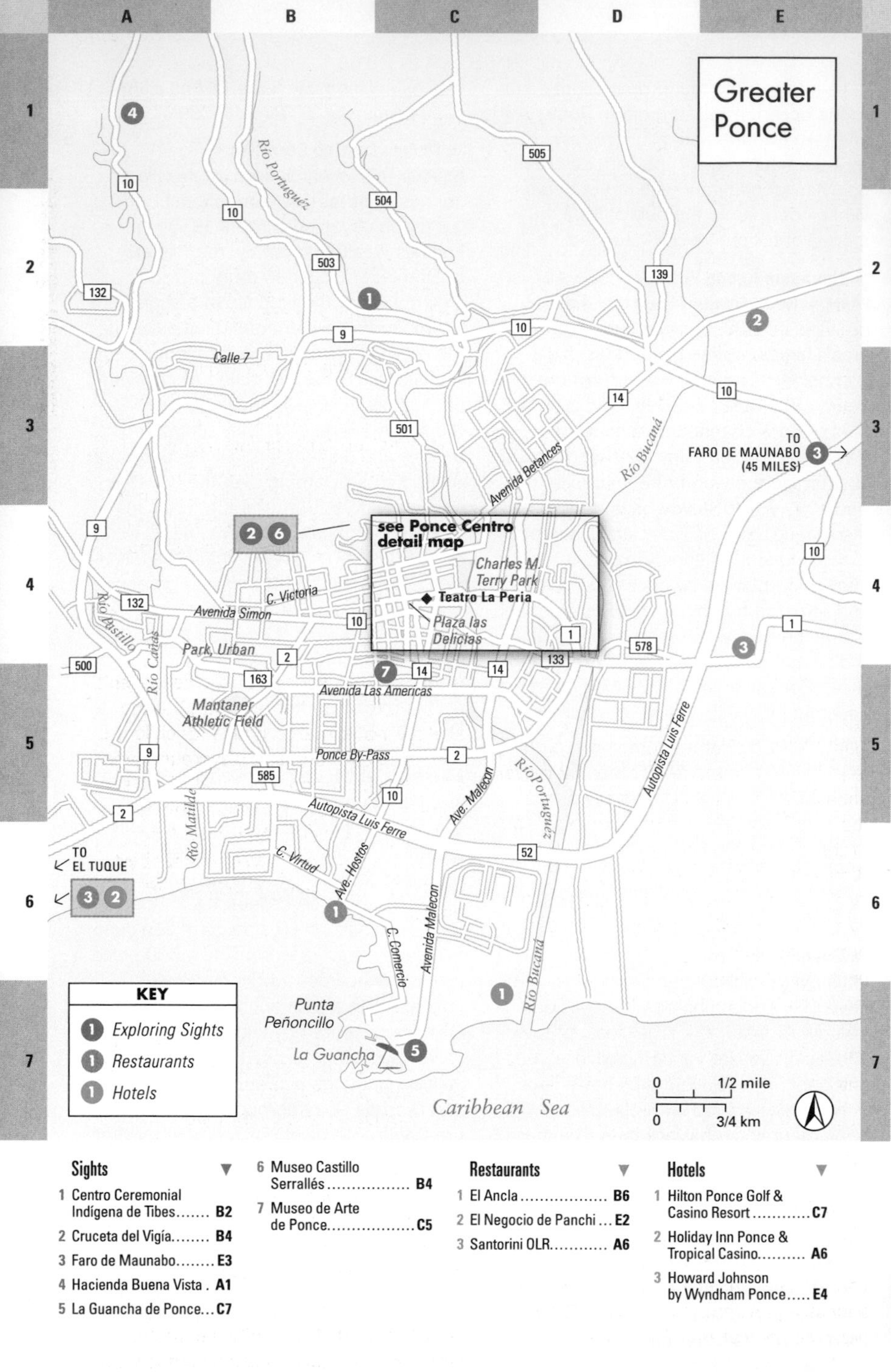

Sights

1 Centro Ceremonial Indígena de Tibes....... **B2**

2 Cruceta del Vigía........ **B4**

3 Faro de Maunabo........ **E3**

4 Hacienda Buena Vista . **A1**

5 La Guancha de Ponce... **C7**

6 Museo Castillo Serrallés................. **B4**

7 Museo de Arte de Ponce.................. **C5**

Restaurants

1 El Ancla.................. **B6**

2 El Negocio de Panchi ... **E2**

3 Santorini OLR............ **A6**

Hotels

1 Hilton Ponce Golf & Casino Resort............ **C7**

2 Holiday Inn Ponce & Tropical Casino.......... **A6**

3 Howard Johnson by Wyndham Ponce..... **E4**

A Good Tour: Greater Ponce

The **Museo de Arte de Ponce** is on Avenida Las Américas, south of Plaza de las Delicias and not far from the Luis A. Ferré Expressway (Route 52). Anyone with a taste for art can happily while away many hours in its galleries. East of the museum you can pick up Route 14 south to the Caribbean and **La Guancha**, a boardwalk with food kiosks, a playground, and a child-friendly public beach. It's a good place to relax and let youngsters burn off energy. From here, if you retrace your path north past downtown you'll be heading to Calle Bertoly and El Vigía (Vigía Hill), where the **Cruceta El Vigía** towers over the city and the **Castillo Serrallés**, a former sugar baron's villa, is a popular attraction.

Farther north on Route 503 is the **Centro Ceremonial Indígena de Tibes**, which displays native artifacts dating back more than 1,500 years. You'll have to backtrack to reach Route 10, then head north to **Hacienda Buena Vista**, a former coffee plantation that's been restored by the Conservation Trust of Puerto Rico. (Call ahead to arrange a tour; reservations are required.) You'll need a car or a cab to reach the Centro Ceremonial Indígena de Tibes or Hacienda Buena Vista.

Beaches

Isla Caja de Muertos (*Coffin Island*)
BEACH—SIGHT | Named for its shape, this island, which stretches for 3 km (2 miles) and is 8 km (5 miles) off the coast, has the best beaches near Ponce and some of the best snorkeling in southern Puerto Rico. Due to hawksbill turtle nesting (May–December), the island is protected by the Reserva Natural Caja de Muertos, but you can still swim, snorkel, and dive here. A 30-minute hike across the island leads to a small lighthouse dating to 1887. Scheduled boats leave La Guancha Friday–Sunday at 8:30 am, daily in high season. Island Venture is one outfitter that leaves from La Guancha for Caja de Muertos (*see Diving and Snorkeling in Sports and the Outdoors*). Alternatively, you can ask one of the many boatmen at La Guancha to take you out for about $30 round-trip. You must pack in what you need (food and drink) and pack out your garbage. **Amenities:** toilets. **Best for:** snorkeling; swimming; walking. ✉ *La Guancha, end of Rte. 14, Ponce.*

La Guancha
BEACH—SIGHT | Ponce's public beach isn't anything to write home about, but the shallow water makes it nice for children. You'll find bathrooms, a playground, and a few kiosks selling fried food. There's some shade under thatched umbrellas, but bring sunscreen. **Amenities:** food and drink; parking (no fee); toilets. **Best for:** swimming. ✉ *At the end of Rte. 14, Ponce.*

Restaurants

El Ancla
$$ | **SEAFOOD** | Families favor this laid-back restaurant at water's edge. Generous and affordable plates of fish, crab, and other fresh seafood come with *tostones* (fried plantains), french fries, and garlic bread. **Known for:** fresh seafood; great water views; piña coladas (with or without alcohol). $ *Average main: $20* ✉ *805 Av. Hostos Final, Ponce* ☎ *787/840–2450* 🌐 *www.restauranteelancla.com.*

El Negocio de Panchi
$$ | **CARIBBEAN** | This Caribbean restaurant updates Puerto Rican favorites with

The Spanish-style Castillo Serrallés dates from the 1930s, having been buit for the city's wealthiest family, the makers of Don Q rum.

contemporary touches, and the menu features a rotating cast of daily specials, which include octopus with saffron butter, shrimp stir-fry with coconut rice, and pork satay in peanut sauce. **Known for:** fresh seafood; osso buco; guava cheesecake. *Average main: $20* *Rte. 14, in front of El Monte Town Center, Ponce* *787/848–4788* *Closed Mon. and Tues. No lunch Wed.–Sat.*

Santorini OLR
$$$ | **GREEK** | The only Greek restaurant in Ponce, this open-air establishment has successfully captured the cuisine and atmosphere of its namesake island. Statues of goddesses line the pathway leading to a bi-level dining area, decorated with 1960s-era movie posters from Greece. **Known for:** grilled lobster; churrasco; baklava. *Average main: $25* *Rte. 2, Km 218, Sector Las Cucharas* *939/644–9021* *Closed Mon. and Tues.*

Hotels

Hilton Ponce Golf & Casino Resort
$$ | **RESORT** | **FAMILY** | The south coast's biggest resort sits on a black-sand beach about 6 km (4 miles) south of downtown Ponce. **Pros:** good golf; large casino; game room and pool for kids. **Cons:** isolated location; must drive to off-property restaurants and attractions; fees for both valet and self-parking. *Rooms from: $159* *1150 Av. Caribe, La Guancha* *787/259–7676, 800/445–8667* *www.hiltonponceresort.com* *263 rooms* *No meals.*

Holiday Inn Ponce & Tropical Casino
$ | **HOTEL** | **FAMILY** | This five-story hotel has a 24-hour casino, a huge pool, and a restaurant and bar where live music can be heard on weekends. **Pros:** game room for kids; large pool area; all rooms have refrigerators. **Cons:** 15 minutes by car from the beach; lots of foot traffic from casino and bar; dated room decor. *Rooms from: $146* *3315 Ponce Bypass, west of downtown, Ponce*

☎ 787/844–1200 ⊕ www.holidayinn.com/ponce ⇆ 116 rooms 🍽 No meals.

Howard Johnson by Wyndham Ponce
$ | HOTEL |FAMILY | Two minutes from Mercedita Aeropuerto, this hotel is a good choice if you have an early morning flight, but it is outdated. **Pros:** close to airport; kid-friendly; free Wi-Fi. **Cons:** no elevator; restaurant serves lunch only on weekends; inconsistent cleanliness of rooms. *[$] Rooms from: $135 ✉ 103 Turpó Industrial Park, Ponce ☎ 787/841–1000 ⊕ www.wyndhamhotels.com ⇆ 120 rooms 🍽 No meals.*

Nightlife

CASINOS

The casinos in Ponce can't hold a candle to their counterparts in San Juan.

Hilton Ponce Casino
CASINOS | Hilton Ponce Golf & Casino Resort has a rather cramped casino that's open 24 hours a day. *✉ 1150 Av. Caribe, La Guancha ☎ 787/259–7676 ⊕ www.hiltonponceresort.com.*

Holiday Inn Ponce Casino
CASINOS | This small casino has 346 slot machines and 10 tables. It's open 24/7. *✉ 3315 Ponce Bypass, Ponce ☎ 787/844–1200 ⊕ www.holidayinn.com/ponce.*

Shopping

Plaza del Caribe Mall
SHOPPING CENTERS/MALLS | Located just outside town, this is Ponce's largest mall and has such stores as Chicos, Clarks, Foot Locker, and American Eagle Outfitters. *✉ Rte. 2, Km 224.9, Ponce ☎ 787/259–8989 ⊕ www.plazadelcaribe.net*

Ponce Mall
SHOPPING CENTERS/MALLS | Ponce Mall, with a couple dozen stores, is an older shopping center, with many local clothing and discount stores. It also has a large IKEA, TJ Maxx, and DSW. *✉ Rte. 2, Km 225.8, Ponce ☎ 787/844–6170 ⊕ www.poncemallpr.com.*

Activities

DIVING AND SNORKELING

You'll see many varieties of coral, parrotfish, angelfish, and grouper in the reefs around the island of Caja de Muertos. Snorkeling around La Guancha and the beach area of the Ponce Hilton is also fairly good.

Island Venture
SCUBA DIVING | Island Venture offers two-tank dive excursions, as well as snorkeling trips. The company also takes day-trippers from La Guancha to Caja de Muertos (a 45-minute boat ride) for a day of relaxing on the beach. *✉ Ponce ☎ 787/842–8546 ⊕ islandventurepr.com 🎟 Snorkeling from $35, diving from $65.*

GOLF

Costa Caribe Golf and Country Club
GOLF | Ponce's only golf course has 27 holes, a driving range, and pro-shop adjoining the Ponce Hilton. To get here, take Route 12 to Avenida Caribe. *✉ 1150 Av. Caribe, Ponce ☎ 787/812–2695 ⊕ www.costacaribe-resort.com 🎟 $69–$75 ⛳ 27 holes, 3397 yards, par 36.*

Coamo

34 km (21 miles) northeast of Ponce, 33 km (20 miles) southwest of Cayey, 20 km (13 miles) northwest of Salinas.

Founded by the Spanish in 1579, Coamo was the third city established in Puerto Rico. It dominated the south of the island until the mid-1880s, when political power shifted to Ponce. Coamo town, however, remained an important outpost; several decisive battles were fought here during the Spanish-American War in 1898.

The thermal springs outside Coamo are believed by some to be the Fountain of Youth for which Ponce de León was searching. In the mid-1800s, a fashionable resort was built nearby, and people have been coming to soak in the waters ever since. Coamo is also famous for the San Blás Half-Marathon, which brings competitors and spectators from around the world. The race, held in early February, covers 18 km (13 miles) of the city's hilly streets.

GETTING HERE AND AROUND

Coamo sits fairly close to the Luis A. Ferré Expressway (Route 52), the toll road that connects San Juan and Ponce; it is about 32 km (20 miles) northeast of Ponce. You can take the turnoff onto Route 153, although there is also access from several points in the Cordillera. Públicos from Ponce connect with Coamo's town center.

Iglesia Católica San Blás

RELIGIOUS SITE | On Coamo's main square, the Iglesia Católica San Blás has a gorgeous Neoclassical facade. Dating from 1563, the whitewashed building is one of the oldest churches on the island. ✉ *Calle Mario Braschetti* ☎ *787/825–1122.*

Museo Histórico de Coamo

MUSEUM | Off the main square, the Museo Histórico de Coamo is appropriately housed in the former residence of one of the city's illustrious citizens, Clotilde Santiago, a wealthy farmer and merchant born in 1826. The museum is on the second floor of this sprawling, tangerine-color building, which dates from 1863. Several rooms are decorated with colonial-style furnishings; photographs of the town and the Santiago family line the walls. ✉ *29 Calle José I. Quintón* ☎ *787/825–1150* 🎫 *Free* ⏲ *Closed weekends.*

★ Piscinas Aguas Termales

HOT SPRINGS | In Coamo you can take a dip at the famous Piscinas Aguas Termales, the thermal springs said to have curative powers. There's a changing room at the end of a path. Note that parking is somewhat limited here, especially on weekends, when the attraction is visited by locals from all over the island. ✉ *Rte. 546, Km 1.7* 🎫 *$3.35.*

La Ceiba

$$ | PUERTO RICAN | The highway leading to Coamo is lined by dozens of fast-food restaurants. Luckily, there are a few worthwhile family-owned eateries, one of the best of which is this open-air cantina. **Known for:** seafood-stuffed red snapper; cheesecake in various flavors; great margaritas. $ *Average main: $15* ✉ *Rte. 153, Km 12.8* ☎ *787/825–2299.*

Salinas

41 km (27 miles) east of Ponce.

Most visitors are familiar with Salinas only because they see its name on an exit sign along Route 52. Islanders, however, know that the road from the expressway exit to Salinas leads to some of Puerto Rico's best seafood restaurants. Most of them are along the seafront in the Playa de Salinas area, reached by heading south on Route 701.

GETTING HERE AND AROUND

You can take either the Luis A. Ferré Expressway (Route 52), the toll road that connects San Juan and Ponce, or the more scenic Route 1 along the coast east from Ponce to reach Salinas.

Albergue Olímpico

SPORTS VENUE | Puerto Rico's Olympic training center isn't just for world-class athletes; it's a massive multiuse sports complex that's open to the public and virtually unknown to anyone other than locals. Just off the main highway on the

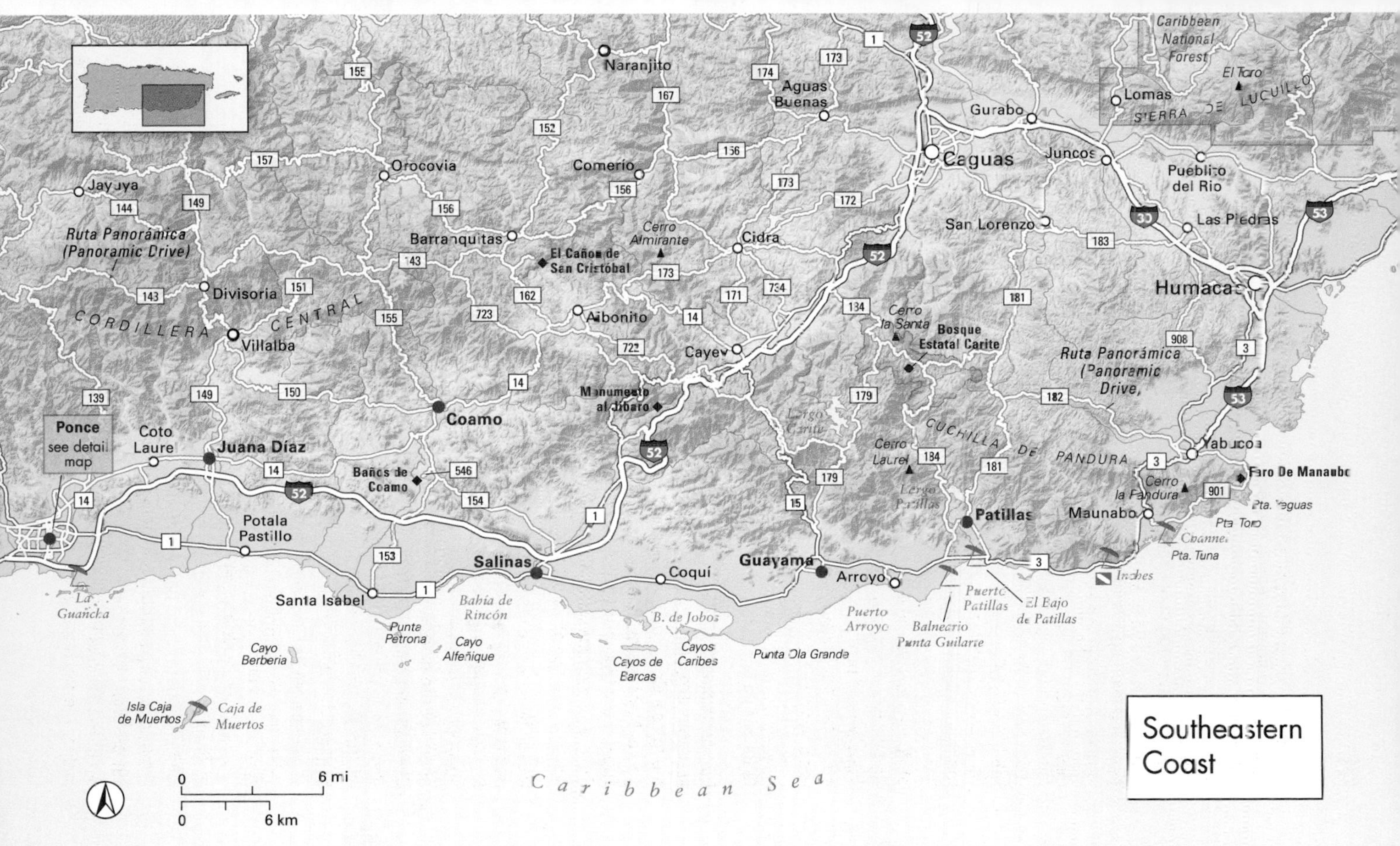
Southeastern Coast
Caribbean National Forest
El Toro
Sierra de Luquillo
Lomas
Gurabo
Juncos
Caguas
Pueblito del Rio
Las Piedras
San Lorenzo
Humacao
Naranjito
Aguas Buenas
Comerío
Orocovia
Jayuya
Ruta Panorámica (Panoramic Drive)
Barranquitas
Cerro Almirante
El Cañon de San Cristóbal
Cidra
Divisoria
Cordillera Central
Villalba
Aibonito
Cayey
Cerro la Santa
Bosque Estatal Carite
Ruta Panorámica (Panoramic Drive)
Manumento al Jíbaro
Coamo
Ponce see detail map
Coto Laurel
Juana Díaz
Baños de Coamo
Cerro Laurel
Cuchilla de Pandura
Yabucoa
Faro De Manaubo
Cerro la Pandura
Maunabo
Pta. Yeguas
Pta Toro
Patillas
Potala Pastillo
Salinas
Coquí
Guayama
Arroyo
Pta. Tuna
Inches
Santa Isabel
La Guancha
Bahía de Rincón
B. de Jobos
Puerto Arroyo
Puerto Patillas
El Bajo de Patillas
Balneario Punta Guilarte
Punte Petrona
Cayo Alfeñique
Cayo Berberia
Cayos de Barcas
Cayos Caribes
Punta Ola Grande
Isla Caja de Muertos
Caja de Muertos
Caribbean Sea
0
6 mi
0
6 km

drive from San Juan to Ponce, the Albergue has 45 different training centers—from gyms and pools to shooting ranges—where visitors can watch athletes train. There's also an Olympic Museum, food and beverage concessions, two water parks, a climbing wall for young kids, and even an 18-hole mini-golf course. Although the center is technically open year-round, the outdoor recreational facilities and public spaces tend to be open only from April to September; at other times of the year, visitors will need to make an appointment if they wish to see the museum, for example. ✉ *Rte. 712, Km 0.3* ☎ *787/824–2200* 🌐 *www.albergueolimpico.com* 🎟 *$16.99 (varies by season)* ⏲ *Some facilities closed seasonally.*

Restaurants

El Balcón de Capitán

$$$ | **SEAFOOD** | This *mesón gastronómico,* hidden among a string of oceanfront restaurants south of the center in the Playa de Salinas area, is one of the most popular on Puerto Rico's southern coast. Sit in either the open-air patio or air-conditioned dining room and bar and sample specialties like *mofongo relleno de mariscos* (seafood-stuffed plantains) or the many preparations of mahimahi, red snapper, *arrayao* (mahogany snapper), octopus, lobster, or conch. **Known for:** seafood-stuffed mofongo; red snapper; seafood paella. $ *Average main: $25* ✉ *Rte. 701, Playa de Salinas* ☎ *787/824–6210.*

El Roble

$$ | **PUERTO RICAN** | In operation since 1961, this restaurant is still considered one of the best in town. Don't be surprised to see flapping fish delivered straight off the boats and into the kitchen, where chefs prepare dishes like grouper fillet stuffed with seafood. **Known for:** fresh seafood, including delicious red snapper; good selection of wine; children's menu. $ *Average main: $18* ✉ *Rte. 701, Playa de Salinas* ☎ *787/824–2377.*

Guayama

29 km (18 miles) east of Salinas, 28 km (17 miles) southeast of Cayey, 49 km (31 miles) southeast of Barranquitas.

Guayama was founded in 1736, but the city was destroyed by fire in the early 1800s. It quickly recovered when the sugarcane industry grew by leaps and bounds, and the wealth that the surrounding plantations brought to town is evident in the number of striking Neoclassical homes on the streets surrounding the main square. Some have been beautifully restored, whereas others are crumbling. One of the finest 19th-century homes, Casa Cautiño, is now a museum.

The nearby countryside is home to Paso Fino horses. Each March at the Marcelino Blondet Stadium you can watch these high-stepping show horses strut their stuff during the Feria Dulce Sueño, a fair named after one of the island's most famous Thoroughbreds. Folk music and crafts are part of the festivities.

GETTING HERE AND AROUND

From the north or west, take either Route 53 or the coastal Route 3 to reach Guayama. On Sunday Guayama has a free trolley that runs to many sights.

CONTACTS Guayama Trolley. ✉ *Alcaldía de Guayama, Calle Vicente Pales* ☎ *787/864–7765.*

Sights

Casa Cautiño

HOUSE | Built for sugar, cattle, and coffee baron Genaro Cautiño Vázquez and his wife, Genoveva Insúa, Casa Cautiño is an elegant Neoclassical home dating from 1887. The painstakingly restored exterior features a balcony with ornate grillwork.

You'll be swept back in time walking through the rooms, which are filled with the original Victorian-era furnishings. Don't miss the modern-for-its-time bathroom, complete with a standing shower. The museum is on the main square. ✉ *1 Calle Palmer, at Calle Vicente Palé Matos* 🎫 *Free* ⏲ *Closed Mon.*

Centro de Bellas Artes

HOUSE | Just a few blocks from the main square, the Centro de Bellas Artes is housed in a beautifully restored Neoclassical building. Paintings by local artists fill its 11 rooms. ✉ *Calle McArthur at Carretera 3* ☎ *787/864–7765* 🎫 *Free* ⏲ *Closed Mon.*

Iglesia San Antonio de Padua

RELIGIOUS SITE | One of the prettiest churches on the southern coast, Iglesia San Antonio de Padua was begun in 1827 but not completed until 40 years later. Don't set your watch by the time on the clock; the hand-painted face is frozen at the time the church was "baptized." The bells in the tower were cast in gold and bronze in 1835. ✉ *5 Calle Palmer.*

GOLF

El Legado Golf Resort

GOLF | This resort, designed by golf legend and native son Chi Chi Rodríguez, is a 7,213-yard, 18-hole course with 12 lakes. The course is closed on Monday. ✉ *Rte. 713, off Rte. 53* ☎ *787/866–8894* 🌐 *www.ellegadopuertorico.com* 🎫 *$60–$65* ⛳ *18 holes, 7213 yards, par 72.*

Juana Díaz

12.5 km (7.7 miles) east of Ponce, 23.4 km (14.6 miles) west of Salinas.

Juana Díaz doesn't figure prominently into the typical travel itinerary, but for the traveler who has a bit of extra time, a stop in this small town is worth the effort, for Juana Díaz is the epicenter of a very important cultural tradition in Puerto Rico: the celebration of the Three Kings. Technically an extension of the municipality of Ponce, Juana Díaz was nicknamed "The Versailles of Ponce" by famed Puerto Rican poet Luis Lloréns Torres. While some of the glory that earned it that name may be faded, the massive Three Kings sculpture in the town's main square and its Three Kings Museum make for an interesting layover on a drive between Salinas and Ponce.

Three Kings Museum

LOCAL INTEREST | No doubt, Christmas is an important holiday in Puerto Rico, but Three Kings Day, celebrated on January 6, is perhaps even more important, observed with a special parade and other festivities across the island. Every day is Three Kings Day at this small museum in Juana Díaz, where Puerto Rico's Three Kings tradition started in 1884 and where it continues today. Visitors can learn more about the holiday and see traditional costumes, sculptures, and other displays, as well as hear about local folklore from on-site guides. ✉ *Rte. 14 (Calle Comercio), Km 13.9, Juana Díaz* ☎ *787/260–0817* 🌐 *www.reyesdejuanadiaz.com* 🎫 *$3.*

Patillas

6 km (4 miles) northeast of Arroyo.

Patillas, the so-called Emerald of the South, is a tranquil city of about 19,000, with a small plaza and steep, narrow streets. The best sightseeing is along the coast east of town, where Route 3 skirts the Caribbean. This stretch passes rugged cliffs and beautiful beaches, many of which have not yet been discovered by visitors.

A Guide to Puerto Rico's Carved Saints 

Hand-carving wooden *santos* (saints) is one of Puerto Rico's oldest traditional art forms, but to find authentic examples, you have to know where to find the artisans—and their handiwork. Authentic santos will simply not be found in most souvenir shops.

History of the Santos

The history of these figures can be traced back to the arrival of Spanish missionaries in the late 15th and early 16th centuries. The missionaries spread God's word by telling stories animated and illustrated with carved santos. According to carver Miguel Díaz, missionaries left santos behind with prospective converts since churches were few and far between. Santos placed on home altars could help keep the spirit of God alive between their visits. Although missionaries are long gone, santos still enjoy a place of honor in many Puerto Ricans' homes and are highly prized by collectors on the island and abroad.

About the Saints

They are not unique to Puerto Rico; just as Spanish missionaries brought santos here, they also carried them to many other countries as well. In Puerto Rico, the most common figures are the Three Kings, Saint Barbara, Saint Francis, and *La Mano Poderosa* (The Powerful Hand, in which a member of the Holy Family tops each finger of a hand bearing the stigma). Typically carved in cedar, they are brushed with a coat of gesso and then painted. Some santos are ceramic.

Where to Find Them

Artisans can often be found working wood and selling their santos during craft fairs held along Old San Juan's **Plaza Dársena**, between the cruise piers and Paseo de la Princesa. Friday and Saturday evenings are sure bets, as are Sunday afternoons. But there are some prominent artisans in the country as well.

Avilés Family. The Avilés family maintains a museum of its generations of craft work. Visits are by appointment only. ✉ *Santurce, San Juan* ☎ *787/455–4217.*

Miguel Díaz. If you're interested in visiting an artisan's workshop, carver Miguel Díaz hosts visitors in his studio in Carolina. ☎ *787/392–8857* ✉ *tallertabonuco@gmail.com.*

Puerto Rican Arts & Crafts. The best source for santos in Old San Juan ensures that its entire stock comes from the hands of artisans who live on the island. The store carries the santos of the late self-taught carver Domingo Orta and of Antonio Avilés Burgos, who represents the third generation of carvers in his family. ✉ *204 Calle Fortaleza, Old San Juan* ☎ *787/725–5596* 🌐 *www.puertoricanart-crafts.com.*

Prices

Prices vary depending on the size and quality of the craftsmanship. Prices for santos begin at $40 but may go up to several hundred dollars for larger or more elaborate pieces. Most of the carvers don't bargain; the first stated price is likely the lowest he or she is willing to go.

GETTING HERE AND AROUND

Patillas is a short drive east of Guayama and Arroyo on Route 53, but there is also access from the east along Route 3 and from the north in Guavate along Route 184. Públicos run from Guayama and Arroyo to the center.

Beaches

★ **Playa Punta Tuna**

BEACH—SIGHT | Punta Tuna Beach is on Puerto Rico's southeast coast. Strong currents make it unsafe to swim here, but this is a beautiful place to relax with a book or take a long walk on the beach. This is also home to the Punta Tuna Reserve, a nesting site for turtles. Nesting season is from March to July. Climbing the rock formations at one of the end beach provides a beautiful view. You can also visit the Punta Tuna Lighthouse perched above the beach. **Amenities:** parking (no fee). **Best for:** solitude; walking. ✉ *PR 7760, Maunabo* ✣ *21 km east of Patillas, 31 km south of Humacao.*

Hotels

Caribe Playa Beach Resort

$ | HOTEL | A good base from which to explore the southeastern coast, this small hotel sits on a crescent-shape beach, which may be a little rocky but still good for a refreshing dip. **Pros:** lovely setting; friendly staff; on-site restaurant. **Cons:** some rooms are dark; mosquitoes and other bugs; some traffic noise. *$ Rooms from: $125* ✉ *Rte. 3, Km 112.1* ☎ *787/839–6339* 🌐 *www.caribeplaya.com* *32 rooms* *Free breakfast.*

Guánica

24 miles (38 km) west of Ponce.

Juan Ponce de León first explored this area in 1508, when he was searching for the elusive Fountain of Youth. Nearly 400 years later U.S. troops landed first at Guánica during the Spanish-American War in 1898. The event is commemorated with an engraved marker on the city's *malecón*, or jetty. Sugarcane dominated the landscape through much of the 1900s, and the ruins of the old Guánica Central sugar mill, closed in 1980, loom over the town's western area, known as Ensenada. Today Guánica's biggest draws are its beaches and forests.

GETTING HERE AND AROUND

From Ponce, Route 2 connects with Guánica via Route 116 and extends to San Germán and Mayagüez. The town hugs Guánica Bay and runs almost immediately into the neighboring village of Ensenada.

Sights

Bosque Estatal de Guánica (*Guánica State Forest*)

FOREST | This 9,900-acre United Nations Biosphere Reserve is a great place for hiking. An outstanding example of a subtropical dry forest, it has some 700 species of plants, from the prickly-pear cactus to the gumbo limbo tree, and offers superb bird-watching; its more than 100 species include the pearly-eyed thrasher, lizard cuckoo, and nightjar.

The popular **Ballena Trail,** which begins at the ranger station on Route 334, is an easy 2-km (1¼-mile) walk that follows a partially paved road past a mahogany plantation to a dry plain covered with stunted cactus. A sign reading "Guayacán centenario" leads you to an extraordinary guayacán tree with a 6-foot-wide trunk. The moderately difficult, 5½-km (3½-mile) **Fuerte Trail** leads to an old fort built by the Spanish Armada. It was destroyed in the Spanish-American War in 1898, but you can see ruins of the old observatory tower.

In addition to using the main entrance on Route 334, you can enter on Route 333, which skirts the forest's southwestern

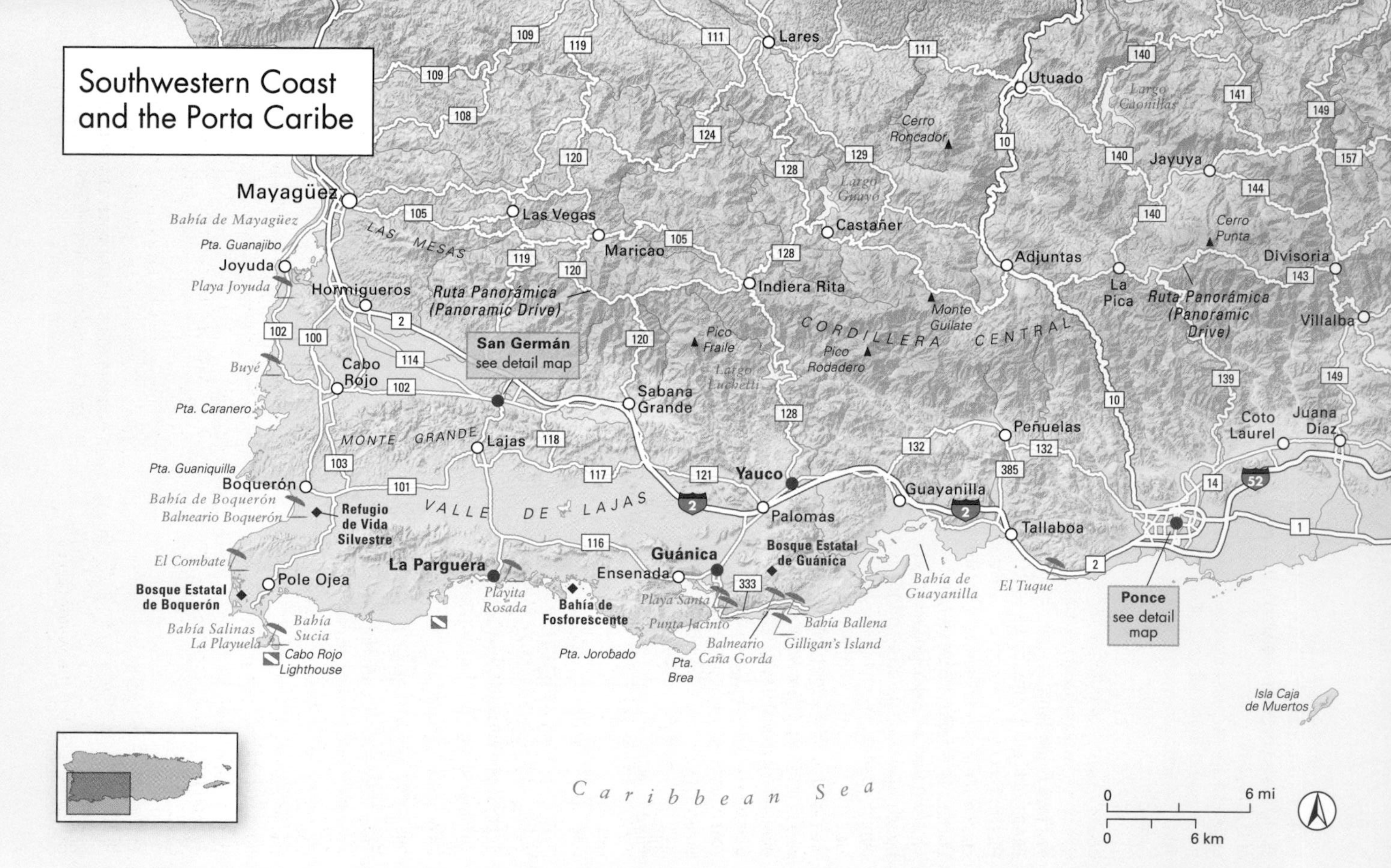
Southwestern Coast and the Porta Caribe
Mayagüez
Bahía de Mayagüez
Pta. Guanajibo
Joyuda
Playa Joyuda
Hormigueros
Buyé
Cabo Rojo
Pta. Caranero
Pta. Guaniquilla
Boquerón
Bahía de Boquerón
Balneario Boquerón
Refugio de Vida Silvestre
El Combate
Pole Ojea
Bosque Estatal de Boquerón
Bahía Salinas
La Playuela
Bahía Sucia
Cabo Rojo Lighthouse
LAS MESAS
Las Vegas
Maricao
Ruta Panorámica (Panoramic Drive)
San Germán see detail map
MONTE GRANDE
Lajas
VALLE DE LAJAS
La Parguera
Playita Rosada
Bahía de Fosforescente
Pta. Jorobado
Sabana Grande
Pico Fraile
Largo Luchetti
Indiera Rita
Castañer
Largo Guayo
Lares
Utuado
Largo Caonillas
Cerro Roncador
CORDILLERA CENTRAL
Pico Rodadero
Monte Guilate
Adjuntas
La Pica
Jayuya
Cerro Punta
Divisoria
Villalba
Ruta Panorámica (Panoramic Drive)
Yauco
Palomas
Ensenada
Guánica
Bosque Estatal de Guánica
Playa Santa
Punta Jacinto
Pta. Brea
Balneario Caña Gorda
Gilligan's Island
Bahía Ballena
Guayanilla
Bahía de Guayanilla
Peñuelas
Tallaboa
El Tuque
Coto Laurel
Juana Díaz
Ponce see detail map
Isla Caja de Muertos
Caribbean Sea
0 6 mi
0 6 km
109
109
108
119
120
105
119
120
105
102
100
2
114
102
103
101
118
117
116
120
124
111
128
128
129
128
121
333
2
111
10
140
141
149
157
140
144
140
143
139
149
10
132
132
385
2
14
52
1
2

quadrant. You may also wish to explore the less-trafficked area west of the town of Guánica, off Route 325. ✉ *Rte. 334* ☎ *787/821–5706* 🎫 *Free.*

Beaches

Balneario Caña Gorda

BEACH—SIGHT | The gentle waters at this beach on Route 333 wash onto a wide swath of sand fringed with palm trees. This is one of the few beaches in Puerto Rico that meets the high environmental standards of the Blue Flag program. There is a designated area roped off for swimmers, and lifeguards remain on duty most afternoons. You'll also find picnic tables, restrooms, showers, and changing facilities. During high season there are beach-chair rentals, food vendors, and paid parking. **Amenities:** food and drink; lifeguards; parking (fee); toilets. **Best for:** snorkeling; swimming; walking. ✉ *Rte. 333, Km 5.9, west of Copamarina Beach Resort.*

Gilligan's Island

BEACH—SIGHT | Off the southwest coast, near Guánica, is Gilligan's Island, a palm-fringed cay skirted by gorgeous beaches. You'll find picnic tables and restrooms but few other signs of civilization on this tiny island, officially part of the Bosque Estatal de Guánica. Wooden boats line up at the small dock in the San Jacinto section of Guánica, off Route 333 just past the Copamarina Beach Resort. Boats depart every hour 9–5. The island is often crowded on weekends and around holidays, but during the week you can find a spot to yourself. Nearby **Isla de Ballena,** reached by the same ferry, is much less crowded. **Amenities:** toilets. **Best for:** solitude (midweek, low season only); swimming. ✉ *Off Rte. 333* ☎ *787/821–4941* 🎫 *Ferry $10.58.*

Playa Jaboncillo

BEACH—SIGHT | Rugged cliffs make a dramatic backdrop for this little cove off Route 333, but the water can be rough. The road down to the beach is extremely steep and rocky and shouldn't be attempted without a four-wheel-drive vehicle. **Amenities:** parking (no fee). **Best for:** solitude; sunset. ✉ *Rte. 333, west of Copamarina Beach Resort.*

Playa Santa

BEACH—SIGHT | You can rent canoes, kayaks, and pedal boats at this beach at the end of Route 325 in the Ensenada district. This beach is popular with local teenagers and can get congested, but the mile-long shoreline is kept clean. **Amenities:** food and drink; parking (no fee); water sports. **Best for:** sunset; swimming; walking. ✉ *Rte. 325, west of town, Ensenada.*

Restaurants

Restaurante Alexandra

$$$$ | **CARIBBEAN** | Puerto Ricans drive for miles to reach this restaurant in the Copamarina Beach Resort. The kitchen takes traditional Puerto Rican dishes and turns them into something extra special, and the elegant dining room looks out onto well-tended gardens. **Known for:** fresh seafood; great lobster; Sunday brunch. $ *Average main: $32* ✉ *Copamarina Beach Resort, Rte. 333, Km 6.5* ☎ *787/821–0505* 🌐 *www.copamarina.com* ⏲ *Closed Mon. and Wed. No dinner Sun. No lunch.*

Hotels

★ Copamarina Beach Resort and Spa

$$ | **RESORT** | The most beautiful resort on the southern coast is set on 16 palm-shaded acres facing the Caribbean. **Pros:** plenty of activities; great dining options; only 10 minutes from Gilligan's Island. **Cons:** somewhat distant from other attractions; expensive 20% resort fee; beach just OK. $ *Rooms from: $190* ✉ *Rte. 333, Km 6.5* ☎ *787/821–0505, 800/468–4553* 🌐 *www.copamarina.com* *104 rooms* 🍽 *Free Breakfast.*

Fish the waters off La Parguera for blue marlin, tuna, or reef fish.

Mary Lee's by the Sea

$ | **RENTAL** | This meandering cluster of apartments sits on quiet grounds full of brightly colored flowers. **Pros:** home away from home; warm and friendly owner; near pristine beaches and forests. **Cons:** weekly maid service unless requested daily; no pool; rooms a bit dated. *Rooms from: $130 ⊠ Rte. 333, Km 6.7 ☎ 787/821–3600 🌐 www.maryleesbythe-sea.com 10 apartments No meals.*

Parador Guanica 1929

$ | **HOTEL** | This 1929 colonial-style building is very pretty, with lovely arches adding more character than you usually find along the southern coast, but sadly it's not on the beach. **Pros:** historic setting; pretty pool area; basketball and volleyball courts. **Cons:** no beach; slightly off the beaten path; rooms are small. *Rooms from: $113 ⊠ Rte. 3116, Km 2.5, Ensenada ☎ 877/821–0099 🌐 www.tropical-innspr.com/parador-guanica-1929 27 rooms No meals.*

Activities

DIVING AND SNORKELING

Dramatic walls created by the continental shelf provide great diving off the Guánica coast. Shallow gardens around Gilligan's Island and Cayo de Caña Gorda (off Balneario Caña Gorda) also attract snorkelers and divers.

Dive Copamarina

SCUBA DIVING | Dive Copamarina offers instruction and trips. *⊠ Copamarina Beach Resort, Rte. 333, Km 6.5 ☎ 787/821–0505 🌐 www.copamarina.com.*

La Parguera

13 km (8 miles) west of Guánica, 24 km (15 miles) southwest of Yauco.

La Parguera is best known for its bioluminescent bay. Although it is not nearly as spectacular as the one in Vieques, it's still a beautiful sight on a moonless night. Boats, including some glass-bottom vessels, line up at the town dock and depart several times each evening for 45-minute trips across the bay. During the day you can explore the nearby mangrove forest.

The town bursts at the seams with vacationers from other parts of the island on long holiday weekends and throughout the summer. The dock area feels a bit like Coney Island, and not in a good way; vendors in makeshift stalls hawk cheap souvenirs, and ear-splitting salsa music pours out of open-air bars. There are signs warning people not to drink alcoholic beverages in the street, but these are cheerfully ignored.

If you're driving through the area between February and April, keep your eyes open for roadside vendors selling the area's famous pineapples, called *piñas cadezonas*. In late June there's the colorful Fiesta de San Pedro, honoring the patron saint of fishermen.

GETTING HERE AND AROUND

You can reach La Parguera from Guánica via Route 116, which turns into Route 318 when it heads to San Germán. Públicos depart from the turnoff at Route 304 and head to Lajas, where connections can be made to San Germán.

Sights

Bahía Fosforescente (*Phosphorescent Bay*)
LOCAL INTEREST | On moonless nights, large and small boats line the dock to take visitors out to view the Bahía Fosforescente. Microscopic dinoflagellates glow when disturbed by movement, suffusing the waves with thousands of starlike points of light. The bay's glow has been diminished substantially by pollution—both light pollution from nearby communities and water pollution from toxic chemicals dumped into the bay. (And, yes, the smoke-belching boats that take tourists to the bay do their part, too.) If you've seen the bioluminescent bay in Vieques, give this one a pass; if not, you may find it mildly interesting. While it's not necessary to make a reservation—plenty of operators try to rustle up customers on the docks around sunset—**Paradise Scuba** runs the most reputable excursions in the area. Visit their dive shop for more information. ✉ *Rte. 304, Km 3.5* ☎ *787/899–7611* 🌐 *www.paradisescubasnorkelingpr.com.*

Bosque Estatal de Boquerón (*Boquerón State Forest*)
NATURE PRESERVE | The eastern section of the Bosque Estatal de Boquerón is made up of miles of mangrove forests that grow at the water's edge. Boats from the dock in La Parguera can take you on cruises through this important breeding ground for seabirds. You can also organize a kayak trip. ✉ *La Parguera marina, off Rte. 304.*

Beaches

Isla Mata la Gata
BEACH—SIGHT | For about $5 per person, boats will ferry you to and from this small island just off the coast for a day of swimming and snorkeling. There are changing rooms and grilling areas. **Amenities:** showers; toilets. **Best for:** snorkeling; swimming. ✉ *La Parguera marina, off Rte. 304* ⏲ *Closed Mon.*

Playita Rosada
BEACH—SIGHT | The small beach doesn't compare to some of the longer beaches on the southwestern coast, but it's a convenient place for a quick swim. There's also a square dock built like a picture frame where locals gather to splash in the center of this natural swimming pool. **Amenities:** none. **Best for:** swimming. ✉ *End of Calle 7.*

Restaurants

La Casita
$$ | **SEAFOOD** | The so-called Little House isn't little at all—it's a sizable

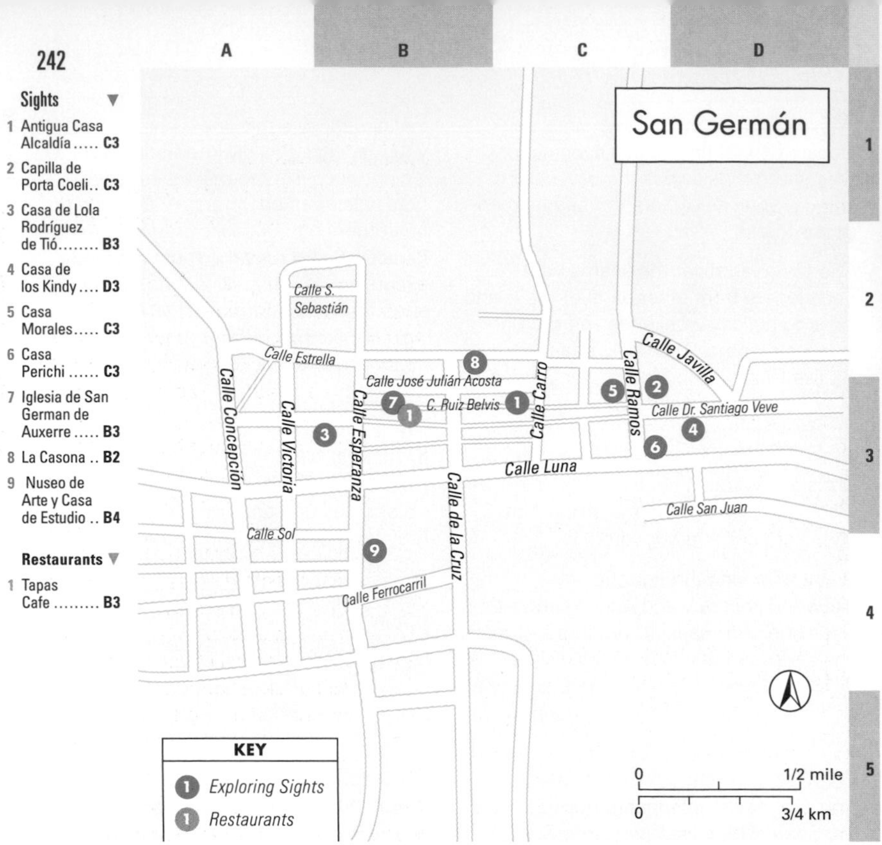

Sights

1 Antigua Casa Alcaldía C3
2 Capilla de Porta Coeli.. C3
3 Casa de Lola Rodríguez de Tió........ B3
4 Casa de los Kindy.... D3
5 Casa Morales..... C3
6 Casa Perichi C3
7 Iglesia de San German de Auxerre B3
8 La Casona .. B2
9 Nuseo de Arte y Casa de Estudio .. B4

Restaurants

1 Tapas Cafe B3

San Germán

A B C D
1 2 3 4 5

Calle S. Sebastián
Calle Estrella
Calle Concepción
Calle Victoria
Calle Esperanza
Calle José Julián Acosta
C. Ruiz Belvis
Calle Carro
Calle Ramos
Calle Javilla
Calle Dr. Santiago Veve
Calle Luna
Calle de la Cruz
Calle San Juan
Calle Sol
Calle Ferrocarril

KEY
Exploring Sights
Restaurants

0 1/2 mile
0 3/4 km

establishment that sits smack in the middle of the town's main road. Generous portions make this family-run restaurant one of the town's favorites. **Known for:** seafood asopao; mofongo with octopus in garlic sauce; views from the terrace. *Average main: $20* *Rte. 304, Km 3.3* *787/899–1681* *Closed Mon. and Wed.*

Hotels

Villa Parguera

$ | **HOTEL** | **FAMILY** | The rooms in this gingerbread-trimmed hotel are clustered around small courtyards filled with bright tropical flowers. **Pros:** family atmosphere; on-site entertainment options; walking distance to the marina. **Cons:** bland, dated rooms; pool area gets crowded; noise from nearby bars. *Rooms from: $107* *Rte. 304, Km 3.3* *787/899–7777* *www.villaparguerapr.com* *74 rooms* *No meals.*

Performing Arts

La Parguera's dock area heats up after sunset, when crowds come to take excursions to the Bahía Fosforescente.

Villa Parguera

CABARET | The live floor show on Saturday night includes a buffet. The show, which claims to be the longest-running live variety show on the island, changes frequently but includes live music, dancing, and comedy of the seltzer-in-your-pants variety. *Villa Parguera, Rte. 304, Km 2.3* *787/899–7777.*

Shopping

Outdoor stands near the docks sell all kinds of souvenirs, from T-shirts to beaded necklaces.

Activities

BOATING

Alelí Tours

BOATING | One alternative to the ubiquitous party boats in La Parguera, Alelí Tours and its staff have a earned a reputation for their personal touch, knowledgeable commentary, and the good condition and safety of their watercraft. ✉ *Rte. 304, Km 3.2* ☎ *787/390–6086* 🌐 *www.alelitours.com.*

DIVING AND SNORKELING

Endangered leatherback turtles, eels, and an occasional manatee can be seen from many of the sites that attract divers and snorkelers from all parts. There are more than 50 shore-dive sites off La Parguera, including the famous Black Wall that starts out at 60 feet and then suddenly drops 150 into a vast canyon.

Paradise Scuba

SCUBA DIVING | Paradise Scuba offers classes and trips, including night-snorkeling excursions in phosphorescent waters. Divers will enjoy the 150-foot vertical drop at the Black Wall, considered one of the most spectacular dive sites in Puerto Rico. Their most popular package is the sunset snorkel tour, which includes snacks, drinks, and a trip to the bioluminescent bay. ✉ *Rte. 304, Km 3.5* ☎ *787/899–7611* 🌐 *www.paradisescubasnorkelingpr.com.*

FISHING

Parguera Fishing Charters

FISHING | You can spend a half or whole day fishing for blue marlin, tuna, or reef fish with Capt. Mickey Amador at Parguera Fishing Charters. Lunch is included in the price. ✉ *Rte. 304, Km 3.8* ☎ *787/382–4698, 787/899–4698* 🌐 *www.puertoricofishingcharters.com.*

San Germán

10 km (6 miles) north of La Parguera, 166 km (104 miles) southwest of San Juan.

During its early years, San Germán was a city on the move. Although the first settlement's exact founding date and location remains at issue, the town is believed to have been established in 1510 near Guánica. Plagued by mosquitoes, settlers moved north along the west coast, where they encountered French pirates and smugglers. In the 1570s they fled inland to the current location, but they endured further harrassment. Determined and creative, they dug tunnels and moved beneath the city (the tunnels are now part of the water system). Today San Germán has a population of 35,000, and its intellectual and political activity is anything but underground. This is very much a college town, and students and professors from the Inter-American University often fill the bars and cafés.

Around San Germán's two main squares—Plazuela Santo Domingo and Plaza Francisco Mariano Quiñones (named for an abolitionist)—are buildings in every conceivable style of architecture found on the island, including mission Victorian, criollo, and Spanish colonial. The city's tourist office offers a free guided trolley tour. Most of the buildings are private homes; two of them—the Capilla de Porta Coeli and the Museo de Arte y Casa de Estudio—are museums. Strip malls surround the historic center.

GETTING HERE AND AROUND

San Germán sits just off Highway 2 between Ponce and Mayagüez on Route 122. This university town is something of a transportation hub, with públicos departing to nearby cities and towns, like Mayagüez and Lajas, from the intersection of Calle Luna and Route 122. A trolley tour of San Germán is available by appointment by calling city hall (☎ *787/892–3500*). On weekends there are free

A Good Tour: San Germán

The best place to start is Plazuela Santo Domingo, the sun-baked park in the center of the historic district. At the eastern edge of the park is the **Capilla de Porta Coeli,** perched at the top of an imposing set of stairs. From the top you get a good view of the rest of the city. Several historic homes, none of them open to the public, are within a block of the Capilla de Porta Coeli. Across the street is the **Casa Morales,** striking for its Victorian-style gables. It would not look out of place in any New England hamlet. Half a block east on Calle Dr. Santiago Veve are two criollo-style houses, **Casa de los Kindy** and **Casa Acosta y Forés.** A block south of the Capilla de Porta Coeli is one of the most beautiful homes in San Germán, **Casa Perichi.**

Head west through Plazuela Santo Domingo. The hulking yellow building you see at the northwest corner of the park is the rear of the **Antigua Casa Alcaldía.** It faces the town's other park, the Plaza Francisco Mariano Quiñones. This park is more popular with locals, as the tree-shaded benches are a pleasant place to watch the world go by. On the park's northern edge is **La Casona,** one of the town's best-preserved criollo-style buildings. The most imposing structure on the park, however, is **Iglesia de San Germán de Auxerre.**

A block and a half west of the church is the **Casa de Lola Rodríguez de Tió,** on Calle Dr. Santiago Veve. It's one of the best examples of criollo-style architecture in the city. Backtrack to Calle Esperanza and head two blocks south to where you'll find the **Museo de Arte y Casa de Estudio.**

Timing

San Germán's historic district is compact, so you can cover all the sights in about an hour. You'll want to budget a bit more time to stroll around the nearby streets. Be sure to wear comfortable shoes, as there will be a lot of walking uphill and downhill on cobbled streets.

horse-and-carriage rides around the plaza. Or you could just walk—all downtown sights are within a few blocks of the main square.

San Germán Trolley
⊠ *Alcaldía de San Germán, 136 Calle Luna* ☎ *787/892–3500.*

Sights

Antigua Casa Alcaldía (*Old Municipal Building*)
GOVERNMENT BUILDING | At the eastern end of Plaza Francisco Mariano Quiñones, this Spanish-colonial-style building served as the town's city hall from 1844 to 1950. Once used as a prison, it is now the headquarters for the police department. ⊠ *East end of Plaza Francisco Mariano Quiñones.*

Capilla de Porta Coeli (*Heaven's Gate Chapel*)
RELIGIOUS SITE | One of the oldest religious buildings in the Americas, this mission-style chapel overlooks the long, rectangular Plazuela de Santo Domingo. It's not a grand building, but its position at the top of a stone stairway gives it a noble air. Queen Isabel Segunda decreed that the Dominicans should build a church and monastery in San Germán, so a rudimentary building was erected in 1609, replaced in 1692 by the structure seen today. (Sadly, most of

The Iglesia de San Germán de Auxerre is a 17th-century church that's still in use today

the monastery was demolished in 1866, leaving only a vestige of its facade.) The chapel functions as a museum of religious art, displaying painted wooden statuary by Latin American and Spanish artists. ✉ *East end of Plazuela Santo Domingo* ☎ *787/892–5845* 🎫 *$3* ⏲ *Closed weekends.*

Casa de Lola Rodríguez de Tió

HOUSE | Part of the San Germán Historic District, which is listed on the National Register of Historic Places, this house bears the name of poet and activist Lola Rodríguez de Tió. A plaque claims she lived in this criollo style house, although town officials believe it actually belonged to her sister. Rodríguez, whose mother was a descendant of Ponce de León, was deported several times by Spanish authorities for her revolutionary ideas. She lived in Venezuela and then in Cuba, where she died in 1924. The museum, which houses Rodríguez's desk and papers, doesn't maintain regular hours; call ahead to schedule a tour. ✉ *13 Calle Dr. Santiago Veve* ☎ *787/892–3500* 🎫 *Free.*

Casa de los Kindy

HOUSE | East of the Plazuela de Santo Domingo, this 19th-century home is known for its eclectic architecture, which mixes Neoclassical and criollo elements. Note the elegant stained glass over the front windows. It's now a private residence. ✉ *64 Calle Dr. Santiago Veve.*

Casa Morales

HOUSE | Facing Plazuela de Santo Domingo, this Victorian-style house was designed in 1913 by architect Pedro Vivoni for his brother, Tomás. The gleaming white structure has numerous towers and gables. The current owners have kept it in mint condition. It is not open to the public. ✉ *38 Calle Ramos.*

Casa Perichi (*Casa Ortiz Perichi*)

HOUSE | You'll find an excellent example of Puerto Rican ornamental architecture in this elegant mansion, which sits a block south of Plazuela Santo Domingo. This gigantic white home, part of the San

Germán Historic District, which is on the National Register of Historic Places, was built in 1920. Note the sensuous curves of the wraparound balcony and wood trim around the doors. It's not open to the public. ✉ *94 Calle Luna.*

Iglesia de San Germán de Auxerre
RELIGIOUS SITE | Dating from 1739, this Neoclassical church has seen many additions over the years. The impressive crystal chandelier, for example, was imported from Barcelona and added in 1866. Be sure to take a look at the carved-wood ceiling in the nave. This church is still in use, so the only time you can get a look inside is during services. ✉ *West side of Plaza Francisco Mariano Quiñones* ☎ *787/892–1027.*

La Casona
BUILDING | On the north side of Plaza Francisco Mariano Quiñones, this two-story home was built in 1871 for Tomás Agrait. (If you look closely, you can still see his initials in the wrought-iron decorations.) For many years it served as a center of cultural activities in San Germán. Today, it holds several shops. ✉ *Calle José Julien Acosta at Calle Cruz.*

Museo de Arte y Casa de Estudio
MUSEUM | This early-20th-century home—built in a criollo style with some obvious Neoclassical influences—has been turned into a museum. Displays include colonial furnishings, religious art, and artifacts of indigenous peoples; there are also rotating exhibits by local artists. ✉ *7 Calle Esperanza* ☎ *787/673–2210* *Free* *Closed Mon. and Tues.*

Restaurants

Tapas Café
$ | SPANISH | One of the biggest surprises in San Germán is this wonderful little restaurant facing Plaza Santo Domingo. The dining room looks like a Spanish courtyard, complete with blue stars swirling around the ceiling. **Known for:** beef medallions with blue cheese; yam-and-cod fritters; charming atmosphere. *Average main: $8* ✉ *50 Calle Dr. Santiago Veve* ☎ *787/264–0610* *Closed Mon. and Tues. No lunch Wed. and Thurs.*

Index

A

B

C

O

P

R

S

T

U

V

Photo Credits

Front Cover: Lumiere / eStock Photo [Description: Puerto Rico, San Juan, Old San Juan, Street Scene.] Back cover, from left to right: Dennisvdwater | Dreamstime.com; Joseph/Shutterstock; Dennisvdwater | Dreamstime.com. Spine: Sepavo | Dreamstime.com. Interior, from left to right: Jorge Moro/Shutterstock (1). Martin Wheeler III/Shutterstock (2-3). Franz Marc Frei / age fotostock (5). **Chapter 1**: Experience Puerto Rico: Sean Pavone/Shutterstock (6-7). Chad Zuber/Shutterstock (8-9). Eric Rivera | Dreamstime.com (9). Sorin Colac | Dreamstime.com (9). Marina Movschowitz / Alamy Stock Photo (10). In collaboration with Discover Puerto Rico (10). Stevengaertner | Dreamstime.com (10). Czuber | Dreamstime.com (10). In collaboration with Discover Puerto Rico (11). Sorin Colac | Dreamstime.com (11). Ioana Catalina E/Shutterstock (12). Littleny | Dreamstime.com (12). Hacienda Santa Ana, Bayamón, Puerto Rico. (12). Arena Creative/Shutterstock (12). Dennis van de Water/Shutterstock (13). Peter Kim/Shutterstock (14). In collaboration with Discover Puerto Rico (14). Frank FF47 (CC BY-NC 2.0) / Flickr (14). Edgar Torres, (CC BY 3.0) / Wikimedia Commons (14). Terri Butler Photography/Shutterstock (15). Dennis Van De Water | Dreamstime.com (15). gowithstock/Shutterstock (18). Perednianking/Shutterstock (18). In collaboration with Discover Puerto Rico (18). focal point/Shutterstock (18). Arturoosorno | Dreamstime.com (19). nehophoto/Shutterstock (19). etorres/Shutterstock (19). In collaboration with Discover Puerto Rico (19). In collaboration with Discover Puerto Rico (20). Planetpix / Alamy Stock Photo (20). Shutterstock (20). AVN Photo Lab/Shutterstock (20). Courtesy of Don Collins (21). Rog01 (CC BY-SA 2.0) / Flickr (21). Roberto Galan | Dreamstime.com (21). In collaboration with Discover Puerto Rico (21). GP Images / Alamy Stock Photo (22). Dennis van de Water/Shutterstock (22). By Discover Marco (22). Photo Spirit/Shutterstock (23). Andre Nunez (23). **Chapter 3:** San Juan: emperorcosar/Shutterstock (51). Sepavo | Dreamstime.com (65). Marek Poplawski (68). Franz Marc Frei / age fotostock (73). Lawrence Roberg/Shutterstock (73). Franz Marc Frei / age fotostock (73). iStockphoto (74). Flickr, [CC BY-ND 2.0] (74). runneralan2004/Flickr, [CC BY-ND 2.0] (75). Franz Marc Frei / age fotostock (75). runneralan2004/Flickr, [CC BY-ND 2.0] (75). Prknlot/Flickr, [CC BY-ND 2.0] (75). Atlantide S.N.C. / age fotostock (76). Oliver Gerhard / age fotostock (78). Shutterstock (80). Dennisvdwater | Dreamstime.com (85). Spphotos | Dreamstime.com (103). Craig Lovell / Eagle Visions Photography / Alamy (104). Pietro Scozzari / age fotostock (105). Wikimedia.org (105). Wikimedia.org (105). Stephane - Fotodeclic / age fotostock (105). Wikimedia.org (106). Wikimedia.org (106). **Chapter 4**: El Yunque and The Northeast: Ken Welsh / age fotostock (111). Kreder Katja / age fotostock (120). Katja Kreder / age fotostock (123). Rolf Nussbaumer / age fotostock (125). Ken Welsh / age fotostock (128-129). Katja Kreder / age fotostock (132). Larry Lambrecht (137). **Chapter 5**: Vieques and Culebra: Katja Kreder / age fotostock (139). Michele Falzone / age fotostock (149). Frank Llosa (155). Starwood Hotels & Resorts (156). Starwood Hotels & Resorts (157). Courtesy of Kayaking Puerto Rico (158). SuperStock (159). **Chapter 6**: The North Coast and The Cordillera Central: Dennis van de Water/Shutterstock (169). Dorado Beach, a Ritz-Carlton Reserve (178). Dennisvdwater | Dreamstime.com (180). Michele Falzone / age fotostock (183). **Chapter 7**: Rincón and The Porta Del Sol: Marlise Kast (185). Fotoamateur49 | Dreamstime.com (194). Israel Pabon/Shutterstock (204). Ken Welsh / age fotostock (209). **Chapter 8**: Ponce and The Porta Caribe: Jozoam | Dreamstime.com (213). Lagustin | Dreamstime.com (216). Nicholas Gill (217). Lagustin | Dreamstime.com (217). Franz Marc Frei / age fotostock (224). Greg Vaughn / Alamy (226). Albertoloyo | Dreamstime.com (230). Jozoam | Dreamstime.com (240). Morales / age fotostock (245).

All photos are courtesy of the writers except for the following: Julie Schwietert Collazo, courtesy of Francisco Collazo.

**Every effort has been made to trace the copyright holders, and we apologize in advance for any accidental errors. We would be happy to apply the corrections in the following edition of this publication.*

Notes

Fodor's PUERTO RICO

Publisher: Stephen Horowitz, *General Manager*

Editorial: Douglas Stallings, *Editorial Director*; Margaret Kelly, Jacinta O'Halloran, Amanda Sadlowski, *Senior Editors*; Kayla Becker, Alexis Kelly, Teddy Minford, Rachael Roth, *Editors*;

Design: Tina Malaney, *Design and Production Director*; Jessica Gonzalez, *Graphic Designer*; Mariana Tabares, *Design & Production Intern*

Production: Jennifer DePrima, *Editorial Production Manager*; Carrie Parker, *Senior Production Editor*; Elyse Rozelle, *Production Editor*; Jackson Pranica, *Editorial Production Assistant*

Maps: Rebecca Baer, *Senior Map Editor*; David Lindroth, Mark Stroud (Moon Street Cartography), *Cartographers*

Photography: Jill Krueger, *Director of Photo*; Namrata Aggarwal, Ashok Kumar, Carl Yu, *Photo Editors*; Rebecca Rimmer, *Photo Intern*

Business & Operations: Chuck Hoover, *Chief Marketing Officer*; Robert Ames, *Group General Manager*; Tara McCrillis, *Director of Publishing Operations*; Victor Bernal, *Business Analyst*

Public Relations and Marketing: Joe Ewaskiw, *Senior Director Communications & Public Relations*; Esther Su, *Senior Marketing Manager*; Ryan Garcia, Thomas Talarico, Miranda Villalobos, *Marketing Specialists*

Fodors.com Jeremy Tarr, *Editorial Director*; Rachael Levitt, *Managing Editor*

Technology: Jon Atkinson, *Director of Technology*; Rudresh Teotia, *Lead Developer*; Jacob Ashpis, *Content Operations Manager*

Writers: Julie Schwietert Collazo, Paulina Salach

Editor: Douglas Stallings

Production Editor: Elyse Rozelle

9th Edition

ISBN 978-1-10188-002-9

ISSN 1531-0396

Library of Congress Control Number 2018914625

SPECIAL SALES

This book is available at special discounts for bulk purchases for sales promotions or premiums. For more information, e-mail SpecialMarkets@fodors.com.

PRINTED IN THE UNITED STATES OF AMERICA

10 9 8 7 6 5 4 3 2 1

About Our Writ

A culin… entrepr… is a co… Group, … to cura… and of Spoon F… travel experienc… is also a license… consultant, event produ… freelance writer. Paulina has contributed to *Have Fork Will Travel,* a handbook for food and drink tourism. Most recently, Paulina was invited to participate in the Global Ambassadors Program, which fosters economic empowerment and entrepreneurship for women. She is a native of Poland and a New Yorker at heart, who has called Puerto Rico home for over 10 years.

…Collazo is a … Award–winning … writer interested … people and … lly in Latin … Chinese … in … ous … movements in Mexico City, and environmental issues in Chile and Puerto Rico. She was one of only a handful of journalists to visit the U.S. detention facility at Guantanamo Bay in Cuba in 2008. Julie has lived in Mexico City and San Juan, Puerto Rico. She's cowriter of *Tender Mercies,* the first memoir by one of the detained migrant mothers whose children were separated from them at the border during the zero-tolerance period.